A History Of Conferences And Other Proceedings: Connected With The Revision Of The Book Of Common Prayer

Edward Cardwell

A

HISTORY OF CONFERENCES

AND OTHER PROCEEDINGS

CONNECTED WITH THE REVISION OF

THE BOOK OF COMMON PRAYER;

FROM THE YEAR 1558 TO THE YEAR 1690.

BY

EDWARD CARDWELL, D.D.

PRINCIPAL OF ST. ALBAN'S HALL.

THIRD EDITION.

OXFORD,
AT THE UNIVERSITY PRESS.
MDCCCXLIX.

THIS volume is a sequel to the one entitled "The two Books of Common Prayer, set forth by authority of Parliament in the reign of King Edward VI, compared with each other;" and the two volumes jointly are intended to contain a complete documentary history of the English liturgy from the period of the Reformation down to the present time.

CONTENTS.

INTRODUCTION.

The state of religious opinions and parties during the
reigns of Edward VI. and Mary.

The two objects of the English reformers.... the different parts
they were allowed to take.... their incidental advantages....
the character of the sovereign.... the state of religious controversy.... illustrated from the cases of the eucharist and
clerical vestments.... the progress of change.... exemplified
in the second Service-book of king Edward.... changes made
in the communion service.... in the rubric respecting vestments.... principles involved in those changes.... opinion of
lord Bacon.... the English reformers in exile.... the exiles
at Frankfort.... at Geneva.... state of religious opinions on
the accession of Elizabeth.... sentiments of moderation....
divines who had remained in England.... archbishop Parker
.... influence of the exiles.... character of Elizabeth.... the
tendency of her measures.

CHAPTER I.

The revision of the liturgy in the reign of Elizabeth.

The queen's neutrality.... efforts of the two great religious
parties.... the queen's proclamation.... committee of revision.... the only prudent method.... of whom composed....

CHAPTER II.

Documents connected with the revision of queen Elizabeth.

CHAPTER III.

The revision of the liturgy in the reign of James I.

CHAPTER IV.

Documents connected with the revision of king James I.

CHAPTER V.

Interpolations charged against archbishop Laud.

CHAPTER VI.

The proceedings of the conference at the Savoy.

effect of their concessions .... ordinances proscribing the
Common Prayer Book.... their natural results .... aided by
collateral circumstances .... strong principles of church-
ascendancy.... the king's declaration.... an exclusive desire
for a strong government .... boldness of the dissenters....
their unreasonable demands.... the king's refusal.... proceedings of the episcopal clergy.... anxiety of the king's ministers
respecting them.... the advice they gave as to the dissenters
.... restoration of the liturgy.... critical circumstances of
the times.... the king's method of proceeding.... a conference resolved upon.... good policy of the court.... conciliating
demeanour of the king.... the dissenters invited to make overtures... they deliver in proposals.... the groundless nature of
their basis.... the answer of the bishops.... influence of ex-
traneous circumstances.... the king's ample concessions....
his private reasons.... success of his stratagem.... satisfaction
of the dissenters.... commission for the revision of the liturgy
.... the instructions provided.... proper interpretation of them
.... proper course of proceeding.... dissenters required to
tender their exceptions.... the policy of such a method....
uncompromising principle of the dissenters.... their list of exceptions and new liturgy.... their high tone of language....
the bishops determine to act as judges .... their answers....
the rejoinder of the dissenters.... its peremptory nature....
ten days only remaining.... a personal debate.... its natural
consequences.... bishop Cosin's proposal.... disputation on
one single topic.... general reflections as to toleration.

CHAPTER VII.

Documents connected with the conference at the Savoy.

CHAPTER VIII.

The revision of the liturgy in the reign of Charles II.

CHAPTER IX.

The attempt made to revise the liturgy in the reign of William and Mary.

CHAPTER X.

Documents connected with the attempted revision of William and Mary.

CONCLUSION.

INTRODUCTION.

The state of religious opinions and parties during the reigns of Edward VI. and Mary.

THE English reformers during the reign of king Edward VI. were engaged in the distinct, though 5 kindred, objects of renouncing the corruptions and authority of the Romish Church, and reconstructing the Church of England. But the means that they had of accomplishing these two portions of their work were extremely different. Having been the principal 10 agents and conductors of the one, it seemed as if they were considered to have neither right nor interest in the other. They had exposed the errors and renounced the jurisdiction of the court of Rome ; but the powers which that court had exercised were transferred, as 15 of necessity, to their sovereign, and no inquiry was made, whether some of them were not part of his original prerogative, and others inconsistent with the nature of his office. It appeared as if the Church of England, having drifted away from the shores of the 20 papacy, was treated by the statesmen of those times as a waif[a] or an estray, and claimed, like all other *bona vacantia,* as the property of the crown.

With respect, then, to the future condition and

[a] This view of the case, though resting on other grounds, was doubt-25 less confirmed by the act of submission, 25 Henry VIII. c. 19.

the positive reformation of the national church, the
powers of the reformers were at an end, as soon as
they had shaken off the tyranny of Rome.   But though
excluded by the nature of the case from any direct
interference in the reconstruction of the Church, their 5
difficulties were mitigated and in great measure removed by the circumstances of the time and the
character of the sovereign.   Edward VI. had adopted
the principles of the reformation to a greater extent
and in a more religious spirit than most of his con- 10
temporaries.   Independently of his general attain-
ments, and the wonderful proficiency he had made in
every branch of sacred knowledge, his youth, his
ingenuous disposition, and even the delicacy of his
physical constitution, were the occasion of placing 15
considerable power in the hands of the reformers,
by inducing him to confide in their integrity and
wisdom.   As yet, moreover, this spirit of confidence,
a spirit least likely to flourish in those exalted regions,
was not repressed by the existing condition of religious 20
controversy, or by the appearance of disunion among
the reformers themselves.   The cause in which they
were engaged had not yet been so successful in its
warfare against the power of Rome, as to afford them
time for turning away their attention from the com- 25
mon enemy, and fixing it upon their own differences.
Being a time of general danger, calling for their
constant and united activity, it left no room for the
exercise of curious and idle speculation ; and the party
zeal and bitter hatred, which gradually made their 30
appearance, as the points in dispute were more nar-
rowly examined, were still latent among the elements
of the contest, and unknown and unsuspected by the
parties that were engaged in it.

And this may be distinctly shewn from the two controversies on the nature of the eucharist, and the proper use of clerical vestments, which were the most remarkable at the present period. The dispute respect-
5 ing the real presence in the eucharist, which more than any other occupied the thoughts and exercised the skill of the reformers, gave them the first opportunity for pursuing new and more subtle subjects of discussion, but found them so much in fear of the
10 Romish tenet of transubstantiation, that their confidence in each other continued hitherto unshaken. Even the objections against the use of clerical vestments, objections that were levelled at an early period by the reformers against each other, and have since
15 become a fruitful source of discord and disunion, appear to have been laid aside for the time by general consent, from an implicit reliance on the prevailing wisdom and moderation of their counsels.

From these causes, then, from the character and
20 circumstances of the sovereign, combined with the peculiar state and the limited development of religious controversy, ensued a general sense of trustworthiness and a direct influence of public opinion, which, notwithstanding the demands of the prerogative, enabled
25 the reformers to take their part in removing the errors and filling up the void of their national church, as well as in establishing their independence of the court of Rome.

It is not necessary to inquire whether the mutual
30 confidence entertained by the reformers of this period, and their consequent readiness to include as many as possible within the terms of communion, were not owing to a peculiar and transitory state of feeling, rather than to a condition of things likely to become

permanent. It is sufficient to observe that, after an
interval of no great length, whatever was the cause,
whether the fear of surrendering some essential truth,
or the jealousy arising from past dissensions, the
terms of communion were narrowed, and the national 5
church had then to encounter a new description of
enemies.

But the rapid progress of change during the short
reign of Edward, and the earnest endeavour that was
made to include all degrees of reformers within the 10
pale of the Church, may be easily traced in the alterations introduced into the Book of Common Prayer
in the year 1552. The earlier edition of 1549,
although constructed wisely and with due regard to
the existing state of public sentiment, was soon found 15
to adhere too closely to the ancient learning. The
encouragement, which had in the mean time been
given to the exercise of private judgment, and the
necessity that followed and was readily obeyed, of
appealing to the sole authority of Scripture, had swept 20
away the foundations of Romanism, and brought into
the minds of men principles and motives powerful
enough to throw down the strongholds of their early
associations. The older and more thoughtful among
the reformers were well aware that there was a moral 25
force in the practice of past ages, and a Christian duty
connected with the sense of God's government of his
Church, which should make them fearful of change,
and distrustful of their own impressions. But how
could they forsake the very principle on which their 30
religious freedom had been obtained, or abandon their
more ardent brethren, who had been the most effectual
instruments in obtaining it? On this impression, then,
they still continued to act in concert, enlarging, as

occasion needed, the pale of their communion ; but
they seem to have forgotten that some of the special
tenets they were renouncing, were still an important
part of public opinion, and that in extending their
5 limits for the purpose of admitting persons, who had
few articles of faith, [b] they were unavoidably excluding
others, who believed accurately and completely. It
may be doubted whether in such cases the converts,
who are newly admitted into communion, are more
10 valuable members than those who are displaced by
them. It is certainly not improbable that if the reign
of Edward had been prolonged, and his counsels had
continued to be directed on the same principle, an
attempt would have been made to establish an ecclesi-
15 astical polity after the model of some foreign churches,
and would have terminated either in civil discord, or
in the permanent loss of some of the best properties in
our church-government.

Two principal alterations introduced into the Liturgy
20 on the revision of 1552, and connected with the two
important points of controversy already noticed, will
illustrate what has been stated. The service of the
communion had previously been so constructed as to
accord with the belief of the real presence of Christ
25 in the sacred elements, and even in some respects to
favour the doctrine of his substantial and corporal
presence. It was declared, for instance, in one of the
rubrics, after describing the kind of bread to be used,

---

[b] " The doctrine of the Lord's supper hath been so slenderly
30 taught by some, that a number have conceived with themselves that
they receive nothing but the external elements in remembrance that
Christ died for them. And these their cogitations have they uttered
to other to their great misliking." Bp. Cooper's Admonition to
the People of England, p. 121.

and the manner in which it was to be divided, " men must not think less to be received in part than in the whole, but in each of them the whole body of our Saviour Jesus Christ." This service accordingly was approved by the advocates of the ancient learning, and the sacrament, as thus administered, was received by many who considered themselves in communion with the Church of Rome. But the alterations of 1552 were of such a nature as to be consistent with the belief that the sacred elements had no new virtues whatever imparted to them, and that Christ was present in the eucharist in no other manner than as he is always present to the prayers of the faithful. That this important change was actually intended, is evident from the words addressed individually to the communicants, which may fairly be considered as the cardinal point of the whole service. Those words were no longer " The body of our Lord Jesus Christ, which was given for thee, preserve thy body and soul unto everlasting life," but merely " Take and eat this in remembrance that Christ died for thee, and feed on him in thy heart by faith with thanksgiving :" and the new form appears to have been suggested from the ritual of a church of foreigners [c] then resident in England, who were among the most remarkable for their rejection of ancient practices and distinct confessions of faith. Here, then, was a difference in a question of religious belief, where, for the sake of enlarging the pale of communion, several shades of opinion were excluded from the public ritual, and exposed to the imputation of being publicly condemned.

The other important alteration was in regard to the

[c] See the two Liturgies of King Edward VI. preface, p. xxix. note.

use of clerical vestments. The vestments used by the Romanists in divine service, and more especially the further decorations required in the sacrifice of the mass, had hitherto been retained by the reformers in 5 their corresponding offices, and probably were not without effect in moderating the hostility of their opponents. But it was owing to the reverence in which these vestments were held by the people, that they were odious to the more earnest reformers, and 10 that the removal of them was declared to be essential to the purity of Christian worship. It was accordingly enjoined in a rubric of 1552 " that the minister at the time of the communion, and at all other times in his ministration, shall use neither alb, vestment nor 15 cope: but being archbishop or bishop he shall have and wear a rochet: and being a priest or deacon he shall have and wear a surplice only."

Now this alteration involved an important victory, not merely because it departed still further from the 20 practice of the Romanists, but much more because it led to the admission of a new principle among the reformers themselves, a larger interpretation being given to the right of private judgment. Unlike the other subject of controversy, which was altogether a 25 question of faith and conscience, and was left on both sides to be solved by an appeal to Scripture, the proper use of vestments was an ordinance of the Church. Being indifferent in its nature, it had merely the force of a human regulation, and became binding on the 30 conscience only so far as the Church had authority to make it so. Such, at least, was the opinion which men in general would entertain respecting it. In favour, then, of the ancient practice were the authoritative decision of the Church, the conscientious feeling that was unwilling to disturb it, the approbation of those semi-converts who were attached to the ancient worship, and the calm assent of the greater portion of the faithful : opposed to them were the convictions of a small minority of the reformers, but those convic-5 tions combining an unconquerable activity, an utter hatred of Romanism, and a deep persuasion of the sinfulness of acquiescence. The strong feelings of the few prevailed against the judgment of the many, and the sense of individual responsibility was allowed to 10 overpower the voice of Church-authority. And yet, in such a case, where the considerations on the two sides were so different in their moral nature, where no religious advantage was gained by maintaining the ancient practice, and provision was effectually made 15 for the decent performance of public worship, who shall say that the alteration was unwisely granted, or unworthy of the high authority that consented to it?

This view of the matter may be confirmed by the 20 judgment of Lord Bacon, which he expressed at a later period in the following emphatic language : [d] " For the cap and surplice, since they be things in their nature indifferent, and yet by some held super-stitious, and that the question is between science and 25 conscience, it seemeth to fall within the compass of the Apostle's rule, which is, ' that the stronger do descend and yield to the weaker.' Only the difference is, that it will be materially said, that the rule holdeth between private man and private man ; but not be- 30 tween the conscience of a private man and the order of a church. But yet since the question at this time is of a toleration, not by connivance, which may en-

[d] Of the Pacification of the Church. Works, vol. ii. p. 541.

courage disobedience, but by law, which may give
a liberty; it is good again to be advised whether it fall
not within the equity of the former rule : the rather,
because the silencing of ministers by this occasion, is,
5 in this scarcity of good preachers, a punishment that
lighteth upon the people as well as upon the party.
And for the subscription, it seemeth to me in the
nature of a confession, and therefore more proper to
bind in the unity of faith, and to be urged rather for
10 articles of doctrine, than for rites and ceremonies, and
points of outward government. For howsoever politic
considerations and reasons of state may require uniformity, yet Christian and divine grounds look chiefly
upon unity."

15 Such was the condition of things in the year 1553,
when king Edward died, and a zealous member of the
Church of Rome succeeded to the throne. The history of the English reformers may now be considered
as transferred to those places on the Continent, where
20 the exiles were permitted to establish themselves, and
to observe their own forms of religious worship.
Amounting in number, as is generally computed, to
more than 800, and consisting of almost all that were
eminent, whether for station or for energy, among
25 the English protestants, they formed small communi-
ties at Embden, Frankfort, Strasburg, Basil, Arau,
Zurich, Geneva, and other places, and communicated
with each other, as occasion required, on all matters
of religious interest. From the places that have
30 been mentioned, it would not be expected that the
reformers would imbibe a more patient spirit than
they had hitherto shewn, or more temperate views
of religious liberty. At Zurich indeed, and Strasburg,
under the influence of such men as Bullinger and

Martyr, moderate sentiments appear to have constantly prevailed, and to have been followed by mutual harmony. Building themselves on their most holy faith, the exiles in those places were also laying a foundation for future usefulness. But the history of the churches [5] at Frankfort and Geneva is a continued narrative of restlessness and discord, of disorderly passions that were exhibited without restraint, in places conspicuous for ecclesiastical license and republican modes of thinking.

It is worthy of remark that, with the exception of [10] the Lutherans and the followers of Bucer, the English reformers had universally acquiesced in the doctrinal alterations of the year 1552, and that the real presence, which had previously been so fertile in controversy, ceased from that period to be a subject of violent [15] dispute. The ceremonies of the Church, and through them, implicitly and eventually, the government of the Church, were now the question of universal interest. The exiles of Frankfort, being led by the circumstances of their case to discuss that question [20] to the uttermost, were unable to detach from it many feelings of personal animosity and a general spirit of distrust and jealousy, which exposed themselves and their followers to a life of perpetual discord. At Geneva the same question of ceremonies, less perverted [25] by any strife among the exiles, but more inflamed by the influence of republican principles, glided naturally into a desire for some new scheme of ecclesiastical polity, and a settled dislike for monarchical forms of government. The Genevan [e] notes on the English [30] Bible first published in 1560, and commending instances of resistance to authority, the two publications of Knox and Goodman which appeared during the

[e] Docum. Annals, vol. ii. p. 12, note.

reign of Mary and countenanced rebellion, and the
ritual adopted by the whole Church, after the model of
that of Calvin, are abundant evidence of the direction
and the extremity to which ecclesiastical questions
5 were carried by the exiles at Geneva.

What then was the state of religious opinion
and of parties in England on the accession of Elizabeth? The fierce persecutions of the last reign
had certainly repressed the public exhibition of
10 protestantism, but at the same time had laid a
foundation for the future increase of it, in the
strong testimony presented by the martyrs to the
truth of their cause, and the compassion and sympathy excited by their sufferings. During this trying
15 interval the minds and consciences of men were
gradually acquiring the solemn conviction that Romanism was as unfavourable to moral virtue as it
was destructive of civil freedom. There was already
therefore a numerous party that still professing the
20 leading doctrines of the Church of Rome, but actuated by a charitable spirit, were anxious for a more
catholic confession of faith. And these persons, as
well from the nature of their sentiments as from
their general character and condition of life, were a
25 main constituent of public opinion. But there was
also another party, not perhaps so numerous, but
supported by the reputation of greater learning and
more intimate acquaintance with the subject, who,
though opposed to ceremonies and lax as to princi-
30 ples of church-government, held a midway station in
points of doctrine between the Lutherans and the
divines of Zurich, and may be considered as the
followers of Bucer and Martyr. When they attempted
an exposition of their opinions, and more especially

on the nature of the eucharist, their distinctions were so subtle, and blended with so much of metaphysical refinement, that they made little impression upon general hearers. Even Grindal acknowledged in speaking of the writings of Bucer, [f] " ita sunt scripta, ut divinatore potius opus sit quam lectore."[5] But when they shewed it was their object to embrace the different parties of the Church under one common confession, so that both Lutherans and Sacramentaries might equally partake with them in their public worship, they created among common observers [10] a strong feeling in their favour, and the sanguine of all parties wished for their success. Hilles, [g] for instance, a well known merchant and generous friend of the exiles, acknowledged to Bullinger, that from the study of the Fathers he had learnt to differ [15] from the divines of Zurich on some important doctrines, having formed a decided preference for the confession of Augsburg; and yet gave no intimation of a division in the protestant body. Gualter also, the friend and colleague of Bullinger, writing [20] to the queen's physician early in the year 1559, and alluding to the attempts at comprehension, entreats " that they would not hearken to the counsels [h] of those men, who, when they saw that popery could not be honestly defended nor entirely retained, would [25] use all artifices to have the outward face of religion to remain mixed, uncertain and doubtful: so that

[f] In a letter to Conrad Hubert, Hess, Catal. vol. iii. p. 118. Zur. lett. 2 Ser. p. 18.

[30]

[g] Hess, Catal. vol. ii. p. 113. Zur. lett. 2 Ser. p. 15. Comp. a letter from Bullinger to Utenhovius in Strype, Ann. vol. i. p. i. pp. 76. 259.

[h] Burnet, Hist. Ref. vol. iii. p. 524. P. 2. p. 353. Hess, Cat. vol. ii. p. 111. Zur. lett. 2 Ser. p. 11.

while an evangelical reformation is pretended, those things should be obtruded on the Church, which will make the returning back to popery, to superstition and to idolatry, very easy."

5 . These sentiments of moderation may be considered as entertained by the more valuable portion of the English laity on the accession of Elizabeth. But the divines who now came forth from their con-cealments, and began to exercise the influence be-10 longing at once to their station and their private character, contributed on their part to the same general impression. They were among the more cautious and prudent of their order, and wherever they had been conspicuous for their talents or learning, 15 had also shewn great forbearance towards their oppo-nents, acquiring such an interest in their good opinion, as enabled them to pass with safety through the time of persecution. The whole class may be well repre-sented by one of the ablest and most eminent of 20 them, Dr. Parker, the future archbishop of Canter-bury. He was a man of learning, of moderation, of system, and of piety, cautious in the formation of his opinions, and firm in maintaining them, but retiring in his habits, slow in his apprehensions, 25 perplexed in his statements, and disqualified for public speaking; " I am often put," said Bp. Sandys[1]

[1] Strype, Parker, vol. iii. p. 41. The archbishop in a private letter to secretary Cecil gives the following characteristic account of him-self : " I cannot be quyet tyl I have disclosed to youe, as to one 30 of my best willing frends, in secrecye myn imperfection. Which greavyth me not so moche to utter in respect of my own rebuke, as it greavyth me, that I am not able to answer your frendly report of me before tyme : wherebi to my moche gryef of hart I pass forth my life in hevynes, beyng thus intruded, notwithstanding my reluctation bi oft letters to my frendes, to be in such rome, which

in a letter to the Primate, " to a doubtful interpretation by reason of your sundry dark sentences." He naturally betook himself to the study of antiquities, and at a subsequent period, when every interest both of church and state was exposed to hazard, and his elevated office made him constantly liable to partake in the burdens of the government, he found at all times a relief and a solace from his cares in his favourite occupation.[k] But in addition to his general habits of prudence and moderation, there were two other points which would be thought likely at that critical period to qualify him for the exercise of church-authority. He had a profound respect for the prerogative of the crown, and dreaded the " *Germanical natures*," [l] as he styled them, of the English exiles.

These exiles were become, on the accession of Elizabeth, a most active constituent of public opinion. Remembered with affection for their own personal qualities, for the learning, the energy, and the devotion which they had constantly shewn in their ministrations,

I cannot susteyne agreably to the honor of the realme, yf I should be so far tryed. The truth is, what with passing those hard yeris of Mary's reigne in obscuritie, without al conference, or such maner of studye as nowe might do me service, and what with my natural vitiositie of overmoche shamfastness, I am so abashed in my self, that I cannot reyse up my hart and stomake to utter in talk with other, which (as I maye saye) with my pen I can express indifferently, without great difficultie. And agayn, I am so evyl acqueynted with strangers, both in their maner of utterance of their speche, and also in such foreyn affayres, that I cannot wynne of my self eny wayes to satisfye my fancye in such kynde of interteynments." Strype, Parker, vol. iii. p. 355.

k Isaac Walton gives a similar account of the recreations of Bishop Sanderson. Wordsw. Lives, vol. v. p. 534.

l Strype, Parker, vol. i. p. 156.

their character was invested with a still greater degree
of sacredness from its connection, to which they
seemed especially entitled, with the memory of Cranmer, of Latimer, of Ridley, and of their fellow-martyrs.
5 To aid these strong feelings in favour of the exiles
there was now the reputation they had contracted
from their intimacy with learned foreigners, and the
great fathers of the German reformation. There were
many of them in whom the sufferings they had under-
10 gone, and the religious differences they had witnessed,
had still failed to subdue their vehemence of temper,
or to moderate the severity of their opinions. Such
were Knox, Whittingham, Fox the martyrologist,
Goodman, Sampson, Whitehead, and others, who after-
15 wards became distinguished in the early history of
puritanism. But the exiles in general, having learnt
wisdom in adversity, and being supported by the
advice of such men as Martyr, Bullinger, Gualter, and
in some degree of Calvin and Beza, were prepared
20 to adopt a tone of moderation, and even to comply
with some observances which they positively disliked,
in the hope that they might be able at no distant
period to remove the remaining errors. " Id enitimur,"[m]
said Bp. Horne, in a letter subsequently addressed to
25 Bullinger, " ut licet male vestiti, bene certe cordati in
opere Domini conficiendo simus.—Alii se ab Ecclesia
separantes perinde faciunt ac ii qui cum auram sibi
adversam aliquantulum sentiant, nec possint statim,
quo volunt, pervenire, ad meliorem sese ventum re-
30 servare nolunt, sed exsilientes e navi in pelagus se
præcipitant ac submergunt."
  Over all these elements of public sentiment, attract-
ing, and in some degree absorbing them within its own

---

[m] Hess, Catal. vol. ii. p. 220. Zur. lett. 1 Ser. p. 248.

commanding influence, was the great character, moral and intellectual, of the sovereign. It would be idle to enlarge on the history of Elizabeth; but it is necessary to observe that owing partly to her natural disposition, and partly to the circumstances in which she had 5 been placed, she combined these several qualities—a consciousness of her own capacity, a love and a fitness for the exercise of power, a fondness for display, a reverence for old observances, and a jealous maintenance of her prerogative—together with a sincere 10 desire for the welfare of her subjects. With a character thus constituted, Elizabeth was placed in the possession of sovereign power at a time when every one felt the necessity for the firm and vigorous employment of it. No conjuncture could have been 15 more unfavourable for the views of those who were adverse to authority or lovers of change. But decisive as the case was in matters of civil government, it bore with cumulative force on questions connected with the Church. On such subjects the judgment and the pas- 20 sions of Elizabeth were equally engaged in resisting the progress of innovation. She was proud of her scholarship, and gave it a direction to the study of the Fathers,[m] from which arose an increasing respect for the maxims of the ancient learning. She had con- 25

[m] " About this time, the better to inform herself in the truth of Christian doctrine, and the government of the Church in the primitive times, she [the queen] was very diligent in reading the Fathers: of which Sir William Cecil, her secretary, wrote to Cox, bishop of Ely, in his correspondence with him. Concerning which that 30 bishop in answer gave his judgment in these words : ' that when all was done, the Scripture is that that pearseth. Chrysostom and the Greek Fathers *Pelagianizant*. Sometimes Bernard *Monachizat.*' And he trusted her Grace meddled with them but *succisivis horis.*" Strype, Ann. vol. i. p. i. p. 540.

tracted a personal offence against Knox and Goodman[n] for their works published at Geneva on the subject of female government, and by an easy transition a portion of the same resentment was conveyed to all the disciples
5 of the school of Calvin.   Under such circumstances it is not difficult to foresee what would be the tendency of the ecclesiastical measures adopted during the reign of Elizabeth.

[n] In a letter written to sir W. Cecil in Nov. 1559, Calvin laments
10 " officium suum in offerendis Commentariis in Isaiam Reginæ non adeo fuisse gratam ob libellum Goodmanni de imperio muliebri Genevæ ante biennium editum.   Quæ olim cum Knoxo de eodem imperio privatim contulerit, candide exponit, seque culpa omni hac in causa vacare multis evincit rationibus." Goodman himself writing
15 to Calvin in Feb. 1561 says, " Cum Anglis, qui Genevæ erant, durius in Anglia agitur." Hess, Catal. vol. ii. pp. 123. 149. Zur. lett. 2 Ser. p. 34. Sadler. i. 532.

CHAPTER I.

The revision of the Liturgy in the reign of Elizabeth.

ELIZABETH succeeded to the throne on the 17th of November, in the year 1558; and the earliest, as it was the most important, of her duties appears to have been to provide for the peculiar condition of the 5 Church. Although neither of the two great religious parties had as yet reason to look for her unqualified support, each of them was willing to interpret in its own favour the line of strict neutrality, which the queen thought it prudent to adopt. The Romanists were in 10 all the places of power and influence, and were not only left in the quiet occupation of them, but had also discovered that there were many circumstances, connected with the character of Elizabeth and the security of her crown, which would make her desirous of 15 retaining their good opinion. The protestants, on the other hand, had the best reason for believing her private sentiments to be in accordance with theirs, and were publicly supported by those eminent men, who were known to be in possession of her confidence. 20 Under these impressions the utmost exertions were made on both sides to improve their respective advantages. Disorder naturally ensued; and the queen, anxious to maintain her reputation for neutrality, and to take no decisive step in favour of either party, until 25 the whole question had been fully examined, issued a

proclamation,[o] commanding " all maner of her subjects, as well those that be called to ministery in the
Church, as all others, that they do forbear to preach or
teach, or to gyve audience to any maner of doctrine
5 or preachyng, other than to the gospels and epistels,
commonly called the gospel and the epistel of the day,
and to the Ten Commaundements in the vulgar tongue,
without exposition or addition of any maner sense or
meaning to be applyed or added ; or to use any other
10 maner of publick prayer, rite, or ceremony in the
Church, but that which is alredy used, and by law
received; or the common letany used at this present in
her majesty's own chappel, and the Lords Prayer, and
the Crede in English ; until consultation may be had
15 by parlament, by her majesty and her three estates of
this realme, for the better conciliation and accord of
such causes as at this present are moved in matters
and ceremonies of religion."

In the mean time a committee of divines had been
20 instructed " to review the Book of Common Prayer,
and order of ceremonies and service in the Church,"
with the design that their report should be laid before
the queen and receive her approval, before it should
be submitted to parliament. At a time when the
25 benefices of the Church were occupied by Romanists,
no assistance could be obtained from a convocation in
such an undertaking ; and accordingly no questions of
the kind were laid before them. It does not even
appear that the committee of divines had any authority
30 given to them under the great seal, being merely a
private assembly meeting at the house of sir Thomas
Smith, a doctor of civil law, and under his presidency,

[o] Strype, Ann. vol. i. p. ii. p. 392.

with the power of calling in " other men of learning
and gravity" to assist them.   And this was probably
the only method that the circumstances of the case
admitted.   To have referred the whole question to the
convocations of the two provinces would have been to 5
put an end to the progress of the reformation : to have
appointed a royal commission after the example of
Henry and Edward, at a time when Henry's statute of
supremacy, having been repealed by Mary, was no
longer in force, would have been to acknowledge the 10
necessity for a power which it might be doubted
whether the crown possessed : and the only alternative
remaining was to take such measures of prudence, and
so to combine the judgments of pious and temperate
men, as to preoccupy the public mind, and to create a 15
kind of moral necessity for the consent of the parliament and the approbation of the people..

The committee thus assembled consisted of eight
members, selected in equal numbers from the exiles,
and those who had remained in England, but giving a 20
preponderance to the opinions entertained by the
queen.   The exiles were Cox, Whitehead, Grindal,
and Pilkington, of whom the two last were fair representatives of the party in general, Whitehead was
resolute in requiring further alterations, and Cox, from 25
his early connexion with king Edward, and his intimate acquaintance with the evils of dissent, was likely
to comply with the wishes of the court ; all of them
however were men of high reputation, and well qualified for the important duty entrusted to them.   The 30
other divines, Parker, May, and Bill, with the civilian
at their head, were personally devoted to the queen,
and desirous of adapting their plans of church-government to the general institutions of the kingdom.

The first question that would naturally offer itself to this committee, would be the choice between the two Service-books of king Edward ; and this question doubtless gave rise to much discussion in an assembly 5 so variously disposed.   They soon called in other men of eminence to assist them, among whom was Guest, soon afterwards made bishop of Rochester, a divine who had been much engaged in the earlier history of the reformation, and held sentiments on doctrinal 10 matters congenial with those of the queen.   When the whole review was completed, and the new Book of Common Prayer was presented to sir William Cecil, this divine accompanied it with a paper setting forth the reasons on which he had assented to several of the 15 proposed alterations.   It appears from that paper that he had received instructions from Cecil in favour of the first Service-book of king Edward, but had not found himself able in every instance to comply with them.

But the fact of greatest interest that we learn from 20 this document, is, that after the divines had completed their work and delivered it to sir W. Cecil, some important changes were still made, before the book received the sanction of the legislature.   It is sup- 25 posed by some[p] that these changes were introduced during its progress through parliament ; but it is more probable from the known sentiments and subsequent conduct of the queen,[q] that they were inserted previ-

[p] Collier, Hist. vol. ii. p. 430, &c.

[q] There is reason to believe that the queen exercised her royal 30 prerogative in a similar manner with regard to the 39 Articles, after they had been approved by convocation in the year 1562. The first clause of the 20th article respecting the positive authority of the Church, which at a subsequent period drew down much unmerited indignation on archbishop Laud, appears to have been

ously by herself and her council. This however is certain, that the committee of divines disapproved of any distinction, as to the use of vestments, between the celebration of the communion and the other services of the Church; and by a still bolder act of [5] concession left it to every man's choice to communicate either standing or kneeling: both these changes however were withdrawn before the book was eventually published, the practice which was adopted in the second year of king Edward being in each case [10] completely restored.

On the 24th of January, 1559, the day after the meeting of parliament, the convocation of the southern province was opened by Bonner, bishop of London. Much doubt would naturally exist as to the right of [15] convocation to enter upon any business without express directions from the crown, the statute of Henry, that prohibited a convocation from doing so, having been repealed during the last reign. This doubt prevailed more especially among the members of the lower [20] house; and when the bishops asked them, if they had any thing to propose, they answered that they knew not for what cause they were assembled, or on what matters they were to treat. Being advised by the bishops to make a supplication to the queen, they also [25] drew up certain articles for the disburdening of their conscience, as they said, and the declaration of their faith, requesting that the bishops would adopt them, and present them in the name of the whole convo-

added by command of Elizabeth. See Lamb's Articles, p. 35. [30] Synodalia, vol. i. p. 38. This is not surprising, as it was the belief of those times that the proper ratification of all ecclesiastical laws was solely in the act of the sovereign. See Docum. Annals, vol. ii. p. 171. note.

cation to the upper house of parliament. They were afterwards informed that their articles, had been presented in parliament by the keeper of the great seal, and with the exception of the last article had received 5 the further approbation of the universities of Oxford and Cambridge.[r]

The articles were the following:

1. That in the sacrament of the altar, by virtue of the words of Christ, duly spoken by the priest, is 10 present realiter under the kinds of bread and wine, the natural body of Christ, conceived of the Virgin Mary, and also his natural blood.

2. That after the consecration there remains not the substance of bread and wine, nor any other substance, 15 but the substance of God and man.

3. That in the mass is offered the true body of Christ and his true blood, a propitiatory sacrifice for the living and dead.

4. That to Peter the apostle, and his lawful successors 20 in the apostolic see, as Christ's vicars, is given the supreme power of feeding and ruling the Church of Christ militant, and confirming their brethren.

5. That the authority of handling and defining concerning the things belonging to faith, sacraments, and 25 discipline ecclesiastical, hath hitherto ever belonged

---

[r] Bp. Burnet (H. R. vol. iii. p. 527) says, "Bonner told the clergy that all their articles, except the last, were approved by the two universities." But there is no record in the registers at Oxford that any thing was done by the university in this matter as a cor- 30 porate act. The case is expressed more accurately in the following note on Wood's Annals, vol. ii. p. 140: "In the latter end of this year (1558) several articles were sent to the universities from the convocation of the clergy, containing matters flat against reformation, which were subscribed by most of the university."

and ought to belong only to the pastors of the Church; whom the Holy Ghost for this purpose hath set in the Church ; and not to laymen.

Such was the only measure in connection with the Church adopted by the convocation of 1559; and it [5] was evident from this measure that the queen's government must proceed with the utmost caution in their plans of reformation. It was doubtless occasioned in a great degree by the report that had been made to the council by the committee of divines ; as a bill of [10] uniformity had already been submitted to the house of commons, and the designs of the court with regard to the liturgy were made publicly known. Warned therefore by these strong tokens of hostility, and by the great influence of the Romanists in the country at [15] large, Elizabeth resolved upon withdrawing the bill of uniformity for the present, and adopting some method of turning the stream of public opinion more strongly in favour of the reformers. She decided upon a conference between the most eminent divines of the two [20] rival parties, to be held at Westminster in the presence of her privy council; being convinced that whatever in other respects might be the issue of it, much advantage would be obtained for the direction of her future measures.   [25]

The following were the questions proposed for discussion :

1. It is against the word of God, and the custom of the ancient Church, to use a tongue unknown to the people in common prayer and the administration of [30] the sacraments.

2. Every Church hath authority to appoint, take away, and change ceremonies and ecclesiastical rites, so the same be done to edification.

3. It can not be proved by the word of God, that there is in the mass offered up a sacrifice propitiatory for the quick and the dead.

The divines appointed to conduct the discussion 5 were White, Watson, Baine, and Scot, bishops of Winchester, Lincoln, Lichfield, and Chester, with the four doctors, Cole, dean of St. Paul's, Langdale, Harpsfield, and Chedsey, archdeacons of Lewes, Canterbury, and Middlesex, on the side of the Romanists; and 10 Scory, (late bishop of Chichester,) Whitehead, Jewel, Ælmer, Cox, Grindal, Horne, and Guest, on the side of the reformers.

The proceedings of this important conference may be stated in the words of the report published by au- 15 thority of the privy council soon afterwards for general circulation :

The declaration [s] of the proceeding of a conference begun at Westminster, the last of March, 1559, concerning certain articles of religion; and the breaking up of the said con- 20 *ference, by default and contempt of certain bishops, parties of the said conference.*

THE queen's most excellent majesty having heard of diversity of opinions in certain matters of religion, amongst sundry of her loving subjects, and being very desirous to have the same 25 reduced to some godly and Christian concord, thought it best, by advice of the lords, and others of her privy council, as well for the satisfaction of persons doubtful, as also for the knowledge of the very truth, in certain matter of difference, to have a convenient chosen number of the best learned of either part,

30   [s] This is taken from an original among abp. Parker's papers in the Library of Corpus Christi College Cambridge, vol. 121. entitled, "Synodalia." Comp. Burnet, H. R. vol. ii. p. ii. p. 483. A longer and more minute account of this conference is given by Fox, Acts and Mon. vol. 2. p. 2119. edit. 1583.

and to confer together their opinions and reasons; and thereby
to come to some good and charitable agreement. And hereupon, by her majesty's commandment, certain of her privy
council declared this purpose to the archbishop of York,
(being also one of the same privy council,) and required him, 5
that he would impart the same to some of the bishops, and to
make choice of eight, nine, or ten of them; and that there
should be the like number named of the other part; and further
also declared to him, (as then was supposed) what the matters
should be: and as for the time, it was thought meet to be as 10
soon as possible might be agreed upon; and then after certain
days past, it was signified by the said archbishop, that there
was appointed, by such of the bishops to whom he had imparted this matter, eight persons; that is to say, four bishops
and four doctors, who were content, at the queen's majesty's 15
commandment, to shew their opinions, and, as he termed it,
render account of their faith in those matters which were
mentioned, and that specially in writing: although, he said,
they thought the same so determined, as there was no cause
to dispute upon them. It was hereupon fully resolved, by the 20
queen's majesty, with the advice aforesaid, that, according to
their desire, it should be in writing on both parts, for avoiding
of much altercation in words. And that the said bishops
should, because they were in authority of degree superiors,
first declare their minds and opinions to the matter, with their 25
reasons, in writing. And the other number, being also eight
men of good degree in schools, and some having been in dignity
in the Church of England, if they had any thing to say to the
contrary, should the same day declare their opinions in like
manner. And so each of them should deliver their writings 30
to the other to be considered what were to be improved therein;
and the same to declare again in writing at some other convenient day; and the like order to be kept in all the rest of
the matters.

All this was fully agreed upon with the archbishop of York, 35
and so also signified to both parties; and immediately hereupon divers of the nobility, and states of the realm, understanding that such a meeting and conference should be, and

that in certain matters, whereupon the court of parliament
consequently following, some laws might be grounded, they
made earnest means to her majesty, that the parties of this
conference might put and read their assertions in the English
5 tongue, and that in the presence of them, of the nobility,
and others of her parliament-house, for the better satisfaction,
and enabling of their own judgments to treat and conclude
of such laws as might depend thereupon. This also being
thought very reasonable, was signified to both parties, and
10 so fully agreed upon; and the day appointed for the first
meeting to be the Friday in the forenoon, being the last of
March, at Westminster church, where, both for good order,
and for honour of the conference, by the queen's majesty's
commandment the lords and others of the privy council were
15 present, and a great part of the nobility also.

And notwithstanding the former order appointed and consented unto by both parts, yet the bishop of Winchester and
his colleagues, alleging they had mistaken that their assertions and reasons should be written, and so only recited out of
20 the book, said, their book was not ready then written, but
they were ready to argue and dispute, and therefore they would
for that time repeat in speech that which they had to say to
the first proposition.

This variation from the former order, and specially from that
25 which themselves had, by the said archbishop, in writing
before required, (adding thereto the reason of the apostle, that
*to contend with words is profitable to nothing, but to subversion
of the hearer,*) seemed to the queen's majesty's council somewhat
strange; and yet was it permitted, without any great repre-
30 hension, because they excused themselves with mistaking the
order, and agreed, that they would not fail, but put it in
writing, and, according to the former order, deliver it to
the other part.

And so the said bishop of Winchester and his colleagues
35 appointed Dr. Cole, dean of Paul's, to be the utterer of their
minds, who partly by speech only, and partly by reading of
authorities written, and at certain times being informed of his
colleagues what to say, made a declaration of their meanings
and their reasons to their first proposition.

Which being ended, they were asked by the privy council, If any of them had any more to be said? and they said, No. So as then the other part was licensed to shew their minds, which they did accordingly to the first order, exhibiting all that which they meant to be propounded in a book written. 5 Which, after a prayer, and invocation made most humbly to Almighty God, for the enduing of them with his Holy Spirit, and a protestation also to stand to the doctrine of the catholic church, builded upon the Scriptures, and the doctrine of the prophets and the apostles, was distinctly read by one Robert 10 Horn, bachelor in divinity, late dean of Duresme. And the same being ended, (with some likelyhood, as it seemed, that the same was much allowable to the audience,) certain of the bishops began to say, contrary to their former answer, that they had now much more to say to this matter; wherein, although 15 they might have been well reprehended for such manner of cavillation, yet for avoiding any more mistaking of orders in this colloquy, or conference, and for that they should utter all that which they had to say, it was both ordered, and thus openly agreed upon of both parts, in the full audience, that 20 upon the Monday following the bishops should bring their minds and reasons in writing to the second assertion, and the last also, if they could, and first read the same; and that done, the other part should bring likewise theirs to the same; and being read, each of them should deliver to other the same 25 writings. And in the mean time the bishops should put in writing, not only all that which Dr. Cole had that day uttered, but all such other matters as they any otherwise could think of for the same; and as soon as they might possible, to send the same book, touching that first assertion, to the other part; 30 and they should receive of them that writing which master Horn had there read that day; and upon Monday it should be agreed what day they should exhibit their answers touching the first proposition.

Thus both parts assented thereto, and the assembly quietly 35 dismissed. And therefore upon Monday the like assembly began again at the place and hour appointed; and there, upon what sinister or disordered meaning is not yet fully known, (though in some part it be understanded,) the bishop of

Winchester and his colleagues, and especially Lincoln, refused to exhibit or read, according to the former notorious order on Friday, that which they had prepared for the second assertion; and thereupon, by the lord keeper of the great seal, they being 5 first gently and favourably required to keep the order appointed, and that taking no place, being secondly, as it behoved, pressed with more earnest request, they neither regarding the authority of that place, nor their own reputation, nor the credit of the cause, utterly refused that to do.

10 And finally, being again particularly every one of them apart distinctly by name required to understand their opinions therein; they all, saving one, (which was the abbot of Westminster, having some more consideration of order, and his duty of obedience, than the other,) utterly and plainly denied to have 15 their book read, some of them as more earnestly than other some, so also some other more indiscreetly and irreverently than others.

Whereupon giving such example of disorder, stubbornness, and self-will, as hath not been seen and suffered in such an 20 honourable assembly, being of the two estates of this realm, the nobility and the commons, beside the presence of the queen's majesty's most honourable privy council, the same assembly was dismissed, and the godly and most Christian purpose of the queen's majesty made frustrate : and afterwards, for the 25 contempt so notoriously made, the bishops of Winchester and Lincoln, having most obstinately both disobeyed common authority, and varied manifestly from their own order, and specially Lincoln, who shewed more folly than the other, were condignly committed to the Tower of London ; and the 30 rest, saving the abbot of Westminster, stand bound to make daily their personal appearance before the council, and not to depart the city of London and Westminster, until further order be taken with them for their disobedience and contempt.

N. Bacon, cust. sigill.

35   F. Shrewsbury.   F. Bedford.   Pembrook.

                                               E. Clynton.

G. Rogers.   F. Knollys.   W. Cecill.   A. Cave.

Strengthened and directed by the proceedings and the issue of this conference, the queen's government again brought into the house of commons a bill of uniformity, with a copy of the Book of Common Prayer annexed to it. So decided was now the 5 impression in its favour, that it was read in that house on three successive days, and passed apparently without any difference of opinion. It was sent to the house of lords on the 26th of April, and was passed by them on the 28th of the same month, 10 having there encountered great but ineffectual opposition. The speeches of the bishop of Chester and the abbot Feckenham are still preserved, and may be read in the ensuing chapter; and the Romanist party on the last division were eighteen in number, 15 consisting of all the spiritual lords then present, with the addition of the marquis of Winchester, the earl of Shrewsbury, viscount Montague, and the barons Morley, Stafford, Dudley, Wharton, Rich, and North. It was ordered that the book should begin to be 20 in use from the following festival of St. John the Baptist.

It is necessary to mention the points of difference between this book and the second Service-book of king Edward, as they will clearly denote the par-25 ticulars in which Elizabeth, whether expressing her own opinions or summing up the wants of her subjects, deviated from the sentiments of her royal brother. They point out at once what were then considered the most vulnerable places in the ritual of the Church, 30 and the additional defences that were thought necessary for their protection. These differences were afterwards stated by archbishop Whitgift, in answer to an inquiry[t] from lord treasurer Burghley, in the following manner:

[t] Strype, Ann. vol. i. P. 1. p. 123. Besides the alterations noticed
in this list of abp. Whitgift, there were several changes made in the
5 Calendar, such as the appointment of proper lessons for Sundays,
as well as for several holidays, for which there were previously
epistles and gospels, but no proper lessons. The alterations are
described in the following manner in the act of uniformity, (1 Eliz.
c. 2. §. 3.) " That all and singular ministers in any cathedral or parish
10 church, or other place within this realm of England, Wales and the
Marches of the same or other the queen's dominions, shall from and
after the feast of the nativity of St. John Baptist next coming, be
bounden to say and use the mattens, evensong, celebration of the
Lord's supper, and administration of each of the sacraments, and all
15 the common and open prayer, in such order and form as is mentioned
in the said book, so authorized by parliament in the said 5th and 6th
years of the reign of king Edward VI. with one alteration or addition of certain lessons to be used on every Sunday in the year, and
the form of the litany altered and corrected, and two sentences only
20 added in the delivery of the sacrament to the communicants, and
none other, or otherwise."   But the tables of proper lessons were
not yet satisfactorily arranged, and in the following year (1560) the
queen issued a warrant authorizing her ecclesiastical commissioners
" to peruse the order of the said lessons throughout the whole yere,
25 and to cause some new calendars to be imprinted, whereby such
chapters or parcels of less edification may be removed, and other
more profitable may supply their roomes."   It seems that the bishops
were willing to leave this discretion to be exercised by the clergy at
large ; for in the year 1564, when the second book of Homilies was
30 published, the following admonition was prefixed to it : " Where it
may so chance some one or other chapter of the Old Testament to
fall in order to be read upon the Sundays or holidays, which were
better to be changed with some other of the New Testament of more
edification, it shall be well done to spend your time to consider well
35 of such chapters beforehand."   And this discretion continued to be
exercised at a later period ; for " Dr. G. Abbot (afterwards abp. of
Canterbury) did reckon this liberty, granted in the said admonition,
to be in force even in his time . . . saying, ' It is not only permitted
to the minister, but commended to him, if wisely and quietly he do

" 1. King Edward's second book differeth from her majesty's book in the first rubric, set down in the beginning of the book; for king Edward's second book hath it thus:

'The morning and evening prayer shall be used 5 in such place of the church, chapel or chancel, and the minister shall turn him, as the people may best hear. And if there be any controversy therein, the matter shall be referred to the ordinary, and he or his deputy shall appoint the place. And the' &c.   10

" Whereas the queen's book hath it thus:

'The morning and evening prayer, shall be used in the accustomed place of the church, chapel or chancel, except it shall be otherwise determined by the ordinary of the place. And the chancels shall 15 remain as they have done in times past.'

" Again, king Edward's second book hath it thus:

'Again, here is to be noted that the minister at the time of the communion, and all other times in his ministration, shall use neither alb vestment nor 20 cope: but being archbishop or bishop shall have and wear a rochet; and being a priest or deacon, he shall have and wear a surplice only.'

" The queen's book hath it:

'And here is to be noted that the minister at 25 the time of the communion, and at all other times in his ministration, shall use such ornaments in the

read canonical Scripture, where the apocryphal upon good judgment seemeth not so fit; or any chapter of the canonical may be conceived not to have in it so much edification before the simple, as some other 30 parts of the same canonical may be thought to have." Strype, Ann. vol. i. p. ii. p. 105. Docum. Ann. vol. i. p. 260. It is clear however that no such discretion is allowed under the act of uniformity 13 and 14 Charles II. c. 4.

church, as were in use by authority of parliament in the second year in the reign of king Edward VI. according to the act of parliament set forth in the beginning of this book.'

5 2. " In king Edward's second book in the litany there are these words, ' From the tyranny of the bishop of Rome, and all his detestable enormities ;' which are not in her majesty's book.

3. " In the litany, her majesty's book hath these 10 words more than are in king Edward's second book, viz. ' strengthen in the true worshipping of thee, in righteousness and true holiness of life.'

4. " In the end of the litany there is no prayer in king Edward's second book for the king nor for the 15 state of the clergy. And the last collect set in her majesty's book next before the first Sunday in Advent, and beginning, ' O God, whose nature and property is ever to have mercy,' is not in king Edward's second book. Further, there are two collects ap- 20 pointed for the time of dearth and famine; whereas her majesty's book hath but one. And in king Edward's second book this note is given of the prayer of St. Chrysostom, ' The litany shall ever end with this collect following ;' which note is not in her majesty's 25 book.

5. "King Edward's second book appointeth only these words to be used when the bread is delivered at the communion, ' Take and eat this in remembrance that Christ died for thee, and feed on him in thine heart 30 by faith with thanksgiving.' And when the cup is delivered, ' Drink this in remembrance that Christ's blood was shed for thee, and be thankful.' Whereas in her majesty's book at the delivering of the bread these words must be said, ' The body of our Lord Jesus

D

Christ, which was given for thee, preserve thy body
and soul unto everlasting life. Take and eat this' &c.:
and at the delivery of the cup these words, ' The blood
of our Lord Jesus Christ, which was shed for thee,
preserve thy body and soul unto everlasting life. Drink 5
this &c.' "

From this comparison then of the two Books of
Common Prayer it appears to have been the persuasion
of the queen and her council that in the important
questions of the eucharist and clerical vestments too 10
much had been done in the reign of king Edward in
the way of innovation : that the mysteries of religion
had been impugned by excluding words that might
suggest, though they would not necessarily involve,
the doctrine of the real presence, and the authority 15
of the Church had been injured in the alteration
respecting vestments.   On the first point accordingly
the form of words addressed individually to the communicants was now made to combine the two separate
forms of the time of king Edward.   With the same 20
view also was expunged the rubric[u] which had been

---

[u] The rubric, after stating in its preamble the necessity for
kneeling, and the misconstruction put upon it, proceeds thus : "We
do declare that it is not meant thereby that any adoration is done
or ought to be done either unto the sacramental bread and wine 25
there bodily received, or unto any real and essential presence there
being of Christ's natural flesh and blood.   For as concerning the
sacramental bread and wine, they remain still in their very natural
substances, and therefore may not be adored ; for that were idolatry
to be abhorred of all faithful Christians ; and as concerning the 30
natural body and blood of our Saviour Christ, they are in heaven
and not here ; for it is against the truth of Christ's true natural
body to be in more places than in one at one time."   This rubric
does not appear in either of the editions printed by Whitchurch in
1552, copies of which are now in the Bodleian ; but it does appear 35
in each of two editions by Grafton, printed in August 1552, copies

added to the Communion Service by that king on his
own authority after the publication of his second
liturgy, declaring " that no adoration was done or
ought to be done to any real or essential presence
5 there being of Christ's natural flesh and blood." To
these changes no reasonable objection could be made
on either side. The Romanists could not disapprove
of what they held to be improvements, although they
did not amount to all that was desired : and the
10 sacramentaries could not complain of the combined
form of words addressed to communicants, unless they
would condemn the use of scripture language, or
require the continuance of a rubric which had never
received the authority of the legislature. On this
15 point therefore there was little important controversy
for the future, although the demand made in the time

of which may also be seen in the same library. The act of parliament, which ratified the second Service-book, was passed in April
1552; and the order of council requiring the insertion of the rubric
20 bears date on the 27th of October, only four days before the book
was to be generally used throughout the kingdom. It is found
accordingly to have been inserted by cancelling the leaf, or some
similar contrivance; and the issuing of this order is a strong evidence
of the alarm in which Cranmer and the council were held on the
25 subject of the real presence, even after the great alteration they had
made respecting it in the service of the communion. The fate of the
rubric is worthy of notice. It was excluded by queen Elizabeth in
1559; and its removal clearly shews that the Church could not then
be brought to express an opinion adverse to the real presence : it
30 was restored in 1661, on the revision of King Charles II.; and its
reappearance may likewise be employed to shew that the Church at
that time also was unwilling to make any declaration on that important tenet. To prevent misapprehension on this point, the words
" or unto any real and essential presence there being of Christ's na-
35 tural flesh and blood," were altered to the very different expression
" or unto any corporal presence of Christ's natural flesh and blood."
Comp. the two Liturg. of Edw. VI. pref. p. xxxvii.

of king Edward for the restoration of the communion service, as it existed in his first liturgy, was occasionally renewed.

But the controversy respecting vestments immediately became formidable. It had hitherto confined[5] itself to the evil associations arising from a long and vicious practice, and their tendency to encourage in vulgar minds some of the worst corruptions of Romanism. It had also been much abated by the alterations made in the second Service-book, when the[10] more objectionable habits had been prohibited, and a hope had been created that even the use of the surplice might eventually be discontinued. But the rubric of 1559, that restored the ornaments and vestments of the second year of King Edward, was ex-[15]tremely galling to the exiles, and would probably have prevented the greater number of them from becoming ministers of the Church, had not the act of uniformity furnished them with a plea for complying. It had been enacted[x] that the queen, with the advice of her[20] commissioners or the metropolitan, might make such changes in the rubrics as might afterwards be found requisite. The reformers[y] therefore were not without some reason for hoping that their brethren who might be advanced to high stations in the Church would[25] retain their present spirit of moderation, and exercise

[x] 1 Eliz. c. 2. §. 25, 26.

[y] Strype, Ann. vol. i. P. 1. p. 122. Burnet, H. R. vol. ii. P. 2. p. 465. Bp. Sandys said in a letter to the archbishop, " The last book of service is gone through with a proviso, to retain the ornaments[30] which were used in the 1st and 2nd year of king Edward, until it please the queen to take other order for them : our gloss upon this text is, that we shall not be forced to use them ; but that others in the meantime shall not convey them away, but that they may remain for the queen."

a salutary influence on the future proceedings of the court. But the clauses in question, however available for such purposes, were probably introduced with very different designs. It appears that they were added to
5 the bill at the express direction of the queen, and were intended to assist her in carrying forward the high views of doctrine and authority which she was known to entertain.

It is impossible at this distant point of time to
10 collect together and to give their several values to the many elements of the question then at issue ; although it has never ceased at any period to be a subject of interest and contention. We must remember that the religious discord was then so predominant in its na-
15 ture, that like the pestilence recorded by the Athenian historian, it drew within it all the other grievances of the period, and was aggravated by their additional bitterness. We must remember that great scandal had arisen to the cause of the reformers from the
20 insubordination it had occasioned, and the divisions which appeared to be inseparable from it ; that it was calculated generally to encourage principles unfavourable to the received maxims of civil government and the admitted claims of the prerogative ; and in one of
25 its most important sections, the school of Geneva, was hostile to the institutions of a monarchy : that, to add to the contrast, the opposite party had the sanction of antiquity and the force of established usages in their favour; that they might naturally look for assistance
30 in the interference of foreign courts; and above all, that the next in succession at that time to the throne, separated from it by a life which was often deemed precarious, was a Romanist, devotedly attached to the principles of her Church. In pondering then the

religious question, the queen and her council would be
influenced by these considerations in a manner independent of the real merits of the argument, and to
a degree that would prevent them from being justly
appreciated.   Even the divines themselves, though less 5
likely to be misled by secular interests, could not be
insensible to the difficulties of their position, wearied,
as they were, with their past dissensions, and dreading,
not without much reason, the total extinction of protestantism.   It appears accordingly, that together with 10
those divines who approved entirely of the existing
state of things, there were two distinct parties con-
forming to the national Church; the first under the
direction of Parker, Horne, and Cox, who were persuaded that in so feverish and fluctuating a state of 15
public opinion no better terms could be obtained; the
other represented by Grindal, Sandys, and Jewel, who
acceded to the terms proposed, with the avowed intention of employing all honest methods for moulding
them according to their own principles.   The first of 20
these two parties possessed the confidence of the court,
and was employed during the reign of Elizabeth in all
the important measures she adopted for the government of the Church.   But the wishes of the other
party were also consulted, in the removal, for instance, 25
of the crucifix from the queen's chapel, in the alteration [*] of the rubric respecting vestments, and in other

---

[*] The Advertisements issued by the archbishop and bishops in
commission in the year 1564, though they did not overcome the
objections of the violent puritans, moderated the ancient rubric 30
respecting vestments, by removing the distinction between the
eucharist and other services in parish churches and retaining it in
cathedrals only.   The orders then were " In the ministration of the
holy communion in cathedral and collegiate churches the principal

matters then considered of importance.   And these
gradual alterations would probably have been carried
to a greater extent, had not intemperate designs and
theories dangerous to civil order been mingled with
5 the controversy, a result, which may be apprehended
in all periods of excitement, and which in those days
of high prerogative could not but be fatal to the
progress of reformation.

What were the sentiments of the clergy in general
10 respecting the Book of Common Prayer, thus published
by authority of parliament, may be learned from the
proceedings of the memorable convocation of 1562.
After the discussions connected with the 39 Articles
of religion, the convocation proceeded to consider the
15 measures proposed to them for the reformation of the
public liturgy.   Bishop Sandys moved that the queen
should be prayed, agreeably with the provisions of the
act of uniformity, to make such alterations as would
exclude women from administering the sacrament of
20 baptism, and put an end to the practice of signing the
infant with the cross ; and that, in conformity with the
plans of the late kings Henry and Edward, a commission should be appointed to draw up a code of

minister shall use a cope with gospeller and epistoler agreeably ;
25 and at all other prayers to be sayde at that communion table, to
use no copes but surplesses.   Item, that every minister sayinge any
publique prayers or ministringe the sacramentes or other rites of the
Churche shall weare a comely surples with sleeves to bee provided
at the charges of the parishe." It is true that these Advertisements
30 were not binding in law, as they had not been sanctioned under the
great seal : but it is clear they were considered binding, as they
certainly were approved by the queen ; and it had not yet been
ruled, that edicts issued by the queen's commission were not binding unless they were confirmed by the queen officially.   See
35 Document. Annals, vol. i. p. 287. Croke's Rep. 2 Jac. p. 37.

ecclesiastical laws.   A memorial was presented by
thirty-three members of the lower house containing
seven articles, which exhibit all the changes called for
at that early period of the controversy, and the wishes
entertained by the general body of the exiles.   These 5
articles were afterwards modified and reduced to six,
and on the 13th of February were proposed in the
lower house in the following order:

1. That all the Sundays in the year, and principal
feasts of Christ, be kept holidays; and all other 10
holidays to be abrogated.

2. That in all parish churches the minister in common prayer turn his face toward the people; and
there distinctly read the divine service appointed,
where all the people assembled may hear and be 15
edified.

3. That in ministering the sacrament of baptism,
the ceremony of making the cross in the child's forehead may be omitted, as tending to superstition.

4. That forasmuch as divers communicants are not 20
able to kneel during the time of the communion, for
age, sickness, and sundry other infirmities; and some
also superstitiously both kneel and knock; that order
of kneeling may be left to the discretion of the ordinary
within his jurisdiction.   25

5. That it be sufficient for the minister, in time of
saying divine service and ministering of the · sacraments, to use a surplice; and that no minister say
service, or minister the sacraments, but in a comely
garment or habit.   30

6. That the use of organs be removed.

The number in favour of these articles were forty-
three present, and fifteen proxies; the number opposed
to them were thirty-five present, and twenty-four

proxies; so that the articles were rejected by the majority of one. In the former list were all those members who had been brought into friendly contact with the practice of foreign churches in the reign of Mary, including several, as Lever and Sampson, who afterwards became nonconformists; in the latter were the friends of the archbishop and of bishops Horne and Cox, together with reformers who had remained in England during the reign of Mary, and several who had at the same period relapsed into Romanism.

CHAPTER II.

Documents connected with the revision of queen Elizabeth.

I. The device for alteration of religion in the first year of queen Elizabeth, (supposed to have been drawn up by sir Thomas Smith). Cotton Libr. Julius F. 6.

II. Dr. Guest to sir William Cecil, the queen's secretary, concerning the Service-book newly prepared for the parliament. Corp. Chr. Coll. Camb. vol. 106.

III. The first proposition upon which the papists and protestants disputed in Westminster Abbey. The discourse of Dr. Horne. Foxe's Acts and Mon. and Corp. Chr. Coll. Camb. vol. 121. Synodalia.

IV. The answer of Dr. Cole to the first proposition of the protestants. Corp. Chr. Coll. Camb. vol. 121. Synod.

V. The protestants' discourse prepared to have been read in the public conference at Westminster on the second question. Corp. Chr. Coll. Camb. vol. 121. Synod.

VI. Dr. Cox's letter to Wolfgang Weidner, with an account of the disputation at Westminster. Corp. Chr. Coll. Camb. vol. 241.

VII. A letter of Jewel's to Peter Martyr, concerning the disputation at Westminster. Burnet, Hist. Ref. vol. iii. part ii. pp. 360—362.

VIII. The oration of abbot Feckenham in the parliament house, 1559, against the bill for the liturgy. Corp. Chr. Coll. Camb. vol. 121. Synod.

IX. Another oration made by Dr. Scot, bishop of Chester, in the parliament house, 1559, against the bill for the liturgy. Fox, MSS. Vespasian, D. 18.

X. An extract out of the journal of the lower house of convocation. Burnet, Hist. Ref. vol. iii. part ii. pp. 419—422.

I.

The device for alteration of religion in the first year of queen Elizabeth.

I. WHEN the alteration shall be first attempted?

At the next parliament: so that the dangers be fore-
5 seen, and remedies therefore provided. For the sooner that religion is restored, God is the more glorified, and as we trust wilbe more merciful unto us, and better save and defend her highness from all dangers.

II. What dangers may ensue upon the alteration?

10 The bishop of Rome, all that he may, wilbe incensed. He will excommunicate the queen's highness, interdict the realms, and give it to prey to all princes, that will enter upon it; and incite them therto by all manner of means.

The French king will be encouraged more to the war, and
15 make his people more ready to fight against us, not only as enemies, but as heretics. He wilbe in great hope of aid from hence, of them that are discontented with this alteration, looking for tumult and discord. He will also stay concluding peace upon hope of some alteration.

20 Scotland will have some causes of boldness; and by that way the French king wil seem soonest to attempt to invade us.

Ireland also will be very difficultly stayed in their obedience, by reason of the clergy that is so addicted to Rome.

Many people of our own wilbe very much discontented;
25 especially these sorts:

All such as governed in the late queen Marie's time, and were chosen thereto for no other cause, or were then most esteemed for being hot and earnest in the other religion, and now remain unplaced and uncalled to credit, will think themselves discredited, and all their doings defaced, and study all the ways they can to maintain their former doings, and despise all this alteration.

Bishops and all the clergy wil se their own ruine. In 5 confession and preaching, and all other ways they can, they wil perswade the people from it. They wil conspire with whomsoever that wil attempt, and pretend to do God a sacrifice, in letting the alteration, tho' it be with murther of Christen men, or treason.   10

Men which be of the papist sect ; which late were in maner all the judges of the law ; the justices of the peace, chosen out by the late queen in all the shires ; such as were believed to be of that sect ; and the more earnest therin, the more in estimation.   These are like to joyn and conspire 15 with the bishops and clergy.

Some, when the subsidy shalbe granted, and money levied, (as it appeareth that necessarily it must be don,) wilbe therewith offended ; and like enough to conspire and arise, if they have any head to stir them to it, or hope of gain 20 and spoil.

Many such as would gladly have the alteration from the Church of Rome, when they shal se peradventure, that some old ceremonies shalbe left still, or that their doctrine, which they embrace, is not allowed and commanded only, and all 25 other abolished and disproved, shall be discontented, and call the alteration *a cloaked papistry*, or *a mingle mangle*.

III. What remedy for these matters!

First, for France, to practice a peace ; or if it be offered, not to refuse it. If controversy of religion be there among 30 them, to help to kindle it.

Rome is less to be doubted ; from whom nothing is to be feared, but evil will, cursing, and practising.

Scotland will follow France for peace. But there may be practised to help forward their divisions ; and especially 35 to augment the hope of them, who incline them to good religion. For certainty, to fortify Berwick, and to employ demilances and horsemen for the safety of the frontiers. And some expence of money in Ireland.

The fifth divided into five parts.

The first is of them which were of queen Mary's council, elected and advanced then to authority, only or chiefly for being of the pope's religion, and earnest in the same.   Every 5 augmentation or conservation of such men in authority or reputation is an encouragement of those of their sect, and giveth hope to them that it shall revive and continue, although it have a contrary blast.   Seeing their pillars to stand still untouched, [will be] a confirmation to them that 10 are wavering papists, and a discouragement of such that are but half enclined to that alteration.   " Dum in dubio est animus, paulo momento huc illuc impellitur."   These must be searched by all law, as far. as justice may extend ; and the queen's majesty's clemency to be extended not before they 15 do fully acknowledge themselves to have fallen in the lapse of the law.

They must be based of authority, discredited in their countries, so long as they seem to repugn to the true religion, or to maintain their old proceedings.   And if they 20 should seem to allow or to bear with the new alteration, yet not likely to be in credit, *quia neophyti.*   And no man but he loveth that time wherein he did flourish.   And when he can, and as he can, those ancient laws and orders ho will maintain and defend with whom and in whom he was 25 in estimation, authority, and a doer.   For every man natu- rally loveth that which is his own work and creature.

And contrary, as those men must be based, so must her highness's old and sure servants, who have tarryed with her, and not shrunk in the last storms, be advanced with 30 authority and credit : that the world may see that her highness is not unkind nor unmindful.   And throughout all England such persons as are known to be sure in religion, every one, according to his ability to serve in the common- wealth, to be set in place.   Whom, if in the cause of 35 religion, God's cause, they shall be slack, yet their own safety and state shall cause to be vigilant, careful, and earnest for the conservation of her state, and maintenance of this alteration.   And in all this, she shall do but the same that the late queen Mary did, to maintain and establish her religion.

The second of these five is the bishops and clergy, being in manner all made and chosen, such as were thought the stoutest and mightiest champions of the pope's church, who in the late times [by] taking from the crown, impoverishing it, by extorting from private men, and all other means possible, *per fas et nefas*, have thought to enrich and advance themselves; these her majesty, being enclined to so much clemency, yet must seek as well by parliament, as by the just laws of England, in the *præmunire*, and other such penal laws, to bring again in order. And being found in default, not to pardon, till they confess their fault, put themselves wholly to her highness's mercy, abjure the pope of Rome, and conform themselves to the new alteration. And by this means well handled, her majesty's necessity of money may be somewhat relieved.

The third is to be amended even as all the rest above, by such means as queen Mary taught, that none such, as near as may be, be in commission of peace in the shires, but rather men meaner in substance and younger in years; so that they have discretion to be put in place. A short law made and executed against assemblies of people without authority. Lieutenants made in every shire: one or two men known to be sure at the queen's devotion. In the mean time musters and captains appointed, viz. young gentlemen which earnestly do favour her highness. No office of jurisdiction or authority to be in any discontented man's hand, as far as justice or law may extend.

The fourth is not to be remedied otherwise than by gentle and dulce handleing, by the commissioners, and by the readiness and good-will of the lieutenants and captains to repress them, if any should begin a tumult, murmur, or provide any assembly, or stoutness to the contrary.

The fifth, for the discontentation of such as could be content to have religion altered, but would have it go too far, the straight laws upon the promulgation of the book, and severe execution of the same at the first, will so repress them, that it is great hope it shall touch but a few. And better it were that they did suffer, than her highness or commonwealth should shake, or be in danger. And to this they must well take heed that draw the book.

5   And herein the universities must not be neglected; and the hurt that the late visitation in queen Mary's time did must be amended. Likewise such colleges where children be instructed to come to the university, as Eaton and Winchester: that as well the encrease hereafter, as at this 10 present time, be provided for.

IV. What shall be the manner of the doing of it?

This consultation is to be referred to such learned men as be meet to shew their minds herein; and to bring a plat or book hereof ready drawn to her highness. Which being ap- 15 proved of her majesty may be so put into the parliament-house: to the which for the time it is thought that these are apt men; Dr. Bill, Dr. Parker, Dr. May, Dr. Cox, Mr. Whitehead, Mr. Grindal, Mr. Pilkington.

And sir Thomas Smith do call them together, and to be 20 amongst them. And after the consultation with these, to draw in other men of learning and gravity, and apt men for that purpose and credit, to have their assents.

As for that is necessary to be done before, it is thought most necessary, that a straight prohibition be made of all 25 innovation, until such time as the book come forth; as well that there should be no often changes in religion, which would take away authority in the common people's estimation; as also to exercise the queen's majesty's subjects to obedience.

30   V. To the fifth, What may be done of her highness for her own conscience openly, before the whole alteration: or, if the alteration must tarry longer, what order be fit to be in the whole realm, as an interim?

To alter no further than her majesty hath, except it be to 35 receive the communion as her highness pleaseth on high feasts. And that where there be more chaplains at mass, that they do always communicate in both kinds. And for her highness's conscience till then, if there be some other devout sort of prayers or *memory* said, and the seldomer mass.

VI. To the sixth, What noblemen be most fit to be made
privy to these proceedings, before it be opened to the
whole council?

The lord marquiss Northampton, the earl of Bedford, the
earl of Pembroke, and the lord John Grey.   5

VII. To the seventh, What allowance those learned men
shall have, for the time they are about to review the
Book of Common Prayer, and order of ceremonies, and
service in the church, and where they shall meet?

Being so many persons which must attend still upon it, 10
two mess of meat is thought yet indifferent to suffice for
them and their servants.

The place is thought most meet [to be] in some set place,
or rather at sir Thomas Smith's lodgings in Chanon Row.
At one of these places must provisions be laid in of wood, 15
and coals, and drink.

———◆———

II.

*Guest to sir William Cecyl, the queen's secretary, concerning the
Service-book, newly prepared for the parliament to be confirmed;
and certain ceremonies and usages of the Church.*

Right honourable,   20

THAT you might well understand, that I have neither
ungodly allowed any thing against the Scripture, neither
unstedfastly done any thing contrary to my writing, neither
rashly without just cause put away it which might be well
suffered, nor undiscreetly for novelty brought in that which 25
might be better left out; I am so bold to write to your
honour some causes of the order taken in the new service:
which enterprise, though you may justly reprove for the
simple handling, yet I trust you will take it well for my good
meaning. Therefore, committing your honourable state to 30
the great mercy of God, and following the intent of my
writing, thus I begin the matter:

OF CEREMONIES.

Ceremonies once taken away, as evil used, should not be taken again, though they be not evil of themselves, but might be well used.   And that for four causes.

5   The first, because the Galatians c were reproved of Paul for receiving again the ceremonies which once they had forsaken : d bidding them to stand in the liberty wherein they were called ; and forbidding them to wrap themselves in the yoke of bondage ; saying, e they builded again that which
10 they had destroyed ; and reproving Peter, for that by his dissembling he provoked the gentiles to the ceremonial law, which they had left ; looking back hereby from the plough which they had in hand.

The second cause, because f Paul forbids us to abstain not
15 only from that which is evil, but also from all that which is not evil, but yet hath the appearance of evil.   For this cause Ezekias destroyed the g brazen serpent ; and Epiphanius the picture of Christ.

The third cause, because the h gospel is a short word, put-
20 ting away the law, which stood in i decrees and ceremonies ; and k a light and easy yoke, delivering us from them.   Therefore is it said, that we should l *worship God in spirit and truth*, and not in ceremonies and shadows also, as did the Jews.   And m Paul likeneth us Christians, for our freedom
25 from ceremony, to men which live in all liberty ; and the Jews, for their bondage in them, to men living in all thraldom.   Wherefore Augustyn, n writing to Januarius against the multitude of ceremonies, thus saith ; " Christ hath bound us to a light burthen, joyning us together with sacraments in
30 number most few, in keeping most easy, in signification most passing."   And in the next epistle following he bewaileth the multitude of ceremonies in his time, and calleth them *presumptions*.   Which yet were but few in respect of the number of ours.

c Gal. 5.   d Gal. 5.   e Gal. 2.   f Phil. 2.   g 2 Kings 18.   h Rom. 10·
i Eph. 2.   k Matt. 11.   l John 4.   m Gal. 4.   n Epist. 118, 119.

E

The fourth cause, because these ceremonies were devised of men, and abused to idolatry. °For Christ with his apostles would not wash their hands before meat, though of itself it was an honest civil order, because it was superstitiously used. Paul forbad the Corinthians P to come to the gentiles tables, 5 where they did eat the meat which was offered to idols : though an idol was nothing, nor that which was offered to it any thing.

OF THE CROSS.

Epiphanius, in an epistle which he wrote to John, bishop 10 of Jerusalem, and is translated by ꝗ Hierom, sheweth how he did cut in pieces a cloth in a church, wherein was painted the image of Christ, or of some saint, because it was against the scriptures ; and counsels the bishop to command the priests of the same church to set up no more any such cloth 15 in the same place, calling it a superstition to have any such in the church. Leo, the emperor, with a council holden at Constantinople, decreed, that all images in the church should be broken. The same was decreed long before in the provincial council at Elibert in Spain, cap. 36. 20

OF PROCESSION.

Procession is superfluous, because we may, as we ought to do, pray for the same in the church that we pray for abroad ; yea, and better too. Because when we pray abroad, our mind is not so set upon God for sight of things, (as experience 25 teacheth,) as when we pray in the church, where we have no such occasion to move our mind withal.

OF VESTMENTS.

Because it is thought sufficient to use but a surplice in baptizing, reading, preaching, and praying, therefore it is 30 enough also for the celebrating of the communion. For if we should use another garment herein, it should seem to teach us, that higher and better things be given by it than

° Matt. 25.   P 1 Cor. 10.   ꝗ Hieron. 2 tom. epi.

be given by the other service; which we must not believe.
For in baptism we put on Christ: in the word we eat and
drink Christ, as Hierom and Gregory write[r]. And Austin
saith, the word is as precious as this sacrament, in saying,
5 " He sinneth as much which negligently heareth the word, as
he which willingly letteth Christ's body to fall on the ground."
And Chrysostom[s] saith, " He which is not fit to receive is
not fit to pray." Which were not true, if prayer were not of
as much importance as the communion.

10 OF THE DIVIDING THE SERVICE OF THE COMMUNION INTO TWO PARTS.

Dionysius Areopagita[t] saith, "That after the reading of
the Old and New Testament, the learners of the faith before
they were baptized, mad men, and they that were joyned to
penance for their faults, were shut out of the church, and
15 they only did remain which did receive." Chrysostom witnesseth also[u], that these three sorts were shut out from the
communion. Therefore Durant writeth[x], that the mass of
the learners is from the *introite* until after the *offertory*,
which is called *missa, masse*, or *sending out :* in that it sendeth
20 out: because, when the priest beginneth to consecrate the
sacrament, the learners be sent out of the church. The mass,
or *sending* out of the faithful, is from the offering till after
communion; and is named *missa, a sending out*, because when
it is ended, then each faithful is sent forth to his proper
25 business.

OF THE CREED.

The Creed is ordained to be said only of the communicants, because Dionysius, and Chrysostom, and Basil, in their
liturgies, say, that the learners were shut out or the Creed
30 was said; because it is the prayer of the faithful only, which
were but the communicants. For that they which did not
receive were taken for that time as not faithful. Therefore
Chrysostom[y] saith, " That they which do not receive be as
men doing penance for their sin."

---

[r] Supp. Eccle. sup. ca. 6. Joh.
[s] Lib. 50. Homiliarum; Homiliar. 26. tom. 10. Chrysost. Hom. 61. ad pop.
Antioch.   [t] Dionys. in coelest. Hierar. cap. 3. part. secunda tertia.
[u] Chrysost. secunda expos. in Mat. Hom. 72.
[x] Durant in rationali Divinor. lib. 4. cap. 1.   [y] Chr. Hom. 61. ad pop. Antioch.

OF PRAYING FOR THE DEAD IN THE COMMUNION.

That praying for the dead is not now used in the communion, because it doth seem to make for the sacrifice of the dead.   And also because, (as it was used in the first book,) it makes some of the faithful to be in heaven, and to need no 5 mercy ; and some of them to be in another place, and to lack help and mercy.   As though they were not all alike redeemed, and brought to heaven by Christ's merits : but some deserved it, (as it is said of martyrs ;) and some, for lack of such perfectness, were in purgatory, (as it is spoken of the 10 meaner sort.)   But thus to pray for the dead in the communion was not used in Christ and his apostles time, nor in Justin's time; who [z], speaking of the manner of using the communion in his time, reporteth not this.   So that I may here well say with Tertullian[a], "That is true which is first; 15 that is false which is after : that is true which is first; that is first which is from beginning ; that is from beginning, which is from the apostles."

OF THE PRAYER IN THE FIRST BOOK FOR CONSECRATION.

O merciful Father, &c.   20

This prayer is to be disliked for two causes.   The first, because it is taken to be so needful for the consecration, that the consecration is not thought to be without it.   Which is not true : for petition is no part of consecration.   Because Christ, in ordaining the sacrament [b], made no petition, but 25 a thanksgiving.   It is written [c], "When he had given thanks," and not, "When he had asked."   Which Christ would have spoken, and the evangelists have written, if it had been needful, as it is mistaken.   And though Mark saith, "that Christ blessed, when he took bread," yet he meaneth by 30 *blessed*, gave thanks, or else he would have said also, He gave thanks, as he said, He blessed, if he had meant thereby divers things.   And speaking of the cup, he would have said, Christ blessed when he took the cup, as he saith, He gave thanks, if *gave thanks* and *blessed* were not all one. 35 Or else Christ should be thought to have consecrated the bread and not the wine, because in consecrating the bread

[z] Secunda Apolog. pro Christianis.   [a] Tertull. contr. Prax. contra Mar.
[b] Matt. 26.   [c] Mar. 14.   Luke 22.   1 Cor. 11.

he said *blessed*, and in consecrating the wine he left it out.
Yea, by Matthew, Luke, and Paul, he should neither have
consecrated the one nor the other. For that they report not
that he blessed.

5 Gregory[d] writeth to the bishop of Syracusa, that the
apostles used only the Lord's Prayer at the communion,
and none other; and seemeth to be displeased, that it is
not there still so used, but instead thereof the canon which
Scholasticus made. Therefore, in that he would the Lord's
10 Prayer to be used at the making of the communion, which
making nothing for the consecration thereof, and not
Scholasticus' prayer, which prayeth for the consecration of
the same, it must needs be that he thought the communion
not to be made by invocation.

15 Chrysostom saith[e], that this sacrament is made by the
words of Christ once spoken; as every thing is gendered
by the words of God, that he once spake, " Increase and fill
the earth."

Bessarion saith[f], that the consecration stands on Christ's
20 ordinance, and his words, and not on the prayer of the
priest; and that for three causes. The first, because the
priest may pray without faith, without which his prayer
is not heard. The second, because the prayer is not all
one in all countries. The third, because baptism is without
25 prayer.

Justin[g], in shewing how the communion was celebrated
in his time, maketh no mention of invocation. No more
doth Irenee[h].

The second cause why the foresaid prayer is to be refused,
30 is for that it prays that the bread and wine may be Christ's
body and blood; which makes for the popish transubstantiation: which is a doctrine that hath caused much idolatry:
and though the Doctors so speak, yet we must speak otherwise, because we take them otherwise than they meant, or
35 would be taken. For when their meaning is corrupted, then
their words must be expounded. In one place it is said,
This is the new testament in my blood; and in another

---

d Lib. 6. Epist. 63.　　e De Perdit. Judæ. Hom. 30.　　f Libr. de Prec.
Eucharist.　　g 2d Apol. pro Christian.　　h Lib. 4. cap. 34.

place, This is my blood of the new testament : there Christ's words be diversely reported, that we should expound them when they be mistaken. And both he and his apostles allege not after the letter, but after the meaning.

OF RECEIVING THE SACRAMENT IN OUR HANDS.   5

Christ gave the sacrament into the hands of his apostles, "Divide it," saith he, "among yourselves [k]." It is decreed [l], that the priest should be excommunicated which did suffer any man to take it with any thing saving with his *hands ;* as then they made instruments to receive it withall. Am- 10 brose [m] thus speaketh to Theodosius the emperor, "How wilt thou with such hands receive the body of Christ?" "If we be ashamed," saith Austin, "and afraid to touch the sacrament with foul hands, much more we ought to fear to take it with an unclean soul." 15

OF RECEIVING STANDING OR KNEELING.

Justin saith, we should rather stand than kneel when we pray on the Sunday, because it is a sign of resurrection; and writeth that Irenee [n] saith, it is a custom which came from the apostles. And Austin [o] thus writeth, "We pray 20 standing, which is a sign of resurrection : therefore on every Sunday it is observed at the altar." It is in plain words in the last chapter of the last book, (which Gaguens, a Frenchman, hath put to Tertullian's works as his,) that Christ's body is received standing. Though this is the old 25 use of the church to communicate standing, yet because it is taken of some by itself to be sin to receive kneeling, whereas of itself it is lawful; it is left indifferent to every man's choice to follow the one way or the other; to teach men that it is lawful to receive either standing or kneeling. 30

Thus, as I think, I have shewed good cause why the service is set forth in such sort as it is. God, for his mercy in Christ, cause the parliament with one voice to enact it, and the realm with true heart to use it.

---

[k] Luke 22.   [l] Concilio 6. Constan. cap. 101. cap. 31. Tripart. Hist.   [n] Quæstio ad Orthod. 115.   [m] Theod. Bes. lib. 4.   [o] Epla. ad Jan. 118.

III.

Dr. Horne's preface to his discourse, read at the conference at Westminster abbey.

FORASMUCH as it is thought good unto the queen's most excellent majesty, (unto whom in the Lord all obedience is 5 due,) that we should declare our judgment in writing upon certain propositions; we, as becometh us, do herein most gladly obey.

Seeing that Christ is our only master, whom the Father hath commanded us to hear; and seeing also his word is the 10 truth, from the which it is not lawful for us to depart one hair's breadth, and against the which, as the apostle saith, " we can do nothing ;" we do in all things submit ourselves unto this truth, and do protest that we will affirm nothing against the same.

15 And forasmuch as we have for our mother the true and catholic church of Christ, which is grounded upon the doctrine of the apostles and prophets, and is of Christ the head in all things governed; we do reverence her judgment; we obey her authority as becometh children; and we do devoutly 20 profess, and in all points follow the faith, which is contained in the three creeds, that is to say, of the apostles, of the council of Nice, and of Athanasius.

And seeing that we never departed, neither from the doctrine of God, which is contained in the holy canonical 25 scriptures, nor yet from the faith of the true and catholic church of Christ, but have preached truly the word of God, and have sincerely ministered the sacraments according to the institution of Christ, unto the which our doctrine and faith the most part also of our adversaries did subscribe, not 30 many years past, (although now, as unnatural, they are revolted from the same,) we desire that they render account of their backsliding, and shew some cause wherefore they do

not only resist that doctrine which they have before professed,
but also persecute the same by all means they can.

We do not doubt but through the equity of the queen's
most excellent majesty, we shall in these disputations be
entreated more gently than in years late past, when we were 5
handled most unjustly, and scantly after the common manner
of men.

As for the judgment of the whole controversy, we refer
unto the most holy scriptures, and the catholic church of
Christ, (whose judgment unto us ought to be most sacred.) 10
Notwithstanding, by the *catholic* church we understand not
the *Romish* church, whereunto our adversaries attribute such
reverence; but that which St. Augustin and other fathers
affirm ought to be sought in the holy scriptures, and which
is governed and led by the Spirit of Christ.   15

---

*The first proposition upon which the papists and protestants
disputed in Westminster-abbey. With the arguments which
the reformed divines made upon it.*

*It is against the word of God, and the custom of the primitive
church, to use a tongue unknown to the people in common-* 20
prayers and administration of the sacraments.

By these words (*the word*) we mean only the written word
of God, or canonical scriptures.

And by *the custom of the primitive church*, we mean, the
order most generally used in the church for the space of five 25
hundred years after Christ; in which times lived the most
notable fathers, as Justin, Ireneus, Tertullian, Cyprian, Basil,
Chrysostom, Hierome, Ambrose, Augustine, &c.

This assertion, above-written, hath two parts:

First, That the use of a tongue not understood of the 30
people, in common prayers of the church, or in the administration of the sacraments, is against God's word.

The second, That the same is against the use of the
primitive church.

The first part is most manifestly proved by the 14th chapter of the First Epistle to the Corinthians, almost throughout the whole chapter; in the which chapter St. Paul intreateth of this matter, *ex professo*, purposely: and although 5 some do cavil, that St. Paul speaketh not in that chapter of praying, but of preaching; yet it is most evident, to any indifferent reader of understanding, and appeareth also by the exposition of the best writers, that he plainly there speaketh not only of preaching and prophesying, but also 10 of prayer and thanksgiving, and generally of all other public actions which require any speech in the church or congregation.

For of praying he saith, " I will pray with my spirit, and I will pray with my mind; I will sing with my spirit, and 15 I will sing with the mind." And of thanksgiving, (which is a kind of prayer,) " Thou givest thanks well, but the other is not edified; and how shall he that occupieth the room of the unlearned say Amen to thy giving of thanks, when he understandeth not what thou sayest?" And in the end, ascending 20 from particulars to universals, concludeth, " That all things ought to be done to edification."

Thus much is clear by the very words of St. Paul; and the ancient doctors, Ambrose, Augustine, Hierome, and others, do so understand this chapter, as it shall appear by their 25 testimonies, which shall follow afterward.

Upon this chapter of St. Paul we gather these reasons following:

1. All things done in the church, or congregation, ought so to be done, as they may edify the same.

30 But the use of an unknown tongue in public prayer or administration of sacraments doth not edify the congregation:

Therefore the use of an unknown tongue in public prayer or administration of the sacraments is not to be had in the church.

35 The first part of this reason is grounded upon St. Paul's words, commanding all things to be *done to edification.*

The second part is also proved by St. Paul's plain words. First, by this similitude; " If the trumpet give an uncertain sound, who shall be prepared to battel?" Even so likewise

when ye speak with tongues, except ye speak words that have
signification, how shall it be understood what is spoken? for
ye shall but speak in the air, that is to say, in vain, and
consequently without edifying.

And afterward, in the same chapter, he saith, "How can 5
he that occupieth the place of the unlearned say Amen at
thy giving of thanks, seeing he understandeth not what thou
sayest? For thou verily givest thanks well, but the other is
not edified."

These be St. Paul's words, plainly proving that a tongue 10
not understood doth not edify.

And therefore both the parts of the reason thus proved by
St. Paul, the conclusion followeth necessarily.

2. Secondly; nothing is to be spoken in the congregation
in an unknown tongue, except it be interpreted to the people, 15
that it may be understood. For, saith Paul, "if there be
no interpreter to him that speaketh in an unknown tongue,
taceat in ecclesiâ, let him hold his peace in the church." And
therefore the common prayers, and administration of sacraments, neither done in a known tongue, nor interpreted, are 20
against this commandment of Paul, and not to be used.

3. The minister, in praying, or administration of sacraments, using language not understood of the hearers, is to
them barbarous, an alien, which of St. Paul is accounted a
great absurdity.   25

4. It is not to be counted a Christian common-prayer
where the people present declare not their assent unto it
by saying *Amen*; wherein is implyed all other words of
assent.

But St. Paul affirmeth, that the people cannot declare their 30
assent in saying *Amen* except they understand what is said,
as afore:

Therefore it is no Christian common-prayer where the people
understandeth not what is said.

5. Paul would not suffer, in his time, a strange tongue to 35
be heard in the common-prayer in the church, notwithstanding that such a kind of speech was then a miracle, and a
singular gift of the Holy Ghost, whereby infidels might be
persuaded and brought to the faith: much less is it to be

suffered now among Christian and faithful men, especially being no miracle, nor especial gift of the Holy Ghost.

6. Some will peradventure answer, That to use any kind of tongue in common-prayer or administration of sacraments is
5 a thing indifferent.

But St. Paul is to the contrary; for he commandeth all things to be " done to edification :" he commandeth to keep silence, if there be no interpreter. And in the end of the chapter, he concludeth thus ; " If any man be spiritual, or a
10 prophet, let him know, that the things which I write are the commandment of the Lord." And so, shortly to conclude, the use of a strange tongue, in prayer and ministration, is against the word and commandment of God.

To these reasons, grounded upon St. Paul's words, which
15 are the most firm foundation of this assertion, divers other reasons may be joined, gathered out of the scriptures, and otherwise.

1. In the Old Testament, all things pertaining to the public prayer, benedictions, thanksgivings, or sacrifice, were always
20 in their vulgar and natural tongue.

In the second book of Paraleipomenon, cap. 29, it is written, " That Ezechias commanded the Levites to praise God with the Psalms of David and Asaph the prophet ;" which doubtless were written in Hebrew, their vulgar tongue. If
25 they did so in the shadows of the law, much more ought we to do the like, who (as Christ saith) must pray *in spiritu et veritate*.

2. The final end of our prayer is, (as David saith,) " Ut populi conveniant in unum, et annuncient nomen Domini in
30 Sion, et laudes ejus in Hierusalem."

But the name and praises of God cannot be set forth to the people, unless it be done in such a tongue as they may understand :

Therefore common prayer must be had in the vulgar
35 tongue.

3. The definition of public prayer out of the words of St. Paul ; " Orabo spiritu, orabo et mente. Publicè orare, est vota communia mente ad Deum effundere, et ea spiritu, hoc est linguâ, testari." Common-prayer is, to lift up our common

desires to God with our minds, and to testify the same out-
wardly with our tongues. Which definition is approved of
by St. Augustine de Magist. c. 1. " Nihi lopus est (inquit)
loquutione, nisi forte ut sacerdotes faciunt, significandæ mentis causâ, ut populus intelligat."   5

4. The ministrations of the Lord's last supper and baptism
are, as it were, sermons of the death and resurrection of
Christ.

But sermons to the people must be had in such language
as the people may perceive, otherwise they should be had in 10
vain.

5. It is not lawful for a Christian man to abuse the gifts of
God.

But he that prayeth in the church in a strange tongue
abuseth the gift of God ; for the tongue serveth only to ex- 15
press the mind of the speaker to the hearer. And Augustine
saith, de Doct. Christ. lib. 4. cap. 10. " Loquendi omnino
nulla est causa, si quod loquimur non intelligunt, propter quos,
ut intelligant, loquimur." There is no cause why we should
speak, if they, for whose cause we speak, understand not our 20
speaking.

6. The heathen and barbarous nations of all countries and
sorts of men, were they never so wild, evermore made their
prayers and sacrifice to their gods in their own mother-tongue;
which is a manifest declaration, that it is the very light and 25
voice of nature.

Thus much upon the ground of St. Paul, and other reasons
out of the scriptures ; joining therewith the common usage of
all nations, as a testimony of the law of nature.

Now for the second part of the assertion, which is,   30

That the use of a strange tongue, in public prayer, and
    administration of sacraments, is against the custom of
    the primitive church. Which is a matter so clear, that
    the denial of it must needs proceed either of great
    ignorance or of wilful malice.   35

For, first of all, Justinus Martyr[a], describing the order of
the communion in his time, saith thus ; " Die solis urbanorum
et rusticorum coetus fiunt, ubi apostolorum, prophetarumque

               [a] Justinus, Apol. 2.

literæ, quoad fieri potest, præleguntur : deinde cessante lectore præpositus verba facit adhortatoria, ad imitationem tam honestarum rerum invitans. Post hæc consurgimus omnes, et preces offerimus, quibus finitis, profertur (ut dixi-
5 mus) panis, vinum et aqua ; tum præpositus quantum potest preces offert, et gratiarum actiones ; plebs vero Amen accinit." Upon the Sunday, assemblies are made both of the citizens and countrymen ; whereas the writings of the disciples and of the prophets are read as much as may be.
10 Afterwards when the reader doth cease, the head-minister maketh an exhortation, exhorting them to follow so honest things. After this we rise all together, and offer prayers ; which being ended, (as we have said,) bread, wine, and water are brought forth ; then the head-minister offereth prayers
15 and thanksgiving, as much as he can, and the people answereth, Amen.

These words of Justin, who lived about 160 years after Christ, considered with their circumstances, declare plainly, That not only the scriptures were read, but also that the
20 prayers and administration of the Lord's supper were done in a tongue understood.

Both the liturgies of Basil and Chrysostom declare, That in the celebration of the communion, the people were appointed to answer to the prayer of the minister, sometimes
25 "Amen;" sometimes, "Lord have mercy upon us; "sometimes, " And with thy Spirit ;" and, "We have our hearts lifted up unto the Lord, &c." Which answers they would not have made in due time, if the prayers had not been made in a tongue understood.

30 And for further proof, let us hear what Basil[b] writeth in this matter to the clerks of Neocæsarea ; " Cæterum ad objectum in psalmodiis crimen, quo maximè simpliciores terrent calumniatores, &c." " As touching that is laid to our charge in psalmodies and songs, wherewith our slanderers
35 do fray the simple, I have this to say, That our customs and usage in all churches be uniform and agreeable. For in the night, the people with us riseth, goeth to the house of prayer: and in travel, tribulation, and continual tears, they confess

b Basil. Epist. 63.

themselves to God ; and at the last rising again, go to their
songs, or psalmodies, where being divided into two parts,
sing by course together, both deeply weighing and confirming
the matter of the heavenly saying ; and also stirring up their
attention and devotion of heart, which by other means be 5
alienated and plucked away.   Then appointing one to begin
the song, the rest follow; and so, with divers songs and
prayers, passing over the night, at the dawning of the day,
all together, even as it were with one mouth and one heart,
they sing unto the Lord a song of confession, every man 10
framing to himself meet words of repentance.

" If ye will flee us from henceforth for these things, ye must
flee also the Egyptians, and both the Libyans, ye must eschew
the Thebans, Palestines, Arabians, the Phenices, the Syrians,
and those which dwell besides Euphrates.   And to be short, 15
all those with whom watchings, prayers, and common singing
of psalms are had in honour."

[Then follow other testimonies from Ambrose, Jerome, Basil,
Chrysostom, Cyprian, Augustin and Justinian's Novell.]

These are sufficient to prove, that it is against God's word, 20
and the use of the primitive church, to use a language not
understood of the people, in common prayer, and ministration
of the sacraments.

Wherefore it is to be marvelled at, not only how such an
untruth and abuse crept, at the first, into the church, but also 25
how it is maintained so stiffly at this day ; and upon what
ground these that will be thought guides and pastors of
Christ's church are so loth to return to the first original
of St. Paul's doctrine, and the practice of the primitive
catholic church of Christ.   30

J. Scory.	R. Cox.	The God of patience and
D. Whithead.	E. Grindal.	consolation give us grace
J. Juel.	R. Horn.	to be like minded one to-
J. Almer.	E. Gest.	wards another, in Christ
		Jesus, that we all agree- 35
		ing together, may, with
		one mouth, praise God,
		the Father of our Lord
		Jesus Christ. *Amen.*

IV.

The answer of Dr. Cole to the first proposition of the protestants,
at the disputation before the lords at Westminster.

Est contra verbum Dei et consuetudinem veteris ecclesiæ lingua
populo ignota uti in publicis precibus et administratione sa-
5 *cramentorum.*

Most honourable ;

WHEREAS these men here present have declared openly,
That it is repugnant and contrary to the word of God to have
the common-prayers and ministration of the sacraments in
10 the Latin tongue here in England, and that all such common-prayer and ministration ought to be and remain in the
English tongue ; ye shall understand, that to prove this
their assertion they have brought in as yet *only one place* of
scripture, taken out of St. Paul's First Epistle to the Corinth-
15 ians, chap. 14, with certain other places of the holy doctors ;
whereunto answer is not now to be made: but when the book,
which they read, shall be delivered unto us, according to the
appointment made in that behalf, *then, God willing, we* shall
make answer, as well to the scripture, as other testimonies
20 alledged by them, so as all good men may evidently perceive
and understand the same scripture to be misconstrued, and
drawn from the native and true sense : and that *it is not St.*
Paul's mind there to treat of common-prayer, or ministration
of any sacraments.   And therefore we now have only to de-
25 clare, and open before you briefly (which after, as opportunity
serves in our answer, shall appear more at large) causes which
move us to persist and continue in the order received, and to
say, and affirm, that to have the common-prayer or service,
with the ministration of the sacraments in the Latin tongue,
30 is convenient, and (as the state of the cause standeth at this
present) necessary.

SECOND SECTION.

1. And *this we affirm*, first, because *there is no scripture manifest* against this our assertion and usage of the church. And though there were any, yet it is not to be condemned that the church hath received. Which thing may evidently 5 appear in many things that were sometime expressly commanded by God and his holy apostles.

2. As for example, (to make the matter plain,) ye see the express command of Almighty God, touching the observation *of the sabbath-day*, to be changed by authority of the church 10 (*without any word of God written* for the same) into the *Sunday*. The reason whereof appeareth not to all men ; and howsoever it doth appear, and is accepted of all good men, without any controversy of scripture, yea, without any mention of the day, saving only that St. John in his Apocalypse 15 nameth it *diem Dominicum :* in the change whereof, all men may evidently understand the authority of the church, both in this cause and also in other matters, to be of great weight and importance, and therein esteemed accordingly.

3. *Another* example we have given unto us by the mouth 20 of our Saviour himself, who, washing the feet of his disciples, said, " I have herein given you an example, that as I have done, even so do you." Notwithstanding these express words, the holy church hath left the thing undone without blame : not of any negligence, but of great and urgent causes, which 25 appeareth not to many men, and yet universally without the breach of God's commandment (as is said), left undone. Was not the fact also, and, as it seemeth, the express commandment of Christ our Saviour, changed and altered, by the authority of the church, in the highest mystery of our faith, the blessed 30 sacrament of the altar ? For he ministereth the same (as the scripture witnesseth) after supper. And now if a contentious man would strain the fact to the first institution, St. Augustine answereth (not by scripture, for there is none to improve it, but indeed otherwise) even as the apostles did, " Visum est 35 Spiritui Sancto ut in honorem tanti sacramenti, in os Christiani hominis prius intret corpus Dominicum quam exteri cibi."

It is determined (saith St. Augustine) by the Holy Ghost, that in the honour of so great a sacrament, the body of our Lord should enter first into the mouth of a Christian man before other external meats. So that notwithstanding it was 5 the fact of Christ himself, yet the church moved by the Holy Ghost, (as is said,) hath changed that also, without offence likewise. By the which sentence of St. Augustine manifestly appeareth, that this authority was derived from the apostles unto this time; the which same authority, according to Christ's 10 promises, doth still abide and remain with his church.

4. *And hereupon* also resteth the alteration of the sacrament under one kind, whenas the multitudes of the Gentiles entered, the church instructed by the Holy Ghost, understood inconveniences, and partly also heresy to creep in through the 15 ministration under both kinds; and therefore, as in the former examples, so in this now, (the matter nothing diminished, neither in itself nor in the receivers, and the thing also being received before, by a common and uniform consent, without contradiction) the church did decree, that from henceforth it 20 should be received under the form of bread only ; and whosoever should think and affirm, that whole Christ remained not under *both kinds*, pronounced him to be in heresy.

5. *Moreover*, we read in the Acts, whereas it was determined in a council holden at Hierusalem by the apostles, that the 25 Gentiles should abstain from strangled, and blood, in these words, " Visum est Spiritui Sancto, et nobis, &c." " It is decreed, by the Holy Ghost, and us, (say the apostles,) that no other burden be laid upon you, than these necessary things, That ye abstain from things offered up unto idols, and from 30 blood ; and from that is strangled, and from fornication." This was the commandment of God, (for still it is commanded, upon pain of damnation, to keep our bodies clean from fornication,) and the other part joined by the Holy Ghost with the same, not kept nor observed at this day.

35   6. Likewise in the *Acts of the Apostles* it appeareth, that among them in the primitive church, all things were common. They sold their lands and possessions, and laid the mony at the feet of the apostles, to be divided to the people as every man had need ; insomuch that Ananias and Saphira, who

kept back a part of their possession, and laid but the other
part at the apostles' feet, were declared by the mouth of St.
Peter to be tempted by the Devil, and to lye against the
Holy Ghost, and in example of all other, punished with sudden
death. By all which examples, and many other, it is manifest, 5
that though there were any such scripture which they pretend,
as there is not, yet the church, wherein the Holy Ghost is
alway resident, may order the same, and may therein say as
truly, " Visum est Spiritui Sancto, et nobis," as did the
apostles ; for Christ promised unto the church, that the Holy 10
Ghost should teach them all truth, and that he himself would
be with the same church unto the world's end. And hereupon we do make this argument with St. Augustine, which
he writeth in his Epistle *ad Januarium*, after this sort,
" Ecclesia Dei inter multam paleam multaque zizania consti- 15
tuta, multa tolerat ; et tamen quæ sunt contra fidem, vel
bonam vitam, non approbat, nec tacet, nec facit."

To this *major* we add this *minor :* But the catholic church
of God neither reproveth the service, or common-prayer, to
be in the learned tongue, nor yet useth it otherwise.   20

Therefore it is most lawful and commendable so to be.

THIRD SECTION.

Another cause that moveth us to say and think, is, that
otherwise doing, (as they have said,) there followeth neces- 25
sarily the breach of unity of the church, and the commodities
thereby are withdrawn and taken from us ; there follows
necessarily an horrible schism and division.

In alteration of the service into our mother-tongue, we
condemn the church of God, which hath been heretofore, we 30
condemn the church that is present, and namely the church
of Rome.

To the which, howsoever it is lightly esteemed here among
us, the holy saint and martyr Ireneus saith in plain words
thus : "Ad hanc ecclesiam propter potentiorem principali- 35
tatem, necesse est omnes alias ecclesias convenire ; hoc est
omnes undique fideles." It is necessary (saith this holy man,
who was nigh to the apostles, or rather in that time, for he
is called σύγχρονος *apostolorum*) that all churches do conform

themselves, and agree with the see or church of Rome, all
churches, that is to say, (as he declareth himself,) all Christian
and faithful men.   And he alleadgeth the cause why it is
necessary for all men to agree therewith, (*propter potentiorem*
5 *principalitatem*) for the greater preeminence of the same, or
for the mightier principality.

From this church, and consequently from the whole universal church of Christ, we fall undoubtedly into a fearful
and dangerous schism, and therewith into all incommodities
10 of the same.

That in this doing, we fall from the unity of the church,
it is more manifest than that we need much to stand upon.
St. Augustine, " Contra Cresconium grammaticum," putting
a difference between *heresis* and *schisma*, saith, " Schisma est
15 diversa sequentium secta, Heresis autem schisma inveteratum."

To avoid this horrible sin of schism, we are commanded,
by the words of St. Paul, saying, " Obsecro vos ut id ipsum
dicatis omnes, et non sint in vobis schismata."

And that this changing of the service out of the learned
20 tongue, is doing contrary to the form and order universally
observed, is plain and evident to every man's eye.

They are to be named *hereticks* (saith he) which obsinately
think and judg in matters of faith otherwise than the rest
of the church doth.   And those are called *schismaticks* which
25 follow not the order and trade of the church, but will invent
of their own wit and brain other orders, contrary or diverse
to them which are already, by the Holy Ghost, universally
established in the church.   And we being declined from God
by schism, note what follows ; There is then no gift of God,
30 no knowledg, no justice, no faith, no works, and finally, no
vertue that could stand us in stead, though we should think
to glorify God by suffering death, (as St. Paul saith) 1 Cor.
13.   Yea, there is no sacrament that availeth to salvation, in
them that willingly fall into schism, that without fear separate
35 and divide themselves from the sacred unity of Christ's holy
spouse, the church, as St. Augustine plainly saith ; " Quicun-
que ille est, qualiscunque ille est, Christianus non est qui in
ecclesia Christi non est ;" that is, Whosoever he be, whatso-

ever degree or condition he be of, or what qualities soever he
hath ; though he should speak with the tongues of angels,
speak he never so holily, shew he never so much vertue, yet is
he not a Christian man that is guilty of the crime of schism ;
and so no member of the church.   5

Wherefore this is an evident argument ; every Christian
man is bound, upon pain of damnation, by the plain words
of God, uttered by St. Paul, to avoid the horrible sin of
schism.

The changing of the service out of the learned tongue, it 10
being universally observed through the whole church from the
beginning, is a cause of an horrible schism ; wherefore every
good Christian man is bound to avoid the change of the
service.

Now to confirm that we said before, and to prove that to 15
have the common-prayer, and ministration of the sacraments
in English, or in other than in the learned tongue, let us behold the first institution of the west church, and the particulars thereof.

And first, to begin with the church of France : Dyonisius, 20
St. Paul's scholar, who first planted the faith of Christ in
France : Martialis, who (as it is said) planted the faith in
Spain : and others which planted the same here in England,
in the time of Eleutherius : and such as planted the faith
in Germany, and other countries : and St. Augustine, that 25
converted this realm afterwards, in the time of Gregory,
almost a thousand years ago : it may appear that they had
interpreters, as touching the declaration and preaching of
the gospel, or else the gift of tongues : but that ever, in any
of these west churches, they had their service in their own 30
language, or that the sacraments, other than matrimony,
were ministred in their own vulgar tongue ; that does not
appear by any ancient historiographer. *Whether* shall they
be able ever to prove that it was so generally, and thereby
by continuance, in the Latin tongue, the self-same order 35
and words remain still ; whereas all men do consider, and
know right-well, that in all other inferiour and barbarous
tongues, great change daily is seen, and specially in this our

English tongue, which *in quovis seculo fere*, in every age, or hundred years, there appeareth a great change and alteration in this language.

For the proof whereof, there hath remained many books 5 of late in this realm, (as many do well know,) which we, that be now Englishmen, can scarcely understand or read. And if we should so often (as the thing may chance, and as alteration daily doth grow in our vulgar tongue) change the service of the church, what manifold inconveniences and errors would 10 follow, we leave it to all mens judgments to consider. So that hereby may appear another invincible argument, which is, the consent of the whole catholick church, that cannot err in the faith and doctrine of our Saviour Christ, but is (by St. Paul's saying) " the pillar and foundation of all truth."

15   *Moreover,* the people of England do not understand their own tongue better than Eunuchus did the Hebrew ; of whom we read in the Acts, that Philip was commanded to teach him ; and he reading there the prophesy of Esay, Philip (as it is written in the 8th chapter of the Acts) 20 enquired of him, whether he understood that which he read, or no? he made answer, saying, " Et quomodo possum, si non aliquis ostenderit mihi ;" in which words are reproved the intolerable boldness of such as will enterprize without any teacher (yea, contemning all doctors) to unclasp the 25 book, and thereby, instead of eternal food, drink up present poison. For whereas the Scripture is misconstrued, and taken in a wrong sense, that it is not the Scripture of God, but as St. Hierom saith, writing upon the Epistle to the Galathians, it is the Scripture of the Devil : and we do not contend with 30 hereticks for the Scripture, but for the true sense and meaning of the Scripture.

We read of ceremonies in the Old Testament, as the circumcision, the bells and pomegranates of Aaron's apparel, with many other, and kinds of sacrifices ; which all were, as 35 St. Paul saith unto the Hebrews, *justitia carnis ;* and did not inwardly justify the party before God that observed them, in protestation of their faith in Christ to come : and although they had the knowledge of every fact of Christ, which was signified particularly by those ceremonies. And it is evident and plain, that the high priest entred into the inner part of the temple, (named *sancta sanctorum,*) whereas the people might not follow, nor lawful for them to stand but there where they could neither see nor hear what the priest either said or did, as St. Luke in the first chapter of his Gos-5 pel rehearseth in the history of Zachary.

Upon conference of these two testaments may be plainly gathered this doctrine, That in the church of Christ many things may be said and done, the mysteries whereof the people knoweth not, neither are they bound to know. Which 10 thing, that is, that the people did not hear and understand the common prayer of the priest and minister, it is evident and plain by the practice of the ancient Greek church, and that also that now is at Venice or elsewhere.

In that east church, the priest standeth, as it were, in a 15 travice, or closet, hanged round about with curtains, or vails, apart from the people. And after the consecration, when he sheweth the blessed sacrament, the curtains are drawn, whereof Chrysostom speaketh thus; " Cum vela videris retrahi, tunc superne cœlum aperiri cogita ;" When thou seest 20 the vails or curtains drawn open, then think thou that heaven is open from above.

It is also here to be noted, that there is two manners of prayings, one publick, another private ; for which cause the church hath such considerations of the public prayer, that 25 it destroyeth not, nor taketh away the private prayer of the people in the time of the sacrifice, or other divine service ; which thing would chance, if the people should do nothing but hearken to answer and say *Amen.* Besides the impossibility of the matter, whereas, in a great parish, every man 30 cannot hear what the priest saith, though the material church were defaced, and he left the altar of God, and stood in the midst of the people.

Furthermore, If we should confess that it were necessary to have common-prayer in the vulgar tongue, these two heresies 35 would follow upon it ; that prayer profiteth no man but him that understandeth it, and him also that is present and heareth it ; and so, by consequent, void was the prayer for St. Peter in prison by the church abroad.

Now consider the practice of this realm.

If we should grant the service to be in English, we should
not have it in the same form that it is in now, being in
Latin; but by likelihood we should have it as it was of late
5 days. The matter of which service is taken out of the Psalms,
and other part of the Bible, translated into English, wherein
are manifest errors, and false translations, which all by de-
pravation of God's Scripture, and so, *verè mendacia*. Now
if the service be so framed, then may men well say upon us,
10 that we serve God with lyes.

Wherefore we may not so travel and labour to alter the
form of our common-prayer, that we lese the fruit of all
prayer, which by this barbarous contention, no doubt, we shall
do. And the church of God hath no such custom, as St.
15 Paul alledgeth, in such contentions. And may not the whole
world say unto us, as St. Paul said unto the Corinthians,
1 Cor. 14, "An à vobis verbum Dei processit, aut in vos solos
pervenit?" As though the whole church had been ever in
error, and never had seen this chapter of St. Paul before:
20 and that the Holy Ghost had utterly forsaken his office, in
leading it into all truth, till now of late, certain, boasting of
the Holy Ghost, and the sincere word of God, hath enter-
prised to correct and overthrow the whole church.

Augustinus, lib. 1. contra *Julianum Pelagium, à Græcis*
25 *pro suâ heresi profugum, querentem, ad hunc modum respondit:*
"Puto (inquit) tibi eam partem orbis debere sufficere, in quâ
primum apostolorum suorum voluit Dominus gloriosissimo
martyrio coronari." *Et idem paulo post;* "Te certe (Julianum
alloquitur) occidentalis terra generavit, occidentalis regene-
30 ravit ecclesia. Quid ei quæris inferre, quod in eâ non inve-
nisti, quando in ejus membra venisti? Imò, Quid ei quæris
auferre, quod in eâ tu quoque accepisti?" *Hæc ille.*

A number of authorities out of the doctors we could rehearse, that maketh for the unity of the church, and for not
35 disturbing the quiet government of the same; which all im-
pugn this their first assertion by way of argument. But because they have framed their assertion so, that we be compelled
to defend the *negative*, (in the probation whereof, the doctors
use not directly to have many words;) therefore of purpose

we leave out a number of the sayings of the doctors, (which all, as I said before, would prove this first matter by way of argument,) lest we should be tedious, and keep you too long in a plain matter.

And therefore now to conclude, for not changing the divine 5 service, and the ministration of the sacraments from the learned tongue (which thing doth make a schism, and a division between us and the catholick church of God), we have brought in the Scripture that doth forbid all such schism; and also the consent and custom of the whole church, which cannot 10 err, and maketh us bold to say as we do; with other things, as ye have heard, for confirmation of the same. And in answering to the first matter, we intend (God willing) to say much more; beseeching Almighty God so to inspire the heart of the queen's majesty, and her most honourable council, with 15 the nobility of this realm, and us that be the pastors of the people in these causes, that so we may dispose of the service of God as we may therein serve God: and that we do not, by altering the said service from the uniform manner of Christ's church, but also highly displease God, and procure 20 to us infamy of the world, the worm of conscience, and eternal damnation; which God forbid: and grant us grace to acknowledge, confess and maintain his truth. *To whom be all glory. Amen.*

V.

The protestants' discourse, prepared to have been read in the 25 *public conference at Westminster, upon the second question,* viz.

> *Every particular church hath authority to institute, change, and abrogate ceremonies and rites in the church, so that it be to edify.*

For avoiding ambiguity in terms, it is not amiss to declare 30 what is meant by the words of the proposition.

By these words, "every particular church," we understand every particular kingdom, province, or region, which by order make one Christian society or body, according to the distinction of countries, and orders of the same.

By "ceremonies and rites of the church," we understand those ceremonies and rites, which neither expressly, neither
5 by necessary deduction or consequence, are commanded or forbidden in the Scriptures, but are things of their own nature indifferent. As for example, the form and manner of prayers before and after baptism, and at the administration of the sacrament of the body and blood of Christ, the ap-
10 pointing of times and places for the hearing of God's word, ministration of sacraments, public prayer, number of holydays, times of fasting, and such like. All which may by God's word, not only by general councils, but also by particular provinces, regions, and societies of Christians, accord-
15 ing to the state of the times, be instituted and ordained, changed and removed upon such just grounds, causes and considerations, as the state of the times, places, people, and other circumstances shall require; so that it be done to edify God's people.
20   Having thus made declaration of the proposition, we will proceed to the proof of the same by God's word, by ancient writers, and by examples.

First, all ecclesiastical rites and ceremonies are things which pertain unto order and decency. But St. Paul[a] committed
25 to the particular church of Corinth the disposition of all things which appertain to decency and order. And committing such authority to the particular church of Corinth, he consequently committeth it to all other particular churches. For with God there is no respect of persons; and as there is in Christ
30 neither Jew nor Gentile, so there is neither Corinthian nor Venetian nor Englishman, but all we in Christ are one, and have like privilege.

Whereupon it followeth, that St. Paul committeth the disposition of all outward ecclesiastical rites and ceremonies to
35 every particular church.

Let this reason be well weighed, for it is plain and evident. For that ceremonies are things of order and decency, and not

---

[a] 1 Cor. 14.

things of necessity to salvation, is a thing confessed of all men. For they have had their beginning of men, and have been changed, as shall appear at large hereafter.

But things of necessity to salvation are immutable, and have their original from God.   5

And further, that the words of St. Paul to the Corinthians pertain to the ordering and disposition of such things, the adversaries cannot deny; saving, that whereas St. Paul committeth it in plain terms to the particular church of Corinth, they bind it and restrain it to an universal determination, 10 contrary to St. Paul's meaning, as shall appear by our answers to their reasons hereafter.

Secondly, the principal foundation whereupon it may be gathered, that any council or assembly hath authority to change or institute rites and ceremonies, stands upon this 15 proof of Christ, "Wheresoever two or three are gathered together in my name, there am I in the midst of them." But in a particular church, not only two or three, but also great numbers may be assembled in the name of Christ. Therefore a particular church hath promise that Christ will be in the 20 midst of them. And consequently that assembly that hath Christ in the midst of it, and the assistance of his Spirit according to his promises, hath authority to institute, alter, and change rites and ceremonies, to the edifying of the people.

Therefore a particular church hath authority to institute, 25 alter, and change ceremonies, to the edifying of the people.

Thirdly, the authority of the church, both universal and particular, to institute, abrogate, and to change rites and ceremonies, dependeth only upon obedience to Christ and his word, in directing of all things to the edification of faith and 30 charity. "For my sheep hear my voice,"[b] saith Christ. And again, "You are my friends, if you do those things which I command you." But particular churches both have, and may obey Christ and his word, in directing all things to the edifying of faith and charity, as shall appear by divers examples 35 hereafter. And therefore particular churches have authority to institute and change rites and ceremonies.

b John 10.

Fourthly, Furthermore it is manifest, that ceremonies, although they were profitable at the first, may grow by continuance to abuse, and be hurtful; as the watching of men and women together in the night at the graves of martyrs, which
5 St. Hierom did so highly commend, at length was tried to be an occasion of much disorder and dissolute life.

Now if every particular church had not authority to abrogate such ceremonies, being hurtful, then should it follow, that Christ, who is the head, not only of the universal church, but
10 also of every particular church, had left the same church destitute of necessary remedies to redress vice and sin.

For as for the general councils, they come together but seldom. It was more than 300 years after Christ or the Nicene Council was called, which was the first general council after
15 the apostles' time. And sith that time, by reason of wars and troubles in the world, sometimes of a long space together no general councils have been called. So that if particular churches may not remove rites tending to sin or idolatry, a great number of souls might perish before the general coun-
20 cils come together. Which were a thing against God's word: for St. Paul saith, God hath given no power to destroy, but to edify.

Fifthly, Look what authority the seven several pastors and churches in Asia had to reform the things that were amiss
25 among every of them, the same authority hath now the several pastors and churches in all kingdoms and provinces. For Aretas, bishop of Cæsarea, and Primasius, episcopus Uticensis in Africa, upon the first chapter of the Revelation of St. John, do teach, that the seven churches in Asia do represent
30 the multitude of the particular churches scattered over the world. Also the Son of man, the universal pastor and head over all churches, was shewed unto John in a vision, present in every of the seven golden candlesticks; that is, in every several and particular church; holding in his right hand all
35 and every the seven stars; that is, governing and defending all and every angel, messenger, and pastor of the several churches.

But every of the said seven pastors in Asia had authority

to reform all things that were amiss among them, as manifestly appears by the seven several epistles which Christ
commanded John to write, and to send unto them. Therefore every several pastor and church, in all kingdoms and
provinces, hath authority to reform such things as be amiss 5
among them.

Sixthly, If a particular church were bound to retain and
exercise, and might not abrogate and remove, evil and hurtful
rites and ceremonies, instituted by men, then were the same
church also bound to obey men more than God; who hath 10
commanded, by his apostle St. Paul, that all things should
be done in the church to edify. But no particular church is
bound to obey men more than God. Therefore a particular
church is not bound to retain, but may remove hurtful ceremonies, instituted by men.   15

These few reasons we have brought out of the Scriptures,
not because we have no more to allege, but partly because
we thought any one saying of Christ sufficient to persuade
any Christian man; and partly, for that we know many men
nowadays stay themselves chiefly upon the decrees of old 20
councils, and the writings and judgments of the doctors and
fathers: and forasmuch as our adversaries will stand most
upon those grounds, we have thought it good to match them
with their own weapons, and in that field wherein they think
themselves best appointed. Wherefore, the rest of our pro- 25
cess shall stand upon the authority of the doctors, and upon
the examples and practice of ancient churches. But first,
we will allege a natural reason or two, and then come to the
authority of the doctors, and examples.

That the proposition is true, very natural reason would 30
suffice a man that would be ruled by reason. But reason
would that things should be restored by like order as they
fell in decay. But it is not likely that any ceremony, being
not wicked of itself, can grow to corruption and abuse in all
places throughout the world at one time, but must of force 35
have both his beginning and his proceeding, and so at length
overwhelm the whole. Wherefore, as the corruption is first
particular, so must there also be first a particular redress.

Yea, and if the abuse happen to be so great, that it over-run the whole body of the church, even very nature would us to do as the good husband is wont to do. The husband, saith St. Augustin, if he see his corn-field overgrown with 5 weeds, goeth not about by and by to weed out altogether, but beginneth in one corner first, and so proceedeth to the whole.

But some man perhaps will say, that the ceremonies of the holy church are sanctified and privileged in such sort that 10 they cannot be abused. But you must understand, that as the nature of man is mutable and corrupt, even so all ordinances devised by men are subject to mutability, and ready to receive corruption. And therefore albeit they were well, and upon some godly zeal received at the beginning, yet after-15 wards, by little and little, they fall to abuse.

The brazen serpent was set up by Moses for the people to behold, that they might receive health. Afterwards it was abused to idolatry. And therefore the good king Ezekias pulled it down, and beat it to powder. And so ceremonies 20 sometimes are taken for things necessary to the worshipping of God ; and of such Christ saith, " Frustra me colunt, docentes doctrinas præcepta hominum." And again, he warn-eth his disciples to beware of the leaven of the scribes and pharisees.

25 Sometimes they grow to such a number, that the multi-tude of them is intolerable. And therefore St. Augustin, in his time, which was more than 1100 years ago, complaineth to his friend Januarius, "Omnia, inquit, sunt plena humanis præsumptionibus ;" All, saith he, is now full of men's pre-30 sumptions. And he saith further, " That the Jews, being under the law, and in servitude of ceremonies, were in far better case than the Christians of his time." And his reason is, " Quia etsi illi tempus libertatis non agnoverint, legalibus tamen sarcinis, non humanis præsumptionibus servierint."

35 This is St. Augustin's reason, for the which he thinketh that the Christians in his time were in worse taking for the bond-age of ceremonies, than ever were the Jews under the shadow of the law. And we be such, you mark it well ; for, saith he, notwithstanding the Jews knew not the time of liberty, yet

they were captive, not as we are to *men's presumptions*, (for
so he calleth the inordinate number of ceremonies devised by
men,) but unto the law of God.

Sometimes they are idle and dumb, and teach nothing;
and are, as I might say, signs without signification. And 5
such are the most part of the ceremonies which now so stiffly
are defended. For the most part of them are such as, I will
not say the poor lay people, or your ignorant priests, but, if
we may be so bold to speak it, you yourselves are not able to
give a reason for them.   10

And sometimes they are devised only for filthy lucre, under
a show of holiness to get money. And whether this have
been practised any time heretofore, we remit the matter to
any indifferent judge.

These many ways may ceremonies be abused. First, if 15
they be taken as things pertaining to the worshipping of
God. Next, if they grow to an inordinate number. Thirdly,
if they teach nothing, nor no man can have understanding of
them. And to conclude, if they be invented for lucre's sake,
to get money. Now ceremonies thus used lack their soul, 20
as I might say, and are become dead: and therefore there
remaineth no more, but that they be had out of the way, and
buried.

There is as great a difference between a particular member
of a general council and the council, as between a particular 25
church and a general council. But in a general council, a
truth hath been revealed to a particular member, for the
edification of the church, which was hid from the whole
council. Unto the which truth and persuasion of the particular member, the whole council gave place, as appeareth 30
in the council of Nice; whereas was revealed unto Paphnu-
tius that which was hid from all the rest. Unto whose
persuasion, notwithstanding that he was but one particular
man, the whole council gave place, because they perceived it
to be for the edification of the church. Therefore the truth 35
of God, whereby things may be instituted, abrogated, or
changed, for the edification of the church, may be sometimes
revealed unto particular churches, which are hid from general
councils.

The apostles' successors had the same authority that the apostles had. For that the adversaries grant; else under what colour drive they men to obey the pope and his decrees? But all bishops be the apostles' successors, and 5 have like power, as appeareth by St. Hierom[c], which saith, "Omnes episcopos apostolorum successores esse:" and by Cyprian, who affirmeth that each one had the like authority; "Hoc utique, inquit, erant cæteri apostoli, quod fuit Petrus, pari consortio prædriti, et honoris et potestatis." Therefore 10 all bishops have the same authority, which is, to dispose things to edification; as Paul saith, "Cætera, cum venero, disponam."

And that the very particular churches had this liberty to retain or to remove ceremonies, as it may seem good for 15 them, it may appear by an infinite number of examples, and in manner by the continual course of the old church. For thus writeth Irenæus of the order of Lenten-fast in his time, as it is reported by Eusebius, "Neque de die tantum disceptatio est," &c. "Neither do they differ only about the 20 day, but also about the manner of their fasting. For some think they should fast one day, some two days, and some more. Some reckon their day of 40 (sic) hours long, accounting altogether the hours of day and night." By this it appeareth, that notwithstanding there was an order taken 25 for fasting, yet was it lawful for men to receive it or leave it, as they listed; and that without breach of charity. For Irenæus straightway addeth these words, "Nihilo tamen minus," &c. "This notwithstanding," saith Irenæus, (an old father, that lived a thousand and four hundred years 30 ago,) "they kept peace and unity among themselves. And so do we until this day. And the diversity of our fasting setteth forth the more the agreeance of our faith." Likewise was there great diversity in keeping of Easter-day. For the Latins kept it upon one day, after the tradition of St. Peter, 35 as they said; and the churches of Asia kept it on another day, after the tradition of St. John; yet notwithstanding, agreed in Christian peace and unity.

[c] Hier. ad Evagr.

Socrates, in the fifth book and twenty-second chapter of his history, prosecuteth this matter at large. And the chapter were worthy to be recited whole, saving for short-ness of time a portion thereof only shall suffice. "Nusquam igitur apostolus nec ipsa evangelia," &c. "Neither the 5 apostle nor the gospels themselves do any where lay upon them which come to preaching (of the gospel, he means) the yoke of bondage. But every one in their own countries have upon a certain custom, as they would themselves, kept the feast of Easter, and other festival days, that they might cease 10 from labour, and remember the healthful passion, (he means, of the Lord;) neither hath our Saviour or the apostles by any law commanded this to be observed of us; neither do the gospels or apostles threaten unto us any pain or punishment, as Moses' law did unto the Jews: but it is written in the 15 gospels only, after the manner of an history, in the repre-hension of the Jews, because they committed murder on the festival days, and because Christ suffered in the time of sweetbread. Wherefore the scope of the apostle was not to make laws for holydays, but to bring in good life and 20 godliness. But it seemeth unto me that likewise, as many other things in every place grew unto a custom, even so also did the feast of Easter. Because none of the apostles, as I have said, decreed any thing of the matter. That certain things, even from the beginning, began to be observed in 25 every place rather by custom than by law, the matter itself declareth. As in Asia the Less, many after the old custom contemning the Saturday, observed the fourteenth day. And they thus doing did never strive with them which did keep the feast of Easter otherwise, until Victor, bishop of Rome, 30 being too earnest, decreed that the Quartodecimans should be excommunicate. For the which deed, Irenæus, being bishop of Lyons in France, wrote a sharp epistle unto Victor, wherein he both reprehendeth his earnestness, and also declareth that none of them which in old time did 35 diversely celebrate the feast of Easter, were by any means separated from the communion. And that Polycarpus, bishop of Smyrna, (which in conclusion suffered martyrdom under

Gordianus,) did not eschew the communion of Anicetus, bishop of Rome, nor did for the festival day's sake fall out with him; although he, according to the custom of Eucharius, bishop of Smyrna, did celebrate Easter the fourteenth
5 day; as Eusebius saith in the fifth book of the Ecclesiastical History."

And a little after; "Romani namque tres ante Pasca septimanas," &c. "For the Romans do fast three weeks together before Easter, except the Saturday and the Sunday.
10 The Illyrici, and all Hellada, and they of Alexandria, do fast their fast six weeks before Easter, and call it *Quadragesimam*, forty days fast, or Lent. But it is a marvel to me, how these men, differing about the number of days, do call it by one name of forty days fast. A man shall find some, which do
15 not only dissent about number of days, but also do not retain one kind of abstinence. For some do utterly abstain from things having life. Some, of those things which have life, eat only fishes; some, besides fishes, eat also birds, and say, after Moses, they came of the waters. Some abstain both from
20 berries and eggs; some do eat only dry bread; some not that: some there be which, fasting to the ninth hour, do use divers meats: in divers nations they fast diversely. Of which there be innumerable causes. And because no man is able to shew any written commandment of this matter, it is plain
25 that the apostles have left it free to every man's judgment and will, lest any man should do a good thing either of fear or necessity. Such is the diversity of fasts through the churches: and about the communion is a much like diversity." And so the author proceedeth in shewing certain diversities about
30 the ministration of the communion, baptism, marriage, and other ecclesiastical observances.

Again, St. Augustin writeth unto Januarius, "Alii quotidie communicant," &c. "Some," saith St. Augustin, "receive the communion of the body and blood of Christ every day;
35 some others upon certain days. Some there be that miss no day without the oblation; some other communicate only upon the Saturday and Sunday, others only upon the Sunday."

G

"ᵈNunquid ergo cæteri apostoli prandere Christianos," &c.
"Did then the other apostles teach the Christians through-
-out the whole world to dine contrary to Peter? Like as
therefore Peter and his fellow-disciples lived in concord
among themselves, even so let them which fast on the Satur- 5
day, and were planted by Peter, and those which dine on
Saturday, and were planted by his fellow-disciples, live together in unity and concord."

And a little after, in the same place, "Sit ergo una fides,"
&c. "Therefore, let the faith of the universal church, which 10
is there spread abroad as inwardly in the inward parts be
one; although the same unity of faith be kept with divers
rites or observations; wherewith in no wise the truth in faith
is hindered. For all the beauty of the king's daughter is
inward. But those rites which are kept diversely, are under- 15
standed in his garment. Whereupon it is said to her, *covered
round about with variety in the golden edge,* or skirts *of his
garments.* But let that vesture also be so divers in variable
rites, that it be not torn in sunder with contentious dissensions." 20

Yet followeth in the same place, "Si autem quoniam huic,"
&c. "But because I think for my part I have sufficiently
answered this, if thou wilt ask my judgment of this matter,
considering this in my mind, I see, that fasting of the
evangelists and apostles, and in the whole Testament, (which 25
is called the New Testament,) is commanded: but on what
days we must not fast, and on what days we must fast, I do
not find determined by the commandment of the Lord or the
apostles. And by this I judge, that liberty is more apt and
convenient, than constraint, of fasting; although truly not 30
to the obtaining the righteousness which faith obtaineth;
wherein consisteth the beauty of the king's daughter inwardly; but yet to signify the eternal rest, which is the true
sabbath."

"ᵉNon omnes quamvis ejusdem opinionis," &c. "All men, 35
though they were of one faith, yet observed they not in their
churches like traditions. Yea, they that had all one faith,

ᵈ De jejun. Sabbath. Augustin. ad Casulan.   ᵉ Nicephor. lib. 12. cap. 34.

yet oft in the observation of usages they differed much.
Which thing was no hinderance to true godliness."

Likewise it is noted in the decrees of pope Stephen, and
alleged in Gratian, dist. 31. as followeth; "Aliter se habet
5 orientalium ecclesiarum traditio," &c. "The tradition of the
east church is far otherwise than the tradition of this holy
church of Rome. For their priests, deacons, and subdeacons
are married : but in this church, none from a subdeacon unto
a bishop hath license to marry a wife." And here is to be
10 marked, that pope Stephen took not the single life of priests
in the Latin church as a thing commanded by God, but only
as a tradition, and such a tradition as the Grecians lately
refused.

"Quæstio Augustini ad Gregorium fuit ista, Cum una sit
15 fides, cur sunt ecclesiarum diversæ consuetudines? et aliter
consuetudo missarum in S. Romana ecclesia, atque aliter
in Galliarum ecclesiis tenetur? Cui Gregorius respondit, 12.
dist. cap. Novit fraternitas tua," &c. "Your brotherhood
knoweth the custom of the church of Rome, wherein you have
20 been trained up. But this way pleaseth me well, that if you
find any thing, whether it be in the church of Rome, or in
the church of France, or else in any other church, that may
more please God, that you diligently choose the same. And
forasmuch as the church of England is new in constitution
25 and in ceremonies, that you pour into it the best ordinances
that you can gather of many others. For we may not love
the things for the places, but the places for the things. Wherefore, gather you out of every church such things as be godly,
religious, and right; and the same, being knit up as it were
30 in a bundle, cause you to be put and to be brought in ure in
the church of England."

Here we may note, that Gregory, being then bishop of
Rome, would not drive other churches to the observations of
the ceremonies and rites of Rome; but suffered each nation
35 quietly to retain and keep such orders as should be most
convenient for them.

Yea, Sozomenus writeth in his seventh book, "Eædem cere-
moniæ non possunt," &c. "One kind of ceremonies cannot
be found in every church."

And moreover Socrates writeth in his fifth book, "Non inveniuntur," &c. "You cannot find two churches, (saith Socrates, writing of the order of the church in his time,) that in rites and ceremonies agree together."

Likewise Theodoretus, upon the fourteenth chapter to the 5 Romans, entreating on these words, "Let every man abound in his own sense, or judgment," writeth as followeth : "Non enim hoc posuit generaliter," &c. "He hath not put this generally, nor yet commandeth he to judge thus of God's decrees. For he doth accurse them that go about to teach 10 any thing contrary unto the truth : 'If any man preach unto you any other doctrine than that ye have received, let him be accursed.'

"And therefore only of meats he left to every man freedom of his own mind. For this custom remaineth in the churches 15 until this day ; and one chooseth abstinence, and another eateth all kinds of meat without scruple of conscience. And neither this man judgeth that man, nor the one reproveth the other, but the law of concord and charity doth make them notable." 20

And all this diversity rose of that, that it was lawful for every particular church either to receive or to leave such ordinances as were devised and thought good by other churches. For if all places had been bound to one order, then could never have been such diversity. 25

Now of this may we thus conclude ; that church that hath liberty, whether it will receive a ceremony or no at the first, may by the same liberty afterwards remove it, when it shall be thought good. Yea, and a great deal more reasonable it is to remove a ceremony, when it is corrupt and abused, than 30 at the first not to receive it, when it was incorrupted and judged profitable. For as St. Augustin writeth to Januarius, "Quod non est contra fidem," &c. that is, "Whatsoever is not against faith and good manners, it is to be taken as a thing indifferent." Now if it be to be taken for a thing 35 indifferent to keep or to refuse, when it is best, much more reason it is to refuse, when it is corrupt and grown out of kind.

For any thing, that cannot necessarily be gathered out of

the word of God, may be changed, as St. Cyprian writeth to
Pompeius; "Nihil innovetur, inquit, quod traditum." Oh!
said the adversary to St. Cyprian, "Nothing that is once
delivered us, may be altered." St. Cyprian makes answer,
5 "Unde est ista traditio?" "May it not be changed?" saith
Cyprian. "Wherefore? From whence came this tradition?
Came it from the authority of the Lord and gospel, or from
the commandments and writings of the apostles?" As if he
should say, If it came from the epistles of the apostles, or
10 the gospels, then it may not be changed; if it came otherwise by the decrees of men, it may. And in another place
he saith, "Non est absurdum," &c. "It is not against reason, that such things as have been received be changed for
the better."

15 For such is the nature of ceremonies, that as it is sometimes profitable to receive them, so sometimes it is profitable
to put them away. And here we have to shew you the wise
answer of a gentleman and counsellor of the city of Athens,
named Theramenes. The Lacedæmonians, after they had
20 given the Athenians a great overthrow in the field, commanded them to pull down the walls of the town, otherwise
they threatened them utter undoing. When this matter came
to deliberation in the council-house of Athens, Theramenes
gave counsel that the walls should be pulled down. Straight-
25 way there stood up another gentleman; And will you, said
he, give your assent to the pulling down of the walls, that
were builded up by the counsel of that worthy man, and great
captain, Themistocles? Yea, said Theramenes: for Themistocles caused the walls to be builded for the safeguard of the
30 city; and for the safeguard of the same city, I give counsel
to throw them down. Even so may we answer by ceremonies: they were brought in at the first for to profit the
church; but after they be once corrupted, and do not that
office for which they were invented, for the profit of the same
35 church they must be removed. And if this be true of such
ceremonies which at the first were indifferent, much more
it is to be thought of such ceremonies that were never good
nor indifferent, but were brought in in the corrupt state of
the church.

And therefore St. Augustin hath a marvellous good saying, writing ad Marcellinum, cap. 5. "Non itaque verum est, quod dicitur," &c. "It is not true that some men say, that such a thing as is once well done, may in no wise be altered. For after the cause or occasion of time is changed, good reason requireth, that that be changed, which otherwise before was well done. That whereas they say, it were not well to have it changed; contrariwise, the truth saith, it were not well but it should be changed: for then shall both be well, if that for the diversity of time they shall be divers." 10

Thus much for proofs out of the Scripture and ancient writers. Now remains to shew the same by example.

Basilius, being a bishop, took upon him to devise a several form of prayers and ceremonies, to be used about the administration of the communion; and by the consent of his church 15 practised the same, without any authority of general council. Chrysostom also did the like; so that it beareth his name until this day, and is called *Liturgia Chrysostomi.* If particular bishops had authority to vary from other churches, and to institute rites and ceremonies about the administra- 20 tion of the holy communion, which be ceremonies of most weight, and most in controversy at this day; how unreasonable is it to deny the like authority to a whole kingdom or province, to the ordinary powers and learned of the same!

Furthermore, the church of the Æthiopians, called *Pres-* 25 *byter Johannes land,* have at this day their own ceremonies, and that in the vulgar tongue.

Those churches that remain yet in the east parts differ, and always have done, from the west churches in rites and ceremonies. 30

Yea, and the west churches themselves vary one from another.

There were in Gregory's time three canons or orders, to minister the holy communion; the canon of Ambrose, the canon of Scholasticus, the canon of Gregory. 35

At Rome, every Saturday was fasting-day. At Milan, St. Ambrose and the whole church kept it no fasting-day. And both St. Augustin and his mother, by St. Ambrose's advice, when they came to Milan, did not fast Saturdays.

So that it may be reasonably gathered, that the old council thought it a thing commodious for the church to have variety in ceremonies, and to leave their churches at their liberty to reform them when they grew to abuse. Otherwise they would 5 have decreed, that all churches should have had like and the same ceremonies and rites; which they never did.

Therefore such uniformity of rites and ceremonies as now is seen in the popish churches was not in the church when it was most pure, but was brought in after, when the bishop of 10 Rome had aspired to the unjust primacy: and so have been continued rather for a public recognition of their subjection to the monarchy of the see of Rome than for any edification.

For it is more profit for the church to have some diversity of ceremonies in divers places, than to have all one; for these 15 causes:

First, that the liberty of the church may remain; that in these indifferent things every particular church may *abundare in suo sensu,* "abound in his own sense," as St. Paul writeth.

Secondarily, That ceremonies be not too much esteemed 20 of the simple, and so grow to be made equal with God's word. As experience declareth, that great numbers make more conscience of breach of an outward ceremony than of one of God's commandments. Such affection is termed of some men *devotion.* But St. Augustin calleth such offence, conceived 25 upon such alteration of ceremonies, *superstition.*

But to proceed with more examples. Ambrose, according to the example of Athanasius, who did the like at Alexandria, did first institute the rite or ceremony of singing psalms at Milan, as St. Augustin reporteth in his Confession.

30 But where is authority to institute, there is also authority to abrogate. That is true, will some say, when it is made by his own authority. Nay also, when it is established by a more general consent, if the practice declare it hurtful, as by the examples following.

35 Nectarius, bishop of Constantinople, did abrogate and remove the office of the penitentiary and auricular confession; which was a constitution almost generally received, and remained still at Rome, notwithstanding his abrogation of it. And that he did well in it, it may be proved by two reasons.

1. That Sozomenus writing the history, saith, that "fere omnes episcopi eum sunt secuti;" "almost all bishops followed his example." Where is to be noted by the way, that particular reformations do much good, and provoke others to follow. 5

2. The second reason is, that St. John Chrysostom succeeding Nectarius did not restore that rite of confession again: for it remained abrogated in Sozomenus's days, who lived after Chrysostom. And it is not to be thought but Chrysostom would have restored it, if it had been unorderly 10 removed. So that this example of Nectarius, and the particular church of Constantinople, abrogating a general consent upon just causes of abuse, approved by the imitation of so many bishops, and especially of the notable father St. John Chrysostom his successor, is a most plain declaration, that 15 particular churches may abrogate abused rites and ceremonies, although they have been instituted by a more general authority.

Likewise in St. Augustin's time, as appeareth in his Confessions[f], there was an ordinance in Afric, and elsewhere, 20 that meat, bread, and wine should be brought to the place of meetings at the *memories* of martyrs. Which ordinance St. Ambrose did abrogate; and the reason is there declared in these words; "Ne ulla occasio se ingurgitandi daretur," &c. "Lest any occasion should be given to drunkards to 25 overcharge themselves with drink:" and also, because that observance was most like to the superstition of the heathen, who kept *parentalia*, burial feasts for their dead parents.

Here, beside that Ambrose, one man, abrogated a common rite, let this also be marked, that the common reason used of 30 men nowadays took no place with this ancient father; which is, Take away the abuse, and let the thing remain. But St. Ambrose took away the abuse by removing the thing.

Moreover, the common watchings, or *wakes*, of men and women at the martyrs' graves, which St. Hierom so highly 35 commends, and doth most sharply inveigh against Vigilantius, who wrote against the said wakes, calling Vigilantius his

---

[f] Lib. 6. cap. 2.

assertion an heresy, was afterwards abrogated and rejected. And of such kind of wakes there is a canon in a particular council holden in Spain, called *Concilium Eliberenum*, in the 35th chap. with these words, " Placuit prohiberi ne fæminæ
5 in cœmiterio pervigilent, &c. " It hath pleased us to forbid, that women should wake the night through in the burial place; because that oftentimes, under pretence of prayer, heinous offences be secretly committed."

Moreover, the late experience within this our country doth
10 declare, that the abrogation of many ceremonies established by general authority is lawful and profitable. For in the time of king Henry VIII. of famous memory, many super-stitious observations and idolatrous rites were abolished; and that by consent of many of them which now are, and of late
15 have been, adversaries; as pilgrimage, stations, pardons, many superstitious opinions of purgatory, holy water, of masses for cattle, and *scala cœli*, innumerable lies out of the church legends of feigned miracles, and saints' lives. All which things were once established by catholic authority, as
20 they term it, and in other regions are yet maintained under the same colour, and the gainsayers accounted by the see of Rome and her patrons, heretics. Which things are so gross, that they need no confutation.

And in this late time, as appeareth, they were ashamed to
25 restore the same. Wherefore it is no inconvenience, that unprofitable and superstitious rites be abrogated and removed by the authority of a particular church.

And because we are entered into this matter, it shall not be amiss to make rehearsal of a few, among a great many, of
30 their vain superstitious fables, which have been in times past propounded to the people for wholesome doctrine.

In the Festival, (a book, as it is in the prologue, gathered out of *Legenda aurea*, for curates that lack books and cun-ning,) in the sermon of *Corpus Christi* day, it is written, that
35 a man hath nine commodities by hearing of mass. One is, that he shall not that day lose his sight. Another, all idle oaths that day shall be forgiven him. Another, he shall die no sudden death. Another, so long as he heareth mass, he

shall not wax old; and his good angel reckons his steps to
and fro the church, to his salvation. It were too long to
reckon them all; let this be enough for a taste.

In the said book, in the sermon on All Souls day, there is
a narration of a priest, which was suspended of his bishop, 5
because he could say none other mass, but mass of *requiems*.
One day the dead bodies rose, and came about the bishop,
for taking away their chaplain from them. And so he was
restored to his office.

In the sermon on Candlemas-day, there is also an history 10
of a woman, which never did good deed, but only that she
had continually kept a candle before our lady: after her
death, by the appointment of our lady, a candle was kept
burning before her in hell, which the devils could not abide;
and by reason thereof she was restored to life, and became 15
a good woman.

What occasion of dissolute life and sin may be ministered
to simple people by these and an infinite number of such like
fables, it is easy to perceive.

But the answer will be, these books were never allowed 20
by public authority. Well, these books were openly printed,
and within memory of men commonly credited, and yet be
of some. And in these late days, there hath been much
preaching against reading the Scriptures in the vulgar tongue;
who hath heard any great invection against such books? And 25
strait inquisition hath been of English Bibles and Testaments
to be burned; whether the like diligence hath been used for
abolishing these, let all men judge.

But to return again to the proofs by ancient examples, that
particular churches may alter and institute ceremonies. 30

In all times there hath been provincial councils holden.
Which were in vain, if they might not allow the good, and
reject the evil. Particular and provincial councils have always
had authority to reject and condemn wicked doctrine; and
by that means many heresies have been suppressed without 35
general councils.

In the provincial council of Gangra, divers wicked opinions

5 Which was for the dead.

against the Christian liberty for marriage, for eating of meats, for bondmen that would not obey their masters under pretence of Christian religion, were condemned.

The heresy of Pelagius was condemned in divers provincial
5 synods in Afric before it was condemned by any general council. But doctrine is a matter of more weight than rites and ceremonies. And so provincial synods having authority of the more, have also of the less.

And to be short, three hundred years after the apostles'
10 time, there were no general councils, and the church well governed all that time, every province ruling their own churches according to the Scriptures, only with the help of provincial councils.

The fathers of the sixth council of Carthage, writing to
15 the bishop of Rome, who would have intermeddled with their matters in Afric, have a notable sentence for this purpose. "The council of Nice," say they, "perceived most justly and wisely, that all controversies ought to be ended there where they first began, and the grace of the Holy Ghost shall not
20 be wanting to any particular province." The words be these: "Prudentissime enim justissimeque viderunt, quæcunque negotia in suis locis ubi orta sunt finienda; nec unicuique provinciæ gratiam S. Spiritus defuturam."

Moreover, testimonies of the Scriptures and doctors may
25 be brought, and many more examples of the ancient churches, for further confirmation hereof. But for this time we have thought this sufficient. Hereafter, as cause shall be moved, we shall have occasion to say more. In the mean season, by these proofs, that we have here shortly alleged, we doubt not
30 but it may appear to the indifferent hearer, that a particular church hath authority to make or change, and remove and abolish ceremonies in such sort as may be most for the edifying of God's people.

We are not ignorant what may be objected against this
35 assertion. As namely, concerning the authority of general councils. But because that matter requireth a long tract, we will in our answer to the reasons on the other part, by God's grace, declare by sufficient authority, in what points

general councils (whose authority we acknowledge with St. Augustin to be right wholesome in the church) are to be universally holden, and in what points they are not.

Again, where they allege continuance of time and their possession in the church, let this be for this time shortly 5 answered; they should first prove their things true, and then allege time. For against the eternal truth of God's word no continuance of time can make prescription; as St. Cyprian saith, " Consuetudo sine veritate est vetustas erroris;" "Custom without truth is an ancient error." 10

And as for their possession in the church, seeing it is also a long matter, and no orderly kind of disputation, that they should bring in one matter in controversy to prove another, that matter shall for this present be referred to this issue; If they be not able to prove that the bishop of Rome is the 15 head of the universal church of Christ, and under his obedience all Christians ought to live, under pain of damnation; and that neither by decrees of general councils, neither by consent of princes, but by the authority of Scriptures, and by the word of God, (for by that title of God's word the pope 20 claimeth his supremacy;) if they be not able to prove that, I say, which they shall never do, as it hath been often proved in this realm, and elsewhere; then is the authority of their church nothing, and their possession unjust.

These and other objections shall be by God's grace 25 answered more at large, when the contrary book shall be exhibited.

The God of peace and consolation give us grace to be like minded one towards another in Christ Jesus, that we all agreeing together, may with one mouth praise God the Father 30 of our Lord Jesus Christ.

VI.

Richard Cox to Wolfgang Weidner, at Wormes, concerning the same subject with the former ; with an account of the disputation at Westminster.

Viro eximio, eruditione et pietate insignito, D. D. Wolfgango
5 *Weidnero Wormaciensi, amico meo observandissimo,* Wor-
maciæ.

Cum Wormacia discederem, venerande senex, et frater in
Christo plurimum observande, semper apud me decrevi ad te
scribere, certioremque te facere tandem aliquando de rerum
10 nostrarum statu et conditione ; quod te audire non ingratum
esse existimavi, propter ardentem sincerumque zelum, quo
indies afficeris erga Christi Jesu evangelium. Coactus sum
hactenus, fateor, invitus silere, ne parum tibi grata referrem.
Sub sævo Mariæ imperio ita crevit invaluitque papismus ad
15 quinquennium tantum, ut incredibile fuerit quantopere pectora
papistarum obduruerint ; adeo ut non sine magna difficultate
pientissima nostra regina una cum suis, qui a veritate strenue
steterunt, sinceræ Christi religioni locum obtinere potuerit.
Restiterunt in summo nostro concilio, (quod *parlamentum*
20 Gallico vocabulo appellamus,) pontifices, scribæ et pharisæi.
Et, quia eo loci paucos habebant, qui contra vel hiscere pos-
sent, vincere perpetuo videbantur. Interim nos, pusillus grex,
qui apud vos in Germania hoc quinquennio, Dei beneficio,
latuimus, in suggestis, maxime coram regina nostra Elizabetha,
25 contra intonamus ; pontificem Romanum vere Antichristum,
et traditiones pro maxima sui parte meras esse blasphemias.
Tandem paulatim resipiscere cœperunt ex nobilibus multi, ex

plebe innumeri, ex clero prorsus nullus. Immotus enim stat
clerus totus,

       "Tanquam dura silex, aut stet Marpesia cautes,"

ut poeta canit. Denique huc est res perducta, ut octo ex ip-
sorum antesignanis, seu episcopi, seu ex doctis selectissimi, 5
cum octo nostrûm abjectorum scilicet atque profugorum, de
quibusdam religionis capitibus dissererent. Et ut vitaretur
verborum pugna, scriptis agi constitutum est. Statuta est
dies. Adsumus omnes. Adsunt reginæ consiliarii. Adest
tota fere nobilitas. Decretum est, ut ipsi primum de con- 10
troversiis sententiam suam proponant. Unusquispiam illorum
nomine, tanquam Goliath contra Davidem, sua venditat, pro-
pugnat, et argumentis irrefragabilibus (ut videbatur) confirmat, sibique plaudit, tanquam jam victor evadens. Respondit nostrûm unus veritate fretus, non ampullis verborum, 15
in timore Domini, non in doctrinæ venditatione. Finita re-
sponsione, incredibilis mox audientium applausus excitatus
est, non sine magna adversariorum perturbatione et con-
fusione. Venit alter dies simili tractationi destinatus. Ro-
gantur adversarii nostri a consultationis præside[h], ut eo ordine 20
progrederentur, quo decretum antea fuerat; nimirum ut ipsi
primum inciperent in altera controversia sua sententiam dicere, nosque sequeremur. Illi vero contra contendunt, territi
scilicet primi diei successu parum prospero : clamitantque iniquum esse, ut ipsi primum dicere incipiant, cum ipsi jam tot 25
annis perstiterint in possessione catholicæ ecclesiæ. Si quid
habeamus contra ipsos, proferamus nos, ut ipsi pro sua autori-
tate nos refutent, atque compescant tanquam filios degeneres,
ut qui ab ecclesiæ unitate jam diu exciderimus. Gratia
Christo Domino nostro; dum illi mandato obsistunt, merito 30
coercentur, et sua causa cadunt. Itaque stabilitur apud nos,
per omnia regni loca, sincera Christi religio, eadem prorsus
ratione, qua sub Edwardo olim nostro, beatissimæ memoriæ,
promulgata erat. Hæc pauca, sed certa, visum est ad te
scribere, quem scio nostra solide gaudere gaudia, ut nobiscum 35
gratias Domino Deo nostro agas, qui nos in ista humiliatione

       [h] D. scil. custode sigilli magni.

et cruce, vere paterna sua commiseratione respexit et conso-
latus est.   Det ipse ut tanta et incredibilia ejus beneficia e
mentibus nostris nunquam elabantur.   Gratam rem fecerit
tua humanitas, si ista D. Jacobo Cornicio, medico, et Vespa-
5 siano Fitich, amicis meis summis communicare dignetur.

Jamjam aggredimur septa papistica disrumpere atque dis-
sipare, et vineam Domini felicibus auspiciis restaurare.   Jam
sumus in opere; at *messis multa, operarii pauci.*   Rogemus
Dominum, ut mittat operarios in messem.   Hæc paucula
10 habeo tibi pro officio in te meo impertiri.   Dominus Jesus te
sospitet, pietatemque tuam servet augeatque ad ultimum usque
spiritus halitum.   Londini in Anglia, 20 Maii, 1559.

Tui studiosissimus, Rich. Coxus.

VII.

A letter of Jewell's to Peter Martyr, concerning the disputation
15 *with the papists at Westminster.*

Jo. Juellus ad P. Martyrem.
S. P.

DE illis disputationibus inter nos, et episcopos, quas proxi-
mis literis scripsi indictas fuisse in ante calendas Aprilis, quid
20 factum sit, paucis accipe.   Sic enim visum est continuare
orationem sine procemio.   Primum ergo, ut omnis causa jur-
giorum et otiosæ contentionis tolleretur, senatus decrevit, ut
omnia utrinque de scripto legerentur, et ita describerentur
tempora, ut primo die assertiones tantum utrinque nudæ pro-
25 ponerentur: proximô autem conventu, ut nos illis responderemus, et illi vicissim nobis.   Pridiè ergò kal. April. cum
magna expectatione, majori credo frequentia, convenissemus
Westmonasterii, episcopi, pro sua fide, nec scripti, nec picti

quicquam attulerunt, quod dicerent, se non satis temporis
habuisse ad res tantas cogitandas : cum tamen habuissent
plùs minùs decem dies, et interea copias auxiliares Oxonio et
Cantabrigiâ, et undique ex omnibus angulis contraxissent.
Tamen ne tot viri viderentur frustra convenisse, D. Colus 5
subornatus ab aliis venit in medium, qui de prima quæstione,
hoc est, de peregrina lingua, unus omnium nomine peroraret.
Ille verò cum omnibus nos contumeliis et convitiis indignis-
simè excepisset, et omnium seditionum authores et faces
appellâsset, et supplosione pedum, projectione brachiorum, 10
inflexione laterum, crepitu digitorum, modò dejectione modò
sublatione superciliorum, (nôsti enim hominis vultum et
modestiam) sese omnes in partes et formas convertisset, huc
postremò evasit, ut diceret, Angliam ante mille trecentos
annos recepisse evangelium ; et quibus, inquit, literis, quibus 15
annalibus, quibus monumentis constare potest, preces tum
publicas in Anglia habitas, fuisse Anglicè.   Postea cùm in
illo circulo sese satis jamdiu jactavisset, adjecit seriò, et vero
vultu, atque etiam admonuit, ut omnes hoc tanquam quiddam
de dictis melioribus diligenter attenderent, atque annotarent, 20
apostolos ab initio ita inter sese distribuisse operas, ut alii
orientis ecclesias instituerent, alii occidentis.   Itaque Petrum
et Paulum, in Romana ecclesia, quæ totam propè Europam
contineret, omnia Romano sermone, hoc est, Latinè docuisse ;
reliquos apostolos in oriente, nullo unquam alio sermone usus 25
fuisse, nisi Græco.   Tu fortasse ista rides : atqui ego ne-
minem audivi unquam, qui solenniùs et magistratiùs insaniret.
Si adfuisset Julius noster, centies exclamâsset, *Poh! horson
knave.*   Verùm ille, inter alia, nihil veritus est, mysteria ipsa
et penetralia, atque adyta prodere religionis suæ.   Non enim 30
dubitavit graviter et seriò monere, etiamsi alia omnia maximè
convenirent, tamen non expedire, ut populus, quid in sacris
ageretur, intelligat.   Ignorantia enim, inquit, mater est veræ
pietatis, quam ille appellavit devotionem.   O mystica sacra,
atque opertanea bonæ deæ ! Quid tu me putas interim de 35
Cotta pontifice cogitâsse ? Hoc videlicet illud est, in spiritu
et veritate adorare.   Mitto alia.   Cum ille jam calumniando,
convitiando, mentiendo magnam partem illius temporis, quod
nobis ad disputandum datum erat, exemisset ; nos postremò

nostra pronunciavimus de scripto, ita modestè, ut rem tantum
ipsam diceremus, nihil autem læderemus adversarium.   Postremò ita dimissa est disputatio, ut vix quisquam esset in
toto illo conventu, ne comes quidem Salopiensis, quin victo-
5 riam illius diei adjudicaret nobis.   Postea inita est ratio, ut
proximo die lunæ, de secunda quæstione eodem modo diceremus; utque die Mercurii, nos illorum primi diei argumentis
responderemus, et illi vicissim nostris.

  Die lunæ, cum frequens multitudo ex omni nobilitate cupi-
10 dissima audiendi convenisset, episcopi, nescio pudorene su-
perioris diei, an desperatione victoriæ, primùm tergiversari,
habere se quod dicerent de prima quæstione, nec oportere
rem sic abire.   Responsum est à senatu, Si quid haberent,
id tertio post die, prout ab initio convenerat, audiri posse:
15 nunc hoc potius agerent, neve turbarent ordinem.   Dejecti de
hoc gradu tamen huc evaserunt, si dicendum omnino sit, nolle
se priores dicere; se enim in possessione constitisse: nos, si
quid vellemus, priori loco experiremur.   Magnam enim se
facturos injuriam causæ suæ, si paterentur, nos posteriores
20 discedere cum applausu populi, et aculeos orationis nostræ
recentes in auditorum animis relinquere.   Senatus contrà,
Hanc ab initio institutam fuisse rationem, ut illi, quòd dignitate priores essent, priori etiam loco dicerent; nec eam nunc
mutari posse.   Mirari verò se, quid hoc sit mysterii, cùm
25 omnino necesse sit, alterutros priores dicere; alioqui enim
nihil posse dici: et præsertim, cum Colus in primis disputationibus etiam injussus, ultrò prior ad dicendum prosiluerit.
Postremò, cum altercationibus magna pars temporis extracta
esset, nec episcopi ullo pacto concedere vellent de secundo
30 loco, ad extremum sine disputatione discessum est.   Ea verò
res, incredibile dictu est, quantum imminuerit opinionem
populi de episcopis: omnes enim cœperunt jam suspicari,
quod nihil dicere voluissent, ne potuisse quidem illos quicquam dicere.   Postero die, Vitus Vintoniensis, amicus tuus,
35 et Vatsonus Lincolniensis, de tam aperto contemptu et con-
tumacia, damnati sunt ad turrim: ibi nunc castrametantur,
et ex infirmis præmissis concludunt fortiter. Reliqui jubentur
quotidiè præstò esse in aula, et expectare quid de illis senatus
velit decernere.   Habes ἔντευξιν ἀτελῆ et penè ἀνέντευκτον;

H

quam tamen, quô meliùs rem omnem intelligeres, descripsi
pluribus, fortasse, quam oportuit. Benè vale, mi pater, decus
meum, atque etiam animi dimidium mei. Si quid est apud
vos novarum rerum hoc tempore, id malo esse proximarum
literarum argumentum. Saluta plurimùm, meo nomine, ve- 5
nerandum illum virum, et mihi in Christo dominum colen-
dissimum, D. Bullingerum, D. Gualterum, D. Simlerum,
D. Lavaterum, D. Wolphium, D. Gesnerum, D. Hallerum,
D. Frisium, D. Hermannum, et Julium tuum meumque.
Nostri omnes te salutant, et tibi omnia cupiunt. Londini, 10
6. April. 1559.   Jo. Juellus tuus.

       Post-script'
Istæ sunt secundæ, quas ad te scribo, ex quo redii in Angliam.

INSCRIPTIO.

D. Petro Martyri, professori sacræ theo-   15
logiæ in ecclesia Tigurina, viro doctis-
simo, et domino suo in Christo colen-
dissimo.   *Tiguri.*

VIII.

The oration of the reverend father in God Mr. Dr. Fecknam,
abbott of Westminster, in the parliament-howse, 1559, against 20
the bill for the liturgy.

HONOURABLE and my very good lordes; having at this present two sundry kindes of religion here propounded and set
forthe before you, and your honours being allready in possession of th'one of them, and your fathers before you, for the 25
space of 14 hundrethe yeres past here in this realme, lyke as
I shall hereafter prove unto you; the other religion is here
set forth in a booke to be receyved and establisshed by
th'aucthoritie of this high courte of parliament, and to take
his effecte here in this realme at Mydsomar nexte comynge. 30
And you beinge (as I knowe right well) dissirous to have some

perfect and sure knowledge, which of both these religions is
the better, and most worthy to be establisshhed here in this
realme, and to be preferred before the other; I shall for my
part, and for the discharge of my dewtie, first unto God,
5 secondly unto our soveraigne lady the quene's highness,
thirdly unto your honours, and to the whole commons of this
realme, here sette forthe, and expresse unto you, three brief
rules and lessons, wherby your honours shalbe able to putte
difference betwixt the true religion of God and the counter-
10 feyte, and therin never to be deceyved. The first of these
three rules or lessons is, that in this your search and tryall
making, your honours must observe, which of them bothe
hathe ben most observed in the churche of Christ of all men,
and at all tymes and seasons, and in all places. The second,
15 which of them bothe is of it self the more staid religion, and
allwayes forth one and agreeable with it self. The third and
last rule to be considered of your wisdoms is, which of these
religions dothe brede the more humble and obedient subjects,
first unto God, second to our soveraigne ladie the quene's
20 highness, and all superiour powers.

Concerninge the first rule and lesson, it cannot be truly
affirmed or yet thought of any man, that this new religion,
here nowe to be sett forthe in this booke, hathe not bene observed in Christ's churche of all Christian men, at all tymes
25 and in all places; when the religion expressed in this book
hathe ben observed only here in this realme, and that for a
shorte tyme, as not muche passing the space of two yeres,
and that in king Edward the 6th dayes: whereas the religion, and the very same maner of servinge and honoringe
30 of God, of the which you are at this present in possession, did
begin here in this realme 1400 yeres past in kinge Lucius's
dayes, the first Christian kinge here in this realme; by whose
humble letters sent unto the pope Eleutherius, he did send
into this realme two holye monkes, the one called Damianus,
35 and th'other Faganus: and they, as embassadors sent from
the sea apostolike of Rome, did bringe into this realme so
many yeres past the very same religion wherof we are now in
possession; and that in the Latin tonge, like as Gildas the
ancyent historiographer of the Brittan-stories witnessethe in

H 2

the beginynge and prologue of his booke. And the same religion so longe ago begune, hath been observed ever sythence
here in this realme, not onely of th'inhabytaunce therof, but
also generally of all Christian men, and in all places of Christendom, untill the late daies of kinge Edward the 6th, as is 5
aforesaid. Wherby it appearethe unto all men that lyst to
see, howe that by this first rule and lesson the auncyent religion and manner of servinge of God (wherof we are allreddye
in possession) is the very true and perfect religion, and of God.

Towchinge the second rule and lesson of tryall and proba- 10
tion, whether of bothe these religions is the better and most
worthy observation here in this realme, is this, that your
honours must observe which of them bothe is the more stayed
religion, and allwayes forthe one, and agreeable with it self.
And that this new religion, here now to be set forthe in this 15
booke, is no stayed religion, nor allwayes forth one, nor
agreeable with it self, who seeth not; when in the late practise therof in kinge Edward the 6th dayes, howe changeable
and variable was it unto it self? Every other yere havinge a
newe booke devysed therof; and every booke beinge sette 20
furthe (as they professed) accordinge to the sincere word of
God, never an one of them did in all pointes agree with the
other: the firste booke affirminge the seven sacraments, and
the reall presence[i] of Christe's body in the holy euchariste,
the other denyinge the same; th'one booke did admit the 25
reall presence of Christe's body in the sacrament to be receyved in one kinde, with kneeling downe, and great reverence, and that in unleavned bread; th'other booke would
have the communyon receyved in bothe the kindes, and that
in leaven bread sitting, without any reverence, but only to the 30
bodye of Christe which is in heaven. And the thinge most
worthy to be observid of your honours is, howe that every
booke made a shewe to be set furthe accordinge to the syn-
cere word of God, and not one of them did agree with
another. And what great marvell, I praye you, when the 35
awthors and devisers of the same bookes coulde not agree

---

[i] This is utterly false, as may be seen in that first book, called The Order of
the Communion, in bishop Sparrow's Collections. STRYPE.

amongest themselves, nor yet any one man of them myght
there be founde that did longe agree with himself? And
for proofe therof, I shall firste begyne with the Germayne
wryters, the cheffe schoolemasters and instructors of our
5 countreymen in all these novelties.

I do read, in an epistle which Philippe Melancthon did
write unto one Frederico Miconio, howe that one Carolostadius was the first mover and begynner of this late sedition in
Germany, towchinge the sacrament of th'altar, and the denyal
10 of Chryst's real presence in the same. And when he should
come to interpret those wordes of our Saviour Chryste;
"'Accepit panem, benedixit, dedit discipulis suis, dicens,
Accipite, et comedite, hoc est corpus meum, quod pro vobis
tradetur; Digito," inquit, " ille, monstrabat visibile suum
15 corpus." By which interpretation of Carolostadius, Chryste
shoulde with the one hand give unto his disciples bread for
to eat, and with the other hand pointe unto his visible bodye
that was ther present, and say, " This is my bodye, which
shall be betrayed for you." Martyn Luther, muche offended
20 with this foolish exposition, made by Carolostadius, of these
wordes of Chryste, " Hoc est corpus meum," he geveth another
sense; and saithe, that " Germanus sensus verborum Christi"
was this, " Per hunc panem, vel cum isto pane, en ! do vobis
corpus meum." Zwinglius, findinge muche faulte with this in-
25 terpretation of Martyn Luther, writeth, that Luther therin
was deceyved : and how that in these wordes of Chryst, " Hoc
est corpus meum," this verbe substantyve *est* must be taken
for *significat*, and this word *corpus*, " quod pro vobis tradetur,"
must be taken *pro figura corporis*. So that the true sense of
30 these wordes of Chryst, " Hoc est corpus meum," by Zwinglius's supposal, is, " Hoc significat corpus meum, vel est
figura corporis mei." Peter Martyr, beinge of late here in
this realme, in his booke by him set furthe, of the disputation
which he had in Oxenforde, with the learned students ther,
35 of this matter, he gevith another sense of these wordes of
Chryst, contrarye to all the reste, and ther saythe, " Quod
Christus accipiens panem dixit, ' Hoc est corpus meum,'
quasi diceret, corpus meum fide perceptum erit vobis pro
pane, vel instar panis." Of whose sense the Englishe is this,

that *Chryst's bodye receyved by faithe, shall be unto the receivers
as bread, or instead of bread.*

But here, to ceasse any further to speake of these Germayne wryters, I shall drawe now near home, as unto doctor
Cranmer, late archbyshoppe of Canterburye in this realme; 5
howe contrary was he unto hymself in this matter! When
in one yeare he did set furthe a catechisme in the Englishe
tongue, and dedicated the same book to kinge Edward the
Sixth, wherin he doth most constantly affirme and defend the
real presence of Chryst's bodye in the holie euchariste; and 10
very shortely after he did set furthe another booke, wherin
he did most shamefullie denye the same, falsifinge bothe the
Scriptures and doctors, to no small admiration of all the
learned readers.   Dr. Ridleye, the notablest learned of that
opinion within this realme, did set furthe at Paul's Crosse 15
the real presence of Chryst's body in the sacrament, with
these wordes, which I heard beynge ther present. "How
that the Devil did beleve that the Sonne of God was able to
make of stones bread; and we Englishe people, which do
confess that Jesus Chryst was the very Sonne of God, yet 20
will not beleve that he did make of bread his verye bodye,
fleashe and blood.   Therefore we are worse than the Devil;
seying that our Saviour Chryste, by expresse wordes, he doth
most plainlie affirme the same, when at his last supper he
tooke the bread, and said unto his disciples, ' Take, eat, this 25
is my bodye, which shall be geven for you.' "   And shortely
after, the said doctor Ridleye, notwithstandinge this most
plaine and open speeche at Paul's Crosse, did deny the same.
And in the last book that doctor Cranmer and his complices
did set furthe of the communion, in kinge Edward's dayes, 30
these plaine wordes of Chryst, " Hoc est corpus meum," did
so encomber them, and troubled their wittes, that they did
in the same last booke leave out this verbe substantive *est*[1];
and made the sense of Chryst's wordes to be there englished,
"Take, eat this my body," and left out there *this is my bodye* ; 35
which thinge beinge espyed by others, and great faulte founde
withal, then they were faine to patche uppe the matter with
a little piece of paper clappid over the foresaid wordes,

1 This very probably was no more but an error of the printer. STRYPE.

wherin was writtyn this verbe substantive *est*. The dealinge
thereof beinge so uncertaine, bothe by the Germayne and
Englishe writers, and one of them against another, your
honours maye be well assured, that this religion, which by
5 them is set fourthe, can be no constant nor stayede religion,
and therfore of your honours not to be receyved; but great
wisdome it were for your honours to refuse the same, untyll
you shall perceyve more better agreement amongest the
awthors and setters furthe thereof.

10   Towchinge the thirde and laste rule of tryall makinge,
and puttinge of difference between religions, it is to be considered of your honours which of them bothe dothe brede
the more obedyent, humble, and better subjects; firste and
cheffelye unto God; second unto our soveregne ladye the
15 quene's highness, and to all other superior powers.   And for
some tryall and probation herof, I shall dissier your honours
to consider the sudayne mutation of the subjects of this
realme, sythence the deathe of good quene Marye, onely
caused in them by the preachers of this newe religion: when
20 in quene Marye's daies your honours do know right well,
howe the people of this realme did live in an order; and wolde
not runne before lawes, nor openlye disobey the quene's highness's proclamations.   There was no spoyling of churches,
plucking downe of aultars, and most blasphemously tredinge
25 of sacrament under their feet, and hanging up of the knave
of clubs in the place therof.   There was no scotchinge or
cuttinge of the faces, legs and arms of the crucifix and the
images of Christ.   There was no open flesh eatinge, nor
shambles kepeinge, in Lent and daies prohibitid.   The sub-
30 jects of this realme, and in especial the nobilitye, and suche
as were of her honourable councell, did in quene Mary's daies
knowe the waye unto the churches and chappels, there to
begyne their daies worke, with callinge for helpe and grace,
by humble prayers, and servinge of God.   And nowe, sithence
35 the comynge and reigne of our most soveraigne and dear
lady quene Elizabeth, by the onely preachers and scaffold
players of this newe religion, all thinges are changed and
turned upsidowne, notwithstandinge the quene's highness most
godly proclamations made to the contrarye, and her most

vertuous example of lyvinge, sufficyent to move the hearts of all obedyent subjects unto the due service and honour of God. But obedyence is gone, humylitie and meekness clean abolyshed, vertuous chastity and straight livinge, as thoughe they had never ben heard of in this realme; all degrees and 5 kindes of men beynge desirous of fleshely and carnall lybertie, wherby the yong springalls and children are degennerate from their naturall fathers, the servants contemptors of their masters commandments, the subjects disobedyent unto God and all superior powers. 10

And therfore, honourable and my very good lordes, of my parte to mynnyster some occasion unto your honours to avoid and expell owte of this realme this newe religion, whose fruites are already so manifestly knowen to be, as I have repetid; and to perswade your honours, as muche as in me lyethe, to 15 persevere and continue the same religion, wherof you are in possession, and have allredye made profession of the same unto God; I shall rehearse unto you foure things, wherby the holie doctor St. Augustine was contynued in the catholicke faith and religion of Christe, which he had receaved, 20 and woulde by no means change nor aulter from the same. The firste of these four things was, "ipsa authoritas ecclesiæ Christi miraculis inchoata, spe nutrita, charitate aucta, vetustate firmata." The second thing was, "populi Christiani consensus et unitas." The third was, "perpetua sacerdotum 25 successio in sede Petri." The fourthe and last thing was, "ipsum Catholici nomen." If these foure thinges did cawse so noble and learned a clarke as St. Augustyn was, to continue in his professed religion of Christe without all chaunge and alteration, howe much then ought these foure pointes to 30 worke the like effect in your honours; and not to forsake your professed religion! Firste, becawse it hathe the aucthoritie of Christe's churche. Second, it hathe the consent and agreement of all Christian people. Third, it hathe confirmation of all Peter's successors in the sea apostolike. Fourth, 35 it hathe "ipsum Catholici nomen," and in all times and seasons called *the catholike* religion of Christ. Thus bolde I have ben to trouble your honours with so tedyouse and longe an oration, for the disch99arginge (as I said before) of my

dewtie, first unto God, second unto our soveraigne lady the
quene's highness, third and laste, unto your honours, and all
other subjects of this realme : most humbly beseeching your
honours to take it in good parte, and to be spoken of me for
5 th'onely cawses aforesaid, and for none other.

IX.

*Another oration made by Dr. Scot, bishop of Chester, in the
parliament howse, against the bill of the liturgy.*

THIS bill, that hathe ben here read now the third tyme,
dothe appeare unto me suche one, as that it is muche to be
10 lamentid, that it shoulde be suffered either to be read, yea, or
anye eare to be gevin unto it of Christian men, or so honour-
ble an assemblye as this is : for it dothe not only call in question and doubte those thinges which we ought to reverence,
without any doubt movinge ; but maketh fourther earneste
15 request for alteraunce, yea, for the clear abolyshinge of the
same. And that this maye more evydently appear, I shall
desire your lordships to consider, that our religion, as it was
here of late discretely, godly, and learnedly declared, dothe
consiste partely in inward things, as in faithe, hope, and cha-
20 ritie ; and partely in outward things, as in common prayers,
and the holie sacraments uniformly mynystred.

Nowe as concernynge these outward thinges, this bill dothe
clearly in very dede extinguishe them, settinge in there places
I cannot tell what.   And the inward it dothe also so shake,
25 that it leavithe them very bare and feble.

For firste, by this bill, Christian *charitie* is taken awaye,
in that the unitie of Christe's churche is broken : for it is
said, " Nunquam relinquunt unitatem, qui non prius amittunt
charitatem."   And St. Paul saythe, that charitye is " vincu-
30 lum perfectionis," *the bond or chayne of perfection,* wherewith
we be knytte and joyned together in one.   Which bond
beynge loosed, we muste nedes fall one from another, in divers
parties and sects, as we see we do at this present.   And as

towchinge our *faythe,* it is evident that dyvers of the articles
and mysteryes therof be also not onlye called into doubt, but
partely openlye, and partely obscurely; and yet in verye dede,
as the other, flatlye denyed.   Nowe these two, I mean faithe
and charitie, beinge in this case, *hope* is eyther lefte alone, or 5
else presumption sett in her place : whereupon, for the moste
parte, desperation dothe followe ; from the which I praye God
preserve all men.

   Wherfore these matters mentioned in this bill, wherin our
whole religion consistethe, we ought, I saye, to reverence, and 10
not to call into question.   For as a learned man wrytethe,
" Quæ patefacta sunt quærere, quæ perfecta sunt retractare,
et quæ definita sunt convellere, quid aliud est, quin de adeptis
gratiam non referre :" that is to saye, " To seke after the
things which be manifestly opened, to call back or retract 15
things made perfect, and to pulle upp againe matters defyned;
what other thing is it, then not to geve thankes for benyfits
receaved ?" Lykewise saythe holie Athanasius, " Quæ nunc
a tot ac talibus episcopis probata sunt ac decreta, clareque
demonstrata, supervacaneum est denuo revocare in judicium." 20
" It is a superfluous thinge, saythe Athanasius, to call into
judgment againe matters which have ben tried, decreed, and
manyfestlye declared by so many and suche bisshoppes, (he
meaneth, as were at the councell of Nice.)   For no man will
denye, saythe he, but if they be new examyned againe, and 25
of new judged, and after that examyned againe and againe,
this curiositie will never come to any end."   And as it is
said in Ecclesiastica Historia, " Si quotidie licebit fidem in
quæstionem vocare, de fide nunquam constabit :"   " If it
shalbe lawfull every daye to call our faithe in question, we 30
shall never be certeyne of our faithe."   Nowe if that Athanasius did thinke, that no man ought to doubt of matters
determyned in the councell of Nice, where there was present
three hundred and eighteen bisshoppes ; howe muche less
ought wee to doubt of matters determyned and practyssed 35
in the holie catholike churche of Christe by three hundrethe
thowsande bisshoppes, and how manye more we cannot tell.

   And as for the certeyntie of our faithe, whereof the storye
of the churche dothe speke, it is a thinge of all other most

necessarye; and if it shall hange uppon an acte of parliament, we have but a weake staff to leane unto.   And yet I
shall dissire your lordeshippes not to take me here as to
speke in derogation of the parliament, which I knowledge to
5 be of great strengthe in matters whereunto it extendethe.
But for matters in religion, I do not thinke that it ought to
be medelled withall, partely for the certeintye which ought
to be in our faithe and religion, and the uncerteyntie of the
statutes and actes of parliaments.   For we see, that often-
10 tymes that which is established by parliament one yere, is
abrogatid the next yere followinge, and the contrarye allowed.
And we see also that one kinge disallowithe the statutes
made under the other.   But our faithe and religion ought to
be most certeyn, and one in all tymes, and in no condition
15 waveringe: for, as St. James saithe, "he that doubtethe, or
staggerithe in his faithe, is like the waves of the sea, and
shall obteyne nothinge at the handes of God."   And partelye
for that the parliament consistethe for the moste parte of
noblemen of this realme, and certeyn of the commons, beyinge
20 laye and temporall men: which, allthough they be bothe of
good wisdom and learninge, yet not so studied nor exercised
in the scriptures, and the holie doctors and practysses of the
churche, as to be competent judges in suche matters.   Neyther
dothe it apperteine to their vocation; yea, and that by youre
25 lordshippes own judgment; as may welbe gathered of one
fact, which I remember was donne this parliament time,
which was this: There was a nobleman's sonne arrested and
commytted unto warde; which matter, beinge opened here
unto your lordeshippes, was thought to be an injurye to this
30 howse.   Whereuppon, as well the yonge gentleman, as the
officer that did arrest hym, and the partie by whose means
he was arrested, were all sent for; and commandid to appeare
here before your lordshippes: which was donne accordynglye.
Yet before the parties were suffered to come into the howse,
35 it was thought expedyent to have the whole matter considered, least this howse shoulde entermedelle with matters
not perteinynge unto yt.   In treatinge wherof, there were
found three pointes.   Firste, there was a debte, and that
your lordshippes did remytte to the common lawe.   The

second was a fraude, which was referred to the chauncerye,
because neyther of bothe did apparteyne unto this courte.
And the thirde was the arrest, and commyttinge to ward of
the said gentleman, wherin this howse tooke order. Nowe if
that by your lordshippes own judgments the parliament hathe 5
not aucthoritie to meddell with matters of common lawe,
which is grounded upon common reason, neyther with the
chauncery, which is grounded upon considerance, (which two
things be naturally given unto man,) then muche lesse maye
it intermeddell with matters of faithe and religion, farr pass- 10
inge reason, and the judgment of man, suche as the contents
of this bill be: wherin there be three thinges specyally to be
consideryd; that is, the *weyghtiness* of the matter; the *darkness* of the cawse, and the *dificultie* in tryinge out the truthe;
and thirdly, the *daunger* and *perill* which dothe ensue, if we 15
do take the wronge waye.

As concernynge the firste, that is, the *weyghtiness* of the
matter conteined in this bill. It is very great: for it is no
money matter, but a matter of inheritaunce; yea, a matter
towchinge liffe and deathe, and damnation dependethe upon 20
it. Here is it set before us, as the scripture saithe, lyfe and
deathe, fier and water. If we put our hand into th'one, we
shall live; if it take holde of th'other, we shall die. Nowe
to judge these matters here propounded, and discerne which
is liffe and whiche is deathe, which is fire that will burne us, 25
and which is water that will refreshe and comforte us, is a
great matter, and not easely perceaved of every man. Moreover, there is another great matter here to be considered,
and that is, that we do not unadvisedly condempne our forefathers and their doings, and justifie our selves and our owne 30
doings; which bothe the scripture forbidithe. This we knowe,
that this doctrine and forme of religion, which this bill pro-
poundethe to be abolished and taken awaye, is that which
our forefathers were born, brought uppe, and lived in, and
have professed here in this realme, without any alteration or 35
chaunge, by the space of 900 yeres and more; and hathe
also ben professed and practised in the universall churche of
Christe synce the apostells tyme. And that which we goe
about to establishe and place for it, is lately brought in,

allowed no where, nor put in practise, but in this realme
onely; and that but a small tyme, and againste the myndes
of all catholycke men.   Nowe if we do consider but the
antiquitie of the one, and the newness of the other, we have
5 juste occasion to have the one in estimation for the longe
continuance therof, unto suche tyme as we see evydent cawse
why we shoulde revoke it; and to suspect the other as never
hearde of here before, unto such tyme as we see juste cawse
why we shoulde receave it, seeynge that our fathers never
10 heard tell of it.

But nowe I do call to remembraunce, that I did here
yesterday a nobleman in this howse say, makinge an answer
unto this as it were by preoccupation, that our fathers lyved
in blyndness, and that we have juste occasion to lament their
15 ignoraunce; wherunto me thinkethe it may be answered, that
if our fathers were here, and heard us lament their doings, it
is very lyke that they woulde say unto us as our Savyour
Christe said unto the women which followed hym when he
went to his death, and weeped after him, " Nolite flere super
20 nos, sed super vos;" i. e. " Weepe not over us for our blind-
ness, but weepe over your selves" for your own presumption,
in takinge upon you so arrogantly to justifie your selves and
your own doings, and so rashely condemnynge us and our
doings.   Moreover, Davyd [m] dothe teache us a lesson cleare
25 contrarye to this nobleman's sayings : for he biddithe us in
doubtfull matters go to our fathers, and learne the truthe of
them, in these wordes; " Interroga patrem tuum, et annun-
ciabit tibi, majores tuos, et dicent tibi :" i. e. " Aske of thy
father, and he shall declare the truthe unto thee, and of
30 thyne auncestors, and they will tell thee."   And after, in the
same psalme, " Filii qui nascentur et exsurgent, narrabunt
filiis suis, ut cognoscat generatio altera:" i. e. " The children
which shalbe borne, and ryse upp, shall tell unto their
children, that it may be knowen from one generation to
35 another."   Davyd here willithe us to learne of our fathers,
and not to contempn their doings.   Wherefore I conclude,
as concernynge this parte, that this bill, conteyninge in it

[m] This bishop mistook David for Moses. For the words are in Deuter. xxxii. 7.
Ps. lxxviii. 6, 7. STRYPE.

matters of great weight and importaunce, it is to be deliberated on with great diligence and circumspection, and
examyned, tryed, and determyned by men of great learnynge,
vertue, and experyence.

And as this matter is *great*, and therfore not to be passed 5
over hastely, but diligentlye to be examyned, so is it *darke,*
and of great difficultie to be so playnlye discussed, as that
the truthe may manyfestlye appeare. For here be, as I have
said, two bookes of religion propounded; the one to be
abolished, as erroneous and wicked; and the other to be 10
establyshed, as godly, and consonant to scripture; and they
be both concernynge one matter, that is, the trewe admynystration of the sacraments, accordinge to the institution of
our Saviour Christe. In the which admynystration ther be
three thinges to be considered. The firste is, the institution 15
of our Savyour Christe for the matter and substaunce of the
sacraments. The seconde, the ordynaunces of the apostles
for the forme of the sacraments. And the thirde is, the
additions of the holie fathers for the adornynge and per-
fitynge of the admynystratyon of the said sacraments. Which 20
three be all dulye, as we see, observed, and that of necessitie,
in this booke of the masse, and old service, as all men do
know, which understand it. The other booke, which is so
much extolled, dothe *ex professo* take away two of these three
thinges, and in very dede makethe the thirde a thinge of 25
nought. For firste, as concernynge the additions of the
fathers, as in the masse, *Confiteor, Misereatur, Kirie Eleeson,
Sequentes preces, Sanctus Agnus Dei*, with suche other thinges :
and also th'ordinaunces of the apostles, as blessings, cross-
ings; and in the admynystration of dyvers of the sacraments, 30
exsufflations, exorcismes, inunctions, prayinge towardes the
east, invocation of saynts, prayer for the dead, with suche
other; this booke takethe awaye, eyther in parte, or else
clearly, as things not allowable. And yet dothe the fawters
therof contende, that it is most perfitt accordinge to Christe's 35
institution, and th'order of the prymytyve churche. But to
let th'ordynaunces of th'apostles, and the additions of the
fathers passe, (which, notwithstandinge, we ought greatly to
esteem and reverence,) lett us come to th'institution of our

Savyour Christe, wherof they taulke so muche, and examyne
whether of those two bookes come nearest unto it. And to
make thinges playne, we will take for example the masse, or,
as they call it, the supper of the Lord; wherin our Savyour
5 Christe (as the holie fathers do gather upon the Scriptures)
did institute three things, which he commanded to be done
in remembraunce of his deathe and passion unto his comynge
againe, sayinge, "Hoc facite," &c. *Do ye this:* wherof the
firste is, the consecratinge of the blessed body and blood of
10 our Saviour Jesus Christe. The seconde, the offeringe up of
the same unto God the Father. And the thirde, the com-
municatinge, that is, the eatinge and drinkinge of the said
blessed body and blood under the formes of bread and wyne.
And as concerninge the firste two, St. Chrysostom saythe
15 thus, "Volo quiddam edicere plane mirabile, et nolite mirari
neque turbamini," &c. "I will," saythe St. Chrysostom,
"declare unto you in very dede a marvellous thinge; but
marvell not at it, nor be not troubled. But what is this? It
is the holie oblation, whether Peter or Paul, or a preste of
20 any desert, do offer, it is the verye same which Christe gave
to his disciples, and which prestes do make or consecrate at
this tyme. This hathe nothinge lesse then that. Whye so?
Bycawse men do not sanctyfie this, but Christe, which did
sanctyfie that before. For lyke as the wordes which Christe
25 did speake, be the very same which the prestes do nowe pronounce, so is it the very same oblation." These be the
wordes of St. Chrysostome; wherin he testifiethe as well the
oblation and sacrifice of the body and blood of our Savyour
Christe, offered unto God the Father in the masse, as also
30 the consecratinge of the same by the preste: which two be
bothe taken away by this booke, as the awthors therof do
willingly acknowledge; cryinge owte of the offering of Christe
oftener than once, notwithstandinge that all the holie fathers
do teach it, manyfestly affirmynge Christe to be offered
35 daylye after an unbloody manner. But if these men did
understand and consider what dothe ensue and followe of
this their affirmation, I thinke they wolde leave their rash-
ness, and returne to the truthe againe. For if it be trewe
that they say, that there is no externall sacrifyce in the

Newe Testament, then dothe it follow, that there is no priesthood under the same, whose office is, saythe St. Paul, "to offer up gyfts and sacrifices for synne[n]." And if there be no priesthood, then is there no religion under the New Testament. And if we have no religion, then be we "sine Deo in hoc mundo;" that is, *we be without God in this worlde.* For one of these dothe necessarily depend and followe uppon an other. So that if we graunt one of these, we graunt all; and if we take away one, we take away all.

Note (I beseeche your lordshippes) th'end of these men's doctryns, that is to sett us withowt God. And the lyke opynion they holde towchinge the consecration: having nothinge in their mouthes but *the holie communion*, which after the order of this booke is *holie* only in wordes, and not in dede. For the thinge is not ther which shoulde make it holie: I mean the body and blood of Christe, as may thus appeare, it may justely in very dede be callid *the holie communion*, if it be mynystred trewly, and accordingly as it ought to be: for then we receave Christe's holie body and blood into our bodies, and be joyned in one with hym, lyke two pieces of waxe, whiche beinge molten and put together, be made one. Which symylitude St. Cyryll and Chrysostom do use in this matter; and St. Paul sayeth, that "we be made his bones and fleshe." But by th'order of this booke this is not done; for Christe's bodye is not there in very dede to be receaved. For th'only waye wherby it is present is by consecration, which this booke hathe not at all[o]; neyther doth it observe the forme prescribed by Christe, nor follow the manner of the churche. The evangelists declare, that our Savyour tooke bread into his handes, and did blesse it, brake it, and gave it to his disciples, saying, "Take and eat, this is my bodye which is gyven for you: do this in remembraunce of me." By these wordes, "Do this," we be commanded to tayke bread into our handes, to blesse it, break it, and havinge a respecte to the bread, to pronounce the wordes spoken by our Savyour, that is, "Hoc est corpus meum."

[n] This is expressly spoken of the high priests of the Old Testament. Vid. Heb. v.

[o] This is notoriously false, the prayer of consecration being evident to all men's eyes that consult the book. STRYPE.

By which wordes, saythe St. Chrysostom, the bread is con-
secratid. Nowe by the order of this booke, neyther dothe
the preste take the bread in his handes, blesse it, nor breake
it, neyther yet hathe any regard or respect to the bread,
5 when he rehearsithe the wordes of Christe, but dothe passe
them over as they were tellinge a tale, or rehearsinge a
storye. Moreover, wheras by the myndes of good wryters
there is requyryd, yea, and that of necessitie, a full mynd and
intent to do that which Christe did, that is, to consecrate his
10 body and blood, with other things followinge : wherfore the
churche hathe appoynted in the masse certeyne prayers, to
be said by the prieste before the consecration, in the which
these wordes be, " Ut nobis fiat corpus et sanguis Domini
nostri Jhesu Christi ;" that is, the prayer is to this end, that
15 the creatures may be made unto us the body and blood of
our Saviour Jesus Christe : here is declared th'intent, as well
of the churche, as also of the prieste which sayeth masse : but
as for this newe booke, there is no such thinge mentyoned in
it, that dothe eyther declare any suche intente, eyther make
20 any suche requeste unto God, but rather to the contrarye ;
as dothe appeare by the request there made in these wordes,
" That we receavinge these thy creatures of bread and wyne,"
&c. which wordes declare that they intende no consecration
at all. And then let them glory as muche as they will in
25 their communion, it is to no purpose, seeynge that the body
of Christe is not there, which, as I have said, is the thinge
that should be communicated.

Ther did yesterdaye a nobleman in this howse say, that
he did beleve that Christe is ther receaved in the commu-
30 nyon set owt in this booke ; and beyng asked if he did
worshippe hym ther, he said, no, nor never woulde, so longe
as he lived. Which is a strange opynyon, that Christe
shoulde be any where, and not worshypped. They say, they
will worshippe hym in heaven, but not in the sacrament :
35 which is much lyke as if a man woulde saye, that when
th'emperor syttethe under his clothe of estate, princely ap-
parelled, he is to be honoured ; but if he come abroad in a
freez coat, he is not to be honoured ; and yet he is all one
emperor in clothe of golde under his clothe of estate, and in a

freez coat abroad in the street. As it is one Christe in
heaven in the forme of man, and in the sacrament under the
formes of bread and wyne. The Scripture, as St. Augustyne
dothe interprete it, dothe commande us to worshippe the body
of our Savyour, yea, and that in the sacrament, in these 5
wordes: "Adorate scabellum pedum ejus, quoniam sanctum
est:" *Worshippe his footstoole, for it is holie.* Upon the which
place St. Augustine wrytethe thus; " Christe tooke fleshe of
the blessed Virgin his mother, and in the same he did walke;
and the same fleshe he gave us to eat unto health; but no 10
man will eat that fleshe, except he worshippe it before. So
is it found owte howe we shall worshippe his footstoole, &c.
we shall not onely not synne in worshippinge, but we shall
synne in not worshippinge." Thus far St. Augustine: but as
concernynge this matter, if we woulde consider all things 15
well, we shall see the provision of God marvellous in it. For
he providithe so, that the verye heretickes, and enymyes of
the truthe, be compellyd to confesse the truthe in this be-
halfe. For the Lutherians writinge against the Zwinglians
do prove, that the true naturall body of our Savyour Christe 20
is in the sacrament. And the Zwinglians against the Lutherians do prove, that then it must nedes be worshipped ther.
And thus in their contention dothe the truthe burst out,
whether they will or no. Wherfore, in myne opynion of
these two errors, the fonder is to say, that Christe is in the 25
sacrament, and yet not to be worshipped, than to say he is
not ther at all. For eyther they do thinke, that eyther he is
ther but in an imagynation or fancye, and so not in very
dede; or else they be Nestorians, and thinke that ther is his
bodye onely, and not his dyvinitie: which be bothe devellishe 30
and wicked.

Nowe, my lordes, consider, I beseche you, the matters here
in varyaunce; whether your lordeshippes be able to discusse
them accordinge to learnynge, so as the truthe may appear,
or no: that is, whether the body of Christe be by this newe 35
booke consecrated, offered, adored, and truly communicated,
or no; and whether these things be required necessarily by
th'institution of our Saviour Christe, or no; and whether
booke goeth nearer the truthe. These matters, my lordes,

be (as I have said) weightie and darke, and not easye to be discussed: and lykewise your lordshippes may thinke of the rest of the sacraments, which be eyther clearly taken awaye, or else mangled, after the same sorte by this newe booke.

5   The third thinge here to be considered, is, the great *daunger* and *peryll* that dothe hange over your heades, if you do take upon you to be judges in these matters, and judge wronge; bringinge bothe your selfes and others from the truthe unto untruthe, from the highwayes unto bypathes.

10 It is daungerous enoughe, our Lord knowethe, for man hymself to erre, but it is more daungerous, not onely to erre hymself, but also to lead other men into error. It is sayd in the Scripture of the kinge Hieroboam, to aggravate his offences, that "peccavit, et peccare fecit Israel:" i. e. *he did*

15 *synne hymself, and caused Israell to synne.* Take heed, my lordes, that the like be not said by you; if you passe this bill, you shall not onely, in my judgement, erre your selves, but ye also shalbe the awthors and cawsers that the whole realme shall erre after you. For the which you shall make an

20 accompte before God.

Those that have read storyes, and knowe the discourse and order of the churche, discussinge of controversies in matters of religion, can testifie, that they have been discussed and determyned in all times by the clergye onely, and never by

25 the temporaltie. The herysie of Arius, which troubled the churche in the tyme of the emperor Constantyne the Great, was condempned in the councell of Nice. The heresye of Eutyches in the councell of Chalcedone under Martin; the heresye of Macedonius in the firste councell of Constantyno-

30 ple, in the tyme of Theodosius; the heresye of Nestorius in the Ephesin councell, in the time of Theodosius the younger. And yet did never none of these good emperors assemble their nobilitie and commons, for the discussing and deter-mynynge of these controversies; neyther asked their myndes

35 in them, or went by number of voices or polles, to determyne the truthe, as is done here in this realme at this tyme. We may come lower, to the third councell of Tolletane in Spayne, in the tyme of Ricaredus, beinge ther; and to the councell in Fraunce, about 800 yeres ago, in the tyme of Carolus

Magnus; which bothe, followinge th'order of the churche,
by licence had of the pope, did procure the clergie of their
realmes to be gathered and assembled, for reformynge of
certeyne errors and enormyties within their said realmes,
wherunto they never callyd their nobilitie nor commons; 5
neyther did any of them take upon themselves eyther to
reason and dispute, in discussinge of the controversies;
neyther to determyne them being discussed; but left the
whole to the discussing and determining of the clergy. And
no mervaill, if these with all other catholick princes used 10
this trade. For the emperors that were hereticks did never
reserve any such matter to the judgment of temporall men,
as may appear to them that read the stories of Constantius,
Valens, &c. who procured divers assemblies, but always of
the clergy, for the stablishing of Arius's doctryn : and of 15
Zeno th'emperor, which did the lyke for Eutyches doctryne,
with many other of that sorte. Yea, yt dothe appeare in the
Actes of the Apostles, that an infidell wolde take no such
matter upon hym. The storye is this: St. Paul havinge
continued at Corynthe one year and an halfe in preachinge 20
of the gospell, certeyn wycked persons did aryse against hym,
and brought hym before their vice-consul, callyd Gallio,
layinge unto his charge, that he tawght the people to worshippe God contrary to their law. Unto whom the vice-
consul answered thus : " Si quidem esset iniquum aliquid aut 25
facinus pessimum, o vos Judæi, recte vos sustinerem ; si vero
quæstiones sint de verbo et nominibus legis vestræ, vosipsi
videritis ; judex horum ego nolo esse :" i. e. *If that this man,*
saithe Gallio, *had committed any wycked acts or cursed cryme,*
O yee Jewes, I myght justely have heard you: but and if it be 30
concernynge questions and doubtes of the wordes and matters of
your lawe, that is to saye, if it be towchinge your religion,
I will not be judge in those matters. Marke, my lordes, this
short discourse, I beseech your lordshippes, and yee shall
perceave, that all catholike princes, heryticke princes, yea, 35
and infidells, have from tyme to tyme refused to take that
upon them, that your lordshippes go about and chalenge
to do.

   But nowe, because I have been longe, I will make an end

of this matter with the sayings of two noble emperors in the lyke affaires. The first is Theodosius, which sayd thus; " Illicitum est enim qui non sit ex ordine sanctorum episcoporum ecclesiasticis se immiscere tractatibus:" i. e. *It is not* 5 *lawfull*, sayeth he, *for hym that is not of the order of the holie busshoppes to entermedell with th'intreatinge of ecclesiasticall matters.* Lykewise sayd Valentinianus th'emperor (beinge desired to assemble certeyne busshoppes together, for examynynge of a matter of doctryn) in this wise; " Mihi qui in 10 sorte sum plebis, fas non est talia curiosius scrutari: sacerdotes, quibus ista curæ sunt, inter seipsos quocunque loco voluerint conveniant:" i. e. *It is not lawfull for me,* quoth th'emperor, *beynge one of the lay people, to searche owte suche matters curyously; but let the prestes, unto whom the charge of* 15 *these things dothe apparteyne, meet together in what place soever they will.* He meaneth for the discoursinge therof. But to conclude; and if these emperors had not to do with suche matters, howe shoulde your lordshippes have to do with all! And thus desiringe your good lordshippes to consider, and 20 take in good parte, these fewe thinges that I have spoken, I make an end.

X.

An extract out of the Journal of the lower house of convocation.

ACTA in inferiori domo convocationis, die sabbati decimo tertio die Februarii, anno 1562.

25 DICTO die sabbati decimo tertio die Februarii, in inferiori domo convocationis cleri provinciæ Cant' post meridiem hora constituta convenerunt frequentes dominus proloquutor cum cæt. infra nominatis ubi post divini Numinis implorationem legebantur quidem articuli approbandi vel reprobandi a cœtu 30 quorum articulorum tenor talis est.

1. That all the Sundays of the year, and principal feasts of Christ, be kept holy-days, and other holy-days to be abrogate.

2. That in all parish churches, the minister in common-prayer turn his face towards the people, and there dis- 5 tinctly read the divine service appointed, where all the people assembled may hear and be edified.

3. That in ministring the sacrament of baptisme, the ceremonie of making of the crosse in the child's forehead may be omitted, as tending to superstition.   10

4. That for as much as divers communicants are not hable to kneel during the time of the communion, for age, sicknes, and sundry other infirmities; and some also superstitiously both kneel and knock; that the order of kneeling may be left to the discretion of the ordinarie, 15 within his jurisdiction.

5. That it be sufficient for the minister, in time of saying of divine service, and ministring of the sacraments, to use a surplice: and that no minister say service, or minister the sacraments, but in a comely garment or 20 habit.

6. That the use of organs be removed.

Unde orta fuit superiorum proband' vel reproband' disceptatio, multis affirmantibus eosdem à se probari, ac multis affirmantibus illos à se non probari; multisque aliis volenti- 25 bus, ut eorum probatio, vel reprobatio, referatur ad reverendissimos dominos, archiepiscopum et prælatos; plurimis item protestantibus, se nolle ullo modo consentire, ut aliqua contenta in his articulis approbentur; quatenus ulla ex parte dissentiant libro divini et communis servicii, jam authoritate 30 senatusconsulti publicè in hoc regno suscepto; neque velle, ut aliqua immutatio fiat contra ordines, regulas, ritus ac cæteras dispositiones in eo libro contentas.

Tandem inceptæ fuerunt publicæ disputationes fieri à nonnullis doctis viris ejusdem domus, super approbatione, vel 35 reprobatione dicti quarti articuli: ac tandem placuit discessionem, sive divisionem fieri votorum, sive suffragiorum singulorum; quæ mox subsecuta fuit: atque numeratis personis pro parte articulos approbante, fuerunt personæ 43; pro

parte verò illos non approbante, neque aliquam immutatio-
nem contra dictum librum publici servicii jam suscepti fieri
petente, fuerunt personæ 35.

Ac deinde, recitatis singulorum votis, sive suffragiis,
5 promptæ sunt quemadmodum in sequenti folio liquet et ap-
paret.

DISPUTATORES.

Decanus Wygorn'.
Mr. Byckley.
10 Archid' Covent'.
Mr. Nebynson.
Mr. Pullen.
Mr. Cotterell.
Mr. Joh. Waker.

Mr. Laur. Neuell.
Mr. Talphill.
Mr. Crowley.
Mr. Tremain.
Mr. Hewet.
Decanus Eliens'.

15 *Pro parte articulos prædictos approbante, fuerunt omnes*
subscripti; viz.

D. Proloquutor, decanus S. Pauli...............	Mr. Joh. Walker.............	2
Mr. Leaver	Mr. Becon	
20 Decan' Heref.	Mr. Proctor..................,	2
Mr. Soreby	Mr. Cockerell	
Mr. Bradbriger	Mr. Todd, archid' Bed......	2
Mr. Peder	Mr. Crouley	
Mr. Watte 3	Mr. Hyll	
25 Decan' Lychef.	Decan' Oxon.	
Mr. Spenser.................	Mr. Savage	
Mr. Beysley	Mr. Pullan	
Mr. Nebinson	Mr. Wilson	
Mr. Bowier	Mr. Burton 2	
30 Mr. Ebden	Mr. Heamond	
Mr. Longlonde..............	Mr. Weyborn	
Mr. Tho. Lancaster	Mr. Day	
Mr. Ed. Weston 2	Mr. Rever	
Mr. Wysdon.................	Mr. Roberts................. 5	
35 Mr. Sall 2	Mr. Calphill 3	
	Mr. Godwyn................. 2	

Mr. Pratt		Mr. Kemper	
Mr. Trenun	2	Mr. Ronayer	
Mr. Leaton		Mr. Abis	

Persons 43.   Voices 58 [a].

5 *Pro parte articulos non approbante, ac protestante ut supra, sunt subscripti ;* viz.

Decan' West.	2	Mr. Cheston	
Mr. Coterell	4	Mr. Chanddelor	
Mr. Latymer	3	Mr. Bonder	
10 Decan' Elien		Mr. Just. Lancaster.........	
Mr. Heuwette	3	Mr. Pondde	
Mr. Ric. Walker	2	Mr. Constantyne	
Mr. Warner		Mr. Calberley	
Mr. Tho. Whyte		Mr. Nich. Smith	
15 Mr. Knouall	2	Mr. Watson	
Mr. Jo. Prise		Mr. Walter Jones............	3
Mr. Bolte	2	Mr. Garth	3
Mr. Hughes	3	Mr. Turnebull................	
Mr. Brigewater	2	Mr. Robynson	
20 Mr. Lougher	3	Mr. Bell	
Mr. Pierson		Mr. Ithel	
Mr. Merick		Mr. Byckley.................	
Mr. Luson		Mr. Hugh Morgan	3
Mr. Greensell	3		

25   Persons 35.   Voices 59.

[a] This is the correct number, although the figures, as given above, would require that it should be 59. The error, wherever it is, has been copied from Burnet, (Hist. Ref. vol. iii. p. ii. p. 419.) The items are given differently by Strype, (Ann. vol. i. p. i. p. 504) but are not more to be relied upon. A search has been 30 made for the original paper in the Petyt collection, but without success.

CHAPTER III.

The revision of the liturgy in the reign of James I.

THE progress that was made by puritanism during the reign of queen Elizabeth must be understood, before we can judge of the real condition of the dispute, as it affected the liturgy, when James I. succeeded to the throne of England. In that, as in every other case of party strife, many different motives were made to bear upon the dispute which had no natural connection with it: as the wind, from whatever quarter it may come, never blows across a glen, but always either up it or down it. The doctrinal puritans, and those who, from whatever cause, took part with them on the ground of conscience, inherited all the antipathy of their predecessors to the cross and the surplice, but looked upon them no longer as badges and tokens of Romanism. They were now the outward signs of an episcopal church in subjection to state authority, and in this light were held in still greater abhorrence, as offending more directly against original principles. It was maintained that in submitting to such a system of church government a man must make the dictates of his conscience subordinate to mere rules of prudence, and place his religious convictions at the mercy

of a human tribunal. And such were the avowed objections of persons who, from the energy of their character, the sincerity of their purpose, and the loftiness
of their pretensions, obtained some consideration for
the cause of puritanism, and formed a centre that at- 5
tracted and united with it various classes of auxiliaries,
some contributing to its strength, others productive
only of discord, but all willing to take part in the warfare, and to join in one common attack upon the church
established. The sentiments that drew to them so 10
many supporters may be expressed in the words of a
petition presented by a body of puritans to the privy
council in the year 1592[a]. "Upon a careful examination of the holy Scriptures, we find the English
hierarchy to be dissonant from Christ's institution and 15
to be derived from antichrist, being the same the pope
left in this land, and to which we dare not subject
ourselves.—We further find that God has commanded
all that believe the gospel to walk in that holy faith
and order which he has appointed in his church: 20
wherefore, in the reverend fear of his name we have
joined ourselves together, and subjected our souls and
bodies to those laws and ordinances, and have chosen
to ourselves such a ministry of pastor, teacher, elders,
and deacons, as Christ has given to his church on earth 25
to the world's end; hoping for the promised assistance
of his grace in our attendance upon him, notwithstanding any prohibition of men, or what by men can be
done unto us."

Sentiments of this description, maintained, however 30
erroneously, on a sense of religious duty, could not be
extinguished by temporal punishments, and might possibly encourage some degree of sympathy, if the treat-

[a] Neal's Hist. of the Purit. vol. i. p. 348.

ment they met with should be considered as a persecution. And such was actually the case under the
impression that prevailed respecting the court of high
commission, and the arbitrary methods it adopted in
5 its examinations and penalties. It administered the
oath "ex officio," and compelled persons to bear evidence against themselves, inflicting fines and imprisonment in case of disobedience; practices these, which
could not be maintained on general principles of jus-
10 tice, and were soon afterwards pronounced to be in
violation of law. Hence arose a large party of auxiliaries, who aided the puritans from feelings of human-
ity, and were most of them too respectable, both in
station and in conduct, to be treated with indifference.
15 But a more numerous and more dangerous body of
supporters was found in that mixed and discordant
multitude of persons who, as at all periods, so especially at that, were dissatisfied with the existing government. Adventurers of every class, those who, from
20 depraved habits or their natural temperament, could
not live in a state of quietude, and those who, as was
peculiarly the case at that period, were willing to enter
into honest occupations, but unable to find them; all
these, together with Romanists, who could pay no alle-
25 giance to a person excommunicated, and anabaptists,
who considered all laws as of the nature of tyranny,
formed a mass of energy incapable of acting in concert
for the promotion of any good purpose, but most powerful in the way of mischief. The case may be illustrat-
30 ed by that strange conspiracy of the year 1603, in
which men of lawless habits and desperate fortunes
were combined with Romish priests and intriguing no-
bles, with lord Cobham, who was a mere instrument in
the hands of others, with lord Gray, a zealous and

determined puritan, and sir Walter Raleigh, a soldier equally intrepid and unscrupulous.

It was not thought possible, at that period, that such an assemblage of the elements of disorder could be treated with any forbearance or discrimination. 5 They were all included under the charge of sedition or treason, and punished as if their offences were committed merely against the state. But there was still another class of puritans, who, though frequently confounded with state offenders, disowned any participa- 10 tion in their projects, and were regarded by many persons in high station with much compassion and respect. They were those nonconformist ministers who, with more of zeal than of judgment, thought it their duty to protest against unnecessary observances, 15 earnestly wishing to exercise their spiritual calling within the pale of the church, but inheriting, from recent controversies, an acute and morbid sensitiveness as to things indifferent. To these men, most of them vehement and indefatigable preachers, and to their 20 numerous followers, who, with a sincere desire for Christian excellence, combined a notion that it was not worth their attainment unless they suffered for its sake, it appeared to be sinful to use a ritual, and much more so to declare their perfect approbation of it, in 25 which they were required to sign with the cross in baptism, to employ the ring in marriage, to bow at the name of Jesus, to observe the holidays of the church, or to read uncanonical Scriptures. Their scruples, though treated with contempt by the great body of 30 conformists, could not be regarded without feelings of respect and sympathy, if not for themselves, at least for the patience, the humility, the disinterestedness and unaffected piety which were frequently found united

with them.   Such are the feelings that have been left
on record by sir Francis Walsingham, by lord Burghley,
by sir Edward Coke [b], and lord Bacon [c], the last of
whom described what he knew and what he feared as
5 to this class of puritans in these expressive words:
" As for any man that shall hereby enter into a contempt of their ministry, it is but his own hardness of
heart.   I know the work of exhortation doth chiefly
rest upon these men; and they have zeal, and hate of
10 sin.   But, again, let them take heed that it be not
true, which one of their adversaries said, that they have
but two small wants, knowledge and love."

In the mean time, the strong arm of authority had
been supported by many able publications, some of
15 them written in such a manner as to mediate between
the rival parties, but the greater number calculated to
fortify the resolutions of the one side without shaking

[b] Sir Ed. Coke, in his charge at Norwich (1607), said of the nonconformists, " The last sort of recusants, though troublesome, yet in
20 my conscience the least dangerous, are those which do with too
much violence contend against some ceremonies used in the church;
with whose indirect proceedings, in mine own knowledge, his majesty is not a little grieved.   But I will hope (as his highness doth)
that in time they will grow wise enough to leave their foolishness,
25 and consider that ceremonies not against the analogy of faith, nor
hindering faith's devotion, are no such bugbears as should scare
them from the exercises of divine duties, nor cause them to disturb
the peace of our church, whose government is more consonant to
Scripture than all the best reformed churches at this day in the
30 world."   This opinion, as compared with that of bishop Cooper, will
illustrate the difference between the two professions of the church
and the law in their conduct towards the nonconformists; a difference which was evident at this early period, and which gradually
led, as lord Clarendon has noticed, to a complete alienation between
35 the members of the two professions.—Hist. Reb. vol. i. p. 400. ed.
4to. 1816.

[c] Works, vol. ii. p. 522.

the convictions of the other. In the year 1589, Cooper, bishop of Winchester, published his "Admonition to the People of England," in which he replied in detail to the charges brought against the bishops and the clergy, and endeavoured, with much mildness, 5 and by appealing to the plain sense and pious feelings of his countrymen, "to satisfy, not all kind of men, but the moderate and godly." But it is plain, from the following passages, that he had no sympathy with those of his opponents who would appear to common ob- 10 servers to be most deserving of it, and that he sought for the active interposition of the civil power in suppressing them and their followers. "He [Satan] worketh his devices by sundry kinds of men : first, by such as be papists in heart, and yet can clap their 15 hands and set forward this purpose, because they see it the next way, either to overthrow the course of the gospel, or, by great and needless alteration, to hazard and endanger the state of the common weal. The second sort are certain worldly and godless epicures, 20 which can pretend religion and yet pass not which end thereof go forward, so they may be partakers of that spoil which in this alteration is hoped for. The third sort, in some respect the best, but, of all other, most dangerous, because they give the opportunity and 25 countenance to the residue, and make their endeavours seem zealous and godly. These be such which in doctrine agree with the present state, and shew themselves to have a desire of a perfection in all things, and in some respect, indeed, have no evil meaning, 30 but, through inordinate zeal, are so carried, that they see not how great dangers by such devices they draw into the church and state of this realm." (p. 29.) And afterwards (p. 122): "Undoubtedly if God move not the hearts of the chief rulers and governors to seek some end of this schism and faction which now rendeth in pieces this church of England, it cannot be but in short time for one recusant that now is we shall have 5 three, if the increase of that number which I mention be not greater."

A more resolute and uncompromising writer was Bancroft, afterwards archbishop of Canterbury. In the year 1593 he sent forth his book entitled " Dangerous 10 Positions and Proceedings, &c.," in which he traced the opinions of the puritans from Geneva as their fountain-head, through the fanatical insurgents of Scotland, down to the separatists of his own country, collecting, as he descended, all the foul and perilous stuff, 15 whether civil or ecclesiastical, that he met with in their publications, and charging it in its cumulative force of sedition and treason on the unhappy puritans of his own times. In another respect, however, his observations, though somewhat coarse, are just (p. 170.) 20 " If it be true (that I have heard reported), that upon the coming forth of Martin's Epistle, Master Cartwright should say, ' Seeing the bishops would take no warning, it is no matter that they are thus handled;' surely those words from him were enough to set these 25 men agog. So as that which is commonly reported of great robberies may fitly serve to satisfy the bolsterers of such lewdness. There are (say they) in such attempts not only executioners, but also setters, receivers and favourers, and, in matters of treason, concealers, 30 who are all of them within the danger and compass of law." In his other well-known work, published in the same year, and entitled, " A Survey of the pretended holy Discipline," he traced the new system of church government introduced by Cartwright and his

followers through its history of fluctuation and incon-
sistency, and shewed its utter want of foundation in
the proceedings of the apostles or the practice of the
primitive church.

But the master production of the period was the 5
" Ecclesiastical Polity" of Hooker. Of this matchless
work the four first books were published in 1594, the
fifth three years afterwards, and the three remaining
books at different periods long after the death of their
author. The germ of his great argument, displayed 10
afterwards in the three first books of his work, had
been previously delivered by him as preacher at the
Temple in the following words[d]: "It is no small perplexity which this one thing hath bred in the minds of
many who, beholding the laws which God himself hath 15
given abrogated and disannulled by human authority,
imagine that justice is hereby conculcated, that men
take upon them to be wiser than God himself, that
unto their devices his ordinances are constrained to
give place : which popular discourses, when they are 20
polished with such art and cunning as some men's wits
are well acquainted with, it is no hard matter with
such tunes to enchant most religiously-affected souls;
the root of which error is a misconceit that all laws
are positive which men establish, and all laws which 25
God delivereth immutable. No : it is not the author
which maketh, but the matter whereon they are made,
that causeth laws to be thus distinguished."

In the fifth book he proceeds to a close examination
of the charges brought by the puritans against the dis- 30
cipline and worship of the church, objecting against
his opponents their want of consideration for the kind

---

[d] See Keble's Pref. to Hooker's Works, p. 5.

of materials out of which human institutions are constructed, and the multiform nature of the judge to whose decision all such questions must practically be referred. His views may be expressed in the two following maxims, which are not only applicable to his own especial subject, but, when transferred to any other relations, may be said to lie at the foundation of all social wisdom. "In the external form of religion such things as are apparently, or can be sufficiently proved, effectual and generally fit to set forward godliness, either as betokening the greatness of God, or as beseeming the dignity of religion, or as concurring with celestial impressions in the minds of men, may be reverently thought of, some few rare, casual and tolerable, or otherwise curable, inconveniencies notwithstanding." (vol. ii. p. 38.) " In evils that cannot be removed without the manifest danger of greater to succeed in their rooms, wisdom, of necessity, must give place to necessity. All it can do in those cases is to devise how that which must be endured may be mitigated, and the inconveniencies thereof countervailed as near as may be : that when the best things are not possible, the best may be made of those that are." (vol. ii. p. 46.)

But the most remarkable attribute of the " Ecclesiastical Polity" is its uniform superiority, in every department of mind, to the general literature of the period. A theologian might naturally be expected to be well provided with weapons from the armoury of the church, a scholar might have exhausted the stores of ancient learning, a philosopher have explored the principles of his science, and a man of taste have a keen perception of the graces of composition; but these various endowments, each of them a great acqui-

K

sition in itself, and some of them calculated from their nature to be exclusive of the rest, are all displayed at once, and each of them in a high degree of excellence, in the " Ecclesiastical Polity." The reader is surprised and delighted to find that his argument has not only 5 stood aloof from the ribaldry of the times and the casuistry of vulgar minds, but has laid before him the important issues and the governing principles of the whole question, investing them at the same time with the riches of a copious literature, the fascinations of a 10 graceful and majestic style, and, above all, the virtues of a Christian character.

Against the disorders of this period, pressed down at different times, but always arising with new strength and numbers from the pressure, the queen's govern- 15 ment, and more especially her ecclesiastical counsellors, presented the most determined resistance, till near the close of her reign. At that time the vigour of her character was broken by age and disappointment, and her advisers willingly found a reason for 20 their own forbearance in the infirmities of their sovereign. Having lost the impulse they had formerly derived from her greater energy, they also began to reflect that a change of measures might be apprehended from the different religious impressions of her 25 successor.

On the accession of king James, the earliest measure adopted by the puritans in concert was to present to him the following address, which, from the great number of the signatures attached to it, was called the 30 Millenary Petition.

" Most gracious and dread sovereign,
" Seeing it hath pleased the Divine Majesty, to the

great comfort of all good Christians, to advance your
highness, according to your just title, to the peaceable government of this church and commonwealth of
England: We, the ministers of the gospel in this land,
5 neither as factious. men, affecting a popular parity in
the church, nor as schismatics, aiming at the dissolution
of the state ecclesiastical, but, as the faithful servants
of Christ and loyal subjects to your majesty, desiring
and longing for the redress of divers abuses of the
10 church, could do no less, in our obedience to God,
service to your majesty, and love to his church, than
acquaint your princely majesty with our particular
griefs. For, as your princely pen writeth, ' the king,
as a good physician, must first know what peccant
15 humours his patient naturally is most subject unto
before he can begin his cure.' And although divers of
us that sue for reformation have formerly, in respect of
the times, subscribed to the book, some upon protestation, some upon exposition given them, some with con-
20 dition, rather than the church should have been deprived of their labour and ministry, yet now we, to the
number of more than a thousand of your majesty's subjects and ministers, all groaning as under a common
burthen of human rites and ceremonies, do, with one
25 joint consent, humble ourselves at your majesty's feet,
to be eased and relieved in this behalf. Our humble
suit, then, unto your majesty is, that these offences following, some may be removed, some amended, some
qualified:

30   " 1. In the church service: that the cross in baptism,
interrogatories ministered to infants, confirmations, as
superfluous, may be taken away: baptism not to be
ministered by women, and so explained: the cap and
surplice not urged: that examination may go before

the communion: that it be ministered with a sermon: that divers terms of priests and absolution and some other used, with the ring in marriage, and other such like in the book, may be corrected: the longsomeness of service abridged: church-songs and music moderated 5 to better edification: that the Lord's day be not profaned: the rest upon holidays not so strictly urged: that there may be an uniformity of doctrine prescribed: no popish opinion to be any more taught or defended: no ministers charged to teach their people to bow at 10 the name of Jesus: that the canonical Scriptures only be read in the church."

In three other articles the petition treats of church ministers, church living and maintenance, and church discipline, complaining of the want of sufficient preachers, 15 of nonresidence, of the subscription usually required to articles, of commendams pluralities and impropriations, of excommunications, of the powers and practices of ecclesiastical courts; and then concludes in the following words: 20

"These, with such other abuses yet remaining and practised in the Church of England, we are able to shew not to be agreeable to the Scriptures, if it shall please your highness further to hear us, or more at large by writing to be informed, or by conference 25 among the learned to be resolved. And yet we doubt not but that, without any further process, your majesty (of whose Christian judgment we have received so good a taste already) is able of yourself to judge of the equity of this cause. God, we trust, hath ap- 30 pointed your highness our physician to heal these diseases: and we say with Mordecai to Hester, 'Who knoweth whether you are come to the kingdom for such a time?' Thus your majesty shall do that which we are persuaded shall be acceptable to God, honourable to your majesty in all succeeding ages, profitable to his church, which shall be thereby increased, comfortable to your ministers, which shall be no more 5 suspended, silenced, disgraced, imprisoned for men's traditions, and prejudicial to none but those that seek their own credit, quiet, and profit in the world. Thus, with all dutiful submission, referring ourselves to your majesty's pleasure for your gracious answer as God 10 shall direct you, we most humbly recommend your highness to the Divine Majesty, whom we beseech for Christ's sake to dispose your royal heart to do herein what shall be to his glory, the good of his church, and your endless comfort."

15 But James had already contracted, from the treatment he had experienced in Scotland, a strong dislike for Genevan platforms and republican principles. His feeling on these subjects was rapidly increased, as he travelled through his southern provinces, by the cla- 20 morous and reiterated demands of the nonconformists, contrasted with the calm and respectful demeanour of the established clergy. Alarmed by the crowds that sought admission to his presence, and irritated by the importunities of the puritans, he would probably 25 have given them a peremptory refusal, had there not been peculiar elements in his character, which made him consent to mediate between the two contending parties, although his decision respecting them appears to have been already taken. A conference was sought 30 by the puritans between persons selected from each side, to discuss the several points at issue, and more especially the projected revision of the liturgy. To this request the king acceded; although the established clergy naturally opposed it, as being in itself

an imputation of error, and likely, if granted, to lead
to no other result than an increased and embittered
discontent. And such was actually the ground on
which a similar request had been refused by his pre-
decessor. But James was greedy of applause; and
there were two different ways in which this concession
would lead to the gratification of his ruling passion.
He would display his magnanimity by listening to the
prayer of individuals for whom, as he had already
shewn, he felt no personal sympathy; and he would
exhibit his talent and erudition by encountering
learned theologians on their own ground, and foiling
them with their own weapons.

The king acted in this case agreeably with the
advice of lord Bacon[f]; who was now advancing in
royal favour, and took care in recommending a conference, and overruling the objections of the clergy, to
touch the principal chord in his master's character.
" It is said that if way be given to mutation, though it
be in taking away abuses, yet it may so acquaint men
with sweetness of change, that it will undermine the
stability even of that which is sound and good. This
surely had been a good and true allegation in the
ancient contentions and divisions between the people
and the senate of Rome; where things were carried
at the appetites of multitudes, which can never keep
within the compass of any moderation: but these
things being with us to have an orderly passage, under
a king who hath a royal power and approved judgment, and knoweth as well the measure of things as
the nature of them, it is surely a needless fear. For
they need not doubt but your majesty, with the advice

---

[f] Works, vol. ii. p. 528. Docum. Ann. vol. ii. p. 44.

of your council, will discern what things are inter-
mingled like the tares amongst the wheat, which have
their roots so enwrapped and entangled, as the one
cannot be pulled up without endangering the other;
5 and what are mingled but as the chaff and the corn,
which need but a fan to sift and sever them."

In the mean time the two universities felt the
occasion to be one of so much peril as to call for an
express declaration of their opinions; and the univer-
10 sity of Oxford sent forth a paper in which the other
university concurred, replying seriatim to the complaints of the petitioners, and representing the danger
that would follow from their designs, not merely to
the church, but also to the monarchy. " Would it not
15 beseem the supereminent authority and regal person of
a king to be himself confined within the limits of some
particular parish, and then to subject his sovereign
power to the pure apostolical simplicity of an over-
swaying and all-commanding presbytery? Would it
20 not do him much good in a time of need that his
people should be rooted and grounded in this truth,,
viz.: 'That his meek and humble clergy have power
to bind their king in chains, and their prince in links
of iron?' that is (in their learning) to censure him, to
25 enjoin him penance, to excommunicate him; yea, (in
case they see cause), to proceed against him as a
tyrant?—Neither may it be truly said that these are
only speculations. There are some of high place yet
alive, and other some are dead, that have felt the
30 smart hereof in their own experience, and have seen
the worst of all this put in woeful execution."

According to his own confession[g], king James had

g Præmon. to all Christian Monarchs. Works, p. 305.

disliked the proceedings of the Scottish reformers
from a very early period, and had laboured to restore
the government of bishops for six years before his
accession to the throne of England. Finding himself
now enabled to decide according to his own judgment [5]
between the two parties, and constantly acquiring
further reasons[h] for supporting the episcopal clergy, he
declared himself a sincere member of the Church of
England, and thanked God that he had been "brought
to the promised land, to a country where religion was [10]
purely professed, and where he sat among grave,
learned, and reverend men; not as before, elsewhere, a
king without state, without honour, and without order,
and where beardless boys would brave him to his
face."   [15]

King James entered the capital of his new dominions on the 7th of May, 1603, and one of his first
acts was to make preparation for convening an assembly of divines, in which all ecclesiastical differences
might be debated. "We are persuaded," said he, in a [20]
subsequent proclamation[i], "that both the constitution
and doctrine thereof [of the Church of England] is
agreeable to God's word, and near to the condition of
the primitive church; yet forasmuch as experience
doth shew daily that the church militant is never so [25]
well constituted in any form of policy, but that the
imperfections of men, who have the exercise thereof,
do with time, though insensibly, bring in some corrup-

---

[h] The king said during the conference, " I have learned of what
cut they have been, who, preaching before me since my coming into [30]
England, passed over with silence my being supreme governor in
causes ecclesiastical."

[i] Proclamation of Oct. 24, 1603. Wilkins' Conc. vol. iv. p. 371.
Docum. Ann. vol. ii. p. 44.

tions; as also for that informations were daily brought unto us by divers, that some things used in this church were both scandalous to many seeming zealous, and gave advantage to the adversaries, we conceived that 5 no subject could be so fit for us to shew our thankfulness to God, as upon serious examination of the state of this church to redeem it from such scandals, as both by the one side and the other were laid upon it."

Owing to the prevalence of the plague in many parts 10 of the kingdom, and other circumstances of a temporary nature, the meeting did not take place till the following month of January; and the interval was employed by many of the nonconformists in such a manner, presuming so far upon the king's disposition 15 in their favour, and adopting measures so seditious in their character, that they increased the high degree of distaste already conceived against them, and met with a severe rebuke from him.

On the 14th day of January, in the year 1604, the 20 first conference was held in the palace of Hampton Court, in the presence of the king and the lords of the privy council. The persons summoned to attend and permitted to take part in the discussion on behalf of the established clergy, were Whitgift, archbishop of 25 Canterbury, then too old and infirm to take any active part in the proceedings, eight bishops, six deans besides the dean of the chapel royal, and two doctors of divinity. The persons appointed to represent the puritans, remarkable certainly for the smallness of their 30 number, but still the best qualified after the death of Cartwright and Travers to support their opinions, were Dr. Rainolds, Dr. Sparkes, Mr. Knewstubbs, and Mr. Chaderton. Mr. Patrick Galloway, minister of Perth, was permitted to be present at the second day's conference, and has left an account of it in a letter[k] addressed to some friends in Scotland. Dr. James Montague, dean of the chapel royal, who was one of the divines summoned to attend, wrote a short narrative of the three conferences on the 18th of January, the day on which the whole business was concluded. This narrative, the composition of a person devoted to the court, but not chargeable with any remarkable prepossession in his statement, is as follows: (in a letter bearing date 18th Jan. 160¾.[l])

"I am sure you have a longing to hear what becometh of this great business, between the bishops and the ministers. I cannot write you the disputes; my employments at this time would not permit; but in short on Saturday it began: the king assembling only the lords of his council and the bishops, myself had the favour to be present by the king's command. The company met and himself sat in his chair. He made a very admirable speech of an hour long at least, for learning, piety, and prudency I never heard the like; concluded it with a most excellent prayer; entered into the points he meant to stand upon, propounding unto them in general, that if he erred in any thing, he would suffer himself to be corrected by God's word ; if they erred they must yield to him, for he would ever submit both sceptre and crown to Christ's, to be guided by his word.

"His majesty propounded six points unto them: three in the Common Prayer Book, two for the bishops' jurisdiction, and one for the kingdom of Ireland. In the Prayer Book he named the general absolution, the confirmation of children, and the private baptism by women. These three were long disputed between the king and the bishops. In the conclu-

k This letter is printed in the ensuing chapter, as well as the longer and authentic account published by Dr. Barlow, one of the divines present, then dean of Chester, and afterwards bishop of Rochester and Lincoln successively.

l Winwood, vol. ii. p. 13.

sion the king was well satisfied in the two former, so that the manner might be changed, and some things cleared.

" For the private baptism it held three hours at least; the king alone disputing with the bishops, so wisely, wittily, and 5 learnedly, with that pretty patience, as I think never man living ever heard the like.   In the end he won this of them, ' that it should only be administered by ministers, yet in private houses, if occasion required ; and that whosoever else should baptize should be under punishment.' ⸌For the com-10 missaries' courts, and the censures of excommunication and suspension they shall be mended, and the amendment is referred to the lord chancellor and the lord chief justice.   But for their common and ordinary excommunication for trifles, it shall be utterly abolished. ⸌The fifth point was about the 15 sole jurisdiction of bishops; so he gained that of them, that the bishops in ordination, suspension, and degradation, and such like, they shall ever have some grave men to be assistants with them in all censures. ⸌For Ireland, the conclusion was (the king making a most lamentable description of the 20 state thereof) that it should be reduced to civility, planted with schools and ministers, as many as could be gotten. These things done, he propounded matters, whereabout he hoped there would be no controversy, as to have a learned ministry and maintenance for them as far as might be.   And 25 for pluralities and non-residences to be taken away, or at least made so few as possibly might be.   These things were concluded on Saturday between the king and the bishops.

" On Monday the king called the other party by themselves ; made likewise an excellent oration unto them, and 30 then went to the matter ; no body being present, but the lords of the council, and Dr. Reynolds, Dr. Sparkes, Dr. Field, Dr. King, Mr. Chaderton, and Mr. Knewstubbs, all the deans that were appointed and myself.

" They propounded four points ; the first for purity of 35 doctrine ; secondly for means to maintain it, as good ministers, &c. ; thirdly, the courts of bishops, chancellors, and commissaries ; fourthly, the Common Prayer Book.

" For doctrine it was easily agreed unto by all ; for ministers also ; for jurisdiction likewise ; for the Book of Common

Prayer and subscription to it, there was much stir about all the ceremonies and every point in it. The king pleaded hard to have good proof against the ceremonies, and if they had either the word of God against them or good authority, he would remove them : but if they had no word of God against them, but all authority for them, being already in the church, he would never take them away : for 'he came not to disturb the state, nor to make innovations, but to confirm whatever be found lawfully established ; and to amend and correct what was corrupted by time.' They argued this point very long. The bishops of Winchester and London, who of all the bishops were present, laboured this point hard, and divers of the deans, but at length the king undertook them himself, and examined them by the Word and by the Fathers. There was not any of them that they could prove to be against the Word, but all of them confirmed by the Fathers, and that long before popery. So that for the ceremonies I suppose nothing will be altered. And truly the doctors argued but weakly against them : so that all wondered they had no more to say against them. So that all that day was spent in ceremonies ; and I think themselves being judges, they were answered fully in every thing. At last it was concluded that day, that there should be an uniform translation set out by the king of all the Bible, and one catechizing over all the realm, and nothing of the Apocrypha to be read that is in any sort repugnant to the Scripture ; but to be still read, yet as Apocrypha, and not as Scripture ; and for any point of the articles of religion that is doubtful, to be cleared. This was the second day's work.

" The third day, which was Wednesday, the king assembled all the bishops (the lords of the council only being present) and took order how to have these things executed, which he had concluded, that it might not be (as the king said) as smoke out of a tunnel, but substantially done to remain for ever So they were debated to whom they might the more fitly be referred, and by them made fit to be hereafter enacted by parliament. So all the bishops and all the council have their parts given them. This being done, the ministers were called in, Dr. Reynolds and the rest, and

acquainted with what the king had concluded on. They were all exceedingly well satisfied, but only moved one thing: that those ministers who were grave men, and obedient unto the laws, and long had been exempted from the use of cere-
5 monies, might not upon the sudden be obliged unto them, but have some time given them to resolve themselves in using or not using them. The king answered, 'his end being peace, his meaning was not that any man should be cruel in imposing those matters, but by time and moderation win all
10 men unto them: those they found peaceable, to give some connivancy to such, and to use their brethren as he had used them, with meekness and gentleness, and do all things to the edification of God's church.' So they ended these matters till the parliament, and then these matters shall be enacted.
15 " This in haste, with my duty, &c., I humbly take my leave, &c. From the court.

"JAMES MONTAGUE."

To this narrative was added the following " note [m] of such thinges as shal be reformed:

20 " 1. The absolution shal be called, The absolution or general remyssion of sins.

" 2. The confirmation shal be called, The confirmation or furder examination of children's faith.

" 3. The private baptism, now by laymen or women, shall
25 be called, The private baptisme by the ministers only; and all those questions in that baptisme, that insinuate it to be don by women, taken awaye.

" 4. The Apocrypha, that hath some repugnancy to the canonical Scripture, shall not be read; and other places chosen,
30 which either are explanations of Scripture, or suite best for good life and manners.

" 5. The jurisdiction of the bishops shal be somewhat limited, and to have either the dean and chapter or som grave minister assistant to them in ordination, suspension,
35 degradation, &c.

---

[m] This is copied from Strype (Whitgift, v. ii. p. 501) who took it from a paper in the handwriting, as he believed, of bishop Bancroft (of London). The copy published in Winwood is not equally correct.

" 6. The excommunication, as it is nowe used, shal be taken awaye both in name and nature. And a writ out of the Chancerie, to punishe the contumacies, shal be framed.

" 7. The kingdom of Ireland, the borders of Scotland, and all Wales, to be planted with schools and preachers as soon as maye be.

" 8. As manie learned ministers, and maintenance for them, to be provided in such places of England where there is want, as maye be.

" 9. As few double-beneficed men and pluralities as may be; and those that have double benefices to maintain preachers, and to have their livings as neere as may be one to the other.

" 10. One uniform translation of the Bible to be made, and onelye to be used in all the churches of Englande.

" 11. One catechisme to be made and used in all places.

" 12. The articles of religion to be explained and inlardged. And no man to teach or read against anie of them.

" 13. A care had, to observe who do not receave the communion once in the year: the ministers to certifie the bishops, the bishop the archbishops, and the archbishops the kinge.

" 14. An inhibition for popish books to be brought over: and if anie come, to be delivered into their hands onelye that are fitt to have them.

" 15. The highe commission to be reformed, and reduced to higher causes and fewer persons; and those of more honour and better qualities."

The sentiments of the king himself respecting the necessity for these conferences, and the manner of conducting them, were expressed in a proclamation of the following March, in words that bear testimony, at the same time, to his own self-approbation, to the judgment he had formed of the two contending parties, to the general tone that he adopted as moderator, and yet to the bland and indulgent temper which he wished to possess in the estimation of his subjects [n].

[n] Rymer, vol. xvi. p. 574. This proclamation is among the documents of the ensuing chapter.

The alterations it was determined to make in the
Book of Common Prayer were not submitted either to
the parliament or even to the convocations of the
clergy. The king required his metropolitan and others
5 of his commissioners for causes ecclesiastical to make
declaration of the changes agreed upon, and then
issued his letters patent to ratify their act, to provide
for the publication of the liturgy in its new condition,
and to enjoin the exclusive use of it in every parish of
10 the two provinces. He probably thought it hazardous
to refer considerations of so delicate a nature to any
large assembly, whether of laymen or of clergy. He
certainly believed that he possessed ample authority[n]
under the broad shield of his prerogative, and those
15 two important statutes of queen Elizabeth, which annexed the spiritual supremacy for ever to the crown,
and made the use of the public liturgy binding upon
his subjects. In describing the changes he had made
as matters merely of exposition and explanation, he
20 sought to shelter them under the clause introduced,
at the desire of queen Elizabeth, into the act of uniformity, which empowered him, "by the advice of his
commissioners or the metropolitan, to ordain and publish such further ceremonies as may be most for the
25 advancement of God's glory, the edifying of his church,
and the due reverence of Christ's holy mysteries and
sacraments."

The alterations, accordingly, that were actually made
in the new edition of the Book of Common Prayer,
30 were the following: into the title of the absolution
were inserted the words "or remission of sins." In
the gospels for the second Sunday after Easter and

[n] The convocation of the same year recognised his alterations
and the authority by which he made them, in the 8oth canon.

the twentieth after Trinity the opening words, "Christ
[or Jesus] said to his disciples," were changed to
"Christ [or Jesus] said," which were also now printed
in a different letter, to shew that they were not to be
found in the original text.   The rubrics in the office 5
for private baptism were altered so as to restrict the
administration of that sacrament to the minister of the
parish, or some other lawful minister.   The title, "confirmation," was explained by the additional words, "or
laying on of hands upon children baptized and able to 10
render an account of their faith."   The doctrine of the
two sacraments was added to the catechism.   Some few
changes were made in the lessons taken from the Apocrypha, and the History of Bel and the Dragon, which
had hitherto been called the 14th chapter of Daniel, 15
was removed from the calendar; a prayer, now called
the prayer for the royal family, was inserted after that
for the king; and occasional thanksgivings for rain, fair
weather, plenty, &c., were added after their corresponding prayers.   20

  It is evident that these alterations did not remove
the whole or even the principal objections made by the
puritans, and were in some instances matters of indifference to them.   The king himself had called for the
changes that were made respecting absolution, private 25
baptism and confirmation, and had readily assented to
the suggestions of Dr. Rainolds on the subject of the
gospels, the lessons taken from the Apocrypha, and an
enlarged form of catechism.   But what must the puritans have thought of the complete and almost con- 30
temptuous refusal that was given to them respecting
the vestments, the ring in marriage, and the cross in
baptism? observances which, when treated as mere rites,
were held to be unobjectionable, but when considered

on the principle of obedience to church authority, were
pronounced to be indispensable. " I charge you," said
the king, " never speak more to that point, how far you
are to obey the orders of the church."

5   The four puritans who were present at the conference appear to have expressed their concurrence in
the decisions of the king as they were severally delivered, and at the close to have promised obedience
to the future injunctions of the church.   Sincere and
10 conscientious men, and some of them possessing no
common amount of learning and talent, they could not
be insensible to the forcible reasoning of their opponents, and were probably oppressed by their sense of
the august presence and the high spiritual authority
15 arrayed against them.   But to their brethren without,
less capable of forming a correct judgment, and less
likely to be influenced by reverential feeling, the result
of this conference was the occasion of disappointment
and remonstrance.

20   " Matters," said a contemporary writer[o], " were well
calmed by the king's moderation, if no after tempest
should arise."   But the tempest had never ceased: it
had only abated, as if to gather strength for more
desperate encounters.   In the following year was pre-
25 sented to the king a petition from ministers in the
diocese of Lincoln, in which, so far from acknowledging the benefits of the recent examination, they seem
to have increased their demands in proportion to
their disappointment.   Charging the Book of Common
30 Prayer with fifty gross corruptions, and ceremonies
notoriously abused to superstition and idolatry, they
called, in strong and peremptory language, for its total

---

[o] Fabric of the Church, by W. Tooker, Pref. 3.

L

abolition.   And this was the beginning of many sor-
rows.

It has been observed by an able historian [P], "that
there is no middle course in dealing with religious sectaries, between the persecution that exterminates and
the toleration that satisfies."   Now whatever may be
the case in such a frame of society as might certainly
be conceived, but has never yet been realized; or,
again, whatever may actually be the case in some com-
munities where religion has ceased to be a conviction
or a principle (and for such cases it is unnecessary to
contend), it is evident that during the whole period
of the puritanical controversy in England, no method
but one professing moderation on the part of the government was either expedient or even practicable.   It
was as much a matter of conscience on the one side to
preserve what the church had ordained, as it was on
the other to reject what their own private judgment
had condemned.   It might be deemed as sinful for the
one party to retain a creed after their own peculiar
tenets had been expunged, as it would be for the other
to use the same creed with such tenets contained in it.
With antagonists so opposed to each other, no persecution could be carried far enough to exterminate either
of them, and no toleration could completely satisfy both.
The only method remaining, and one which has also
positive reasons in its favour, was to secure, by mild and
temperate measures, the concurrence and cooperation
of the middle classes of men, of those who are always
respectable for their numbers and their character, and
are always reinforced, and more especially at a time
of danger, from the adverse parties on either side of
them.

[P] Hallam, Const. Hist. vol. i. p. 219, 4to.

CHAPTER IV.

Documents connected with the revision of king James I.

I. A proclamation concerning such as seditiously seek reformation in church matters. Wilkins' Conc. vol. iv. p. 371.

II. The opinion of Matthew Hutton, archbishop of York, touching certain matters, like to be brought in question at the conference. Strype, Whitgift, vol. iii. pp. 392—402.

III. King James to some person unknown in Scotland, concerning the conference at Hampton Court. Cott. Libr. Vespasian. F. 3.

IV. A letter from court by Toby Matthew, bishop of Durham, to archbishop Hutton, giving an account of the conference. Strype, Whitgift, vol. iii. pp. 402—407.

V. The sum and substance of the conference at Hampton Court, contracted by William Barlow, D. D., dean of Chester.

VI. A letter from Patrick Galloway to the presbytery of Edinburgh, concerning the conference. Calderwood's Hist. of the Ch. of Scotland, p. 474.

VII. Archiepiscopo Cantuariensi et aliis pro reformatione Libri Communis Precum. Rymer, vol. xvi. p. 565.

VIII. A proclamation for the authorizing of the Book of Common Prayer to be used throughout the realm. Wilkins' Conc. vol. iv. p. 377.

L 2

I.

A proclamation concerning such as seditiously seek reformation in church matters.

AS we have ever from our infancy had manifold proofs of God's great goodness towards us in his protecting of us from many dangers of our person, very nearly threatening 5 us, and none more notorious than his happy conducting us in the late case of our succession to this crown, which contrary to most men's expectation we have received with more quiet and concurrency of good will of our people (otherwise perhaps of different dispositions) than ever in like accident hath been 10 seen; so do we think, that the memory of his benefits ought to be a continual solicitation to us to shew ourselves thankful to his divine majesty wheresoever opportunity shall be offered us to do him service, but especially in things concerning his honour and service, and the furtherance of the gospel, which 15 is the duty most beseeming royal authority. Wherefore after our entry into this kingdom, when we had received information of the state thereof at the decease of the queen our sister of famous memory, although we found the whole body thereof in general by the wisdom of herself, and care of those 20 who had the administration thereof under her, in such good state of health, as did greatly commend their wisdoms, as well in the politic part of it, as also in the ecclesiastical, whereof since we have understood the form and frame, we are persuaded that both the constitution and doctrine thereof 25 is agreeable to God's word, and near to the condition of the primitive church; yet forasmuch as experience doth shew daily, that the church militant is never so well constituted in any form of policy, but that the imperfections of men, who have the exercise thereof, do with time though insensibly, 30 bring in some corruptions; as also for that informations were daily brought unto us by divers, that some things used in this church were both scandalous to many seeming zealous, and

gave advantage to the adversaries; we conceived that no
subject could be so fit for us to shew our thankfulness to
God, as upon serious examination of the state of this church,
to redeem it from such scandals, as both by the one side and
5 the other were laid upon it.   For our instruction wherein, we
appointed a meeting to be had before ourself and our council,
of divers of the bishops and other learned men, the first day
of the next month, by whose information and advice we might
govern our proceeding therein, if we found cause of amend-
10 ment.   But by reason of the sickness reigning in many places
of our kingdom, the unseasonable time of the year for travel,
and the incommodity of the place of our abode for such an
assembly, we were constrained to defer it till after Christmas.
At which consultation we shall both more particularly under-
15 stand the state of the church, and receive thereby light to
judge, whether there be indeed any such enormities as are
pretended, and know how to proceed to the redress.   But
this our godly purpose we find hath been misconstrued by
some men's spirits, whose heat tendeth rather to combustion
20 than reformation, as appeareth by the courses they have
taken; some using public invectives against the state ecclesiastical here established, some contemning their authority
and the processes of their courts, some gathering subscriptions of multitudes of vulgar persons to supplications to be
25 exhibited to us, to crave that reformation, which if there be
cause to make, is more in our heart than in theirs.   All
which courses, it is apparent to all men, are unlawful, and do
savour of tumult, sedition, and violence, and not of such a
Christian modesty, as beseemeth those, who for piety's sake
30 only desire redress of things they think to be amiss, and
cannot but be the occasions of dissentious partialities, and
perhaps of greater inconveniences among our people.
   For preventing whereof, we have thought it necessary to
make public declaration to all our subjects, that as we have
35 reason to think the estate of the church here established, and
the degrees and orders of ministers governing the same, to be
agreeable to the word of God and the form of the primitive
church, having found the same blessed in the reign of the late
queen with great increase of the gospel, and with a most

happy and long peace in the politic state, which two things, the true service of God, and happiness of the state, do commonly concur together; so are we not ignorant, that time may have brought in some corruptions, which may deserve a review and amendment, which if by the assembly intended by 5 us we shall find to be so in deed, we will therein proceed according to the laws and customs of this realm by advice of our council, or in our high court of parliament, or by convocation of our clergy, as we shall find reason to lead us; not doubting, but that in such an orderly proceeding we shall 10 have the prelates and others of our clergy no less willing, and far more able to afford us their duty and service, than any other, whose zeal goeth so fast before their discretion. Upon which our princely care, our pleasure is, that all our subjects do repose themselves, and leave to our conscience that which 15 to us only appertaineth, avoiding all unlawful and factious manner of proceeding; for that hereafter if any shall either by gathering the subscriptions of multitudes to supplications, by contemptuous behaviour of any authority by the laws resting in ecclesiastical persons, by open invectives and inde- 20 cent speeches either in the pulpit or otherwise, or by disobedience to the processes proceeding from their jurisdiction, give us cause to think, that he hath a more unquiet spirit than becometh any private person to have toward public authority, we will make it appear by their chastisement, how 25 far such a manner of proceeding is displeasing to us, and that we find that these reformers under pretended zeal affect novelty, and so confusion in all estates, whereas our purpose and resolution ever was, and now is, to preserve the estate as well ecclesiastical as politic in such form as we have found it 30 established by the laws here, reforming only the abuses, which we shall apparently find proved, and that also to do by such mature advice and deliberation as we have above mentioned. Wherefore we admonish all men hereby to take warning, as they will answer the contrary at their peril. Given under 35 our hand at Wilton the 24th day of October, of our reign of England, France, and Ireland the first, and of Scotland the thirtieth and seventh year, anno Domini MDCIII.

II.

The opinion of Matthew Hutton, archbishop of York, touching certain matters, like to be brought in question before the king's most excellent majesty, at the conference at court. Written October 9. 1ᵐᵒ Jacobi, to the archbishop of Canterbury.

5   QUESTION I.

First, Concerning the *appropriations:* Whether they be to be given over to the ministers of the gospel, or may continue, &c.

This question dependeth of another; viz. Whether tithes
10 now in the time of the gospel are to be paid *jure divino* or *jure positivo.*

Respons. My opinion is with Peter Martyr, 19. *Judicum,* That he that laboureth is worthy of his hire, and that the preachers of the word must have a competent portion to live
15 of; but not precisely of tithes.

To make the matter more plain, we must understand, that the Law of Moses was divided into three parts, moral, ceremonial, and judicial: and that these three laws were (as it were) three adjuncts unto the subjects, (to speak after Ramus
20 his logick.) The *ceremonial* law was tied to the priesthood of Levi. Which being taken away and abrogated, the whole law also is abrogate, as St. Paul saith, Heb. vii. " Mutato sacerdotio, necesse est ut legis mutatio fiat." The *judicial* law was annexed, and given to that nation, or people, and
25 that government; which being cast off, and that government ceasing, the *judicial* law is abrogate: but not so as the ceremonial law is, but made not necessary for any state to be tied unto. (Albeit, Struthius and Monetarius, two notable hereticks of late times, would have all the world to be go-
30 verned by the judicial law of Moyses.) For kingdoms and commonwealths may retain some, and alter some, as in wisdom shall be thought convenient. *Theft* by that law was punished by restitution. In this land, and (almost) in all countries, it is punished with death. As for the *moral* law,

it abideth for ever, because the image of God (though rased and much defaced in all men) doth still remain; and by the law of nature and reason doth owe a duty to God and to all men, &c.

Now by what law were tythes commanded by Moyses?   5

Peter Martyr (*Judic.* 19.) saith, by the ceremonial law: and that tythes did aim at Christ, the giver of all things. But now, (Martyr saith,) " stipendia ministris, sive persolvantur ex agris, sive ex ædibus, sive pecunia numerata, sive in decimis, nihil refert ; modo non sordidè, sed honestè, sus- 10 tententur."

In this ceremonial law of tithes there was something *moral*, that is, that a sufficient portion should be allotted to the ministers, &c. and that abideth still.   But precisely the tenth part, that was *ceremonial*, and bindeth not now.   As in the 15 moral law of the *sabbath*, there was something ceremonial: *moral*, that some day or time should be allotted to God's service; but precisely the seventh day, and not the eighth day, that was *ceremonial*, and is abrogate.   So in the ceremonial law, the moral doth continue, the ceremonials are 20 taken away.

That excellent book, called "The Doctor and Student," (the author whereof was called St. German,) in the 55th chapter saith, that tythes did belong to the *judicials* of Moses, to the government of the nation.   But he is in 25 opinion, that, by the law of reason and nature, (which is the moral law,) the ministers of the New Testament must be sufficiently provided for in land, rent, or otherwise, but not necessarily by tithes.   For he saith, that many whole countries pay no tithes, and that our laws in many cases do allow 30 of a *prescription*, "de non decimando ;" which cannot be against the law of God.

Now as for *appropriations*, I think, superstition was the cause of most of them ; but now they are confirmed by the law of the land, and universally dispersed by the same law ; 35 some in the crown; some belonging to colleges in the universities, (and they are best bestowed ;) some belong to noblemen and bishops ; some to cathedral churches and hospitals; some to gentlemen and others, inferiors of all sorts ;

some are seized of them, as of inheritance; more possessed, as of leases; and all these, *bonæ fidei possessores:* and therefore may keep them with a safe conscience; and the parishioners are bound in conscience, as to the parsons and vicars,
5 so to the approprietaries, or to their farmers, to pay their tithes truly, though they be never so wicked men. "Suum cuique tribuere est proprium munus justitiæ."

I wish better provision were made for godly preachers. But how it may be done, I leave that to his majesty, (who is
10 both learned, wise, and careful for religion,) and to the grave men of state and of the church. Thus much of the first question.

QUESTION II.

As touching the *government* of the church in this kingdom,
15 under his majesty, whether by *bishops* or by *presbyteries*, I will shew my opinion as briefly as I can.

Respons. *Presbytery* is more popular, *bishops* more aristocratical. Presbytery hath a resemblance with a *sanhedrim* of the Jews; which being a part of the judicial law, is so abro-
20 gate, that it is made not necessary to be reteyned in the time of the New Testament: neither the authoritie of that which was the *great sanhedrim;* nor of the twenty-three, the middle; nor of three, which was the lowest, and dealt with smallest matters. But our presbyteries do derive their authority
25 from the apostles' time. Priests and bishops, they say, were all one, as Jerom saith to Evagrius [a], and upon the Epistle to Titus: and they governed the church *communi consilio.* But afterwards, for avoiding of schism, "in toto orbe decretum est," it was decreed in all the world, that one of the number
30 of the priests should be elected to be over the rest, and to have the general care over the priests: but "magis consuetudine, quam dispositionis Dominicæ veritate."

Whereas indeed *bishops* have their authority, not by any custom or decree of man, but from the apostles themselves,
35 as Epiphanius proveth plainly against Arrius the heretick; who, being a proud man, because he could not get to be

---

[a] S. Jerom. in cap. ad Tit.

bishop himself, thought, that "idem est episcopus et presbyter." With this opinion St. Augustine doth charge that
heretick, in his book "De Hæresibus, Ad quod vult Deum."
But Epiphanius doth shew the difference to be, not only
because the bishop hath authority over the priests, but be- 5
cause *presbyter* begetteth children to the church by preaching and baptizing; the *bishop* begetteth fathers to the church
by giving of orders. "Hujus rei gratia reliqui te in Creta,
ut quæ desunt pergas corrigere; constituas oppidatim presbyteros," &c. And so it hath continued in the church ever 10
since. The question then is this:

Whether is better, the *bishops* to continue in England, or
that *presbyteries* be brought into this realm and church of
England?

Aristotle saith, There are three kinds of good states; 15
basilia, the best; *aristocratia*, the next: and *timocratia*, the
meanest of all the three: where one, few, or many govern for
the good of the whole commonwealth. Three other sorts of
evil states, *tyrannis*, *oligarchia*, and *democratia*; where one,
few, or the multitude have care only of their own private, 20
and not of the good of the whole. If the gospel be preached
in any of the evil states, there is hope it will make it good.
If in any of the good states, it is no doubt but it will make
it better. But one ecclesiastical government and discipline
is not fit for all commonwealths. The *sanhedrim* of the Jews 25
was not so convenient in the time of the kings, as it was
before and afterwards. Josephus writes, that when the
people would needs have a king, Samuel was sore offended
thereat [b], because "valdè delectabatur optimatum guberna-
tione; at non amabat regiam potestatem ut nimiam [c]." And 30
Hircanus and Aristobulus, before Pompey, refuse to be under
kings, and desire that the people may be governed by God's
priests, as was the manner of the country. So likewise at
this time, they that so much do magnify the government
by presbyteries, like better of a popular state than of a 35
monarchy. Yea, Calvin himself, the chief patron of presbyteries, as he misliketh that a king should be supream head,

---

[b] Lib. vi. cap. 4. Antiq.   [c] Lib. xiv. cap. 5.

so he commendeth, beyond all other, a mixt state of *aristo-cratia* and *timocratia* [d]. Such was and is at Geneva. And so a popular government by presbyteries is more fit for a popular government than it is for *basilia*.

5 Therefore the king's majesty, as he is a passing wise king, and the best learned prince in Europe, had need to take heed, how he receiveth into his kingdom such a popular government ecclesiastical as is that of the presbyterie; "ne forte, &c. latet anguis in herba." *Basilia*, the worst of the 10 three, &c. And the king to be *supream head* of the church, misliked, &c. Thus much of the second question.

QUESTION III.

Thirdly, I am informed, there is great banding by men of good learning, (but of singular wisdom and learning in their 15 own opinion,) set on by busy-bodies, hot and guiddy heads, who fear nothing more, than lest they should seem to doubt of any thing: these Lucians, or Luciferians, intend to disgrace and deface the Book of Common Prayer and the ministration of the sacraments; either to overthrow it, or (at 20 least) to alter it. But these men, though they make small accompt of the bishops now lyving in this church, yet (me-thinks) should reverence reverend archbishop Cranmer, learned bishop Ridley, and grave bishop Latymer, who at one time yielded their bodies to be burnt, for the defence of that book, 25 and the gospel professed in the church of England, in the time of vertuous king Edward the Sixth.

This matter began almost forty years ago, and hath been answered first and very sufficiently by your grace unto T. C. and since very well by divers others: yet being required, I 30 am content to set down my opinion shortly in some few points.

One chief thing is misliked, that women, midwives, and laymen, seem to be permitted to baptize in time of necessity. *Respons.* I answer briefly. First, That the book doth not 35 allow of it. Secondly, That it was not said to women or laymen, "Ite, prædicate, baptizantes eos in nomine," &c. and

---

d Calvin. in Amos. cap. 7. Institut. lib. iv. cap. 20.

therefore they may not minister the sacrament of baptism.
I say also with Epiphanius, contra Collyridianos, that the
blessed Virgin Mary her self was not permitted to baptize.
And he charged Marcion the heretick, that he gave leave to
women to baptize. And yet I confess, that not only the 5
church of Rome, but all the schoolmen, and almost all the
ancient fathers, do hould it lawful, that laymen may baptize
in time of necessity. Tertullian de baptismo; " Alioquin
laicis jus est dandi : quod enim ex æquo accipitur, ex æquo
dari potest." Augustine also, contra Epist. Parmeniani, and 10
in many other places, alloweth of the baptism ministred
by laymen. Zozomenus writeth ᵉ, that Athanasius, a boy,
playing with boyes, baptized certain of them; and yet Alexander, bishop of Alexandria, would not suffer them to be
baptized again. This erroneous custom and abuse of the 15
holy sacrament did grow from another error, urged especially
by that good father, St. Augustine, (" Quandoque bonus dor-
mitat Homerus,") that children dying without baptism could
not be saved : which hath no sufficient warrant in the word.
The promise is, " Ero Deus tuus, et Deus seminis tui." So 20
that the children of Christian parents are within the covenant before baptism; and by baptism are sealed and declared so to be : as by circumcision were the children of the
Israelites. Yet if they died before the eighth day, they were
not thought to be condemned. David would not have been 25
cheared and comforted, when his son died the seventh day,
and before he was circumcised, if he had thought he had
been condemned : Nay, saith he, (2 Sam. xii.) " I must go to
him," &c.

Why then doth the book allow that women should baptize ? 30
The best answer is, that though the book seem so to do,
yet doth it not commend or allow of that fact. True it is,
that their charitable dealing can do the child no harm, and
their fervent prayer to God may do it good. And the sick,
woful mother receiveth comfort, if it die. But if it live, it 35
is commanded by the book, that the child be brought to
the church, and the witnesses to be examined of all circum-

ᵉ Lib. ii. cap. 16.

stances; and if the minister find a manifest defect, he is commanded to proceed to prayer, and to the ministration of baptism, and (at the least) baptize the child with a condition: viz. " If thou, *N.* be not already baptized, I baptize thee in 5 the name of the Father, Son, and of the Holy Ghost." It is referred to the judgment of the minister, whether he think the baptism sufficient and lawful.

And the fourth general council of Carthage, (canon 100,) whereunto St. Augustin did subscribe, hath these words: 10 " Mulier baptizare non presumat." And I heard divers reverend fathers (who were learned preachers in king Edward's days, and very privy to the doings in the convocation, and themselves dealers, *in anno primo Elizabethæ*) affirm plainly, that there was no meaning to allow, that midwives or women 15 should baptize, no more than to minister the supper of the Lord to the sick in private houses. But would not lay it down in plain words, lest it might hinder the passage in the parliament: tantæ molis erat Romanum tollere ritum.

QUESTION IV.

20 Another thing is misliked, *viz.* that the child is signed with the sign of the *cross* in the forehead.

Respons. I answer, that the sign of the cross is and hath been much abused in popery:

" Per crucis hoc signum, fugiat procul omne malignum."

25 I say further, that it is not necessary to be used in that sacrament. Yea, the papists themselves confess, that it is not of the substance, which standeth of two parts, as Augustine saith, " Accedit verbum ad elementum, et fit sacramentum, etiam visibile verbum [f]." Notwithstanding to the ministra-30 tion thereof five things are required: the party baptizing, the party baptized, a meaning to do that which Christ commanded, the element of water, and the form of the words, &c. Henricus de Vurima in Quartam Sentent. comprehendeth them in these two verses:

35   " Cum tincto tingens, intentio, pòst aqua, forma
   Verborum, faciunt, ut sit baptismatis esse."

[f] 80. Tract. in Joan.

All other things whatsoever, he confesseth not to be of the substance; and he comprizeth many of them in three verses:

> " Sal, oleum, chrisma, cereus, chrismale, saliva,
> Flatus, virtutem baptismatis ista figurant;
> Hæc cum patrinis non mutant esse, sed ornant." 5

The same we say of the cross: baptism may be well without it. But we say also, it may be well used; and is well used in the church of England.

It is a very ould ceremony, used by the best fathers, both without baptism and in baptism. "Insultat Paganus 10 crucifixo Christo: videam ego in frontibus regum crucem Christi [g]. Again, Usque adeo de cruce non erubesco, ut non in occulto loco habeam crucem Christi, sed eam in fronte portem. Ad omnem progressum atque promotum, ad omnem aditum et exitum, &c. frontem crucis signaculo 15 terimus [h]."

It was also used in baptism, "Baptisma quoque per crucem datur. Oportet enim signaculum hoc sumere, &c.[i]" Cyprian also, in his sermon " De Passione Christi," saith, that the sign of the cross was used in all sacraments [k]. 20

Now being set down in this church by publick authority, it may not be spurned at by private men. Humility and obedience to the prince and his laws, in all things not contrary to God's laws, beseem best for all subjects and private men. 25

Question V.

It is much misliked in the litany, that we pray to be delivered from *sudden death*. We ought so to live, that death should never find us unprepared.

Respons. I answer, that *sudden death* to the wicked is said 30 to be part of their happiness in this world; that when they have spent their lives in voluptuousness, and all worldly felicity, they are not tormented with long and lingring sickness, but without pain they are suddenly taken away. So saith Job xxi. "Ducunt in bonis dies suos, et in momentum 35 descendunt in sepulchrum."

---

[g] Augustinus in Psal. cxli.   [h] Ibidem. Tertullian. de Corona Milit.
[i] Chrysost. Hom. 13. in Philipp.   [k] Cyprian. in Sermone de Passion.

I say further, it is sometime a blessing for God's children to be taken away by death, lest they should fall into divers sins. And so saith Cyprian, *De Mortalitate*[1], upon these words of the Book of Wisdom, " Raptus est, ne malitia mu-
5 taret intellectum ejus." He commendeth hasty death, because thereby men are taken away from the danger of sin; and that children by death avoid the danger of slippery age.

And Augustin also saith, " Quomodo homini lapso, et in
10 eodem lapsu istam vitam miserè finienti, atque ad pœnas eunti talibus debitas, non plurimum summeque prodesset, si ex hoc tentationum loco priusquam laberetur, morte rape-
retur[m]. To be by death snatched away from sinning is a blessing, as to dye suddenly in sin is a curse. " Electi non-
15 nulli, accepta gratia, in qualibet ætate periculis hujus vitæ mortis celeritate subtrahuntur[n]." And so are taken away hastily, lest they should sin.

But by *sudden death* to be taken away in the act of sin, without space or grace to repent, is a most fearful and ter-
20 rible thing; as were Core, Dathan, Abiron, Absolon, Ananias and Sapphira, and many more. From such sudden death every man ought to say, *Good Lord deliver us.*

But contrariwise, what a singular blessing is it, when a man hath space and grace, not onely to repent him of his
25 sins, but also to dispose of his things, and make open profession of his faith, that he dieth the servant of God, and so yieldeth his soul into the hands of God? It is a comfortable edifying of them that be present, or shall hear of his godly departure. Who wisheth not to dye the death of Abraham,
30 Isaac, and Jaakob, or David, &c.?

Lastly, There are some things that we must simply pray for without condition; as, that God's name may be hallowed, his will fulfilled, the kingdom of Christ enlarged; that we ourselves may live and die in the favour of God, by the
35 merits of Christ Jesus. These things, and such like, we must pray for without condition. Other things, which belong to this life, and the manner of our death, we may pray

[1] Cyprian. de Mortalit. cap. 4.   [m] August. de Prædest. Sanct. cap. 14.
[n] August. de Corrupt. de Gratia, cap. 7.

for with this condition, if it may so stand with the good will
and pleasure of Almighty God.   And this condition, tho' not
expressed, is understood in very many prayers in the litany.
From *battel* and *murther;* from *plague, pestilence,* and *famine ;*
and from *sudden death.*   From *sudden death* without repent- 5
ance, we must simply pray to be delivered.   But yet indefinitely we may well pray to be delivered from sudden death,
with condition, if it may stand with the good pleasure of our
good God.   And a condition is understood in one petition of
the Lord's Prayer, *Give us this day our daily bread ;* the rest 10
without condition.

The Lord, for his Christ's sake, bless his majesty with his
manifold graces : that he may maintain the gospel in this
church, as his dear sister, most worthy queen Elizabeth, did
leave it ; and that as he, in his golden book to the prince his 15
son, doth shew his dislike both of superstitious papists and
giddy-headed puritans, so God may give him courage and
constancy to withstand them both ; that neither the papists
may obtain their hoped toleration, nor the puritans their
fantastical platform of their reformation.   20

III.

*King James to some person unknown in Scotland ; concerning
the conference at Hampton Court between him and the puritans.*

MY honest Blake, I dare not say, *faced* 3.   The letters 25
talking of *deambulatorie* counsils, and such like satyrike trikis,
did a little chafe me ; but yee may see I answered according
to the old scholar's rule, " In quo casu quæris, in eodem re-
spondere teneris."   For I would be sorry not to be as constant indeed as she was, who called her self, *Semper eadem.* 30
Indeed ye may tell the Beagil, that he had best cease to complain of me being a Peripatetike.   For I will oftentimes walk
so fast about and about with him, that he will be like to fall

down dead upon the floure.   I can give you no other thanks
for lyour daily working and publike smiling upon me; onely
this, do quhat you can, yee can give me no more argumentis
of your faithful affection towards me; and do quhat I can unto
5 you, I cannot never increase a haire the devotion of your service towards me.

We have kept such a revell with the puritans here this
two days, as was never heard the like: quhaire I have pep-
pered thaime as soundlie as yee have done the papists thaire.
10 It were no reason, that those that will refuse the airy sign
of the cross after baptism should have their purses stuffed
with any more solid and substantial crosses.   They fled me
so from argument to argument, without ever answering me
directly, *ut est eorum moris*, as I was forced at last to say unto
15 thaime; that if any of thaime had been in a college disputing
with thair scholars, if any of thair disciples had answered
them in that sort, they would have fetched him up in a place
of a reply; and so should the rod have plyed upon the poor
boyes buttocks.   I have such a book of thaires as may well
20 convert infidels, but it shall never convert me, except by
turning me more earnestly against thayme.

And thus praying you to commend me to the honest chamberlain, I bid you heartily farewel.

James R.

——————————

IV.

25 *A letter written from court by Toby Matthew, bishop of Durham, to Hutton, archbishop of York; giving an account at
large of the conference at Hampton Court before the king, in
January* 1603.

MAY it please your grace: Upon Thursday the 12th of
30 this instant, [January,] my lords grace of Canterbury, with
the bishops of London, [Durham interlined,] Winchester,
Worcester, St. David's, Chichester, Carlisle, Peterborough,
and my self, out of the privy chamber, were sent for by his

M

majesty into an inner withdrawing chamber; where in a very private manner, and in as few words, but with most gracious countenance, he imparted to us, first, the cause wherefore we were called up; which was, for the reformation of some things amiss in ecclesiastical matters, supposed, and by some 5 complained of. Next, how desirous he was, and we ought to be, that the kingdom of Ireland might be reduced to the true knowledge of God, and true obedience. To which latter, without the former, he could never hope to find among them. Lastly, his majesty gave us to understand, that the day was 10 somewhat mistaken, being meant by him to be the Saturday after: at which time his majesty willed us to repair to the court again.

Which when we did accordingly, his highness, about eleven of the clock, in his privy chamber, in the presence of the 15 privy council only, sitting on his right hand, and all the bishops on his left, made an excellent oration of an hour long, declaring, "That religion was the soul of a kingdom, and unity the life of religion. That as both among the Jews and the heathen, so among the Christian emperors, their chiefest 20 care was first to establish God's worship. And that in this realm of England, as sondrie of the kings had been religious in their kynde, of auncient tyme, so in this latter age there had been made divers alterations; as, by king Henry the Eighth in some points; by king Edward in many more; 25 by queen Marie, who crossed them both; and lastly, by queen Elizabeth, who reformed her sister's superstitions, and established the church of God here, in the doctrine of Christ, and discipline agreable to the same. Whereunto, because some preachers in sondrie parts of the realme did not so 30 submit themselves, but that some contradiction and discontentment did arise long since, and increase of late, little less than to a schisme, (a point most perillous as well to the common weale as to the church:) therefore he had convened us, the reverend fathers, to consult with us: first, aparte 35 from our opposites, for avoiding contention towards us and them, and for his own resolutions in some particulars, which the contrary faction imputed partly to the Book of Common Prayer, and partly to the forme of church government here.

Which said particulars were, I. The forme of *absolution* after the publique confession of synnes. II. The manner of *confirmation* of children. III. The toleration of *private baptisme* to be done by laymen or women. IV. Many great 5 errors and abuses, crept in under the title of *excommunication ;* and by the corrupt dealing of chancellors, officials, &c." Against all which his majesty did argue and dispute at large.

And after answer severally made by my lords grace of 10 Canterburie, and the bishops of London and Winchester chiefly, his highness so scholasticallie and effectuallie replied, that what with rejoyninge and surrejoyninge, fower long houres were spent in that daies conference, to our exceeding great admiration of his majesties not only rhetorical and 15 logical, but theological and juridical discourses. As also, in the end, to his good satisfaction in all such objections as he propounded ; giving present order, that for the present clearing of some doubts and misconstructions here and there, some few words, not in the body of the sense, but in the rubricks, 20 or titles, of some of the aforesaid particulars, should, in the next edition of the Common Prayer Book, be inserted, by way rather of some explanation, than of any alteration at all.

Upon Monday his majesty appointed certain of the best learned of the *preciser* sort to be before him in the privy 25 chamber, to hear what they could object; viz. Dr. Reynolds, Dr. Sparke, Mr. Chatterton, and Mr. Knewstubbs : to whom his highness used more shorte and round speech : and admitted only two bishops to be present, to be named by my lords grace of Canterbury ; who sent thither the bishops of 30 London and Winchester, while we the rest were with him, setting down the form of the former points. The doctors named divers abuses, but insisted chiefly upon the *confirmation*, the *cross* in baptism, the *surplice, private baptism, kneeling* at 35 the communion, reading of the *Apocrypha, subscriptions* to the Book of Common Prayer and Articles ; one only translation of the Bible to be authentical, and read in the church ; the censure of *excommunication* for so small causes ; the *corruptions* in the bishops' and archdeacons' courts, committed by their chancellors, commissaries, officials, registers, and such

M 2

like officers; together with their immoderate exactions and
fees, to be reformed. Of all which, as also concerning the
oath (upon many and sundry catching articles unto the
preachers) *ex officio*, to entangle them: which one of them
compared to the Spanish inquisition.   5

After that his majesty had, in most excellent and extraordinary manner, disputed and debated with them, and confuted their objections; being therein assisted now and then,
for variety sake rather than for necessity, by the two bishops
before-named, from eleven of the clock until after fower; 10
with some sharpe words amonge, he favourablie dismissed
them for that tyme; requiring them to give their attendance
here again on the Wednesdaie after, before himself and his
council, and all the bishops, to receive such order and directions as he should be pleased to give therein.   15

According to which appointment, we and they altogether
presented our selves. And after that his majesty had summarily repeated unto us what had passed between him and
them on the Monday, and began to set down the courses he
would have to be observed in some of the foresaid poynts in 20
controversy, Mr. Chatterton and Mr. Knewstubbs moved his
highness, with all submission, to have the *cross* in baptisme
utterly forborn, and *kneeling* at the communion. Which
being utterly for divers causes denied them, yet by their
importunitie on behalf of certain preachers in Lancashire, 25
who had taken great pains against the papists, and doone
much good among the people, his highness was contented,
out of his princely clemencie, so far to condescend unto them
that a letter should be written to the bishop of Chester, to
bear with their weakness for some time, and not proceed over 30
hastilie and roughlie against any of them, until, by conference between the bishop and them, they might be persuaded
to conforme themselves to us, and the rest of their brethren;
advising Mr. Chatterton and Mr. Knewstubbs, by their letters or otherwise, to deal with those preachers to submit 35
themselves to the judgment of the church, and to avoid all
singularitie, the mother of schismes and disorder.

Which done, his majesty assigned his council and all the
bishops forthwith to go and consult together in the council-

chamber, as well upon the premisses that needed any amends, as also how religion might be planted upon the borders of England and Scotland, and likewise in Wales, but especially in his kingdome of Ireland; wherein he made demonstration
5 of his exceeding princely care and godlie zeal, with most vehement and deep impression in all our ears and hearts, for the salvation of the souls of that forelorn people, and for the discharge of his own and all our Christian duties. Naming withall some whom he thought fittest to be employed, to take
10 care for the expedition of that principal design.

Immediately whereupon, all the most honourable privy councel and wee going together, agreed to set down several courses for the better performance of all and every the matters afore-mentioned: some of them and us to employ our
15 selves, some in one thing and some in another. The copy of which general project I will send your grace so soon as I can procure it of my lord Cecill: to whom his highness did deliver it to be recorded in the council book: adding thereunto an earnest exhortation and charge unto both the chancellors
20 of the universities there present, and to the bishoppes, to be much more careful hereafter than heretofore, not to suffer any person in any college, that shall be given to defend any heresie, or disposed to maintaine any *schismatical tricks,* (as he termed them,) what other good giftes or eloquence soever
25 they have. For the more learning, saith he, without humilitie and obedience, the more pernicious to church and commonweale. Lastly, to look better to the education of noblemen and gentlemens sons, many of which he was informed to have been by popish tutors and teachers danger-
30 ouslie corrupted.

And requiring the bishoppes to be so much the more vigilant in their calling, as the adversaries are no less diligent than the devil himself in perverting the people, we were most benignly and graciously dismissed for that tyme.

35 Thus much I thought it my duty in grosse to advertise your grace, as I promised, presuming that some other, as sir John Bennet, hath already or will shortly certify all in more particular: wishing that you had been here at the conference, which in my opinion would have wrought in you as

great comfort and joy as ever happened to you in this mortal life; to see and hear so worthie a kyng and prieste in one person, with so sacred a majesty, to propose, discusse, and determyne so many, so necessarie, and so important matters, so readilie, so soundlie, as I never look to see or hear the 5 like again.   God, even the God of our fathers, prosper and protect his highness and all his posteritie, as he hath rejoyced the hearts of all us, his humble and obedient clergye; hoping also, that it will work, if not perfect contentment, yet much more quietness in all those that were before otherwise 10 affected.

Thus, with my many humble thanks for your grace's late fatherly kindness at Bishopthorp, among the rest of your auncient accustomed favours, and with my most hearty salutations to good Mrs. Hutton, your vertuous yoake-fellow, I 15 take my leave: betaking you both to the grace of God.   At Kingstone upon Thames, this 19th of January, 1603.

Your graces humble at commandment,

and for ever most assured,

Tobie Duresme.   20

When I was in the middest of this discourse, I received a message from my lord chamberlaine, that it was his majesty's pleasure that I should preach before him upon Sunday next; which *Scarborough warning* did not only perplex me, but so puzzel me, as no mervail if somewhat be pretermitted, 25 which otherwise I might have better remembered.

V.

The summe and substance of the conference which it pleased his excellent majestie to have with the lords bishops, and others of his clergie (at which the most of the lords of the councill were present) in his majesties privie-chamber, at Hampton Court,
5 *Jan. 14, 1603. Contracted by William Barlow, doctor of divinity, and dean of Chester.*

TO THE READER.

THIS copy of the conference in January last hath been long expected, and long since it was finished : impeachments, of
10 the divulging, were many; two main above the rest : one, his untimely death, who first imposed it upon me, with whom is buried the famousest glory of our English church, and the most kind incouragement to paines and study [a] : a man happy in his life and death; loved of the best while he lived; and
15 heard of God for his decease; most earnestly desiring, not many dayes before he was stroken, that he might not (yet) live to see this parliament, as neer as it was.

The other, an expectation of this late comitial conference, much threatened before, and triumphed in by many; as if
20 that regal and most honourable proceeding should thereby have received his counterblast, for being too forward. But his majesties constancy having, by the last, added comfort and strength to this former, which now, at length, comes abroad, therein, good reader, thou mayest both see those huge pre-
25 tended scandals (for which our flourishing church hath been so long disturbed) objected and removed ; and withall behold the express and vive image of a most learned and judicious king, whose manifold gifts of grace and nature my scant measure of gift is not able to delineate, nor am I willing to
30 enumerate, because I have ever accounted the personal commendation of living princes, in men of our sort, a verbal symonie; such flies there are too many, which puffe the skin, but taint the flesh. His majesties humble deportment in those sublimities will be the eternizing of his memory, the

[a] Archiepiscopus Cantuar.

rather, because καταπεψαι τὸν ὄλβον, to digest so great felicity without surfeit of surquedry is a virtue, rare in great
personages, and that, which the King of heaven feared even
the king of his own choice would want. The more eminent
he is in all princely qualities, the happier shall we be: our 5
duty, as we are Christians, is prayer for him; as we are subjects, obedience to him; as we are men, acknowledgment of
our settled state in him; our unthankfulnesse may remove
him, as it did the mirror of princes, our late famous Elizabeth. She rests with God, the phœnix of her ashes reignes 10
over us, and long may he so do to God's glory, and the
churches good, which his excellent knowledge beatifieth, and
government adjoyned will beautifie it. An hope of this last
we conceive by his written Βασιλικον: a specimen of the
other, in this interlocutory conference: whereof take this, 15
which is printed, but as an extract, wherein is the substance
of the whole. Intercourse of speeches, there occasioned, would
cause prolixity without profit: what every man said, *point
devise*, I neither could, nor cared to observe; the vigor of
every objection, with the summe of each answer, I guesse I 20
misse not: for the first day, I had no help beyond mine own;
yet some of good place and understanding have seen it, and
not controlled it, except for the brevity: for the two last,
out of divers [b] copies, I have selected and ordered what you
here see: in them all, next unto God, the king's majesty 25
alone must have the glory: yet to say, that the present state
of our church is very much obliged to the reverend fathers,
my lords of London and Winton, their pains and dexterity
in this businesse, were neither detraction from other, nor
flattery of them. His highnesse purposed to compose all 30
quarrels of this kind hereby, and supposing he had settled all
matters of the church, it pleased him so to signifie by proclamation after it was done: but there is a triple generation
in the world, of whom the wise man speaketh [c], marry I say
nothing (for even private speeches cannot now passe without 35
the smeer of a black cole). In one rank whereof you may

---

[b] Ep. Londi., deanes of Christch. Winchest. Windsor, Archdea. Nottingh. and
mine own.

[c] Prov. xxx. 12, 13, 14.

place our Hercules Limbomastix, whom it might have pleased, without this gnathonicall appeal, to have rested his majesties determination, and being a synoptical theologue ἐν πλατεῖ, and angry that he was not so κατ' ἐπιτομήν, have learned the
5 difference in divinity between *viam regis* and *viam gregis.*

Many copies of divers sorts have been scattered and sent abroad, some partial, some untrue, some slanderous. What is here set down, for the truth thereof shall be justified : the onely wrong therein, is to his excellent majesty, a syllable
10 of whose admirable speeches it was pitty to lose, his words as they were uttered by him, being, as Solomon speaketh, "like apples of gold with pictures of silver[d];" and therefore I request thee, good reader, when thou commest to any of his highnesse speeches, to turn Martial his apostrophe upon me,

15   "Tu male jam recitas, incipit esse tuus,"

and I will take it kindly. If thou be honest, and courteous, thou wilt rest satisfied, and that is my content : to lay a pillow for a dog, sorts neither with my leisure nor purpose : farewell.
20   Thine in Christ Jesu,

                          W. BARLOW.

THE

FIRST DAYES CONFERENCE.

The day appointed was, as by his majesties proclamation
25 we all know, Thursday the 12th of January ; on which there met at Hampton Court by nine of the clock, all the bishops and deanes, summoned by letters, namely, the archbishop of Canterbury, the bishops of London, Durham, Winchester, Worcester, S. Davids, Chichester, Carleil, and Peterborow :
30 the deanes of the chapell, Christs-church, Worcester, Westminster, Pauls, Chester, Winsor, with doctor Field, and doctor King, arch-deacon of Nottingham : who, though the night before they heard a rumour that it was deferred till the fourteenth day, yet according to the first summons,

d Prov. xxv. 11.

thought it their duty to offer themselves to the king's presence, which they did. At which time it pleased his highnesse
to signifie unto the bishops, that the day having prevented, or
deceived him, he would have them return on Saturday next
following: on which day, all the deanes and doctors at- 5
tending my lords the bishops into the presence chamber,
there we found sitting upon a form, doctor Reinolds, doctor Sparks, master Knewstubs, and master Chaderton, agents
for the millenary plaintiffes. The bishops entring the privy
chamber staied there, till commandement came from his ma- 10
jesty, that none of any sort should be present, but only the
lords of the privie council, and the bishops, with five deanes,
viz. of the chapel, Westminster, Pauls, Westchester, Salisbury, who being called in, the door was close shut by my
lord chamberlain.   15

After a while, his excellent majesty came in, and having
passed a few pleasant gratulations with some of the lords, he
sat down in his chair, removed forward from the cloth of
state a pretty distance: where, begining with a most grave
and princely declaration of his general drift in calling this 20
assembly, no novel device, but according to the example of
all Christian princes, who in the commencement of their
reign usually take the first course for the establishing of the
church, both for doctrine and policie, to which the very
heathens themselves had relation in their proverb, *A Jove* 25
principium, and particularly in this land, king Henry VIII.
toward the end of his reign; after him king Edward VI. who
altered more; after him queen Mary, who reversed all; and
last the queen of famous memory, so his highnesse added
(for it is worth noting, that his majesty never remembred 30
her, but with some honourable addition) who settled it as
now it standeth. Wherein, he said that he was happier than
they, in this, because they were fain to alter all things they
found established, but he saw yet no cause so much to alter
and change any thing, as to confirm that which he found well 35
setled already; which state, as it seemed, so affected his
royal heart, that it pleased him both to enter into a gratula-
tion to Almighty God, (at which words he put off his hat)
for bringing him into the promised land, where religion was

purely professed, where he sate among grave, learned and reverend men, not, as before, elsewhere, a king without state, without honour, without order, where beardlesse boyse would brave him to his face; and to assure us, that he called not 5 this assembly for any innovation, acknowledging the government ecclesiastical, as now it is, to have been approved by manifold blessings from God himself, both for the increase of the gospel, and with a most happy and glorious peace; yet because nothing could be so absolutely ordered, but some-10 thing might be added afterward thereunto, and in any state, as in the body of man, corruptions might insensibly grow, either through time or persons; and in that he had received many complaints, since his first enterance into the kingdome, especially through the dissentions in the church, of many 15 disorders, as he heard, and much disobedience to the lawes, with a great falling away to popery; his purpose therefore was, like a good physician, to examine and try the complaints, and fully to remove the occasions thereof, if they prove scandalous, or to cure them, if they were dangerous, 20 or, if but frivolous, yet to take knowledge of them, thereby to cast a sop into Cerberus his mouth, that he may never bark again; his meaning being, as he pleased to professe, to give factious spirits no occasion hereby of boasting or glory, for which cause he had called the bishops in severally be 25 themselves, not to be confronted by the contrary opponents, that if any thing should be found meet to be redressed, it might be done, (which his majesty twice or thrice, as occasion served, reiterated) without any visible alteration.

And this was the sum, so far as my dull head could con-30 ceive and carry it, of his majesties general speech. In particular he signified unto them the principal matters, why he called them alone, with whom he would consult about some special points, wherein himself desired to be satisfied; these he reduced to three heads: first, concerning the Book of 35 Common Prayer, and divine service used in this church. Second, excommunication in the ecclesiastical courts. Third, the providing of fit and able ministers for Ireland.

In the book he required satisfaction about three things. First, about confirmation; first for the name, if arguing a

confirming of baptism, as if this sacrament without it were
of no validity, then were it blasphemous: secondly, for the
use, first brought upon this occasion; infants being baptized,
and answering by their *patrini*, it was necessary they should
be examined, when they came to yeares of discretion, and 5
after their profession made by themselves, to be confirmed
with a blessing, or prayer of the bishop, laying his hands
upon their heads, abhorring the abuse in popery, where it
was made a sacrament and corroboration to baptism.

The second was for absolution, which how we used it in 10
our church he knew not, he had heard it likned to the popes
pardons, but his majesties opinion was, that, there being only
two kinds thereof from God, the one general, the other particular: for the first, all prayers and preachings do import
an absolution: for the second, it is to be applied to special 15
parties, who having commited a scandal, and repenting, are
absolved: otherwise, where there precedes not either excommunication or penance, there needs no absolution.

The third was private baptism, if private for place, his
majesty thought it agreed with the use of the primitive 20
church; if for persons, that any but a lawfull minister might
baptize any where, he utterly disliked; and in this point his
highnesse grew somewhat earnest against the baptizing by
women and laikes.

The second head was excommunication, wherein he offered 25
two things to be considered of; first, the matter; second,
the person. In the matter, first, whether it were executed
(as it is complained) in light causes; second, whether it were
not used too often. In the persons, first, why laymen, as
chancellors and commissaries, should do it? second, why the 30
bishops themselves, for the more dignity to so high and
weighty a censure, should not take unto them, for their
assistants, the dean and chapter, or other ministers, and
chaplains of gravity and account: and so likewise in other
censures, and giving of orders, &c.   35

The last, for Ireland, his majesty referred, as you shall
in the last dayes conference hear, to a consultation. His
highnesse, (to whom I offer great wrong, in being as Phocion
to Demosthenes, κοπὶς τῶν λόγων the hatchet to cut short so

amiable a speech) having ended, the lord archbishop, after
that, on his knee, he had signified how much this whole land
was bound to God, for setting over us a king, so wise, learned,
and judicious, addressed himself to enform his majesty of all
5 these points in their several order.

And first, as touching confirmation, he shewed at large the
antiquity of it, as being used in the catholique church ever
since the apostles time, till that of late some particular
churches had unadvisedly rejected it.   Then he declared the
10 lawful use of it, agreeable to his majesties former speech,
affirming it to be a meer calumniation, and a very untrue suggestion, if any had informed his highnesse, that the Church
of England did hold or teach, that without confirmation
baptism was unperfect, or that it did adde any thing to the
15 vertue and strength thereof.   And this he made manifest by
the rubricks in the communion book set before confirmation,
which were there read.

My lord of London succeeded, saying, that the authority
of confirmation did not depend onely upon the antiquity and
20 practice of the primitive church, which out of Cyprian, Ep. 73.
and Hieron. *adversus Luciferian.* he shewed, but that it was
an institution apostolical, and one of the particular points of
the apostles' catechism, set down and named in expresse
words, Heb. vi. 2, and so did master Calvin expound that very
25 place, who wished earnestly the restitution thereof in those
reformed churches where it had been abolished.   Upon which
place the bishop of Carleil also insisted, and urged it both
gravely and learnedly.   His majesty called for the Bible, read
the place of the Hebrews, and approved the exposition.

30   Something also the bishop of Durham noted, out of the
Gospel of Saint Matthew, for the imposition of hands upon
children.   The conclusion was, for the fuller explanation, that
we make it not a sacrament, or a corroboration to a former
sacrament, " That it should be considered of by their lord-
35 ships, whether it might not, without alteration, (whereof his
majesty was still very wary,) be intituled an Examination
with a Confirmation."

Next in order was the point of absolution, which the lord
archbishop cleared from all abuse, or superstition, as it is

used in our Church of England: reading unto his majesty,
both the confession in the beginning of the Communion Book,
and the absolution following it, wherein (saith he) the minister doth nothing else but pronounce an absolution in general. His highnesse perused them both in the book itself, 5
liking and approving them, finding it to be very true, which
my lord archbishop said. But the bishop of London stepping
forward, added, it becometh us to deal plainly with your
majesty: there is also in the Communion Book, another more
particular and personal form of absolution, prescribed to be 10
used in the order for the visitation of the sick: this the king
required to see, and whilst master dean of the chapel was
turning to it, the said bishop alleged, that not only the confessions of Augusta, Boheme, Saxon, which he there cited, do
retain and allow it, but that master Calvin did also approve 15
such a general kind of confession, and absolution as the
Church of England useth, and withall did very well like of
those which are private, for so he terms them. The said
particular absolution in the Common Prayer Book being read,
his majesty exceedingly well approved it, adding, that it was 20
apostolical, and a very good ordinance, in that it was given
in the name of Christ, to one that desired it, and upon the
clearing of his conscience.

The conclusion was, that it should be consulted of by the
bishops, whether unto the rubrike of the general absolution, 25
these words, remission of sins, might not be added for explanation sake.

In the third place, the lord archbishop proceeded to speak
of private baptism, shewing his majesty, that the administration of baptism by women and lay-persons was not allowed 30
in the practice of the church, but enquired of by bishops in
their visitation, and censured; neither do the words in the
book inferre any such meaning. Whereunto the king excepted, urging and pressing the words of the book, that they
could not but intend a permission, and suffering of women 35
and private persons to baptize. Here the bishop of Worcester said, that indeed the words were doubtful, and might
be pressed to that meaning, but yet it seemed by the contrary
practice of our church, (censuring women in this case) that

the compilers of the book did not so intend them, and yet propounded them ambiguously, because otherwise, perhaps, the book would not have then passed in the parliament, (and for this conjecture, as I remember, he cited the testimony
5 of my lord archbishop of York:) whereunto the bishop of London replied, that those learned and reverend men, who framed the Book of Common Prayer, intended not by ambiguous termes to deceive any, but did, indeed, by those words intend a permission of private persons to baptize in case
10 of necessity, whereof their letters were witnesses; some parts whereof he then read, and withall declared that the same was agreeable to the practice of the antient church; urging to that purpose, both Act. 2. where 3000. were baptized in one day, which for the apostles alone to do was impossible, at
15 least improbable; and besides the apostles, there were then no bishops or priests: and also the authority of Tertullian, and Saint Ambrose in the fourth to the Ephesians, plain in that point, laying also open the absurdities and impieties of their opinion who think there is no necessity of baptism,
20 which word necessity he so pressed not, as if God without baptism could not save the child; but the case put, that the state of the infant, dying unbaptized, being uncertain, and to God only known; but if it die baptized, there is an evident assurance that it is saved; who is he that having any reli-
25 gion in him, would not speedily, by any means, procure his child to be baptized, and rather ground his action upon Christ's promise, than his omission thereof upon God's secret judgement?

His majesty replied, first to that place of the Acts, that
30 it was an act extraordinary, neither is it sound reasoning from things done before a church be setled and grounded, unto those which are to be performed in a church stablished and flourishing: that he also maintained the necessity of baptism, and alwaies thought, that the place of S. John,
35 " Nisi quis renatus fuerit ex aqua," &c. was meant of the sacrament of baptism, and that he had so defended it against some ministers in Scotland, and it may seem strange to you my lords, saith his majesty, that I, who now think you in England give too much to baptism, did 14 moneths ago in

Scotland argue with my divines there for ascribing too little
to that holy sacrament. Insomuch that a pert minister
asked me if I thought baptism so necessary, that if it were
omitted the child should be damned? I answered him, No,
but if you, being called to baptize the child, though privately, 5
should refuse to come, I think you shall be damned. But
this necessity of baptism his majesty so expounded, that it
was necessary to be had, where it might be lawfully had, *id
est*, ministred by lawful ministers, by whom alone, and by no
private person, he thought it might not in any case be ad- 10
ministred; and yet utterly disliked all rebaptization, although
either women or laikes had baptized.

Here the bishop of Winchester spake very learnedly and
earnestly in that point, affirming, that the denying of private
persons in cases of necessity to baptize, were to cross all anti- 15
quity, seeing that it had been the ancient and common practice of the church, when ministers at such times could not be
got, and that it was also a rule agreed upon among divines,
that the minister is not of the essence of the sacrament.
His majesty answered, though he be not of the essence of the 20
sacrament, yet is he of the essence of the right and lawful
ministry of the sacrament, taking for his ground the commission of Christ to his disciples, Matt. xxviii. 20, " Go preach
and baptize."

The issue was a consultation, whether into the rubrick of 25
private baptism, which leaves it indifferently to all laikes or
clergy, the words, curate or lawful minister, might not be
inserted, which was not so much stuck at by the bishops.
And so his majesty proceeded to the next point, about excommunication in causes of lesser moment: first, whether the 30
name might not be altered, and yet the same censure be
retained: or secondly, whether in place of it another coercion
equivalent thereunto might not be invented and thought of.
A thing very easily yielded unto of all sides, because it had
been long and often desired, but could not be obtained from 35
her majesty, who resolved to be still *semper eadem*, and to
alter nothing which she had once setled.

And thus the Wednesday succeeding being appointed for
the exhibiting of their determinations in these points, and

the Monday next immediately following this present day for
the opponents to bring in their complaints, we were dismissed
after three hours and more spent, which were soon gone ;
so admirably, both for understanding, speech, and judgement,
5 did his majesty handle all those points, sending us away, not
with contentment only, but astonishment, and, which is
pitiful, you will say, with shame to us all, that a king, brought
up among puritans, not the learnedst men in the world, and
schooled by them, swaying a kingdom full of businesse and
10 troubles, naturally given to much exercise and repast, should
in points of divinity shew himself as expedite and perfect, as
the greatest scholars and most industrious students there
present might not out strip him.   But this one thing I might
not omit, that his majesty should professe, howsoever he
15 lived among puritans, and was kept, for the most part, as a
ward under them, yet since he was of the age of his sonne,
ten years old, he ever disliked their opinions ; as the Saviour
of the world said, " though he lived among them, he was not
of them."

20   *Finis primæ diei.*

SECOND DAYES CONFERENCE.

On Monday, January sixteen, between 11. and 12. of the
clock, were the 4. plaintiffes called into the privy chamber,
25 (the two bishops of London and Winchester being there
before) and after them all the deanes, and doctors present,
which had been summoned, Patr. Galloway sometime minister
of Perth in Scotland, admitted also to be there, the king's
majesty, entring the chamber, presently took his chair,
30 placed as the day before, (the noble young prince sitting by
upon a stool,) where making a short, but a pithy and sweet
speech, to the same purpose which the first day he made,
viz. " Of the end of the conference, meet to be had he said by
every king, at his first entrance to the crown ; not to inno-
35 vate the government presently established, which by long

N

experience he had found accomplished with so singular
blessings of God, 45. yeares, as that no church upon the face
of the earth more flourished than this of England. But first
to settle an uniform order through the whole church. Secondly, to plant unity for the suppressing of papists and 5
enemies to religion. Thirdly, to amend abuses, as natural to
bodies politick, and corrupt man, as the shadow to the body,
which once being entred, hold on as a wheel, his motion once
set going. And because many grievous complaints had been
made to him, since his first entrance into the land, he 10
thought it best to send for some, whom his majesty understood to be the most grave, learned and modest of the
agrieved sort, whom being there present, he was now ready
to hear at large, what they could object or say ;" and so
willed them to begin : whereupon they four kneeling down, 15
D. Reinolds the foreman, after a short preamble gratulatory,
and signifying his majesties summons, by vertue whereof
they then and there appeared, reduced all matters disliked,
or questioned, into these four heads :

1. That the doctrine of the church might be preserved in 20
purity according to God's word.

2. That good pastors might be planted in all churches to
preach the same.

3. That the church government might be sincerely ministred, according to God's word.   25

4. That the Book of Common Prayer might be fitted to
more increase of piety.

I. For the first, he moved his majesty, that the book of
Articles of Religion, concluded 1562, might be explained in
places obscure, and enlarged where some things were defec- 30
tive. For example, whereas art. 16. the words are these :
"after we have received the Holy Ghost, we may depart
from grace :" notwithstanding the meaning be sound, yet he
desired that, because they may seem to be contrary to the
doctrine of God's predestination and election in the 17. ar- 35
ticle, both those words might be explained with this, or the
like addition, "yet neither totally nor finally ;" and also that
the nine assertions orthodoxal, as he termed them, concluded
upon at Lambeth, might be inserted into that book of Articles.

II. Secondly, where it is said in the 23. article, that 'it is not lawful for any man to take upon him the office of preaching or administring the sacraments in the congregation before he be lawfully called, D. Reinolds took exception
5 to these words, "in the congregation," as implying a lawfulnesse for any man whatsoever, out of the congregation, to preach and administer the sacraments; though he had no lawful calling thereunto.

III. Thirdly, in the 25. article, these words touching con- -,
10 firmation, "grown partly of the corrupt following the apostles," being opposite to those in the collect of confirmation in the Communion Book, "upon whom after the example of the apostles," argue, saith he, a contrariety each to other; the first, confessing confirmation to be a depraved imitation of
15 the apostles; the second, grounding it upon their example, Act. 8. and 9. as if the bishop in confirming of children, did by his imposing of hands, as the apostles in those places, give the visible graces of the Holy Ghost; and therefore he desired that both the contradiction might be considered, and
20 this ground of confirmation examined.

Thus farre doctor Reinolds went on without any interruption: but here, as he was proceeding, the bishop of London, much moved to hear these men, who some of them the evening before, and the same morning, had made semblance
25 of joyning with the bishops, and that they sought for nothing but unity, now strike to overthrow (if they could) all at once, cut him off, and kneeling down, most humbly desired his majesty, first, that the ancient canon might be remembred, which saith, that "Schismatici contra episcopos non sunt
30 audiendi." Secondly, that if any of these parties were in the number of the thousand ministers, who had once subscribed to the Communion Book, and yet had lately exhibited a petition to his majesty against it, they might be removed and not heard, according to the decree of a very ancient councel,
35 providing that no man should be admitted to speak against that whereto he had formerly subscribed.

Thirdly, he put D. Reinolds and his associates in minde, how much they were bound to his majesties exceeding great clemency, in that they were permitted, contrary to the

N 2

statute 1 Eliz. to speak so freely against the liturgy and discipline established. Lastly, forasmuch as that he perceived they tooke a course tending to the utter overthrow of the orders of the church, thus long continued, he desired to know the end which they aimed at, alleging a place out of master 5 Cartwright, affirming that we ought rather to conform our selves in orders and ceremonies to the fashion of the Turks than to the papists; which position he doubted they approved, because, contrary to the orders of the universities, they appeared before his majesty in Turky gownes, not in 10 their scholastical habits, sorting to their degrees.

His majesty perceiving my lord of London to speak ·in some passion, said, that there was in it something which he might excuse, something that he did mislike: excuse his passion he might, thinking he had just cause to be so moved 15 both in respect that they did thus traduce the present well setled church government; and also did proceed in so indirect a course, contrary to their own pretence, and the intent of that meeting also: yet he misliked his sudden interruption of D. Reinolds whom he should have suffered to have taken his 20 course and liberty, concluding, that there is no order, nor can be any effectual issue of disputation, if each party might not be suffered, without chopping, to speak at large what he would. And therefore willed that either the doctors should proceed, or that the bishop would frame his answer to these 25 motions already made: although, saith his majesty, some of them are very needlesse. It was thought fitter to answer, lest the number of objections increasing, the answers would prove confused.

Upon the first motion, concerning falling from grace; the 30 bishop of London took occasion to signifie to his majesty, how very many in these daies, neglecting holinesse of life, presumed too much of persisting of grace, laying all their religion upon predestination, If I shall be saved, I shall be . saved; which he termed a desperate doctrine, shewing it to 35 be contrary to good divinity, and the true doctrine of predestination, wherein we should reason rather *ascendendo* than *descendendo*, thus; "I live in obedience to God, in love with my neighbour, I follow my vocation, &c., therefore I trust

that God hath elected me, and predestinated me to salvation:" not thus, which is the usual course of argument,
"God hath predestinated and chosen me to life, therefore
though I sin never so grievously, yet I shall not be damned :
5 for whom he once loveth, he loveth to the end." Whereupon he shewed his majesty out of the next article, what
was the doctrine of the church of England, touching predestination, in the very last paragraph, *scil.* "We must receive
God's promises, in such wise, as they be generally set forth to
10 us in holy Scripture; and in our doings, that will of God
is to be followed which we have expressly declared unto us
in the word of God :" which part of the article his majesty
very well approved, and after he had, after his manner, very
singularly discoursed on that place of Paul, "Work out your
15 salvation with fear and trembling," he left it to be considered
whether any thing were mete to be added, for the clearing of
the doctor his doubt by putting in the word *often*, or the
like, as thus, "We may often depart from grace;" but in the
mean time, wished that the doctrine of predestination might
20 be very tenderly handled, and with great discretion, lest on
the one side, God's omnipotency might be called in question,
by impeaching the doctrine of his eternal predestination, or
on the other, a desperate presumption might be arreared, by
inferring the necessary certainty of standing and persisting in
25 grace.

To the second it was answered, that it was a vain objection, because, by the doctrine and practice of the church of
England, none but a licenced minister might preach, nor
either publikely or privately administer the eucharist, or
30 the Lord's supper. And as for private baptism, his majesty
answered, that he had taken order for that with the bishops
already.

In the third point (which was about confirmation) was
observed either curiosity or malice, because the article which
35 was there presently read, in those words, "These five commonly called sacraments, that is to say, confirmation, penance, orders, &c. are not to be accounted for sacraments of
the gospel, being such as have grown partly of the corrupt
following the apostles," &c., insinuateth that the making of

confirmation to be a sacrament is a corrupt imitation; but
the Communion Book, aiming at the right use and proper
course thereof, makes it to be according to the apostles
example; which his majesty observing, and reading both the
places, concluded the objection to be a meer cavil. And this 5
was for the pretended contradiction.

Now for the ground thereof the bishop of London added,
that it was not so much founded upon the places in the Acts of
the Apostles, which some of the fathers had often shewed,
but upon Heb. vi. 2, where it is made, as the first day he had 10
said, a part of the apostles catechism; which was the opinion,
besides the judgment of the holy fathers, of master Calvin
and D. Fulke, the one upon Heb. vi. 2. as upon Saturday he
had declared, the other upon Acts viii. vers. 27, where with
St. Augustine, he saith that we do not in any wise mislike 15
that antient ceremonie (of imposition of hands, for strength-
ning and confirming such as had been baptized,) but use it
in our selves, being nothing else, but as St. Austen affirmeth,
prayer over a man to be strengthened and confirmed by the
Holy Ghost; or to receive increase of the gifts of the Holy 20
Ghost, as Saint Ambrose saith; and a little after alludeth
unto Heb. vi. 2, &c. Neither need there any great proof of
this (saith my lord). For confirmation to be unlawful, it was
not their opinion who objected this, as he supposed; this was
it that vexed them, that they had not the use thereof in their 25
own hands, every pastor in his parish to confirm, for then it
would be accounted an apostolical institution; and willed
doctor Reinolds to speak herein what he thought : who seemed
to yield thereunto, replying that some diocesse of a bishop
having therein six hundred parish churches (which number 30
caused the bishop of London to think himself personally
touched, because in his diocesse there are 609, or there-
abouts) it was a thing very inconvenient to commit confirmation unto the bishop alone, supposing it impossible that he
could take due examination of them all which came to be 35
confirmed. To the fact my lord of London answered, for his
majesties information, that the bishops in their visitations
give out notice to them who are desirous either to be themselves or to have their children confirmed, of the place where

they will be; and appoint either their chaplaines or some
other ministers to examine them which are to be confirmed,
and lightly confirm none, but either by the testimony or report
of the parsons or curates where the children are bred and
5 brought up. To the opinion he replied, that none of all the
fathers ever admited any to confirm but bishops alone; yea
even Saint Jerome himself, though otherwise no friend to
bishops, by reason of a quarrel between the bishop of Jerusalem and him, yet confesseth that the execution thereof was
10 restrained to bishops only, " Ad honorem potius sacerdotii,
quàm ad legis necessitatem." Whereof, namely of this prerogative of bishops, he giveth this reason, " Ecclesiæ salus in
summi sacerdotis dignitate pendit ; cui si non exors quædam
& ab omnibus eminens detur potestas, tot in ecclesiis effice-
15 rentur scismata, quot sacerdotes." My lord bishop of
Winchester chalenged doctor Reynolds, willing him, of his
learning, to shew where ever he had read, that confirmation
was at all used in ancient times by any other but bishops ;
and added withall, that it was used partly to examine chil-
20 dren, and after examination, by imposition of hands (which
was a ceremonie of blessing among the Jews) to blesse them
and pray over them : and partly to try whether they had
been baptized in the right form or no. For in former ages
baptism was administred in divers sorts : some gave it " In
25 nomine Patris & Filii," &c. ; others, " In nomine Patris ma-
joris, & Filii minoris," as the Arrians did ; some, " In nomine
Patris per Filium, in Spiritu Sancto ;" others, not in the name
of the Trinity, but in the death of Christ, &c. Whereupon
catholick bishops were constrained to examin them who
30 were baptized " in remotis," *far from them*, how they were
taught to believe concerning baptism ; if it were right, to
confirm them ; if amisse, to instruct them.

His majesty concluded this point, first by taxing Saint
Jerome for his assertion, that a bishop was not *divinæ ordi-*
35 *nationis* (the bishop of London thereupon inserting, that
unlesse he could prove his ordination lawful out of the Scriptures, he would not be a bishop 4 hours). Which opinion
his majesty much distasted, approving their calling and use
in the church, and closed it up with this short aphorism,

"No bishop, no king."   Secondly, for confirmation, his highnesse thought, that it sorted neither with the authority nor
decency of the same, that every ordiuary pastor should do it:
and therefore said, that for his part, he meant not to take
that from the bishops, which they had so long retained and 5
injoyed; seeing, as it pleased him to adde, as great reason
that none should confirm without the bishop's licence, as none
should preach without his licence; and so referring, as the
day before, the word *examination* to be added to the rubrick
in the title of confirmation in the Communion Book, if it 10
were thought good so to do, he willed doctor Reinolds to
proceed.

 ̇ ₍Who, after that he had deprecated the imputation of
schism, with a protestation that he meant not to gall any
man, goeth on to the 37. article, wherein he said these words, 15
"The bishop of Rome hath no authority in this land," not
to be sufficient, unlesse it were added, "nor ought to have."
Whereat his majesty heartily laughed, and so did the lords:
the king adding an answer, which the rhetoricians call ἐρώ-
τημα ἐλέγχικον; What speak you of the pope's authority 20
here? "Habemus jure quod habemus;" and therefore, in
as much as it is said, he hath not, it is plain enough, that he
ought not to have.

   This, and some other motions, seeming to the king and
lords very frivolous, occasion was taken, in some by-talk, to 25
remember a certain description, which master Butler of
Cambridge made of a puritan, viz. A puritan is a protestant
frayed out of his wits.   But my lord of London there
seriously put his majesty in mind of the speeches, which the
French embassadour master Rogne gave out concerning our 30
church of England, both at Canterbury after his arrival, and
after at the court upon the view of our solemn service and
ceremonies; namely, that if the reformed churches in France
had kept the same orders among them which we have, he
was assured that there would have been many thousands of 35
protestants more there than now there are; and yet our
men stumble and strain at these petty quillets, thereby to
disturb and disgrace the whole church.

   V. After this, the doctor moved that this proposition,

" The intention of the minister is not of the essence of the sacrament," might be added unto the book of Articles, the rather, because that some in England had preached it to be essential. And here again he remembred the nine orthodoxal
5 assertions concluded at Lambeth. His majesty utterly dis-
— liked that first part of the motion for two reasons; first, think-ing it unfit to thrust into the book every position negative, which would both make the book swell into a volume as big as the Bible, and also confound the reader: bringing for
10 example the course of one master Craig in the like case in Scotland, who with his, I renounce and abhor, his detestations and abrenunciations, did so amaze the simple people, that they, not able to conceive all those things, utterly gave over all, falling back to popery, or remaining still in their former
15 ignorance. Yea, if I, said his majesty, should have been bound to his form, the confession of my faith must have been in my table-book, not in my head. But because you speak of intention, saith his highnesse, I will apply it thus: If you come hither with a good intention, to be informed, and satis-
20 fied where you shall find just cause, the whole work will sort to the better effect; but if your intention be to go as you came (whatsoever shall be said), it will prove that the in-tention is very material, and essential to the end of this pre-sent action. To the other part for the nine assertions, his
25 majesty could not suddenly answer, because he understood not what the doctor meant by those assertions or propositions at Lambeth; but when it was informed his majesty, that by reason of some controversies, arising in Cambridge, about certain points of divinity, my lords grace assembled some
30 divines of especial note, to set down their opinions, which they drew into nine assertions, and so sent them to the uni-versity, for the appeasing of those quarrels; then his majesty answered; first, that when such questions arise among scholars, the quietest proceeding were, to determine them in
35 the universities, and not to stuff the book with all con-clusions theological. Secondly, the better course would be to punish the broachers of false doctrine, as occasion should be offered: for were the articles never so many and sound, who can prevent the contrary opinions of men till they be heard?

Upon this, the dean of Paule's, kneeling down, humbly desired leave to speak, signifying unto his majesty, that this matter somewhat more nearly concerned him, by reason of a controversie between him and some other in Cambridge, upon a proposition which he had deliverd there; namely, that who- 5 soever (although before justified) did commit any grievous sin, as adultery, murder, treason, or the like, did become, *ipso facto*, subject to God's wrath, and guilty of damnation, or were in state of damnation, (*quoad præsentem statum,*) untill they repented; adding hereunto, that those which were called or jus- 10 tified according to the purpose of God's election, howsoever they might, and did sometimes fall into grievous sins, and thereby into the present state of wrath and damnation, yet did never fall, either totally from all the graces of God, to be utterly destitute of all the parts and seed thereof, nor finally from 15 justification, but were in time renewed by God's Spirit unto a lively faith and repentance; and so justified from those sins, and the wrath, curse and guilt annexed thereunto, whereinto they are fallen, and wherein they lay, so long as they were without true repentance for the same. Against which doc- 20 trine, he said, that some had opposed, teaching, that all such persons as were once truely justified, though after they fell into never so grievous sins, yet remained still just, or in the state of justification, before they actually repented of those sins; yea, and though they never repented of them, through 25 forgetfulnesse or sudden death, yet they should be justified and saved without repentance. In utter dislike of this doctrine, his majesty entred into a longer speech of predestination, and reprobation, than before, and of the necessary conjoyning repentance and holinesse of life with true faith: con- 30 cluding, that it was hypocrisie, and not true justifying faith, which was severed from them: for although predestination and election depend not upon any qualities, actions, or works of man, which be mutable, but upon God his eternal and immutable decree and purpose; yet such is the necessity of 35 repentance, after known sins committed, as that, without it, there could not be either reconciliation with God or remission of those sins.

Next to this, doctor Reinolds complained, that the cate-

chism in the Common Prayer Book was too brief; for which
one by master Nowel, late dean of Paul's, was added, and
that too long for young novices to learn by heart : requested
therefore, that one uniform catechism might be made, which,
5 and none other, might be generally received; it was demanded of him, whether, if to the short catechism in the
Communion Book something were added for the doctrine of
the sacrament, it would not serve? His majesty thought the
doctor's request very reasonable : but yet so, that he would
10 have a catechism in the fewest and plainest affirmative terms
that may be: taxing withal the number of ignorant catechisms set out in Scotland, by every one that was the son of
a good man; insomuch, as that which was catechism doctrine in one congregation, was in another scarcely accepted as
15 sound and orthodox; wished, therefore, one to be made and
agreed upon, adding this excellent gnomical and canon-like
conclusion, that in reforming of a church he would have two
rules observed : first, that old, curious, deep and intricate
questions might be avoided in the fundamental instruction of
20 a people : secondly, that there should not be any such departure from the papists in all things, as that because we
in some points agree with them, therefore we should be accounted to be in error.

To the former, doctor Reinolds did adde the prophanation
25 of the Sabbath day, and contempt of his majesties proclamation, made for the reforming of that abuse; of which he
earnestly desired a straighter course for reformation thereof,
and unto this he found a general and unanimous assent.

VII. After that, he moved his majesty that there might be
30 a new translation of the Bible, because those which were
allowed in the reign of king Henry the Eight and Edward
the Sixt were corrupt, and not answerable to the truth of
the original. For example, first, Galatians iv. 25. the Greek
word συστοιχεῖ is not well translated as now it is, *bordereth*
35 neither expressing the force of the word, nor the apostles
sence, nor the situation of the place.

Secondly, psalm cv. 28, " They were not obedient;" the
original being, " They were not disobedient."

Thirdly, psalm cvi. 30, "Then stood up Phinees and prayed,"

the Hebrew hath, "executed judgment." To which motion
there was at the present no gainsaying, the objections being
trivial, and old, and already in print, often answered; only
my lord of London well added, that if every man's humour
should be followed, there would be no end of translating. 5
Whereupon his highnesse wished that some special paines
should be taken in that behalf for one uniform translation,
(professing that he could never yet see a Bible well translated in English, but the worst of all his majesty thought the
Geneva to be,) and this to be done by the best learned in 10
both the universities; after them to be reviewed by the
bishops, and the chief learned of the church; from them to
be presented to the privy councel; and lastly, to be ratified
by his royal authority. And so this whole church to be
bound unto it, and none other. Marry, withall, he gave this 15
caveat, (upon a word cast out by my lord of London,) that no
marginal notes should be added, having found in them which
are annexed to the Geneva translation (which he saw in a
Bible given him by an English lady) some notes very partial,
untrue, seditious, and savouring too much of dangerous and 20
traiterous conceits. As for example, the first chapter of
Exodus and the nineteenth verse, where the marginal note
alloweth disobedience unto kings. And 2 Chron. xv. 16, the
note taxeth Asa for deposing his mother only, and not killing
her: and so concludeth this point as all the rest, with a grave 25
and judicious advice. First, that errors in matters of faith
might be rectified and amended. Secondly, that matters indifferent might rather be interpreted, and a glosse added,
alleging from Bartolus de regno, that, as better a king with
some weaknesse, than still a change; so rather a church with 30
some faults, than an innovation. And surely, saith his
majesty, if these be the greatest matters you be grieved with,
I need not have been troubled with such importunities and
complaints as have been made unto me; some other more
private course might have been taken for your satisfaction, 35
and withall, looking upon the lords, he shook his head,
smiling.

 VIII. The last point (noted by doctor Reinolds) in this first
head, for doctrine, was, that unlawful and seditious books

might be suppressed, at least restrained, and imparted to a
few: for by the liberty of publishing such books so commonly,
many young scholars and unsetled minds in both universities,
and through the whole realm, were corrupted and perverted;
5 naming for one instance that book entitled, " De jure Magi-
stratus in Subditos," published of late by Ficlerus a papist,
and applied against the queen's majesty that last was, for the
pope. The bishop of London supposing, as it seemed, himself
to be principally aimed at, answered, first, to the general,
10 that there was no such licentious divulging of those books as
he imagined or complained of, and that none, except it were
such as doctor Reinolds, (who were supposed would confute
them,) had liberty by authority to buy them: again, such
books came into the realm by many secret conveiances, so
15 that there could not be a perfect notice had of their impor-
tation: secondly, to the particular instance of Ficlerus, he
said, that the author "De jure," &c. was a great disciplina-
rian; whereby it did appear what advantage that sort gave
unto the papists, who *mutatis personis* could apply their own
20 arguments against princes of the religion: but for his own
part he said, he detested both the author and the applier
alike. My lord Cicill here taxing also the unlimited liberty
of the dispersing and divulging these popish and seditious
pamphlets, both in Paul's Church-yard and the universities,
25 instanced one lately set forth, and published, namely, " Spe-
culum Tragicum," which both his majesty and the lord H.
Howard, now earl of Northampton, termed a dangerous book
both for matter and intention: and the lord chancellor, also
dividing all such books into Latine and English, concluded,
30 that these last, dispersed, did most harm: yet the lord se-
cretarie affirmed, that my lord of London had done therein
what might be, for the suppressing of them; and that he
knew no man else had done any thing in that kind but he.
At length, it pleased his excellent majesty, to tell doctor
35 Reinolds that he was a better college-man than a states man:
for if his meaning were, to tax the bishop of London for suffering those books, between the secular priests and Jesuites,
lately published, so freely to passe abroad, his majesty
would have him and his associates to know, and willed them

also to acquaint their adherents and friends abroad therewith, that the said bishop was much injured and slandered in
that behalf, who did nothing therein but by warrant from the
lords of the councel, whereby, both a schism between them
was nourished, and also his majesties own cause and title 5
handled : the lord Cicil affirming thereunto, that therefore
they were tolerated, because, in them, was the title of Spain
confuted.

The lord treasurer added, that doctor Reinolds might
have observed another use of those bookes, viz. that now by 10
the testimony of those priests themselves, her late majesty
and the state were cleared of that imputation, of putting
papists to death for their consciences only, and for their
religion, seeing, in those books, they themselves confess that
they were executed for treason. Doctor Reinolds excused 15
himself, expounding his complaint, not meant of such books
as had been printed in England, but such as came from
beyond the seas, as commentaries both in philosophy and
divinity. And these were the parts of the first head, concerning purity of doctrine.   20

TOUCHING PASTORS, RESIDENT, LEARNED.

To the second general point concerning the planting of
ministers learned in every parish : it pleased his majesty to
answer, that he had consulted with his bishops about that,
whom he found willing and ready to second him in it : inveigh- 25
ing herein against the negligence and carelesnesse which he
heard of many in this land, but as *subita evacuatio* was *peri-
culosa*, so *subita mutatio*. Therefore this matter was not for
a present resolution, because to appoint to every parish a sufficient minister were impossible, the universities would not 30
afford them. Again, he had found already, that he had more
learned men in this realm than he had sufficient maintenance
for ; so that maintenance must first be provided, and then
the other to be required : in the mean time, ignorant ministers, if young, to be removed, if there were no hope of their 35
amendment ; if old, their death must be expected, that the
next course may be better supplied : and so concluded this

point, with a most religious and zealous protestation, of doing
something dayly in this case, because Jerusalem could not be
built up in a day. The bishop of Winchester made known
to the king that this insufficiency of the clergy, be it as it is,
5 comes not by the bishops' defaults, but partly by lay patrons,
who present very mean men to their cures; whereof, in himself, he shewed an instance, how that since his being bishop
of Winchester very few masters of arts were presented to
good benefices; partly by the law of the land, which ad-
10 mitteth of a very mean tolerable sufficiency in any clerk, so
that if the bishop should not admit them then presently a
quare impedit is sent out against him.

Here my lord of London, kneeling, humbly desired his majesty, because he saw, as he said, it was a time of moving peti-
15 tions, that he might have leave to make two or three.

First, that there might be amongst us a praying ministery
another while; for whereas there are in the ministery
many excellent duties to be performed, as the absolving of
the penitent, praying for and blessing of the people, adminis-
20 tring of the sacraments, and the like; it is come to that
passe now, that some sort of men thought it the only duty
required of a minister to spend the time in speaking out of a
pulpit; sometimes, God wot, very undiscreetly and unlearn-
edly; and this, with so great injury and prejudice to the
25 celebration of divine service, that some ministers would be
content to walk in the church-yard till sermon time, rather
than to be present at publick prayer. He confessed, that in
a church new to be planted preaching was most necessary;
but among us, now long established in the faith, he thought
30 it not the only necessary duty to be performed, and the other
to be so profanely neglected and contemned. Which motion
his majesty liked exceeding well, very acutely taxing the
hypocrisie of our times, which placeth all religion in the ear,
through which there is an easy passage; but prayer, which
35 expresseth the hearts affection, and is the true devotion of
the mind, as a matter putting us to overmuch trouble,
(wherein there concurre, if prayer be as it ought, an un-
partial consideration for our own estates, a due examination
to whom we pray, an humble confession of our sins, with an

hearty sorrow for them, and repentance not severed from faith,) is accounted and used as the least part of religion.

The second was, that till such time as learned and sufficient men might be planted in every congregation, that godly homilies might be read, and the number of them increased, 5 and that the opponents would labour to bring them into credit again, as formerly they brought them into contempt. Every man, saith he, that can pronounce well cannot indite well.

The king's majesty approved this motion, especially where 10 the living is not sufficient for maintenance of a learned preacher; as also in places where plenty of sermons are, as in the city and great townes. In the countrey villages where preachers are not near together, he could wish preaching; but where there are a multitude of sermons, there he 15 would have homilies to be read divers times: and therein he asked the assent of the plaintiffs, and they confesse it. A preaching ministery, saith his majesty, was best, but where it might not be had, godly prayers and exhortations did much good. That that may be done, let it, and let the rest 20 that cannot, be tolerated. Somewhat was here spoken by the lord chancellor of livings rather wanting learned men than learned men livings; many in the universities pining, masters, batchelors, and upwards: wishing, therefore, that some might have single coats, before other had dublets: and 25 here his lordship shewed the course that he had ever taken in bestowing the king's benefices; my lord of London, commending his honourable care that way, withall excepted that a dublet was necessary in cold weather: the lord chancellor replied, that he did it not for dislike of the liberty of our 30 church, in granting one man two benefices, but out of his own private purpose and practice, grounded upon the foresaid reason.

The last motion by my lord of London was, that pulpits might not be made pasquils, wherein every humorous or dis- 35 contented fellow might traduce his superiors. Which the king very graciously accepted, exceedingly reproving that as a lewd custome; threatning, that if he should but hear of such a one in a pulpit he would make him an example: con-

cluding with a sage admonition to the opponents, that every
man should solicite and draw his friends to make peace, and
if any thing were amisse in the church officers, not to make
the pulpit the place of personal reproof, but to let his majesty
5 hear of it : yet by degrees.

First, let complaint be to the ordinary of the place, from
him to go to the archbishop ; from him to the lords of his
majesties council, and from them, if in all these places no
remedy is found, to his own self.   Which caveat his majesty
10 put in, for that the bishop of London had told him, that if
he left himself open to admit of all complaints, neither his
majesty should ever be quiet, nor his under-officers regarded :
seeing that now already no fault can be censured, but presently the delinquent threatneth a complaint to the king : and
15 for an instance, he added, how a printer, whom he had taken
faulty, very lately answered him in that very kind.

Doctor Rein. cometh now to subscription, (which concerneth the fourth general head, as he first propounded it, namely,
the Communion Book,) taking occasion to leap into it here,
20 as making the urging of it to be a great impeachment to a
learned ministery, and therefore intreated it might not be
exacted as heretofore, for which many good men were kept
out, other removed, and many disquieted.   To subscribe
according to the statutes of the realm, namely, to the Articles
25 of religion, and the king's supremacy, they were not unwilling.   The reason of their backwardnesse to subscribe
otherwise was, first the books apocryphal, which the Common
Prayer Book injoined to be read in the church ; albeit there
are, in some of those chapters appointed, manifest errors,
30 directly repugnant to the scriptures : the particular instance
which he then inferred was, Ecclus. xlviii. 10. where he
charged the author of that book to have held the same
opinion with the Jewes at this day, namely, that Elias, in person, was to come before Christ, and therefore as yet Christ,
35 by that reason, not come in the flesh ; and so, consequently,
it implied a denial of the chief article of our redemption.   His
reason of thus charging the author was, because that Ecclus.
used the very word of *Elias in person*, which the prophet
Malachy, cap. iv. doth apply to an Elias in resemblance,

o

which both an angel, Luke xix. and our Saviour Christ, Matt. xi. did interpret to be John Baptist. The answer was, as the objection, twofold. First, general, for apocrypha books; the bishop of London shewing, first, for the antiquity of them, that the most of the objections made against those 5 books were the old cavils of the Jewes, renewed by Saint Jerome in his time, who was the first that gave them the name of apocrypha, which opinion, upon Ruffinus his challenge, he, after a sort, disclaimed, the rather, because a general offence was taken at his speeches in that kind, first, 10 for the continuance of them in the church out of Kimedoncius and Chemnitius, two modern writers.

The bishop of Winton remembred the distinction of Saint Jerome, "Canonici sunt ad informandos mores, non ad confirmandam fidem." which distinction, he said, must be held 15 for the justifying of sundry councels. His majesty in the end said, he would take an even order between both, affirming, that he would not wish all canonical books to be read in the church, unlesse there were one to interpret, nor any apocrypha at all, wherein there was any error, but for 20 the other, which were clear, and correspondent to the scriptures, he would have them read; for else, saith his majesty, why were they printed? And therein shewed the use of the books of Machabees, very good to make up the story of the persecution of the Jewes; but not to teach a man either to 25 sacrifize for the dead, or to kill himself.

And here his highnesse arose from his chair, and withdrew himself into his inner chamber a little space: in the mean time a great questioning was amongst the lords about that place of Ecclus., with which, as if it had been their rest and 30 upshot, they began a fresh at his majestie's return; who, seeing them so to urge it and stand upon it, calling for a Bible, first shewed the author of that book, who he was, then the cause why he wrote that book, next analyzed the chapter it self, shewing the precedents and consequents 35 thereof; lastly, so exactly and divine like, unfolded the summe of that place, arguing, and demonstrating, that whatsoever Ben Sirach had said there of Elias, Elias had in his own person, while he lived, performed and accomplished, so that the *susurrus*, at the first mention, was not so great, as the astonishment was now at the king his sudden and sound, and indeed so admirable an interpretation; concluding, first, with a serious check to doctor Reinolds, that it was not good 5 to impose upon a man that was dead a sense never meant by him: secondly, with a pleasant apostrophe to the lords; What, trow ye, make these men so angry with Ecclesiasticus? By my soul, I think he was a bishop, or else they would never use him so.   But for the general, it was appointed by his 10 majesty, that doctor Rein. should note those chapters in the apocrypha books where those offensive places were, and should bring them unto the lord archbishop of Canterb. against Wednesday next, and so he was willing to go on.

The next scruple against subscription was, that old "Crambe 15 bis posita," that in the Common Prayer Book it is twice set down, "Jesus said to his disciples;" when as by the original text it is plain that he spake to the Pharisees.   To which it was answered, that for ought that could appear by the places, he might speak as well to his disciples, they being 20 present, as to the Pharisees.   But his majesty, keeping an even hand, willed that the word *disciples* should be omitted, and the words *Jesus said* to be printed in a different letter, that might appear not to be a part of the text.

The third objection against subscription were interroga- 25 tories in baptism propounded to infants, which being a profound point was put upon master Knewstubs to pursue: who in a long and perplexed speech said something out of Austen, that *baptizare* was *credere*, but what it was his majesty plainly confessed, *Ego non intelligo*, and asked the 30 lords what they thought he meant; it seemed that one present conceived him, for he standing at his back, bad him urge the punct, urge that punct, that is a good point.   My lord of Winton, aiming at his meaning, shewed him the use thereof out of Saint Austen and added the Father's reason for it, 35 " Qui peccavit in altero, credat in altero ;" which was seconded by his majesty, (whom it pleased, for the rest of the matters which followed, himself alone to answer, and justly might he appropriate it to himself, for none present were able with

quicker conceit to understand, with a more singular dexterity
to refute, with a more judicious resolution to determine, than
his majesty : herein being more admirable, that these points,
wherein some thought him prejudicial to the contrary, all of
us supposed him to have been but a stranger to them, he 5
could so intelligently apprehend, and so readily argue about
them,) it was, I say, seconded by his majesty ; first,

By reason that the question should be propounded to the
party whom it principally concerned.

Secondly, by example of himself, to whom interrogatories 10
were propounded when he was crowned in his infancy king
of Scotland.

And here his majesty (as hereafter at the end of every
objection he did) asked them whether they had any more
to say.   15

Master Knewstubs took exceptions to the cross in baptism,
being in number two.

First, the offence of weak brethren, grounded upon the
words of Saint Paul, Rom. xiv. and 1 Cor. viii., viz. "the
consciences of the weak not to be offended :" which places his 20
excellent majesty answered most accutely, beginning with
that general rule of the Fathers : " Distingue tempora, et
concordabunt scripturæ." Shewing here the difference of
those times and ours, then a church not fully planted nor
setled, but ours long established and flourishing ; then 25
Christians newly called from paganism, and not throughly
grounded, which is not the case of this church, seeing that
heathenish doctrine, for many years, hath been hence abandoned.

Secondly, with a question unanswerable, asking them how 30
long they would be weak? whether 45 yeares were not sufficient for them to grow strong? Thirdly, who they were pretended this weaknesse! for we, saith the king, require not
now subscription of laiks and idiots, but preachers and ministers, who are not still, I trow, to be fed with milk, but are 35
enabled to feed others.

Fourthly, that it was to be doubted some of them were
strong enough, if not head-strong, and howsoever they in this

case pretended weakness, yet some, in whose behalf they now spake, thought themselves able to teach him and all the bishops of the land.

His objection against the cross consisted of three interro-5 gatories; first, whether the church had power to institute an external significant sign? to which was replied; first, that he mistook the use of the crosse with us, which was not used in baptism any otherwise than only as ceremony.

Secondly, by their own example, who make imposition 10 of hands in their ordination of pastors to be a sign significant.

Thirdly, in prayer, saith the bishop of Winton, the kneeling on the ground, the lifting up of our hands, the knocking of our breasts, are ceremonies significant; the first, of our 15 humility coming before the mighty God; the second, of our confidence and hope; the other, of our sorrow and detestation of our sins; and these are, and may lawfully be used. Lastly, M. Dean of the chapel remembred the practise of the Jews, who unto the institution of the Passeover, prescribed 20 unto them by Moses, had, as the rabbins witnesse, added both signes and words, eating sowre herbs, and drinking wine, with these words to both, "Take and eat these in remembrance," &c.; "Drink this in remembrance," &c. Upon which addition and tradition of theirs, our Saviour instituted 25 the sacrament of his last supper, in celebrating it with the same words and after the same manner; thereby approving that fact of theirs in particular, and generally, that a church may institute and retain a signe significant: which satisfied his majesty exceeding well.

30 And here the king desired to have himself made acquainted about the antiquity of the use of the crosse, which doctor Reynolds confessed to have been ever since the apostles' times; but this was the difficulty, to prove it of that ancient use in baptism. For that at their going abroad, or entering 35 into the church, or at their prayers and benedictions, it was used by the ancients, desired no great proof: but whether in baptism antiquity approved it, was the doubt cast in by M. Deane of Sarum, whom his majesty singled out, with a special encomion, that he was a man well travelled in the

ancients: which doubt was answered, *obsignatis tabulis*, by
the dean of Westminster, (whom the king's majesty, upon
my lord of London's motion, willed to speak to that
point,) out of Tertullian, Cyprian, Origen, and others, that it
was used in *immortali lavacro:* which words being a little 5
descanted, it fell from one, I think it was my lord of
Winchester, *obiter*, to say, that in Constantine his time it
was used in baptism. What! quoth the king, and is it now
come to that passe, that we shall appeach Constantine of
popery and superstition? If then it were used, saith his 10
majesty, I see no reason but that still we may continue it.

Master Knewstubs his second question was, that put case
the church had such power to adde significant signes, whether
it might there adde them where Christ had already ordained
one: which he said was no lesse derogatory to Christ's 15
institution, as he thought, than if any potentate of this
land should presume to adde his seal to the great seal of
England. To which his majesty answered, that the case
was not alike; for that no sign or thing was added to the
sacrament; which was fully and perfectly finished before any 20
mention of the crosse is made: for confirmation whereof he
willed the place to be read.

Lastly, if the church had that power also, yet the greatest
scruple to their conscience was, how farre such an ordinance
of the church was to bind them, without impeaching their 25
Christian liberty? Whereat the king, as it seemed, was much
moved, and told him he would not argue that point with him,
but answer therein, as kings are wont to speak in parliament,
Le roy s'avisera, adding withall, that it smelled very rankly
of anabaptism: comparing it unto the usage of a beardlesse 30
boy, (one master John Black,) who the last conference his
majesty had with the ministers in Scotland, (in December,
1602,) told him, that he would hold conformity with his
majesties ordinances for matters of doctrine, but for matters
of ceremonie, they were to be left in Christian liberty to every 35
man, as he received more and more light from the illumination
of God's Spirit; even till they go mad, quoth the king, with
their own light: but I will none of that; I will have one
doctrine and one discipline, one religion in substance and in

ceremony : and therefore I charge you never to speak more to that point, (how far you are bound to obey,) when the church hath ordained it.   And so asked them again if they had any thing else to say.

5   Dr. Reynolds objected the example of the brasen serpent, demolished and stampt to powder by Ezechias, because the people abused it to idolatry, wishing that in like sort the cross should be abandoned, because, in the time of popery, it had been superstitiously abused.   Whereunto the king's
10 majesty answered divers wayes.   First, quoth he, though I be sufficiently perswaded of the cross in baptism, and the commendable use thereof in the church so long ; yet, if there were nothing else to move me, this very argument were an inducement to me for the retaining of it, as it is now by
15 order established : for inasmuch as it was abused, so you say, to superstition, in time of popery, it doth plainly imply, that it was well used before popery.   I will tell you, I have lived among this sort of men, (speaking to the lords and bishops,) ever since I was tenne years old, but I may say of my self as
20 Christ did of himself, Though I lived amongst them, yet since I had ability to judge, I was never of them ; neither did any thing make me more to condemn and detest their courses, than that they did so peremptorily disallow of all things which at all had been used in popery.   For my part, I know
25 not how to answer the objection of the papists when they charge us with novelties, but truely to tell them, that their abuses are new, but the things which they abused we retain in their primitive use, and forsake only the novel corruption. By this argument we might renounce the Trinity, and all
30 that is holy, because it was abused in popery : (and speaking to Dr. Reynolds merily) they used to wear hose and shooes in popery, therefore you shall now go barefoot.

Secondly, quoth his majesty, what resemblance is there between the brasen serpent, a material visible thing, and the
35 sign of the crosse made in the aire ?

Thirdly, I am given to understand by the bishops, and I find it true, that the papists themselves did never ascribe any power or spirituall grace to the sign of the crosse in baptism.

Fourthly, you see, that the material crosses, which in time
of popery were made for men to fall down before them, as
they passed by them, to worship them, (as the idolatrous
Jews did the brasen serpent,) are demolished, as you desire.

The next thing which was objected, was the wearing of the 5
surplis, a kind of garment which the priests of Isis used to
wear. Surely, saith his majesty, untill of late, I did not
think that it had been borrowed from the heathen, because
it is commonly tearmed a ragge of popery, in scorn; but
were it so, yet neither did we border upon heathenish na- 10
tions, neither are any of them conversant with us, or com-
morant amongst us, who thereby might take just occasion
to be strengthened or confirmed in paganism, for then there
were just cause to suppresse the wearing of it: but seeing
it appeared out of antiquity, that in the celebration of divine 15
service a different habit appertained to the ministry, and
principally of white linnen, he saw no reason, but that in this
church, as it had been, for comelinesse and for order sake, it
might be still continued.   This being his constant and resolute opinion, that no church ought further to separate it self 20
from the church of Rome, either in doctrine or ceremony,
than she had departed from her self when she was in her flourishing and best estate, and from Christ her Lord and Head.
And here again he asked what more they had to say.

D. Reynolds took exceptions at those words in the Common 25
Prayer Book, of matrimony, *with my body I thee worship.*
His majesty looking upon the place; I was made believe
(saith he) that the phrase did import no lesse than divine
worship and adoration, but by the examination I find that
it is an usual English tearm, as a gentleman of worship, &c. 30
and the sense agreeable unto scriptures, *giving honour to the
wife,* &c.   But turning to doctor Reyn. (with smiling saith
his majesty), Many a man speakes of Robin Hood who never
shot in his bow: if you had a good wife your self, you would
think all the honour and worship you could do to her were 35
well bestowed.

The dean of Sarum mentioned the ring in marriage;
which doctor Reyn. approved, and the king confessed that
he was married withall; and added, that he thought they

would prove to be scarce well married who are not married with a ring.

He likewise spake of the churching of women by the name of purification; which being read out of the book, his majesty
5 very well allowed it, and pleasantly said, that women were loth enough of themselves to come to church, and therefore he would have this or any other occasion to draw them thither.

And this was the substance and summe of that third
10 general point. At which pawse, it growing toward night, his majesty asked again if they had any more to say: if they had, because it was late, they should have another day; but M. doctor Reynolds told him, that they had but one point more, which was the last general head; but it pleased his
15 majesty first to ask what they could say to the cornerd cap! ͪ They all approved it: Well then, said his majesty, turning himself to the bishops, you may now safely wear your caps: but I shall tell you, if you should walk in one street in Scotland with such a cap on your head, if I were not with you,
20 you should be stoned to death with your cap.

In the fourth general head touching discipline, doctor Reyn. first took exception to the committing of ecclesiastical censures unto lay-chancellors; his reason was, that in the statute made in king Henry his time, for their authority,
25 that was abrogated in queen Maries time, and not revived in the late queen's daies: and abridged by bishops themselves 1571; ordering that the said lay-chancellors should not excommunicate in matters of correction; and an. 1584, and 1589, not in matters of instance; but to be done onely by
30 them who had power of the keies: his majesty answered; "he had already conferred with his bishops about that point, and that such order should be taken therein as was convenient, willing him in the mean time to go to some other matter, if he had any." Then he desireth, that according to
35 certain provincial constitutions, they of the clergy might have meetings once every three weekes.

First, in rural deaneries, and therein to have prophecying, according as the reverend father archbishop Grindall and other bishops desired of her late majesty. 1 Cor. xiv.

Secondly, that such things as could not be resolved upon there might be referred to the archdeacon's visitation, and so

Thirdly, from thence to the episcopal synode, where the bishop with his presbytery should determine all such points as before could not be decided.   5

At which speech his majesty was somewhat stirred; yet, which is admirable in him, without passion, or shew thereof; thinking that they aymed at a Scotish presbytery, which, saith he, as well agreeth with a monarchy as God and the Devil. Then Jack and Tom and Will and Dick shall meet, 10 and at their pleasures censure me and my councel, and all our proceedings : then Will shall stand up and say, It must be thus; then Dick shall reply and say, Nay marry, but we will have it thus. And therefore, here I must once reiterate my former speech, Le roy s'avisera: stay, I pray you, for 15 one seven years, before you demand that of me : and if then you find me pursy and fat, and my wind pipes stuffed, I will perhaps hearken to you : for let that government be once up, I am sure I shall be kept in breath, then shall we all of us have work enough, both our hands full. But, doctor Reynolds, 20 till you find that I grow lazy, let that alone.

And here, because that doctor Reynolds had twice before obtruded the king's supremacie; first, in the article concerning the pope; secondly, in the point of subscription; his majesty at those times said nothing : but now growing to an 25 end, he said, I shall speak of one matter more : yet somewhat out of order : but it skilleth not. Doctor Reynolds, quoth the king, you have often spoken for my supremacy; and it is well; but know you any here, or any elsewhere, who like of the present government ecclesiastical, that find fault or dislike 30 my supremacy? Doctor Reynolds said, No. Why then, said his majesty, I will tell you a tale. After that the religion restored by king Edward the Sixth was soon overthrown, by the succession of queen Mary here in England, we in Scotland felt the effect of it. Whereupon master Knox writes to 35 the queen regent, (of whom without flattery I may say, that she was a vertuous and moderate lady,) telling her that she was supream head of the church, and charged her, as she would answer it before God's tribunal, to take care of Christ

his evangill, and of suppressing the popish prelates, who
withstood the same.　But how long, trow ye, did this continue? Even so long, till by her authority the popish bishops
were repressed, he himself and his adherents were brought in,
5 and well settled, and by these meanes made strong enough to
undertake the matters of reformation themselves.　Then loe,
they began to make small account of her supremacy, nor
would longer rest on her authority, but took the cause into
their own hand, and, according to that more light wherewith
10 they were illuminated, made a further reformation of religion.
How they used that poor lady my mother is not unknown,
and with grief I may remember it : who, because she had not
been otherwise instructed, did desire only a private chapell,
wherein to serve God after her manner, with some few se-
15 lected persons, but her supremacy was not sufficient to obtain it at their hands : and how they dealt with me in my
minority you all know ; it was not done secretly, and though
I would, I cannot conceal it.　I will apply it thus.　And then
putting his hand to his hat his majesty said; My lords the
20 bishops, I may thank you that these men do thus plead for
my supremacy ; they think they cannot make their party
good against you but by appealing unto it ; as if you, or some
that adhere unto you, were not well affected towards it.　But
if once you were out, and they in place, I know what would
25 become of my supremacy.　No bishop, no king, as before I
said.　Neither do I thus speak at randome without ground,
for I have observed since my comming into England, that
some preachers before me can be content to pray for James
king of England, Scotland, France, and Ireland, defender of
30 the faith, but as for supream governor in all causes and over
all persons, (as well ecclesiastical as civil,) they passe that over
with silence, and what cut they have been of I after learned.
After this, asking them if they had any more to object, and
doctor Reynolds answering no ; his majesty appointed the
35 next Wednesday for both parties to meet before him, and
rising from his chair, as he was going to his inner chamber,
If this be all, quoth he, that they have to say, I shall make
them conform themselves, or I will harry them out of this
land, or else do worse.

And this was the summe of the second dayes conference, which raised such an admiration in the lords, in respect of the king his singular readynesse and exact knowledge, that one of them said he was fully perswaded his majesty spake by the instinct of the Spirit of God.   My lord Cicil acknow- 5 ledged that very much we are bound to God, who had given us a king of an understanding heart.   My lord chancellor, passing out of the privy chamber, said unto the dean of Chester, standing by the door, I have often heard and read, that "Rex est mixta persona cum sacerdote," but I never 10 saw the truth thereof till this day.

Surely, whosoever heard his majesty might justly think that title did more properly fit him which Eunapius gave to that famous rhetorician, in saying that he was βιβλιοθήκη τὶς ἔμψυχος καὶ περιπατοῦν μουσεῖον, a living library and a walking 15 studie.

Finis secundæ diei.

THE

THIRD DAYES CONFERENCE.

Upon Wednesday, January 18, all the bishops aforenamed 20 attended at the court, and the deanes : who were all called into the privy chamber, and whoso else my lord archbishop appointed, (for such was his majesties pleasure) ; whereupon the knights and doctors of the arches, viz. sir Daniel Dunne, sir Thomas Crumpton, sir Richard Swale, sir John Bennet, 25 and doctor Drury entred in.   As soon as the king was set, the lord archbishop presented unto him a note of those points which his majesty had referred to their consideration upon the first day, and the alteration, or rather explanation of them in our liturgie.   30

1. Absolution or remission of sinnes, in the rubrick of abso-lution.

2. In private baptism, the lawfull minister present.

3. Examination, with confirmation of children.

4. *Jesus said to them,* twice to be put into the Dominical gospels, in stead of *Jesus said to his disciples.*

5   His majesty here taking the Common Prayer Book, and turning to private baptism, willed, that where the words were (in the rubric, the second paragraph), " They baptize not children," now it should be thus read, " They cause not children to be baptized ;" and again in the same paragraph, for
10 those words, " Then they minister it," it should be, " The curate, or lawful minister present, shall do it on this fashion." Concluding very gravely, that in this couference he aimed at three things principally ; first, the setting down of words fit and convenient ; secondly, contriving how things might be
15 best done, without appearance of alteration ; thirdly, practise, that each man may do his duty in his place.

After this, his majesty fell into discourse about the high commission, wherein he said, that he understood how the parties named therein were too many and too mean ; that
20 the matters they dealt in were base, and such as ordinaries at home in their courts might censure ; that the branches granted out to the bishops in their several diocesses were too frequent and large.   To which my lord's grace answered severally.   First, for the number, it was requisite it should
25 be great, for otherwise he must be forced, as oft-times now it fell out, to sit alone ; because that albeit all the lords of the privy counsell were in, all the bishops, many of the judges at law, and some of the clerks of the councel, yet very few, or none of them, sitting with him at ordinary times, some of
30 meaner place, as deanes, and doctors of divinity and law, must needs be put in ; whose attendance his grace might with more authority command and expect.   Secondly, for the matters handled therein, he said, that he oftentimes had complained thereof, but saw that it could not be remedied ;
35 because that the fault may be of that nature, as that the ordinary jurisdiction might censure it ; but eftsoones it falls out, that the party delinquent is too great, and so the ordinary dare not proceed against him ; or so mighty in his state,

or so willful in his contumacie, that he will not obey the summons or censure ; and so the ordinary is forced to crave help at the high commission.   To the third, his grace said, that it concerned not him to make answer thereunto, for such commissions have been granted against his will oftentimes, 5 and without his knowledge for the most part.   My lord chancellor therefore offered it to his majestie's wisdom to consider, if such commissions should not be granted to any bishop, but such as have the largest dioceses, which his majesty well approved ; and added withall, that those bishops who have in 10 their dioceses the most troublesome and refractory persons, either papists or puritans : but of this, as also of the other things found fault with herein, he willed those to consult to whom should be appointed the review of the commission. And here that point had ended, but that one of the lords (I 15 think verily rather upon misinformation than set purpose) pleased to say that the proceeding thereby was like unto the Spanish inquisition, wherein men were urged to subscribe more than law required ; that by the oath *ex officio* they were inforced to accuse themselves ; that they were examined 20 upon twenty or twenty-four articles upon the sudden, without deliberation, and for the most part against themselves : for the evidence thereof, a letter was shewed of an ancient honourable councellor, written to the lord archbishop, anno 1584, of two ministers of Cambridgeshire, then or there 25 abouts, examined upon many articles, and in the end deprived.   The lord archbishop answered, first, to the matter, that in the manner of proceeding and examining his lordship was deceived : for if any article did touch the party any way, either for life, liberty, or scandal, he might refuse to answer, 30 neither was he urged thereunto.   Secondly, to the letter, being in a cause twenty years since determined, he could not answer the particulars, but if his answer to that letter were found out, he doubted not, but as it did satisfie that honourable councellour when he lived, so it would also sufficiently 35 clear this complaint before his majesty.

My lord of London, for the matter of subscription, shewed his highnesse the three articles which the church-men of England are to approve by subscribing ; namely, the king's

supremacy, the Articles of religion, and the Book of Common
Prayer. All which it pleased his majesty himself to read,
(and after a litle glance given, that the mention of the oath
ex officio came in before his due time) he dilated, first, how
5 necessary subscription was in every well governed church ;
that it was to be urged for the keeping of peace : for as laws
to prevent killing did provide there should be no quarrel-
ling, so to prevent greater tumults in the church subscription was requisite.   Secondly, because the bishop is to
10 answer for every minister whom he admitteth into his diocesse, it were fittest for him to know the affection of the
party before his admittance, the best way to know him, and
to prevent future factions, was to urge his subscription at his
first entrance : for, " Turpius ejicitur, quàm non admittitur
15 hospes." Thirdly, as subscription was a good meanes to discern the affection of persons, whether quiet or turbulent,
withall it was the principal way to avoid confusion : concluding, that if any, after things were well ordered, would not
be quiet, and shew his obedience, the church were better
20 without him, he were worthy to be hanged. " Præstat ut
pereat unus, quam unitas."
   Touching the oath *ex officio*, the lord chancellor, and after
him the lord treasurer, spake both for the necessity and use
thereof, in diverse courts and cases.   But his excellent ma-
25 jesty preventing that old allegation, " Nemo cogitur detegere
suam turpitudinem," said, that the civil proceedings only
punished facts, but in courts ecclesiastical it was requisite
that fame and scandals should be looked unto.   That here
was necessary the oath *compurgatorie* and the oath *ex officio*
30 too ; and yet great moderation should be used, first, *in gravi-
oribus criminibus ;* and secondly, in such whereof there is a
publick fame; thirdly, in distinguishing of publick fame,
either caused by the inordinate demeanor of the offendor, or
raised by the undiscreet proceeding in trial of the fact : as
35 namely in Scotland, where the lying with a wench (though
done privately, and known, or scarce suspected, by two or
three persons before) was made openly known to the king,
to the queen, to the prince, to many hundreds in the court,

by bringing the parties to the stool of repentance, and yet
perhaps be but a suspition only. And here his majesty so
soundly described the oath *ex officio*; first, for the ground
thereof; secondly, the wisdom of the law therein; thirdly,
the manner of proceeding thereby, and the necessary and 5
profitable effect thereof, in such a compendious but absolute
order, that all the lords and the rest of the present auditors
stood amazed at it: the archbishop of Canterbury said that
undoubtedly his majesty spake by the special assistance of
God's Spirit. The bishop of London, upon his knee, pro- 10
tested that his heart melted within him (as so, he doubted
not, did the hearts of the whole company) with joy, and made
haste to acknowledge unto Almighty God the singular mercy
we have received at his hands in giving us such a king, as
since Christ his time the like he thought had not been; 15
whereunto the lords with one voice did yield a very affectionate acclamation. The civilians present confessed that
they could not in many houres warning, have so judicially,
plainly, and accurately, and in such a brief manner, have
described it.   20

After this, his majesty committed some weighty matters to
be consulted of by the lords and bishops; first, for excommunication, in causes of lesse moment the name or censure to
be altered; secondly, for the high commission, the quality of
the persons to be named, and the nature of the causes to be 25
handled therein; thirdly, for recusant communicants: for
there are three sorts, saith his majesty, of papists: some,
first, which come to sermons, but not to service and prayer;
secondly, some which come to both them, but not to the
communion; thirdly, a number which abstain from all. That 30
inquiry might be made of all those who were of the first,
second, or third rank, concluding therein, that the weak were
to be informed, the wilful to be punished.

Here my lord chancellor mentioned the writ *De excommu-
nicato capiendo*, which his honor said did most affright the 35
papists of all other punishments, because by reason of that
they were many wayes disabled in law: therefore he would
take order, if his majesty so pleased, to send that writ out

against them freely, without charge, and if they were not executed, his lordship would lay the under-sheriffes in prison; and to this the king assented.

The fourth thing to be consulted of was for the sending 5 and appointing of preachers into Ireland, whereof, saith his majesty, I am but half a king, being lord over their bodies, but their soules seduced by popery he much pittied, affirming, that where there is not true religion, there can be no continued obedience: nor for Ireland only, but for some part of Wales, 10 and the northern borders, so once called, though now no borders: the men to be sent not to be factious or scandalous, for weeds will be weeds, wheresoever they be, and are good for nothing but to be piked over the wall, therefore they should single out men of sincerity, of knowledge, of courage.

15 The last was, for provision of sufficient maintenance for the clergie; and withall, for the planting of a learned and painful minister in every parish, as time shall serve.

To every of these his majesty willed that several commissioners of his councel and bishops should be appointed by the 20 lord upon the dissolving the assembly present.

And thus having conferred of these points with the bishops, and referred other some of them, as you heard, to special committies, his majesty willed, that doctor Reyn. and his associates should be called in, to whom he presently 25 signified what was done, and caused the alterations, or explications, before named, to be read unto them. A litle disputing there was, about the words in marriage, " With my body I thee worship," and arguing no other thing to be meant by the word *worship*, than that which St. Paul willeth, 30 1 Cor. vii. 4. the man thereby acknowledging, that hereby he worshipeth his wife, in that he appropriateth his body unto her alone: nor any more than that which S. Peter counselleth, 1 Pet. iii. 7. that *the man should give honour to his wife, as the weaker vessel;* yet for their satisfaction should 35 be put in, " With my body I thee worship, and honour," if it were thought fit; and so his majesty shut up all with a most pithy exhortation to both sides for unity, perswading diligence in each man's place, without violence on the one party or disobedience on the other, and willed them to

P

deal with their friends abroad for that purpose: for his
majesty feared, and had some experience, that many of them
were ticklish and humorous; nor that only, but labourers
to pervert others to their fancies; he now saw that the
exceptions against the communion book were matters of 5
weaknesse; therefore if the persons reluctant be discreet,
they will be won betimes, and by good perswasions; if
undiscreet, better they were removed: for many by their
factious behaviour were driven to be papists. Now then of
their fruits he shall judge them, obedience and humility being 10
marks of honest and good men, and is expected of them;
and by their example and perswasion of all their sort abroad;
for if hereafter things being thus well ordered, they should be
unquiet, neither his majesty nor the state had any cause to
think well of them.   15

To which they gave all their unanimous assent, taking
exceptions against nothing that was said or done, but promised to perform all duty to the bishops, as their reverend
fathers, and to joyn with them against the common adversaries, and for the quiet of the church.   20

Only master Chatterton, of Emmanuel college, kneeling,
requested that the wearing of the surplis, and the use of the
crosse in baptism, might not be urged upon some honest,
godly, and painful ministers in some parts of Lancashire,
who feared, that if they should be forced to them, many 25
whom they had won to the gospel would slide back, and
revolt unto popery again; and particularly instanced the
vicar of Ratesdale, (he could not have light upon a worse,) for
not many years before, he was proved before my lord archbishop, as his grace there testified, and my lord chancellour, 30
by his unseemly and unreverent usage of the eucharist,
dealing the bread out of a basket, every man putting in
his hand and taking out a peece, to have made many loath
the communion, and wholly refuse to come to church.

His majesty answered, that it was not his purpose, and he 35
durst answer for the bishops, that it was not their intent
presently and out of hand to enforce those things, without
fatherly admonitions, conferences and perswasions premised;
but wished that it should be examined, if those men by their

pains and preaching had converted any from popery, and
were withall men of quiet disposition, honest of life, and
diligent in their calling; if so, letters should be written to the
bishop of Chester (of whom his majesty gave a very good
5 testimony) to that purpose; if not, but that they were of
a turbulent and oposite spirit, both they and others of that
unquiet humour should presently be enforced to a conformity:
and so for that point it was concluded, that my lord archbishop should write to the bishop of Chester his letters for
10 that matter.

My lord of London replieth, that if this were granted,
the copy of these letters (especially if his majesty had written,
as at first it was purposed) would flie over all England, and
then others, for their confines, would make the same request,
15 and so no fruit would follow of this conference, but things
would be worse than they were before.

Therefore he humbly desired his majesty, that a time
should be limited, within which compasse they should conform
themselves. To which his majesty readily assented, and
20 willed that the bishop of the diocesse should set them down
the time, and in the mean while conferre with them, and if
they would not yield, whatsoever they were, to remove them,
after their time expired.

No sooner was that motion ended, but down falls master
25 Knewstubs, and he requests the like favour of forbearance,
for some honest ministers in Suffolk, telling the king it would
make much against their credits in the country, to be now
forced to the surplis, and the crosse in baptism. My lord's
grace was answering; Nay, saith his majesty, let me alone
30 with him. Sir, saith the king, you shew your self an
uncharitable man; we have here taken paines, and in the
end have concluded of an unity, and uniformity, and you
forsooth must preferre the credits of a few private men
before the general peace of the church: this is just the
35 Scotish argument; for when any thing was there concluded
which disliked some humors, the only reason why they would
not obey was, it stood not with their credits to yield, having
so long time been of the contrary opinion. I will none
of that, saith the king, and therefore, either let them conform

themselves, and that shortly, or they shall hear of it. My lord Cicill put his majesty in mind of a word his highnesse had used the day before, namely, of ambling communions, saying, that the indecency thereof was very offensive, and had driven many from the church. And here master 5 Chatterton was told of sitting communions in Emanuel college; which he said was so, by reason of the seats so plac'd as they be, yet that they had some kneeling also.

Finally, they joyntly promised to be quiet and obedient, now they knew it to be the king's mind to have it so. His 10 majestie's gracious conclusion was so piercing, as that it fetched tears from some on both sides. My lord of London ended all, in the name of the whole company, with a thanksgiving unto God for his majesty, and a prayer for the health and prosperity of his highnesse, our gracious queen, the 15 young prince, and all their royal issue.

His majesty departed into the inner chamber: all the lords presently went to the council chamber, to appoint commissioners for the several matters before referred.

VI.

A letter from Patrick Galloway to the presbytery of Edinburgh, 20
concerning the conference.

BELOVED brethren, after my very hearty commendations, these presents are to shew you that I received two of your letters, one directed to his majesty, and another to myself for the using thereof; the same I read, closed, and three days 25 before the conference delivered it into his majesty's hands, and received it back again after some short speeches had upon a word of your letter, as "the gross corruptions of this church;" which then was exponed, and I assured that all corruptions dissonant from the word, or contrary thereto, 30

should be amended. The 12 of Januar was the day of meeting, at what time the bishops called upon by his majesty were gravely desired to advise upon all the corruptions of this church, in doctrine, ceremonies, and discipline;
5 and as they will answer to God in conscience, and to his majesty upon their obedience, that they should return the third day after, which was Saturday. They returned to his majesty, and there apposed as of before, it was answered all was well. And when his majesty in great fervency brought
10 instances to the contrary, they upon their knees with great earnestness craved that nothing should be altered, lest popish recusants, punished by penal statutes for their disobedience, and the puritans, punished by deprivation. from calling and living for nonconformity, should say they had just cause to
15 insult upon them, as men who had traveled to bind them to that, which by their own mouths now was confessed to be erroneous. Always after five hours' dispute had by his majesty against them, and his majesty's resolution for reformation intimated to them, they were dismissed that day.
20 Upon the 16 of Januar, being Monday, the brethren were called to his majesty, only five of them being present, and with them two bishops and six or eight deans. Here his majesty craved to know of them what they desired to be reformed; but it was very loosely and coldly answered. This
25 day ended after four hours talking, and Wednesday the 18 of Januar was appointed for the meeting of both the parties. Whereas before, the parties being called together, the heads were repeated which his majesty would have reformed at this time: and so the whole action ended.
30 Sundry, as they favoured, gave out copies of things here concluded: whereupon myself took occasion, as I was an ear and eye witness, to set them down and presented them to his majesty, who with his own hand mended some things, and eeked other things which I had omitted. Which corrected
35 copy with his own hand I have, and of it have sent you herein the just transumpt word by word,—and this is the whole. At.my own returning, which, God willing, shall be shortly, ye shall know more particularly the rest. So till then taking my leave, I commit you to the protection of the

Most High, and your labours to the powerful blessing of
Christ.   From London this tenth of Februar, 1604.

Your brother in the Lord to his uttermost,

M. P. Galloway.

The cause of my delay to write was my awaiting on his 5
majesty's leisure, to obtain that copy spoken of before, as it
is, that so I might write, as it was allowed to stand, and to
be performed.

A note of such things as shall be reformed.

1. OF DOCTRINE.   10

1. That an uniform short and plain catechism be made, to
be used in all churches and parishes in this kingdom.   There
is already the doctrine of the sacraments added, in most clear
and plain terms.

2. That a translation be made of the whole Bible, as 15
consonant as can be to the original Hebrew and Greek; and
this to be set out and printed without any marginal notes, and
only to be used in all churches of England in time of divine
service.

3. That no popish nor traiterous books be suffered to be 20
brought in this kingdom, and that straight order be taken,
that if they come over, they be delivered or sold to none,
either in country or universities, but to such only as may
make good use thereof, for confutation of the adversaries.

2. OF THE SERVICE BOOK.   25

1. That to the absolution shall be added the word of pronouncing the remission of sins.

2. That to confirmation shall be added the word of catechizing, or examination of the children's faith.

3. That the private baptism shall be called the private 30
baptism by the ministers and curates only; and all these
questions that insinuate women or private persons, to be
altered accordingly.

4. That such apocrypha as have any repugnance to canonical scripture shall be removed and not read; and other 35

places chosen for them which may serve better, either for explanation of scripture, or instruction in good life and manners: and specially the greatest part of such places as were given in writ.

5. The words of marriage to be made more clear.

6. The cross in baptism was never counted any part in baptism, nor sign effective, but only significative.

3. OF DISCIPLINE.

1. The bishops are admonished to judge no ministers without the advice and assistance of some of the gravest deans and chaplains.

2. That none shall have power to excommunicate, but only their bishops in their dioceses, in the presence of these aforesaid; and only upon such weighty and great causes, to which they shall subscribe.

3. The civil excommunication now used, is declared to be a mere civil censure; and therefore the name of it is to be altered; and a writ out of the chancellary to punish the contumacy shall be framed.

4. That all bishops, nominated to that effect, shall set down the matters and manner of proceeding, to be followed hereafter in ecclesiastical courts, and modify their fees.

5. That the oath 'ex officio' be rightly used, id est, only for great and public slanders.

6. That the bishops be careful to cause the ministers note in every parish of their dioceses the names of all recusants; as also the names of such as come to church and hear preaching, but refuse to communicate every year once; and to present the same to the bishop, and the bishop to the archbishop, and the archbishop to the king.

7. That the sabbath be looked to, and better kept throughout all dioceses.

8. That the high commission be rightly used, the causes to be handled, and the manner of proceeding therein to be declared; and that no person be nominated thereto but such as are men of honour and good quality.

4. OF THE MINISTRY.

1. That the reading of ministers that are of age and not scandalous, be provided for and maintained by the person preferred to preach in his room, according to the valor of the living; and that the unlearned and scandalous be tried and 5 removed from these places, and learned and qualified be placed for them.

2. That as many ministers as may be had with convenient maintenance for them, may be placed in such places where there is want of preaching, with all haste.   10

3. That learned and grave ministers be transported from the parts where the gospel is settled and planted, to such parts of the kingdom where greatest ignorance is, and greatest number of recusants are.

4. That ministers, beneficed men, make residence upon 15 their benefices, and feed their flocks with preaching every sabbath day.

5. That pluralists and such as presently have double benefices, make residence upon one of them; and that these their benefices be as near other as he may preach to the people of 20 both their week about: and where they are further distant, that he maintain therein a qualified preacher.

5. FOR SCHOOLS.

1. That schools in cities, towns, and families, throughout all this kingdom, be taught by none but such as shall be 25 tried and approved to be sound and upright in religion: and for that effect, that the bishops, in every one of their dioceses, take order with them, displacing the corrupted, and placing honest and sufficient in their places.

2. That orders be taken with universities for trial of 30 masters and fellows in colleges; and that none be suffered to have the cure of instructing the youth, but such as are approved for their soundness in religion; and that such as are suspected or known to be otherways affected, be removed.

3. That the kingdom of Ireland, the borders of England 35 and Scotland, and all Wales, be planted with schools and preachers as soon as may be.

The ministers have been this long time past, and shall be in all time coming, urged to subscribe nothing but the three articles, which are both clear and reasonable.

[Then are recited the three articles of the 36th canon.]

VII.

5 *Archiepiscopo Cantuariensi et aliis pro reformatione Libri Communis Precum.*

James, by the grace of God, &c. To the most rev. father in God, our right trusty and well beloved councellor, John archbishop of Canterbury, of all England primate and me-
10 tropolitane, the rev. fathers in God our trusty and well beloved Richard bishop of London, Anthony bishop of Chichester, and to the rest of our commissioners for causes ecclesiasticall, greeting.

Whereas all such jurisdictions, rights, priviledges, supe-
15 riorities, and preheminences, spirituall and ecclesiasticall, as by any spirituall or ecclesiasticall power or authority have heretofore beene or may lawfully be exercised or used for the visitation of the ecclesiastical state and persons, and for reformation, order, and correction, as well of the same as of
20 all manner of errors, heresies, schisms, abuses, offences, contemptes, and enormities, to the pleasure of Almighty God, the increase of vertue, and the conservation of the peace and unitie of this our realm of England, are for ever, by authoritie of parliament of this our realme, united and annexed to the
25 imperiall crowne of the same.

And whereas also by act of parliament it is provided and enacted, that whenever we shall cause to take further order for or concerning any ornament, righte, or ceremony appointed or prescribed in the booke commonly called "The
30 Book of Common Prayer, Administration of the Sacraments, and other rites and ceremonies of the Church of England," and our pleasure knowne therein, either to our commissioners, authorized under our great seal of England, for causes

ecclesiasticall, or to the metropolitane of this our realm of England, that then further order should be therein taken accordingly.

We therefore, understanding that there were in the said booke certeyne thinges which might require some declaration [5] and enlargement by way of explanation; and, in that respect, having required you our metropolitane, and you the bishops of London and Chichester, and some others of our commissioners authorized under our great seal of England for causes ecclesiasticall, according to the intent and meaning of the [10] said statute, and of some other statutes alsoe, and by our supreme authoritie and prerogative royall, to take some care and payns therein, have received from you the said particuler thinges in the said book declared, and enlarged by way of explanation, made by you our metropolitane and the rest of [15] our said commissioners in manner and forme following. In the rubricke before Absolution these wordes followinge are to be placed, the Absolution or Remission of Synnes to be pronounced by the minister alone.

John x. 11. being the Gospel "Dominica secunda post [20] Pasch." these wordes (*Christe sayed*) to be printed in letters differing from the text; and these words to be left out, videlicet, *to his disciples.*

Matth. xxii. 1. "Dominica vicesima post Trinitat." These words (*Jesus said*) to be printed in letters differing from the [25] text; and these words to be left out, videlicet, *unto his disciples.*

The whole rubricke before Private Baptism to be in these words:

Of them that are to be baptized in private houses in time [30] of necessitie by the minister of the parish, or any other lawfull minister that can be procured; the pasters and curates shall often admonish the people that they defer not the baptism of infants any longer then the Sonday or other holyday next after the child be born, unless upon a great and reason. [35] able cause declared to the curate, and by him approved; and also they shall warn them that without great cause and necessitie they procure not their children to be baptized at home in their houses; and when great need shall compell

them soe to doe, then baptism shall be administred in this
fashion ; first, let the minister that be present call upon God
for his grace and say the Lord's Prayer, if the time will
suffer : and then, the child being named, by some one of them
5 that is present, the said lawfull minister shall dippe it in
water, or pour water upon it, saying these words, " N. I baptize thee in the name of the Father, and of the Sonne, and of
the Holy Ghost. Amen." And let them not doubte but that
the child so baptized is lawfully and sufficiently baptized, and
10 ought not to be baptized again : but yet nevertheless, if the
child which is after this sort baptized do afterwards lyve, it is
expedient that it be brought into the church, to the intent
that if the priest or minister of the same parishe did himself
baptize that child, the congregation may be certefied of the
15 true form of baptism by him privately before used ; or if the
child were baptized by any other lawfull minister, that then
the minister of the parish where the childe was born or cris-
tened, shal examyne and try whether the child be lawfully
baptized or no : in whiche case if those which bring any child
20 to the church do answer that the same child is already baptized ; then shall the minister examyne them further, saying,
By whom was the child baptized? Who was present when
the child was baptized? And because some thinges effectuall
to this sacramente may happen to be omitted through fear
25 or haste in such times of extremity ; therefore I demande
further of you, With what matter was the child baptized?
With what words was the child baptized? Whether think
you the child to be lawfully and perfectly baptized? And if
the minister shall fynde, by the answers of such as bring the
30 child, that all things were done as they ought to bee, then
shall he not cristen the child againe, but shall receive him as
one of the flock of the true Christian people, saying thus : I
certefy you that in this case all is well done, and according &c.
following the words of the book, as the same was before.   In
35 the last rubrick of Private Baptism these words are to be
placed : But if they which bring the infants to the church do
make such uncertaine answers to the priest's questions as
that it cannot appear that the childe was baptized in the
name of the Father, and of the Sonne, and of the Holy

Ghoste with water, which are essentiall partes of baptism; then let the priest baptize it in form above written concernynge Publique Baptism.

In the rubrick before the Declaration of the use of Confirmation these words are to be placed :   5

The order of Confirmation, or laying on of handes upon children baptized, and able to render an accompte of their faith, according to the Catechism following.

An explanation of Baptism and the Lord's Supper to be added to the end of the Catechism in these questions and 10 answers following :

QUESTION. How many sacraments hath Christ ordained in his church?

ANSWER. Two only as generally necessarie to salvation, (that is to say,) Baptism and the Supper of the Lord.   15

QUESTION. What meanest thou by this word Sacrament?

ANSWER. I mean an outward and visible sign of an inward and spiritual grace given unto us, ordained by Christ himself as a means whereby we receive the same, and a pledge to assure us thereof.   20

QUESTION. How many parts be there in a sacrament?

ANSWER. Two; the outwarde and visible signe and the inward and spirituall grace.

QUESTION. What is the outward visible sign or form in Baptism?   25

ANSWER. Water, wherein the person baptized is dipped or sprinkled with it in the name of the Father, and of the Sonne, and of the Holy Ghoste.

QUESTION. What is the inward and spirituall grace?

ANSWER. A death unto synne and a new birth unto right-30 eousness : for being by nature born in sin, and the children of wrath, we are hereby made the children of grace.

QUESTION. What is required of persons to be baptized?

ANSWER. Repentance whereby they forsake synne, and fayth whereby they stedfastly believe the promises of God 35 made to them in that sacrament.

QUESTION. Why then are infants baptized, when by reason of their tender age they cannot perform them?

ANSWER. Yes, they do perform them by their sureties,

who promise and vow them both in their names, which when they come to age themselves are bound to perform.

QUESTION. Why was the sacrament of the Lord's Supper ordained!

5 ANSWER. For the continuall remembrance of the sacrifice of the death of Chryste, and the benefits which we receive thereby.

QUESTION. What is the outward part or sign of the Lord's Supper?

10 ANSWER. Breade and wyne, which the Lord hath commanded to be received.

QUESTION. What is the inward part or thinge signified!

ANSWER. The body and blood of Christe, which are verily and indeede taken and received of the faithfull in the Lord's 15 Supper.

QUESTION. What are the benefits whereof we are partakers thereby?

ANSWER. The strengthenynge of our souls by the body and blood of Chryste as our bodies are by the breade and wyne.

20 QUESTION. What is required of them which come to the Lord's Supper?

ANSWER. To examyne themselves whether they repent them trulie of their former sins, steadfastly purposinge to lead a new life, have a livelie faith in God's mercies through Christ, 25 with a thankfull remembrance of his death, and be in charity with all men.

The rubricke before the acte of Confirmation shall be in these words:

" Confirmation, or laying on of hands."

30   *In the Kalendar.*

Augusti 26, at morning prayer, note that the 13th of Danyell, touching the historie of Susanna, is to be read unto theis words (And king Astiages, &c.). The same day at evening prayer, instead of the 14th chapter of Daniell, touch-35 ing Bell and the Dragon, read the 30th of the Proverbs.

Octobris primo, at morninge prayer, instead of the fifth chapter of Thobie, read the sixte of Exodus unto theis words

(Theis be the heades, &c.). The same daye at evening prayer, instead of the sixt chaptor of Thobie, read the twentith of Josua.

Octobris secundo, at evening prayer, instead of the eighte chapter of Thobie, read the twoe and twentieth of Josua. 5

The seventeenth of November at evening prayer, note likewise that the six and fortieth chapter of Ecclesiasticus is to be read unto theise words, " After this he told," &c.

A prayer for the queen, the prince, and other the king's and queen's children, to be inserted next under the prayer for the 10 *king.*

Almighty God, which hast promised to be a Father of thine elect and of their seed, wee humbly beseech thee to bless our gracious queen Anne, prince Henry, and all the king's and queen's royal progeny, indue them with thy Holy 15 Spirit, inrich them with thy heavenly grace, prosper them with all happiness, and bring them to thine everlasting kingdom, through Jesus Christe, &c.

Another prayer to be inserted into the litany after these words,
(over all his enemys). 20

That it may please thee bless and preserve our gracious queen Anne, prince Henry, and the rest of the king and queen's royal issue.

An enlargement of thanksgiving for diverse benefits, by way of
explanation. 25

O God our Heavenly Father, who by thy gracious providence dost cause the former and the latter rain to descende upon the earth, that it may bringe forth fruite for the use of man, wee give thee humble thanks that it hath pleased thee in our greatest necessitie to sende us at the last a joyfull 30 rayne upon thine inheritance, and to refresh it when it was drye, to the great comfort of us thy unworthy servants, and to the glory of thy holy name, through thy mercies in Jesus Christ our Lord. Amen.

A thanksgiving for fair weather.

O Lord God, who hath justly humbled us by thy late plague of immoderate rayne and waters, and in thy mercie hast relieved and comforted our souls by this seasonable and
5 blessed change of wether; wee praise and glorify thy holy name for this thy mercie, and will always declare thy loveing kindness from generation to generation, through Jesus Christ our Lord. *Amen.*

A thanksgiving for plenty.

10 O most mercifull Father, which of thy gracious goodness hast heard the devout prayers of thy church, and turned our dearth and scarcitie into cheapnes and plenty: wee give thee humble thanks for this thy especiall bounty: beseeching thee to contynue this thy loving kindnes unto us, that our lande
15 may yeild us her fruite of encrease to thy glory and our comfort, through Jesus Christ our Lord. *Amen.*

A thanksgiving for peace and victorie.

O Almighty God, who art a strong tower of defence unto thy servants against the face of their enemys, we yeild thee
20 praise and thanksgiving for our deliverance from those greate and apparant dangers wherewith wee were compassed, wee acknowledge it thy goodness that wee were not delivered over as a prey unto them, beseeching thee still to continue such thy mercies towards us, that all the world may know that
25 thou art our Saviour and mighty Deliverer, through Jesus Christe our Lord. *Amen.*

A thanksgiving for deliverance from the plague.

O Lord God, which hast wounded us for our synnes and consumed us for our transgressions, by thy late heavy and
30 dreadfull visitation, and nowe in the middest of judgment remembring mercie, hast redeemed our souls from the jawes of death, wee offer unto thy fatherly goodnes our selves, our souls and bodies, which thou hast delivered, to be a lyving sacrifice unto thee, always praysing and magnifying thy

mercies in the middest of the congregation, through Jesus Christ our Lord. *Amen.*

Or this.

We humbly acknowledge before thee (O most mercifull 5 Father) that all the punishments which are threatened in thy lawe might justly have fallen upon us by reason of our manifold transgressions and hardness of heart: yet being it hath pleased thee of thy tender mercie, upon our weak and unworthy humiliation, to assuage the noysome pestilence, 10 wherewith wee latelie have been sore afflicted, and to restore the voice of joy and health into our dwellings; we offer unto thy divyne Majesty the sacrifice of praise and thanksgiving, lauding and magnifying thy glorious Name for such thy preservation and providence over us, through Jesus Christ 15 our Lord. *Amen.*

All which particular poynts and things in the said book, are thus by you declared and enlarged by way of exposition and explanation. Forasmuch as wee having maturely considered of them, do hold them to be very agreable to our own 20 severall directions, upon conference with you and others, and that they are in no part repugnant to the word of God, nor contrarie to anie thinge that is already contained in that book; nor to any of our lawes or statutes made for allowance and confirmation of the same: wee by virtue of the said 25 statutes, and by our supreme authoritie and prerogative royall, doe fully approve, allowe and ratify all and every one of the said declarations and enlargements by way of explanation.

Willing and requiryng, and withall authorising you the 30 archbishop of Canterbury, that forthwith you do command our printer, Robert Barker, newly to print the said Communion Book, with all the said declarations and enlargements by way of exposition and explanation above mentioned: and that you take such order, not only in your own province, but 35 likewise in our name with the archbishop of Yorke for his province, that every parish may provide for themselves the saide booke so prynted and explained, to be onely used by the minister of every such parish in the celebration of divine

service and admynistration of the sacraments. And duely by
him to be observed according to the lawe in all the other
parts, with the rites and ceremonies therein contained and
prescribed for him to observe.

5   And these our letters patents, or the enrollement thereof,
shal be your sufficient warrant for all and every the premisses
contayned in them.

   Witnes our selfe at Westminster the ninth day of February.

                              Per ipsum regem.

VIII.

10 *A proclamation for the authorizing and uniformity of the Book
of Common Prayer to be used throughout the realm*

ALTHOUGH it cannot be unknown to our subjects by the
former declarations we have published, what our purposes
and proceedings have been in matters of religion since our
15 coming to this crown; yet the same being now by us reduced
to a settled form, we have occasion to repeat somewhat of
that which hath passed; and how at our very first entry into
the realm being entertained and importuned with informations
of sundry ministers, complaining of the errors and imper-
20 fections of the church here, as well in matter of doctrine as
of discipline, although we had no reason to presume that
things were so far amiss as was pretended, because we had
seen the kingdom under that form of religion, which by law
was established in the days of the late queen of famous
25 memory, blessed with a peace and prosperity, both extraordinary and of many years' continuance (a strong evidence that
God was therewith well pleased,) yet because the importunity
of the complainers was great, their affirmations vehement,
and the zeal wherewith the same did seem to be accom-
30 panied very specious, we were moved thereby to make it
our occasion to discharge that duty, which is the chiefest
of all kingly duties, that is, to settle the affairs of religion

                              Q

and the service of God before their own; which while we
were in hand to do, as the contagion of the sickness reigning
in our city of London and other places would permit an
assembly of persons meet for that purpose, some of those
who misliked the state of religion here established, presuming 5
more of our intents than ever we gave them cause to do,
and transported with humour, began such proceedings as
did rather raise a scandal in the church than take offence
away. For both they used forms of public serving of God not
here allowed, held assemblies without authority, and did 10
other things carrying a very apparent show of sedition more
than of zeal; whom we restrained by a former proclamation
in the month of October last, and gave intimation of the
conference we intended to be had with as much speed as
conveniently could be, for the ordering of those things of the 15
church; which accordingly followed in the month of January
last, at our honour of Hampton court, where before ourself
and our privy council were assembled many of the gravest
bishops and prelates of the realm, and many other learned
men, as well of those that are conformable to the state 20
of the church established, as of those that dissented; among
whom, what our pains were, what our patience in hearing and
replying, and what the indifferency and uprightness of our
judgment in determining, we leave to the report of those who
heard the same, contenting ourself with the sincerity of our 25
own heart therein. But we cannot conceal, that the success
of that conference was such as happeneth to many other
things, which moving great expectation before they be entered
into, in their issue produce small effect. For we found
mighty and vehement informations supported with so weak 30
and slender proofs, as it appeared unto us and our council,
that there was no cause why any change should have been
at all in that which was most impugned, the Book of Common
Prayer, containing the form of the public service of God here
established; neither in the doctrine, which appeared to be 35
sincere, nor in the forms and rites, which were justified out
of the practice of the primitive church. Notwithstanding we
thought meet, with consent of the bishops and other learned
men there present, that some small things might rather be

explained than changed; not that the same might not very
well have been borne with by men who would have made
a reasonable construction of them, but for that in a matter
concerning the service of God we were nice, or rather jealous,
5 that the public form thereof should be free, not only from
blame, but from suspicion, so as neither the common adversary
should have advantage to wrest aught therein contained to
other sense than the Church of England intendeth, nor any
troublesome or ignorant person of this church be able to take
10 the least occasion of cavil against it: and for that purpose
gave forth our commission under our great seal of England
to the archbishop of Canterbury and others, according to
the form which the laws of this realm in like case prescribe
to be used, to make the said explanation, and to cause the
15 whole Book of Common Prayer, with the same explanations,
to be newly printed. Which being now done and established
anew after so serious a deliberation; although we doubt not
but all our subjects, both ministers and others, will receive
the same with such reverence as appertaineth, and conform
20 themselves thereunto every man in that, which him concerneth; yet have we thought it necessary to make known
by proclamation our authorizing of the same, and to require
and enjoin all men, as well ecclesiastical as temporal, to conform themselves unto it, and to the practice thereof, as the
25 only public form of serving of God established and allowed
to be in this realm. And the rather, for that all the learned
men who were there present, as well of the bishops as
others, promised their conformity in the practice of it, only
making suit to us, that some few might be borne· with for
30 a time.

Wherefore we require all archbishops, bishops, and all
other public ministers, as well ecclesiastical as civil, to do
their duties in causing the same to be obeyed, and in punishing the offenders according to the laws of the realm heretofore
35 established for the authorizing of the said Book of Common
Prayer. And we think it also necessary, that the said archbishops and bishops do each of them in his province and
diocese take order, that every parish do procure to themselves, within such time as they shall think good to limit,

one of the said books so explained. And last of all, we do
admonish all men, that hereafter they shall not expect nor
attempt any further alteration in the common and public
form of God's service from this which is now established;
for that neither will we give way to any to presume, that our 5
own judgment having determined in a matter of this weight,
shall be swayed to alteration by the frivolous suggestions of
any light spirit; neither are we ignorant of the inconveniences that do arise in government by admitting innovation
in things once settled by mature deliberation; and how ne- 10
cessary it is to use constancy in the upholding of the public
determinations of states; for that such is the unquietness
and unsteadfastness of some dispositions, affecting every year
new forms of things, as, if they should be followed in their
inconstancy, would make all actions of states ridiculous and 15
contemptible: whereas the steadfast maintaining of things by
good advice established is the weal of all commonwealths.
Given at our palace of Westminster the fifth day of March,
in the first year of our reign of England, France and Ireland,
and of Scotland the seven and thirtieth, anno Domini MDCIII. 20

CHAPTER V.

Interpolations charged against archbishop Laud.

FROM the light in which the Book of Common Prayer was held by the puritans of the seven-teenth century, it would naturally be expected that any attempt to introduce readings without authority and at variance with their suggestions, would be an occasion for the renewal of hostilities. Little disposed to make use of the liturgy themselves for the offices of public worship, they would still employ it with force and effect as a ground of accusation against their opponents, if it should appear to have undergone any clandestine alterations, whether they were positively unsound, or were merely unauthorized. And such was the vehemence of those times, that whenever an accusation was made, it rarely wanted a tone of confidence to accompany it, or a strong public feeling to give it credence; so that the most improbable reports might pass into general circulation, and grave and sensible men be charged with offences, that involved the most wanton and impracticable foolishness.

Of such a nature was the charge brought against archbishop Laud of corrupting the Book of Common Prayer. It is well known that he had employed his power of granting licenses for publications in such a manner as to alter the character of many of the books 5 submitted to him, and to give them a leaning in favour of his own views of doctrine and discipline. He was of that order of mind which could address itself with much vigour and readiness either to the governing principles of a question, or to the smallest circum- 10 stances connected with it. But the course of his education had given him a strong tendency in the latter direction; and the spirit of the times, which by a kind of moral crystallization had converted all general discussions into a multitude of sharp and 15 uniform points, disposed him to infer great danger from the smallest indications of it, and in all cases alike to apply the remedy of pains and penalties. Acting upon these principles he had carried his vigi_ lance, as censor of the press, to the greatest extent; 20 and authors of all descriptions complained of the liberties that were taken with their works, passages being omitted or reconstructed not merely on subjects of secondary interest, but especially on those questions on which every man at that time thought deeply and 25 passionately. The instructions given by the archbishop to his chaplains with reference to the one subject of popery were; "that[a] all exasperating passages which edify nothing, should be expunged out of such books as by them were to be licensed to the press; and that 30 no doctrines of that [the Romish] church should be writ against, but such as seemed to be inconsistent

---

[a] Heylin's Laud, p. 418.

with the established doctrines of the Church of
England." It is easy to foresee how such instructions,
administered by chaplains, whose theological sentiments had met with the approval of archbishop Laud,
5 would give deep offence to two parties of great activity
and increasing numbers—to the puritans, who independently of their own strength had considerable influence within the pale of the church, and to those
lovers of free discussion, who have at all times a pre-
10 possession in their favour, and had at that time become
a powerful party in the state.

But in such cases his proceedings, however inju-
dicious in the extent to which they were carried, were
in their principle consistent with law, and with the
15 practice of his predecessors. The question would have
been very different, had he of his own authority made
any variations in the text of the public liturgy.

The writer of "The news from Ipswich," a tract
calculated to make much impression at that period,
20 had already charged the archbishop with corrupting
the Book of Common Prayer; but the most direct and
questionable shape, in which the same accusation appeared, was in two sermons preached by H. Burton on
the 5th of November 1636, and in two tracts pub-
25 lished by the same writer soon afterwards, the one
containing the substance of the sermons, and the other
consisting of an appeal against the proceedings of the
ecclesiastical commission.

The principal charge was directed against the
30 alterations that had been made in the form of prayer
provided for the 5th of November. The alterations
were that the words "root out that Babylonish and
antichristian sect which say of Jerusalem" were
changed to " root out that Babylonish and anti-

christian sect of them which say of Jerusalem:" and
the words "cut off those workers of iniquity whose
religion is rebellion" to "cut off those workers of
iniquity who turn religion into rebellion." It was
alleged that the archbishop had violated the act of 5
parliament (3 James I. c. 1.) which appointed that
day to be observed as a religious festival. Now the
facts of the case were, that the act in question provided
no form of worship for the day, but left it to be supplied, according to the customary practice, by an order 10
of the council; that the form actually provided had
not at any time been united with the common editions
of the liturgy, but was printed expressly for the occasion, incorporating with it the usual daily service; and
that if any further justification were necessary, similar 15
alterations had been made at earlier periods by royal
injunctions[b], as well as by authority of parliament. It
is plain then that in this instance if any charge could
be sustained, it would be merely that a change had
been made in the occasional devotions of the people, 20
which was alleged to be in opposition to their wishes.
It could not be pretended that any illegal alteration
had been made in the Book of Common Prayer, or
that any irregular act of any kind whatever had been
done.   25

Of the same nature were the objections taken
against the form of prayer provided for the public
fast of the year 1636, which was declared to differ
in many respects from the forms provided on other
similar occasions, although the king's proclamation, 30
that enjoined the observance of the fast, required the

[b] In the Prayer Book of 1552, and in the Injunctions of Queen
Elizabeth.

publication of the accustomed services. But these objections were extremely futile. The changes were numerous, and whether they were made judiciously or not (although there appears to be no reason for 5 disputing it) they were made by the competent persons, had many precedents in their favour, and were set forth in the usual manner, by his majesty's authority[c].

Forms of prayer or thanksgiving had been provided 10 during the reigns of queen Elizabeth and king James I. for many special occasions; for instance, in the year 1562 during a time of pestilence (Wilkins, Conc. vol. iv. p. 242); in the year 1588 during a time of danger (Wilkins, vol. iv. p. 351); and on several 15 occasions of the queen's recovery from illness. Instances also occurred, as in the case of a great scarcity in the year 1596, (Wilkins, vol. iv. p. 351,) when clergymen appear to have been left to their own discretion in the selection of prayers. But in the year 20 1603, the first year of king James, and a time of great pestilence, certain prayers were collected for the occasion "out of a form of godly meditations," which became the model for future compilations of the same kind. Differences however were frequently 25 introduced; as for instance in the form provided for the pestilence of the year 1625, the first year of king Charles I, to which was added a prayer for the high court of parliament containing those memorable words, "our most religious and gracious king[d]," which are

30   [c] Comp. Heylin's Brief Answer, &c. p. 157, and Dow's Innovations, &c. p. 141.

[d] This prayer in its original shape was probably composed by bishop Laud; for in the year 1625, when it first appeared in any public form, he already stood higher in royal favour than archbishop 35 Abbot; and we find a great part of it adopted by Laud himself in

supposed by many persons to have been used in the first
instance for the purpose of describing king Charles II.
after the revision of 1661.

We come nearer to a grave and substantial accusation, when we find it alleged against the archbishop [5]
that he made important alterations in a prayer of the
public liturgy, commonly entitled the Prayer for the
Royal Family; by striking out the names of " the
prince elector palatine and the lady Elizabeth his
wife," and by substituting the words " the fountain of [10]
all goodness" instead of the ancient clause " which
hast promised to be a father of thine elect and of
their seed." It was urged that in the one case he was
actuated by political motives, and in the other by his
well-known aversion for any language that savoured of [15]
the school of Calvin. But here again the archbishop

a private collection of prayers compiled for his own use, which was
first published in the year 1650. Dr. D'Oyly, in his Life of Archbishop Sancroft, (vol. i. p. 114,) does not trace the prayer higher
than the year 1628; but Dr. Routh in his notes on bp. Burnet's [20]
History of his Own Times, (vol. i. p. 332), assigns it to the earlier
period.

As might naturally be expected, the prayer for the parliament was
not used constantly during the time of Charles I. It appears in a
special form provided in the year 1625, is wanting in a form for the
year 1626, appears again in a form for 1628, when the troubles [25]
were beginning, and is omitted afterwards (in forms, for instance,
issued in 1636, 1640, and 1643) until it was recast for a special
service in the year 1661, and was thence transferred by the convocation of the same period to the Book of Common Prayer.   [30]

In the convocation of 1640 archbishop Laud proposed that a
prayer should be composed for the parliament and the peace and
tranquillity of the kingdom. The task was entrusted to his two
chaplains, Bray and Oliver, who on the 25th of April brought in
their form of prayer; and it was then approved. But this prayer [35]
appears to have been provided for the use of the convocation. Wilk.
Conc. vol. iv. p. 539. Synod. Ang. App. p. 27.

is free from all real imputation. The prayer itself was approved, if not composed, by archbishop Whitgift, and appears for the first time after the revision made by king James on his sole authority in the year 1604 ᵉ.
5 It is not even to be found in the form of service that was provided a few months previously on occasion of the pestilence. Resting therefore exclusively upon the royal mandate, the same authority was competent to alter or remove it. Accordingly in the first form of
10 prayers published by authority in the reign of king Charles I, being the service provided for the fast of the year 1625, the words, "the fountain of all goodness" were introduced for the first time into the prayer for the royal family, and were continued in the Prayer
15 Book published in the year 1627; and for this obvious reason, that the ancient clause, for which they were substituted, was not thought appropriate in the case of a sovereign who was at that time without issue. It appears also that in the year 1632 when there was
20 royal issue, and prince Charles and the lady Mary are mentioned in the prayer by name, the original clause was replaced, as then no longer inapplicable. In the following year however, the first year of the primacy of Laud, the clause was again removed, and
25 was not afterwards restored. For similar reasons it appears that distinct mention of the elector palatine and the princess Elizabeth was made for the last time in the year 1632, other names being introduced of princes more nearly connected with the throne, and
30 the general expression "the royal family" being added to include all the remoter branches. We might infer indeed from these facts that the alterations were permanently made at the suggestion of the archbishop,

ᵉ See above, p. 144. l. 11 ; and Rymer, Fœdera, vol. xvi. p. 567.

as they coincide with the time when he was advanced
to the primacy; but if that inference be correct (and
it is evident from his speech before the star-chamber
that he approved of the change) he is still free from
censure, as the prayer was altered by the same author-[5]
ity, on which it depended for its existence, the mandate of the crown.

Another charge brought against the archbishop was
that in the Epistle for the Sunday before Easter, at
the passage, " in the name of Jesus every knee shall [10]
bow," the word "in" was altered to "at," with the
view, as was alleged, of " making [f] the fairer colour for
their forced bowing to the name of Jesus, for which
there is neither Scripture nor ancient Father." To this
charge the archbishop answered in his speech delivered [15]
in the star-chamber, in the following words : " I do
here solemnly protest to you, I know not how it came.
For authority from the prelates the printers had none ;
and such a word is easily changed in such a negligent
press as we have in England.　Or if any altered it [20]
purposely, for aught I know they did it to gratify the
preciser sort.　For therein they followed the Geneva
translation, and printed at Geneva 1557, where the
words are ' at the name of Jesus.'　And that is
ninety-four years ago, and therefore no innovation [25]
made by us."　The truth is, if it be necessary to pursue
the matter further, that though in an edition of 1607
the word is " in," it was printed " at" during the whole
of the reign of Charles I, as may be seen in editions
of 1627, 1632, 1633, 1634, 1639, &c.: and the prac- [30]
tice of bowing, which had given offence to the puritans,
was no novelty of the archbishop's, but had been required by the Injunctions of queen Elizabeth.

[f] Burton's Sum of two Sermons, p. 130.

Another alteration which has been ascribed to the archbishop in later times, but does not seem to have been made matter of accusation in his own, was the substitution of the word " priest" for " minister" in the
5 rubric prefixed to the Absolution or remission of sins. It is not easy to discover how this charge originated; for on an examination of the editions of the Common Prayer belonging to that period, it is found that the words were used as if no distinct meanings were as-
10 signed to them. Editions of 1607 and 1627 have " minister." The form of prayer for the fast in 1625 and Prayer-books of 1632 and 1633 have " priest." But editions of 1634 and 1639 again have the word " minister," and are therefore sufficient evidence, that
15 if the alleged alteration were made clandestinely, the blame cannot reasonably be imputed to archbishop Laud.

His speech delivered in the star-chamber on the 14th of June, 1637, when Bastwick, Burton, and Pryn
20 received sentence for the libels they had published, appears to have liberated him altogether from the imputation of corrupting the Book of Common Prayer; but the alterations made in the two services for the public fast and the 5th of November, alterations, which,
25 with much appearance of reason, were ascribed to his influence, were kept in remembrance, and were brought forward at his trial in the year 1644, with the view of proving by their constructive evidence the designs which he was said to have conceived in favour of the
30 Church of Rome.

CHAPTER VI.

The proceedings of the conference at the Savoy.

IN the dark interval that now elapsed between the commencement of the rebellion and the restoration of the monarchy, when it is difficult to fix upon any measure, though promoted by the friends of the church, which was not turned by the strong current of the times into an adverse channel, there are several facts to be especially noticed, as connected with the subsequent condition of the Book of Common Prayer. They evidently made a great impression on the character of the times, and though the results that followed, like all results at periods of great excitement, did not fulfil the expectations that had been formed of them, we can trace their operation, whether for good or for evil, in the proceedings of the Savoy conference, and the history of the act of uniformity.

On the 1st of March, 1641, the house of lords appointed a committee consisting of ten earls, ten bishops, and ten lay-barons, to " take into consideration all innovations in the church respecting religion." On the 10th of the same month, they were empowered to associate with them as many learned divines as they

pleased, and archbishop Usher, and Drs. Prideaux,
Warde, Twisse, and Hacket, are particularly mentioned
as selected for the purpose.   But the object for which
they were professedly appointed gives little information
5 as to the extensive powers they possessed.   It would
appear to have been the intention of the house that
they should consider and report upon the minute
regulations adopted by archbishop Laud and other
bishops in their respective dioceses, regulations which
10 had been made the subject of constant complaint, not
merely by all the avowed opponents of the church,
but also by great numbers of its members.   These
were the innovations which the committee were required to examine; but with an understanding on all
15 sides that they were to carry their inquiries into the
whole field of doctrine and discipline, and suggest
such measures as might tend to allay the great and
general feeling of discontent.   Bishop Williams, at
this time dean of Westminster and bishop of Lincoln,
20 presided over the committee, as well as over the sub-
committee, that was appointed soon afterwards, and
proceeded without delay to enter upon its important
duties.

A meeting consisting of such persons as bishops
25 Williams, Moreton (of Durham), and Montague (of
Norwich), archbishop Usher, and the following divines*, Warde, Prideaux, Sanderson, Featley, Brownrigg, Holdsworth, Hacket, Twisse, Burgess, White,
Marshall, Calamy, Hill, many of whom were eminent

30   * Of these divines Warde was one of the translators of the Bible
in 1611, and held the Lady Margaret's professorship at Cambridge,
in which he was succeeded by Holdsworth ; and Prideaux, Sanderson, Brownrigg, and Hacket, were afterwards bishops of Worcester,
Lincoln, Exeter, and Lichfield, respectively.

for their learning and their attachment to the national church, could not fail to attract general notice, and to give much weight and sanction to the measures they recommended. It is probable that the greater number of them entered upon their task with views derived 5 altogether from the strange necessities of the times, rather than in compliance with their own deliberate judgment. They were aware that the torch was already uplifted for the destruction of the sacred edifice, and they were willing to remove those outworks which, 10 though employed formerly in its defence, would be now most likely to fall into the hands of the assailant. Doubtless they were justified in the opinions of many sober and moderate men; but their measures were fruitless in the way of relaxation at the time, and pro-15 bably contributed, in the subsequent combinations of events, to results directly opposite. In the ensuing month of May they found that motions were entertained in the house of commons, which left no further doubt as to the impending ruin of the established church, 20 and their undertaking was then abandoned.

But it was already known that they had agreed upon many important changes in the Book of Common Prayer, some of them likely to be granted, but others destined to meet with the greatest opposition. They 25 advised that the psalms, sentences, epistles, and gospels should be printed according to the new translation; that fewer lessons should be taken from the Apocrypha; that the words "with my body I thee worship" should be made more intelligible; that the 30 immersion of the infant at the time of baptism should not be required in case of extremity; that some saints, which they called legendaries, should be excluded from the calendar; that the "benedicite" should be omitted;

that the words, " which only workest great marvels,"
should be omitted ; that " deadly sins," as used in the
litany, should be altered to " grievous sins ;" that the
words, " sanctify the flood Jordan," and "in sure and cer-
5 tain hope of resurrection," in the two forms of baptism
and burial, should be altered to, " sanctify the element
of water," and " knowing assuredly that the dead shall
rise again." To these and other changes of a like nature they added the following more difficult concessions :
10 " that the rubric with regard to vestments should be altered ; that a rubric be added to explain that the kneeling
at the communion was solely in reference to the prayer
contained in the words 'preserve thy body and soul ;'
that the cross in baptism should be explained or dis-
15 continued ; that the words in the form of confirmation,
declaring that infants baptized are undoubtedly saved,
should be omitted ; and that the form of absolution
provided for the sick should be made declaratory, instead of being authoritative." These concessions, sur-
20 rendering by implication some of the most solemn convictions of a great portion of the clergy, on the authority of the church, the nature of the two sacraments,
and the sanctity of the priesthood, would meet with
the most strenuous opposition, and tend to increase the
25 causes of discontent, instead of abating them.

Such were the alterations approved by the committee of divines ; and their decision, though unavailing with reference to its immediate object, became a
record to be quoted[b] as authority by future noncon-

30   [b] For instance, the nonconformists, in the preface to their " Exceptions," given in at the Savoy conference, reproached the bishops
" for not yielding to that which several bishops voluntarily offered
twenty years before." Afterwards, in their rejoinder to the bishops
at the same conference, they observed, " The primate of Ireland,

R

formists, and to be lamented by the orthodox party as
one of the many causes that weakened the defences of
the church, and led, by certain consequence, to its
overthrow.   As a series of concessions which on pre-
vious occasions had been resolutely refused, which 5
abandoned in the outset the whole principle of church
government, and was so closely followed by the violences it dreaded, that it might be said to have invited
them, it was remembered by the royalists, when they
afterwards acquired the ascendant, with feelings of irri- 10
tation and resentment.

But the most remarkable event of the period, connected with the history of the Book of Common
Prayer, was the ordinance passed by the parliament on
the 3rd of January, 1645, which repealed certain sta- 15
tutes of king Edward VI. and queen Elizabeth, and
provided that the Book of Common Prayer should not
remain or be used thenceforth in any church, chapel,
or place of public worship in England or Wales, and
that the Directory should be used instead of it.   In 20
another ordinance of August 23, in the same year, the
use of the Book of Common Prayer was also forbidden
in any private place or family, all copies of it to be
found in the churches were ordered to be delivered up,
and heavy penalties were imposed upon offenders.   25

There was in these ordinances, and in the measures
they occasioned, something so offensive to the con-

the archbishop of York, and the many others that had divers meetings for the reformation of the liturgy, and who drew up that catalogue of faults, or points that needed mending, which is yet to be 30
seen in print, &c." (Account of the Proceedings of the Commissioners, p. 28.) The same concessions are also quoted in "The
Conformist's Plea for the Nonconformists" (p. 22), at considerable
length, and with the same view of justifying the demands made at
the Savoy conference.

sciences of many devout persons, so tyrannical in the estimation of reasonable men, and so profane in the licentiousness of public worship, which followed as their natural consequence, that as soon as the presbyterian 5 feeling began to subside, the wish for a prescribed ritual returned with additional strength, and the prohibited liturgy was regarded with a degree of veneration such as is felt for a saint who had suffered martyrdom. As presbyterianism fell, and was succeeded by a party 10 less intolerant, but more licentious, this sentiment became more active and resolute. Acquiring more adherents from the many varieties of opinion that readily united in resisting the progress of the Independents, it also combined with the strongest reasons 15 in favour of the ancient mode of worship a feeling of deep personal interest in its restoration.

The impression thus created was increased in force as well as in extent, during the rest of this dark interval, by many collateral influences, often, indeed, 20 failing to accomplish their direct objects, but always making insensible progress in aid of the ancient liturgy. Of these the most remarkable was the question of ecclesiastical government. The presbyterians, who with their rigid observances could not 25 object against the church that it was too precise in its creed, or too exact in its discipline, undertook in defence of their tenets to establish a system that should comprise all classes, and give them an interest in its preservation. They forgot, however, that as the 30 governing party would necessarily be the smaller of the two, any system which included all persons and became strictly imperative upon them on the assumption that they had themselves acquiesced in it, would be certain to occasion disorder in proportion as it was

exact and elaborate. They succeeded in obtaining an
ordinance that all parishes should be brought under
the government of congregational, classical, provincial,
and national assemblies; but when they demanded that
the spiritual authority of the keys should be supported 5
by the power of suspending from the Lord's supper
and excommunicating, with a view also to the imposition of civil penalties, they exposed themselves on all
sides to suspicion and jealousy, and laid a certain train
for their own destruction. The party that succeeded was 10
a hydra of many heads, increasing in a twofold degree,
as any endeavours were made to diminish them.   Old
sects revived, new sects were created, and there ensued
a state of distraction and impiety, the natural tendency
of which was to break up all minor distinctions, and to 15
divide men into two large classes, one of them anxious
to find terms of agreement, in order that religion
might not be utterly extinguished, and the other indifferent whether any form of religion remained.

From this state of things we might anticipate the 20
general result described by king Charles II. in his
Declaration of October 1660, a result that continued
to exist until other causes had cooperated to turn the
stream of public opinion into a more definite channel,
and to shew that strong principles of church-ascend- 25
ancy would ultimately prevail.   As soon as the
parliament of 1661 was assembled, and the sentiments
of the house of commons were ascertained, there
could no longer be any doubt as to the future form
and relations of the national church.   30

" When we were in Holland," [c] said the king in his
Declaration, " we were attended by many grave and

---

[c] Docum. Ann. vol. ii. p. 236.

learned ministers from hence, who were looked upon
as the most able and principal assertors of the presbyterian opinions ; with whom we had as much conference as the multitude of affairs, which were then upon
5 us, would permit us to have, and to our great satisfaction and comfort found them persons full of affection
to us, of zeal for the peace of the church and state,
and neither enemies, as they have been given out to
be, to episcopacy or liturgy, but modestly to desire
10 such alterations in either, as without shaking foundations, might best allay the present distempers, which
the indisposition of the time and the tenderness of
some men's consciences had contracted." Such at that
period was doubtless the case ; but as soon as a few
15 steps more had been taken in reestablishing the
monarchy, different sentiments prevailed. Demands of
a republican tendency having been made by a party
not considerable in numbers, but acquiring importance
from its clamour and turbulence, the public feeling
20 took the alarm, and became insensible to all considerations, except the desire for a strong and permanent
government. It was this exclusive desire, pardonable
under existing circumstances, and perhaps necessary
for the restoration of good order, that inspired the
25 subsequent deliberations both in church and state, and
was finally embodied in the act of uniformity.

When commissioners were sent by the lords and
commons to wait upon the king at the Hague, Reynolds, Calamy, Case, Manton, and other presbyterian
30 divines went with them, as representatives of their
party. They were graciously received, and assured
that the king was desirous of relieving them in matters
of conscience, but that the two houses of parliament
would best judge what degree of indulgence and

toleration was necessary for the peace and quiet of the kingdom. Emboldened by the king's gracious demeanour, by the Declaration he had issued of liberty for tender consciences, and by the temptation offered them to make some specific trial of their strength,[5] they ventured to suggest to the king in some private audiences, that the use[d] of the Book of Common Prayer had long been discontinued; that many of the people had never heard of it, and had become familiar with an opposite method of public worship;[10] and that he would be acting agreeably with the wishes of the nation, if he were to abstain from using the liturgy in strict form in the royal chapel.

This was certainly a bold attempt on the part of the presbyterians, not only because it savoured of the [15] intolerance they were come to condemn, but also because the liturgy had never been laid aside by lawful authority, and would naturally become the order of public worship on the restoration of the regal government. The king[e] replied with some warmth [20] " that whilst he gave them liberty, he would not have his own taken from him; that he had always used that form of service, which he thought the best in the world, and had never discontinued it in places where it was more disliked than he hoped it was by them; that [25] when he came into England, he would not severely inquire how it was used in other churches, though he doubted not he should find it used in many; but he was sure he would have no other used in his own chapel. Then they besought him with more im- [30] portunity ' that the use of the surplice might be discontinued by his chaplains, because the sight of it

---

[d] Clarendon, Hist. Reb. vol. iii. p. 989.   [e] Ibid. p. 990.

would give great offence and scandal to the people.'
They found the king as inexorable in that point as in
the other. He told them plainly ' that he would not
be restrained himself, when he gave others so much
5 liberty; that it had been always held a decent habit in
the church, constantly practised in England till these
late ill times; that it had been still retained by him;
and though he was bound for the present to tolerate
much disorder and indecency in the exercise of God's
10 worship, he would never in the least degree, by his
own practice, discountenance the good old order of the
church in which he had been bred.' Though they
were very much unsatisfied with him, whom they
thought to have found more flexible, yet they ceased
15 further troubling him, in hope and presumption that
they should find their importunity in England more
effectual."

In the mean time the episcopal clergy having ascertained through the lord chancellor (Hyde) that the
20 king was decidedly favourable to the ancient method
of government in the church, had despatched Dr. Barwick, afterwards dean of St. Paul's, with an address
to his majesty, setting forth their devotedness to his
person, and their thankfulness for the great mercies
25 they had experienced. Assuming that they were fully
recognised as the clergy of the national church, they
sought for information as to the time and place,
with all other particulars, at which the king would
be pleased to require their attendance on his landing,
30 and afterwards on his celebration of a public thanksgiving.

The direction that events were taking had so distinctly been foreseen by close observers, and was now
become so evident to men in general, that the king's

ministers at Breda thought it necessary to be upon their guard, lest any of the friends of the established church should conduct themselves rashly and intemperately. The chancellor, in a letter of April 16, 1660[f], addressed to Dr. Barwick, says, "You will find Dr. Morley a very worthy and discreet person, and fit to keep you company in allaying the too much heat and distemper which some of our friends are, in this unseasonable conjuncture, very much accused of; insomuch as this very last post hath brought over three or four complaints to the king of the very unskilful passion and distemper of some of our divines in their late sermons; with which they say that both the general and the council of state are highly offended, as truly they have reason to be, if, as they report, there have been such menaces and threats against those who have hitherto had the power of doing hurt, and are not yet so much deprived of it that they ought to be undervalued." "The king is really troubled at it, and extremely apprehensive of inconvenience and mischief to the church and himself. And truly I hope, if faults of this kind are not committed, that both the church and the kingdom will be better dealt with than is imagined; and I am confident those good men will be more troubled that the church should undergo a new suffering by their indiscretion, than for all they have suffered hitherto themselves."

The sentiments entertained by the court at Breda respecting the presbyterians may be inferred from the following observations of the chancellor[g], written to Dr. Barwick on the 22nd of the same month: "The king desires that he [Dr. Morley] and you, and other

---

f Barwick's Life, p. 517.　　　　g Ibid. p. 525.

discreet men of the clergy, should have frequent conferences with those of the presbyterian party, that, if it be possible, you may reduce them to such a temper as is consistent with the good of the church; and, it may
5 be, it would be no ill expedient to assure them of present good preferments in the church. But, in my own opinion, you should rather endeavour to win over those who, being recovered, will have both reputation and desire to merit from the church, than be over solicitous
10 to comply[h] with the pride and passion of those who propose extravagant things. As what can be said to the divine who is not only so well satisfied with his rebellion, but would require other men to renounce their innocence and justify him, which I am confident
15 no parliament will ever do."

Immediately after the return of the king, the liturgy of the Church of England was restored to his majesty's chapel; and a few days afterwards, the two houses of parliament ordered that prayers
20 should be read before them according to the ancient practice.

---

[h] Lord Clarendon's opinion on this point is expressed in his Life (vol. ii. p. 121), in the following emphatic language: "It is an unhappy policy, and always unhappily applied, to imagine that classis
25 of men can be recovered and reconciled by partial concessions, or granting less than they demand. And if all were granted they would have more to ask, somewhat as a security for the enjoyment of what is granted, that shall preserve their power, and shake the whole frame of the government. Their faction is their religion; nor are those com-
30 binations ever entered into upon real and substantial motives of conscience, how erroneous soever, but consist of many glutinous materials, of will, and humour, and folly, and knavery, and ambition, and malice, which make men cling inseparably together till they have satisfaction in all their pretences, or till they are absolutely broken
35 and subdued, which may always be more easily done than the other."

Although the first great difficulty in the restoration of the monarchy was now overcome, there were still many arrangements to make, any one of which, if incautiously conducted, might terminate fatally for the interests of the church. The disbanding of the army, the restoration of the ejected clergy, the restitution of church property, the future form of church government, the exact observance of the liturgy and its rubrics, were all of them questions in the issues of which the designs of the king and his ministers might be frustrated. It was of the utmost importance that the convention-parliament, which contained much of the republican spirit, should be neither treated with so great a degree of confidence as to consider themselves competent for matters of permanent legislation, nor yet induced by the appearance of distrust, to contract feelings of jealousy or displeasure. In the case, then, of the nonconformists, for which it was necessary to provide immediately, some method must be devised independent of the aid of parliament, and free from the suspicion of encroaching upon its proper jurisdiction. In conformity with these views, three several methods might be suggested, any one of which, if supported by the supremacy of the crown, might possibly be sufficient to secure the present repose of the church, and to establish a claim in favour of its continuance on the same model for the future; the king might issue his warrant for a conference between the clergy and the nonconformists, might address injunctions to the bishops, directing them as to their conduct in their respective dioceses, or might appoint a commission with large powers of revision and amendment. The conference was the plan adopted, and though, from the nature of the case, it would certainly end in disappointment, and probably produce a greater degree of alienation between the contending parties, it was selected wisely under the circumstances of the times, and with the ulterior object which the court appears 5 to have had in view. A conference would naturally beget in eager disputants an increased attachment to their own party, and an incautious and unscrupulous use of argument and authority; but it would satisfy all other minds that such an accommodation as they 10 had hoped for could not be obtained; it would probably, from the advantages actually possessed by the clergy, and the symptoms already manifested by their opponents, leave the odium of the failure attaching to the nonconformists; and, as the result of the whole 15 proceeding, it would create a favourable impression of the discernment and fair dealing of the court.

These plans were promoted by the personal demeanour of the king, who, having private objects to accomplish in favour of the Romanists, assumed the 20 appearance of candour and generosity towards every description of dissenter. He declared to the presbyterians who waited on him, that no coalition could be expected without something of concession and abatement on both sides; that if an agreement were not 25 obtained, it should not be his fault, but their own; and desired them to lay before him proposals for an arrangement respecting church government, the most difficult point at issue, stating, at the same time, the greatest extent to which they could go in the way of 30 concession. With this command they promised to comply, on the two following conditions, to which the king readily assented: that the proposals should be received from themselves as individuals, without prejudice to the great body of dissenters, and that the

clergy should be required to deliver in a similar statement of concessions on their side.

It will be seen that this latter condition was not
strictly observed; and this is not the only instance
where the king was induced, either by the facility of [5]
his nature, or by the under-current of secret motives,
that affected so much of his conduct, to contract engagements in private, which were not found to be
consistent with his public duties. In a few weeks the
presbyterians in London agreed upon a paper drawn [10]
up by Reynolds, Worth, and Calamy, and presented
it, together with archbishop Usher's Reduction of
Episcopacy, to the king. Respecting the liturgy and
ceremonies they expressed themselves in the following
manner: [15]

" [i] We are satisfied in our judgments concerning the
lawfulness of a liturgy or form of worship, provided it
be for matter agreeable to the word of God, and suited
to the nature of the several ordinances and necessities
of the church; neither too tedious, nor composed of [20]
too short prayers or responsals, not dissonant from the
liturgies of other reformed churches, nor too rigorously
imposed, nor the minister confined thereunto, but that
he may also make use of his gifts of prayer and exhortation.   [25]

" Forasmuch as the Book of Common Prayer is in
some things justly offensive, and needs amendment,
we most humbly pray, that some learned, godly, and
moderate divines of both persuasions may be employed
to compile such a form as is before described, as much [30]
as may be in Scripture words; or at least to revise and
reform the old, together with an addition of other

[i] Neal's Puritans, vol. iii. p. 51.

various forms in Scripture phrase, to be used at the minister's choice.

"Concerning ceremonies; we hold ourselves obliged in every part of divine worship to do all things 5 decently and in order and to edification; and are willing to be determined by authority in such things as, being merely circumstantial or common to human actions and societies, are to be ordered by the light of nature and human prudence.

10 "As to divers ceremonies formerly retained in the Church of England, we do in all humility offer to your majesty the following considerations: that the worship of God is in itself pure and perfect and decent without any such ceremonies: that it is then most pure and 15 acceptable, when it has least of human mixtures: that these ceremonies have been imposed and advanced by some, so as to draw near to the significancy and moral efficacy of sacraments: that they have been rejected by many of the reformed churches abroad, and have 20 been ever the subject of contention and endless disputes in this church: and therefore being in their own nature indifferent and mutable, they ought to be changed, lest in time they should be apprehended as necessary as the substantials of worship themselves.

25 "May it therefore please your majesty graciously to grant, that kneeling at the Lord's supper, and such holidays as are but of human institution, may not be imposed on such as scruple them: that the use of the surplice, and cross in baptism, and bowing at the name 30 of Jesus may be abolished: and forasmuch as erecting altars and bowing towards them, and such like, having no foundation in the law of the land, have been introduced and imposed, we humbly beseech your majesty, that such innovations may not be used or imposed for the future."

The expectations they had formed of a meeting to
be conducted on terms of perfect equality with the
episcopal clergy, expectations derived no less from the
sense of their own importance, than from the ready
assent of his majesty, were not warranted either by 5
the relative condition of the two parties, or by any
prospect that such an experiment as a conference
would be successful. The clergy, the liturgy, and the
ceremonies of the church were in legal and rightful
possession; and could not reasonably be ejected or 10
disturbed, or even fettered, unless they either voluntarily abated in their rights, or were proved to have
been disentitled to them. The case was simply one of
plaintiff and defendant, in which the former must
encounter the difficulty and invidiousness of accusing, 15
and the latter would take the exact line of vindication,
merely replying when he had been attacked, and con-
fining himself strictly to the points at issue. This was
the view taken by the clergy themselves, and in this
they were supported by the principal ministers of the 20
crown, and by all the advocates of ancient rights and
established order.

The bishops accordingly, having obtained a copy of
the proposals submitted by the nonconformists, drew
up an answer to the several points successively, de- 25
claring themselves in regard to the liturgy and ceremonies in the following manner[k]: " they pronounce
the offices in the Common Prayer altogether unex-
ceptionable, and conceive the book cannot be too
strictly enjoined, especially when ministers are not 30
denied the exercise of their gifts in praying before
and after sermon; which liberty for extemporary or
private compositions stands only upon a late custom,

[k] Collier, Eccles. Hist. vol. ii. p. 873.

without any foundation from law or canons; and that
the common use of this practice comes only from connivance.   However, they are contented to yield the
liturgy may be reviewed, in case his majesty thinks
5 fit.   As for the ceremonies, they are unwilling to part
with any of them; being clearly of opinion, that the
satisfaction of some private persons ought not to over-
rule the public peace and uniformity of the church :
and that if any abatements were made, it would only
10 feed a distemper and encourage unquiet people to further demands."

But many collateral influences, connected with the
condition of the church, were now beginning to operate
to its disadvantage, increasing, as lord Clarendon [1] has
15 observed, the malignity that was entertained against
it; and the anxiety they occasioned acquired additional force from the known feeling of the convention-
parliament on ecclesiastical matters, and the danger of
intrusting to its decision points of so much delicacy
20 and importance.   The king resolved accordingly to
take the matter into his own hands, and to issue a
declaration, founded on the rights of the prerogative,
which might tend to disentangle some of the growing
intricacies of the times.   It might pacify the greater
25 number of the nonconformists, might coincide with
the general wish expressed in the house of commons,
and yet leave the whole question to be considered and
determined in a future parliament.   To these motives,
coupled with the secret designs of the king, of which
30 he gave several indications during the progress of the
business, we must ascribe the celebrated Declaration of
October 1660.   It was framed as the result of many

---

[1] Life, vol. ii. p. 7.

interviews granted by his majesty to divines of both
parties, and is stated by lord Clarendon to have had
their joint concurrence.   With the exception however
of the point as to the superior order of episcopacy, this
paper seems to have conceded all the urgent demands 5
of the presbyterians, as to the sanctification of the
Lord's day, the admission to the Lord's supper, the
rite of confirmation, the limitation of episcopal jurisdiction, the appointment of suffragans, the non-require-
ment of oaths and subscriptions, the discretionary use of 10
the liturgy, and the nonobservance of the prescribed
ceremonies.   The king rejoiced when he found his
stratagem had succeeded.   The commons were not
only satisfied with his Declaration, but even complied
with his desire that they would not make it the per- 15
manent settlement of the church by an act of the
legislature.   Lord Clarendon too, who did not disguise
his dislike and distrust of the presbyterians, was contented to wait for a more favourable season, when a
new parliament should have assembled, and a con- 20
vocation have been permitted to discuss and determine
the affairs of the church.   Although "the times[m] began
again to be froward, and all degrees of men were hard
to be pleased," he had formed his views from a close
observation of events, and he was not disappointed.   25

To the presbyterians themselves this state of affairs
was so satisfactory, that they joined in addresses of thanks
for his majesty's great condescensions, promised to promote to the utmost of their power the peace and union
of the church, and several of them, including Reynolds 30
and Manton, accepted spiritual appointments, and recognised the authority of the bishops.

[m] Clarendon, Life, vol. ii. p. 10.

On the 25th of March, 1661, the king issued his warrant appointing a commission of divines, who were selected equally from the two parties, to revise the Book of Common Prayer, requiring them to meet at 5 the Savoy, of which the bishop of London was the master, and limiting the commission to the period of four calendar months.

The divines selected were

Episcopal divines.

10 Frewen, archbishop of York.
Sheldon, bishop of London.
Cosin, bishop of Durham.
Warner, bishop of Rochester.
King, bishop of Chichester.
15 Henchman, bishop of Sarum.
Morley, bishop of Worcester.
Sanderson, bishop of Lincoln.
Laney, bishop of Peterborough.
Walton, bishop of Chester.
20 Sterne, bishop of Carlisle.
Gauden, bishop of Exeter.

25

Presbyterian divines.

Reynolds, bishop of Norwich.
Dr. Tuckney, master of St. John's, Cambridge.
Dr. Conant, reg. prof. div. Oxford.
Dr. Spurstow.
Dr. Wallis, Sav. prof. geom. Oxford.
Dr. Manton.
Mr. Calamy.
Mr. Baxter.
Mr. Jackson.
Mr. Case.
Mr. Clarke.
Mr. Newcomen.

Coadjutors.

Dr. Earle, dean of Westminster.
Dr. Heylin.
Dr. Hacket.
30 Dr. Barwick.
Dr. Gunning.
Dr. Pearson.
Dr. Pierce.
Dr. Sparrow.
35 Mr. Thorndike.

Coadjutors.

Dr. Horton.
Dr. Jacomb.
Dr. Bates.
Dr. Cooper.
Dr. Lightfoot.
Dr. Collins.
Mr. Woodbridge.
Mr. Rawlinson.
Mr. Drake.

It was of great importance that the precise object of this commission, and the method to be taken in its proceedings, should be clearly defined. They were expressed in the following manner; " to advise upon and review the Book of Common Prayer, comparing the same 5 with the most ancient liturgies, which have been used in the church in the primitive and purest times : and to that end to assemble and meet together from time to time, and at such times within the space of four calendar months now next ensuing, in the master's lodgings in 10 the Savoy in the Strand, in the county of Middlesex, or in such other place or places as to you shall be thought fit and convenient; to take into your serious and grave considerations the several directions, rules, and forms of prayer, and things in the said Book of Common 15 Prayer contained, and to advise and consult upon and about the same, and the several objections and exceptions which shall now be raised against the same. And if occasion be, to make such reasonable and necessary alterations, corrections, and amendments therein, 20 as by and between you and the said archbishop, bishops, doctors, and persons hereby required and authorized to meet and advise as aforesaid, shall be agreed upon to be needful or expedient for the giving satisfaction unto tender consciences, and the restoring and continuance 25 of peace and unity in the churches under our protection and government; but avoiding, as much as may be, all unnecessary alterations of the forms and liturgy wherewith the people are already acquainted, and have so long received in the Church of England." 30

It is evident from these instructions that the existing Book of Common Prayer was to be the basis of the future liturgy; that it was to be fully considered and examined by both parties; that any objections or

exceptions raised against it were to be entertained and
discussed; that it was to be compared with the primitive liturgies, the acknowledged models of public
worship; that if any changes were made, they should
5 be such only as were reasonable and necessary for the
satisfying of tender consciences and the establishment
of peace and unity; and that no changes should be
made in matters familiar to the people and generally
approved in the church.

10   If this be a fair representation of conditions somewhat inconsistent with each other, it will appear that
the first step to be taken, when the commissioners entered upon their duties, was to call upon the presbyterians for an account of their objections, and to require
15 that they should be drawn up in form and submitted
in writing.   It is clear that the discussion must begin
on this stage of the question, as the orthodox divines
were ready to retain the Prayer Book as it was, and
denied that any change was either necessary or de-
20 sirable.   It is also clear that any objections, which
might be made by either party, could not be profitably
discussed in a strife of tongues, between persons many
in number, all zealously devoted to their respective
opinions, and having no one of greater eminence than
25 the rest to preside and moderate among them.

It was in conformity with these views that at the
first meeting, which, for some reason not satisfactorily
explained, did not take place till the 15th day of
April, the bishop of London stated, that " as the non-
30 conformists and not the bishops had sought for the
conference, nothing could be done till the former had
delivered their exceptions in writing, together with
the additional forms and alterations which they desired." After some objections from the nonconformists,

grounded on their wish for an open conference, and the construction they gave to the language of the king's warrant, but shewing, as they frequently shewed, an unfitness for the transaction of public business, they consented to the plan proposed to them, and met from 5 day to day to draw up a series of exceptions, intrusting Mr. Baxter with the other office of preparing additions to the services.

Bishop Burnet[n] has observed, "Sheldon saw well what the effect would be of putting them to make all 10 their demands at once. The number of them raised a mighty outcry against them, as people that could never be satisfied." It is not improbable that this result was foreseen. But whether foreseen or not, it followed from the only method of proceeding which could have 15 been proposed by reasonable men. It might also have been rendered harmless, if the nonconformists had been equally quicksighted on their part, and had confined their alterations within such limits as were dictated at once by true policy and a Christian spirit. 20 Unhappily for their cause they were governed by the morbid imagination and insatiable energy of Richard Baxter, who was in favour of a bold and full declaration of all their complaints, and persuaded them that they were bound to ask for every thing that they thought 25 desirable, without regard to the sentiments of their opponents. On this principle he himself proceeded in the task intrusted to him. Instead of preparing some additional forms of prayer, such as might be inserted into the ancient service, and be consistent with 30 its other offices, he drew up an entirely new liturgy, shewing no respect either to the primitive models, or

[n] Own Times, vol. i. p. 327.

the long established prepossessions of the people. It is
a strong proof of the influence which his talents, his
industry, and his piety had obtained for him among his
colleagues, that they submitted this new liturgy, as well
5 as their series of exceptions, for the consideration of
the assembled divines.

These papers were introduced by an address, also
composed by Baxter, which was afterwards published
under the title of a Petition for Peace. Its prayer
10 was, that the new liturgy should be adopted, as well
as the old, and either of them be used, at the discretion of the minister; that there should be freedom
from subscription, from oaths and ceremonies, according to the terms of the king's Declaration; and that
15 no ordination, whether absolute or conditional, should
be required from any who had already been ordained
by parochial pastors. But owing to the headstrong
disposition of the nonconformists, even this address
was so constructed as to throw a great degree of
20 odium upon a cause, which had already been rendered
hopeless by their own mismanagement. Proceeding
on the principle, that in all such matters, whether
expressly revealed or otherwise, they owed no deference and would pay no obedience to man's authority,
25 they also indulged in such reflections as the following:
" One would think that a little charity might suffice to
enable you to believe them." (p. 6.) " We accuse none
of the like inclinations; but we must say that it is easy
to make any man an offender, by making laws which
30 his conscience will not allow him to observe." (p. 7.)
" If you should reject, which God forbid, the moderate
proposals which now and formerly we have made, we
humbly crave leave to offer it to your consideration,
what judgment all the protestant churches are likely

to pass on your proceedings, and how your cause and
ours will stand represented to them and to all succeeding ages." (p. 9.)   " We crave leave to remember
you that the Holy Ghost hath commanded you to
oversee the flock, not by constraint, but willingly, not 5
as being lords over God's heritage, but as ensamples to
the flock." (p. 10.)

The bishops were now strong enough to employ the
language of authority.   When they had examined the
exceptions, they gave their answers, not as if the 10
matter were under joint discussion, but as if each
question were submitted to them for their decision;
alleging as their reason, that according to the terms
of the warrant, no alterations could be adopted, unless
they were shewn to be necessary, and were approved 15
by both parties.

The exceptions of the nonconformists and the answers of the bishops must be read at length in order
to do justice to the controversy.   They are accordingly
printed in the ensuing chapter, the first of the two 20
being taken from the copy preserved by Baxter, and
afterwards published in his own narrative of his life.
The answers of the bishops do not appear with the
same advantage as the other paper.   It is not known
that there is any copy of them extant in their original 25
form ; and it has been necessary to extract them in
fragments, though probably comprising the whole of
the arguments, from the lengthy rejoinder of the non-
conformists°, in which it was attempted to refute
them.   30

° These papers were published, together with others, immediately
after the close of the conference, under the title, " An Accompt of
all the proceedings of the Commissioners of both perswasions appointed by his sacred Majesty, according to letters patents, for the

This rejoinder[p], sufficient in itself to form a separate work, it is not thought necessary to republish. In the view taken by the bishops, the discussion had already terminated when they gave in their answers; 5 and the concessions that were offered at the same time were a sufficient proof, from the smallness of their number, and their comparative unimportance, that the two parties were now so remote from each other as to leave no prospect of an agreement. It was 10 probably under this conviction that the rejoinder, also composed by Baxter, was made to assume the character rather of protest and remonstrance than of amicable debate. It seems to have been intended not only to exhaust the argument, but also to leave on record a 15 sense of injury and an expression of indignation, which,

review of the Book of Common Prayer," &c. London, printed for R. H. 1661. Baxter speaks of this publication in the following manner : " All these being surreptitiously printed, save the first piece, by some poor men for gain, without our knowledge and correction, 20 are so falsely printed that our wrong by it is very great. Whole lines are left out; the most significant words are perverted by alterations, and this so frequently, that some parts of the papers, especially our large reply, and our last account to the king, are made nonsense and not intelligible." Life by Sylvester, B. I. P. 2. p. 379. 25   P The preface of this rejoinder enumerates the many points in which the bishops refused to accede to the wishes of the nonconformists, and complains generally of " the paucity of the concessions and the inconsiderableness of them, they being, for the most part, verbal and literal, rather than real and substantial." The rejoinder 30 itself opens thus : " The strain of these papers, we fear, is like to persuade many that your design is not the same with ours. Being assured that it is our duty to do what we can to the peace and concord of believers,—instead of consent or amicable debates, in order to the removal of our differences, we have received from you 35 a paper abounding with sharp accusations, as if your work were to prove us bad and make us odious : which, as it is attempted on mistake by unrighteous means, so were it accomplished, we know

however natural in the minds of eager and disappointed partisans, were lamentably out of place in an attempt to bring two parties of opposite sentiments to a mutual understanding.

Of the four months, to which the commission was limited, only ten days were now remaining. The nonconformists entreated that before their powers expired, an attempt might be made to hold a personal conference, and to conduct a disputation on terms acceptable to both parties. After two days' debating on this preliminary question, the bishops, though unwilling to abandon the ground they had hitherto taken, and foreseeing the inevitable issue of such an experiment, thought it prudent to consent; and three persons were chosen on each side to carry on the business of the conference. Dr. Pearson, Dr. Gunning, and Dr.

not how it will conduce to the concord which ought to be our common end." It contains elsewhere, together with many others, the following caustic observations : " The way to make us think the bishops to be so wise and careful guides and fathers to us, is not for them to seem wiser than the apostles, and make those things of standing necessity to the church's unity which the apostles never made so, nor to forbid all to preach the gospel or to hold communion with the church, that dare not conform to things unnecessary. Love and tenderness are not used to express themselves by hurting and destroying men for nothing." (p. 11.)   " We must protest before God and men against the dose of opium which you here prescribe or wish for, as that which plainly tendeth to cure the disease by the extinguishing of life, and to unite us all in a dead religion." (p. 23.) " If you are resolved to make all that a matter of contention, which we desire to make a means of peace, there is no remedy, while you have the ball before you, and have the wind and sun, and the power of contending without control." (p. 24.)   " O lamentable charity, that smoothes men's way to hell, and keepeth them ignorant of their danger, till they are past remedy !" (p. 127.) The concluding words are, " If those be all the abatements and amendments you will admit, you sell your innocency and the church's peace for nothing."

Sparrow represented the episcopal party; and Dr.
Bates, Dr. Jacomb, and Mr. Baxter appeared on the
side of the nonconformists. A debate conducted indis-
criminately by six eager disputants could not fail to be
5 involved in great confusion; and if from the necessity
of the case it were then left to the management of
those two, who were the most impetuous among them,
occasion would be given for much personal asperity.
Both these consequences actually followed; and if it
10 be said that the bishops had not only foreseen the final
result, but had taken care to secure it by selecting Dr.
Gunning as their champion, it must be said in answer,
that the meeting was altogether in opposition to their
judgment, and that no person of their party could be
15 so little qualified for the office of mediation as was
Richard Baxter, the champion of their opponents.

At length bishop Cosin produced a paper, as from
a considerable person, which greatly narrowed the field
of controversy, and might possibly at an earlier period
20 have opened a way for some permanent arrangement.
It was proposed that the complainers should distinguish between what they charged as sinful, and
what they opposed as inexpedient. But the issue was
now inevitable; and though the controversy was hence-
25 forth reduced to writing, and summed up at last in
one⁹ single topic, "the sinfulness of enjoining ministers

⁹ The nonconformists alleged the eight following points as contrary to the word of God :

1. That no minister be admitted to baptize without the prescribed
30 use of the transient image of the cross.

2. That no minister be permitted to read or pray, or exercise the
other parts of his office, that dare not wear a surplice.

3. That none be admitted in communion to the Lord's supper
that dare not receive it kneeling : and that all ministers be enjoined
35 to deny it to such.

to deny the communion to all that dare not kneel," the nonconformists only added fresh occasions[r] for their own annoyance, and the whole conference became a perpetual monument of the futility and mischief of such experiments.   5

"And so," says bishop Kennett[s], "ended this conference without union or accommodation; the presbyterian divines depending too much on the encouragement[t] they had received from the king and his chief ministers, on the assurances given them by some of the 10 leading members of the parliament, and on the affec-

4. That ministers be forced to pronounce all baptized infants to be regenerate by the Holy Ghost, whether they be the children of Christians or not.

5. That ministers be forced to deliver the sacrament of the body 15 and blood of Christ unto the unfit, both in their health and sickness; and that with personal application putting it into their hands; and that such are forced to receive it, though against their own wills, in the conscience of their impenitency.

6. That ministers be forced to absolve the unfit, and that in abso- 20 lute expressions.

7. That they are forced to give thanks for all whom they bury, as brethren, whom God in mercy hath delivered and taken to himself.

8. That none may be a preacher that dare not subscribe that 25 there is nothing in the Common Prayer Book, the Book of Ordination, and 39 Articles, that is contrary to the word of God. Baxter's Life, by Sylvester, B. I. P. 2. p. 341.

[r] The formal argument in which this question was debated, is given in the ensuing chapter, as a specimen of logical disputation, 30 which was once universally practised by theologians, and is now altogether abandoned.

[s] Complete History, vol. iii. p. 254.

[t] They had the support generally of the earl of Manchester, the earl of Anglesey, and the lord Hollis; of whom, nevertheless, 35 Baxter says, "they would have drawn us to yield further than we did." Life by Sylvester, vol. I. P. 2. p. 278.

tions of the people; in all which they were mistaken, as well as in the merit of their cause." Dr. Calamy [u] complains of the latter portion of this statement; but if we make any alteration in it, it must be to the fol-
5 lowing effect: that their cause, when they undertook the management of it, stood fair in public estimation, and might reasonably be expected to have had some measure of success; but that being made gradually unpopular as the argument was protracted, it finally
10 became odious and insufferable, and sunk to a degree of abasement, from which its real merits ought to have preserved it. The presbyterians sought for an alteration in the established forms of worship on grounds that were considered captious and frivolous, and to an
15 extent calculated, in the judgment of their opponents, to increase the amount of disunion. It was not surprising or unreasonable that their demand should have been refused; but it would seem to follow, as a direct consequence of the refusal, that being prohibited from
20 interfering with the ritual of others, they might confidently ask that their own should be tolerated. And yet no such alternative appears to have been contemplated by either party. However natural it might be according to the principles of later times, nothing would have
25 been more incredible at that period than the supposition that a national religion was compatible with any scheme of general toleration. The Romanists, indeed, in the days of their adversity have appeared to support it, and the Independents have at all times declared it
30 to be the sum and substance of their confession; but at the time of the restoration it would have been generally considered to be inconsistent with the first princi-

u Life of Baxter, p. 170.

ples of reason as well as Scripture. The current of
public feeling had always been on the side of high prerogative and church authority ; and the flood had now
set in with the greater violence, as it had for some
years been obstructed in its progress. Toleration[x], there- 5
fore, in any extensive application of it, was a thing
impossible. The Presbyterians were as unwilling to
accept it now at the hands of the conformists, as they
had resolutely withheld it from others, when they
themselves were in a condition to bestow it : and if the 10
Independents came forward in its support, they only
created a tempest of bitterness and scorn, by invoking
the recollection of that period of confusion, when their
principles had prevailed, the only period when it was
ever known that toleration had been carried into 15
practice.

[x] Baxter, when consulted in the year 1663, "whether the way of
comprehension or indulgence was the more desirable," answered,
"the way desirable is, first, a comprehension of as many fit persons
as may be taken in by law ; and then, a power in his majesty to 20
indulge the remnant so far as conduceth to the peace and benefit of
church and state." It is evident from this answer that he wished
for the comprehension of all classes of presbyterians, and then that
the church so constructed should exercise a control in the toleration
of any other nonconformists. Life by Sylvester, B. I. P. 2. p. 435. 25
Martindale said a few years afterwards, " I did so little like a universal toleration, that I have oft said and once writ, in answer to a
book which Mr. Baxter after more largely answered in print, that if
the king had offered me any liberty, upon condition that I would
consent that Papists, Quakers, and all other wicked sects should have 30
theirs also, I think I should never have agreed to it." Life of Adam
Martindale, p. 198.

CHAPTER VII.

Documents connected with the conference at the Savoy.

I. Proceedings of the committee of divines appointed by the house of lords in 1641. Baxter's Life by Sylvester, B. I. P. 2. p. 369.

II. The first address and proposals of the ministers to king Charles II. Baxter's Life by Sylvester, B. I. P. 2. p. 232.

III. His majesty's declaration to all his loving subjects, bearing date October 25, 1660. Wilkins' Conc. vol. iv. p. 560.

IV. His majesty's letters patents for a commission of divines, bearing date March 25, 1661. Wilkins' Conc. vol. iv. p. 572.

V. The exceptions against the Book of Common Prayer, presented by the ministers May 4, 1661. Baxter's Life by Sylvester, B. I. P. 2. p.316.

VI. The answer of the bishops to the exceptions of the ministers. From the account of the proceedings of the Savoy Commissioners, published in 1661.

VII. The disputation in which the episcopal divines were opponents and the ministers respondents. From an account printed in 1662.

I.

A copy of the proceedings of some worthy and learned divines touching innovations in the doctrine and discipline of the Church of England ; together with considerations upon the Common Prayer Book. (The committee appointed by the house of lords in the year 1641.)[a]   5

INNOVATIONS IN DOCTRINE.

Quære 1. WHETHER in the twentieth article these words are not inserted, "Habet ecclesia authoritatem in controversiis fidei."

2. It appears by Stetfords, and the approbation of the 10 licensers, that some do teach and preach, " that good works are concauses with faith in the act of justification :" Dr. Dove also hath given scandal in that point.

3. Some have preached that works of penance are satisfactory before God.   15

4. Some have preached that private confession by particular enumeration of sins is necessary to salvation, " necessitate medii ;" both those errours have been questioned at the consistory at Cambridge.

5. Some have maintained that the absolution which the 20 priest pronounceth is more than declaratory.

6. Some have published, that there is a proper sacrifice in the Lord's supper, to exhibit Christ's death in the postfact, as there was a sacrifice to prefigure in the old law in the antefact, and therefore that we have a true altar ; and there- 25

[a] Corrected from a MS. in the Dolben papers, and a contemporary printed copy (Pamph. 35.) in the Bodleian.

fore not only metaphorically so called, so Dr. Heylin and others in the last summer's convocation; where also some defended, that the oblation of the elements might hold the nature of the true sacrifice, others the consumption[a] of the 5 elements.

7. Some have introduced prayer for the dead, as Mr. Brown in his printed sermon, and some have coloured the use of it with questions in Cambridge, and disputed that "preces pro defunctis non supponunt purgatorium."

10 8. Divers have oppugned the certitude of salvation.

9. Some have maintained the lawfulness of monastical vows.

10. Some have maintained that the Lord's day is kept merely by ecclesiastical constitution, and that the day is 15 changeable.

11. Some have taught a new and dangerous doctrine, that the subjects are to pay any sums of money imposed upon them, though without law, nay contrary to the laws of the realm, as Dr. Sybthorp, and Dr. Manwaring bishop of 20 St. David's, in their printed sermons, whom many have followed of late years.

12. Some have put scorns upon the two books of Homilies, calling them either popular discourses, or a doctrine useful for those times wherein they were set forth.

25 13. Some have defended the whole gross substance of Arminianism, that "electio est ex fide prævisa," that the act of conversion depends upon the concurrence of man's free-will; that the justified man may fall finally and totally from grace.

30 14. Some have defended universal grace, as imparted as much to reprobates as to the elect, and have proceeded "usque ad salutem ethnicorum," which the Church of England hath anathematized.

15. Some have absolutely denied original sin, and so 35 "evacuated the cross of Christ," as in a disputation at Oxon.

---

[a] consumption.] consummation is the reading of the contemporary copy in the Bodleian. Pamph. 35.

16. Some have given excessive cause of scandal to the church; as being suspected of Socinianism.

17. Some have defended that concupiscence is no sin, either in the habit or first motion.

18. Some have broached out of Socinus a most uncomfortable and desperate doctrine, that late repentance, that is, upon the last bed of sickness, is unfruitful, at least to reconcile the penitent to God.

ADD UNTO THESE SOME DANGEROUS AND MOST REPROVABLE BOOKS.

1. The Reconciliation of Sancta Clara, to knit the Romish and Protestant in one. Memorand. That he be caused to produce bishop Watson's book of the like reconciliation which he speaks of.

2. A book called "Brevis Disquisitio," printed (as it is thought) in London, and vulgarly to be had, which impugneth the doctrine of the Holy Trinity, and the verity of Christ's body (which he took of the blessed Virgin) in heaven, and the verity of our resurrection.

3. A book called "Timotheus Philalethes de Pace Ecclesiæ," which holds that every religion will save a man, if he holds the covenant.

INNOVATIONS IN DISCIPLINE.

1. The turning of the holy table altar-wise, and most commonly calling it an altar.

2. Bowing towards it, or towards the east, many times with three congees, but usually in every motion, access, or recess in the church.

3. Advancing candlesticks in many churches upon the altar so called.

4. In making canopies over the altar so called, with traverses and curtains on each side, and before it.

5. In compelling all communicants to come up before the rails, and there to receive.

6. In advancing crucifixes and images upon the parafront, or altar-cloth, so called.

7. In reading some part of the Morning Prayer at the holy table, when there is no communion celebrated.

8. By the minister's turning his back to the west, and his face to the east, when he pronounceth the creed, or reads prayers.

9. By reading the litany in the midst of the body of the church in many of the parochial churches.

10. By pretending for their innovations, the Injunctions and Advertisements of queen Elizabeth, which are not in force, but by way of commentary and imposition; and by putting to the liturgy printed "secundo, tertio Edwardi sexti," which the parliament hath reformed and laid aside.

11. By offering of bread and wine by the hand of the churchwardens or others, before the consecration of the elements.

12. By having a *credentia*, or side-table, besides the Lord's table, for divers uses in the Lord's supper.

13. By introducing an offertory before the communion, distinct from the giving of alms to the poor.

14. By prohibiting the ministers to expound the Catechism at large to their parishioners.

15. By suppressing of lectures, partly on Sundays in the afternoon, partly on week-days, performed as well by combination, as some one man.

16. By prohibiting a direct prayer before sermon, and bidding of prayer.

17. By singing the *Te Deum* in prose after a cathedral church way, in divers parochial churches, where the people have no skill in such musick.

18. By introducing Latin-service in the communion of late in Oxford, and into some colledges in Cambridge, at Morning and Evening Prayer, so that some young students, and the servants of the colledge, do not understand their prayers.

19. By standing up at the hymns in the church, and always at *Gloria Patri.*

20. By carrying children from the baptism to the altar so called, there to offer them up to God.

21. By taking down galleries in churches, or restraining the building of such galleries where the parishes are very populous.

T

MEMORANDUM.

1. That in all the cathedral and collegiate churches two sermons be preached every Sunday by the dean and prebendaries, or by their procurement, and likewise every holy-5 day, and one lecture at the least to be preached on working-days every week, all the year long.

2. That the musick used in God's holy service in cathedral and collegiate churches be framed with less curiosity, that it may be more edifying and more intelligible, and that no 10 hymns or anthems be used where ditties are framed by private men, but such as are contained in the sacred canonical Scriptures, or in our liturgy or prayers, or have publick allowance.

3. That the reading-desk be placed in the church where 15 divine service may best be heard of all the people.

CONSIDERATIONS UPON THE BOOK OF COMMON PRAYER.

1. Whether the names of some departed saints and others should not be quite expunged in the Kalender.

2. Whether the reading psalms, sentences of Scripture, 20 concurring in divers places, and the hymns, Epistles, and Gospels, should not be set out in the new translation.

3. Whether the rubrick should not be mended, where all vestments in time of divine service are now commanded, which were used 2 Edw. VI. 25

4. Whether lessons of canonical Scripture should be put into the Kalender instead of Apocrypha.

5. That the Doxology should be always printed at the end of the Lord's Prayer, and be always said by the minister.

6. Whether the rubrick should not be mended, where it is, 30 that the lessons should be sung in a plain tune; why not, read with a distinct voice?

7. Whether *Gloria Patri* should be repeated at the end of every psalm.

8. Whether, according to that end of the preface before 35 the Common Prayer, the curate should be bound to read morning and evening prayers every day in the church, if

he be at home, and not reasonably letted ; and why not only on Wednesday and Friday morning, and in the afternoon on Saturday, with holy-day eves ?

9. Whether the hymns, *Benedicite omnia opera,* &c. may not be left out.

10 In the prayer for the clergy, that phrase perhaps to be altered, " which only worketh great marvels."

11. In the rubrick for the administration of the Lord's supper, whether an alteration be not to be made in this, " that such as intend to communicate shall signify their names to the curate over night, or in the morning before prayers."

12. The next rubrick to be cleared, how far a minister may repulse a scandalous and notorious sinner from the communion.

13. Whether the rubrick is not to be mended, where the churchwardens are strictly charged to gather the alms for the poor before the communion begin ; for by experience it is proved to be done better when the people depart.

14. Whether the rubrick is not to be mended, concerning the party that is to make his general confession upon his knees before the communion ; that it should be said only by the minister, and then at every clause repeated by the people.

15. These words in the form of the consecration, " This is my body—This is my blood of the new testament," not to be printed hereafter in great letters.

16. Whether it will not be fit to insert a rubrick, touching kneeling at the communion, that is, to comply in all humility with the prayer which the minister makes when he delivers the elements.

17. Whether cathedral and collegiate churches shall be strictly bound to celebrate the holy communion every Sunday at the least, and might not it rather be added once in a month ?

18. In the last rubrick touching the communion, is it not fit that the printer make a full point, and begin with a new great letter at these words, " And every parishioner shall also receive the sacrament."

19. Whether in the first prayer at the baptism, these

words, "didst sanctify the flood Jordan, and all other waters," should not be thus changed, "didst sanctify the element of water."

20. Whether it be not fit to have some discreet rubrick made to take away all scandal from signing the sign of the cross upon the infants after baptism; or if it shall seem more expedient to be quite disused, whether this reason should be published, That in ancient liturgies no cross was consigned upon the party but where oil also was used; and therefore oil being now omitted, so may also that which was concomitant with it, the sign of the cross.

21. In private baptism the rubrick mentions that which must not be done, that the minister may dip the child in water being at the point of death.

22. Whether in the last rubrick of confirmation, those words be to be left out, "and be undoubtedly saved."

23. Whether the Catechism may not receive a little more enlargement.

24. Whether the times prohibited for marriage are quite to be taken away.

25. Whether none hereafter shall have licenses to marry, nor be asked their banns of matrimony, that shall not bring with them a certificate from their ministers that they are instructed in their Catechism.

26. Whether these words in matrimony, "with my body I thee worship," shall not be thus altered, "I give thee power over my body."

27. Whether the last rubrick of marriage should not be mended, that new married persons should receive the communion the same day of their marriage; may it not well be, or upon the next Sunday following when the communion is celebrated.

28. In the absolution of the sick, were it not plain to say, "I pronounce thee absolved?"

29. The psalm of thanksgiving of women after childbirth, were it not fit to be composed out of proper versicles taken from divers psalms?

30. May not the priest rather read the Commination in the desk, than go up to the pulpit?

31. The rubrick in the Commination leaves it doubtful, whether the litany may not be read in divers places in the church.

32. In the order of the burial of all persons, 'tis said, "We commit his body to the ground, in sure and certain hope of resurrection to eternal life;" why not thus, "knowing assuredly that the dead shall rise again?"

33. In the collect next unto the Collect against the Pestilence, the clause perhaps to be mended: "for the honour of Jesus Christ's sake."

34. In the litany, instead of "fornication and all other deadly sin," would it not satisfy thus? "from fornication and all other grievous sins."

35. It is very fit that the imperfections of the metre in the singing psalms should be mended, and then lawful authority added unto them, to have them publickly sung before and after sermons, and sometimes instead of the hymns of morning and evening prayer.

II.

ª *The first address and proposals of the ministers.*

May it please your most excellent majesty,

WE your majesty's most loyal subjects cannot but acknowledge it is a very great mercy of God, that immediately after your so wonderful and peaceable restoration unto your throne and government, (for which we bless his Name,) he hath stirred up your royal heart as to a zealous testimony against all prophaneness in the people, so to endeavour an happy composing of the differences, and healing of the sad breaches which are in the church. And we shall according to our bounden duty become humble suitors at the throne of grace, that the God of peace who hath put such a thing as this into your majesty's heart, will by his heavenly wisdom and holy Spirit so assist you therein, and bring your

ª This address has been corrected from a MS. copy preserved in the Tanner papers in the Bodleian, vol. xlix. fol. 7.

resolutions unto so perfect an effect and issue, that all the
good people of these kingdoms may have abundant cause to
rise up and bless you, and to bless God who hath delighted
in you to make you his instrument in so happy a work. That
as your glorious progenitor Henry VII. was happy in uniting 5
the houses of Lancaster and York, and your grandfather
king James of blessed memory in uniting the kingdoms of
England and Scotland, so this honour may be reserved for
your majesty as a radiant jewel in your crown, that by your
princely wisdom and Christian moderation, the hearts of all 10
your people may be united, and the unhappy differences and
misunderstandings amongst brethren in matters ecclesiastical
so composed, that the Lord may be one, and his Name one,
in the midst of your dominions.

In an humble conformity to this your majesty's Christian 15
design, we, taking it for granted that there is a firm agreement between our brethren and us in the doctrinal truths of
the reformed religion, and in the substantial parts of divine
worship, and that the differences are only in some various
conceptions about the ancient form of church-government, 20
and some particulars about liturgy and ceremonies, do in all
humble obedience to your majesty represent,—that in as
much as the ultimate end of church-government and ministry
is, that holiness of life and salvation of souls may be effectually
promoted, we humbly desire in the first place that we may be 25
secured of those things in practice, of which we seem to be
agreed in principles.

1. [b] That those of our flocks who are serious and diligent
about the matters of their salvation, may not by words of
scorn, or any abusive usages be suffered to be reproachfully 30
handled; but have liberty and encouragement in those
Christian duties of exhorting and provoking one another unto
love and good works, of building up one another in their
most holy faith, and by all religious and peaceful means of
furthering one another in the ways of eternal life; they being 35
not therein opposite to church-assemblies, nor refusing the

[b] This was put in because the serious practice of religion had been made the
common scorn, and a few Christians praying or repeating a sermon together had
been persecuted by some prelates as a heinous crime. BAXTER.

guidance and due inspection of their pastors, and being responsible for what they do or say.   •

2. ^cThat each congregation may have a learned, orthodox and godly pastor residing amongst them, to the end that the 5 people may be publickly instructed and edified by preaching every Lord's day, by catechising, and frequent administration of the Lord's supper, and of baptism, and other ministerial acts as the occasions and the necessities of the people may require both in health and sickness; and that effectual pro- 10 vision of law be made, that such as are insufficient, negligent, or scandalous, may not be admitted to, or permitted in so sacred a function and employment.

3. ^dThat none may be admitted to the Lord's supper, till they competently understand the principles of Christian reli- 15 gion, and do personally and publickly own their baptismal covenant, by a credible profession of faith and obedience, not contradicting the same by a contrary profession, or by a scandalous life: and that unto such only confirmation (if continued in the church) may be administered: and that the 20 approbation of the pastors to whom the catechising and instructing of those under their charge do appertain, may be produced before any person receive confirmation; which course we humbly conceive, will much conduce to the quieting of those sad disputes and divisions which have greatly troubled 25 the church of God amongst us, touching church-members and communicants.

4. ^eThat an effectual course be taken for the sanctification of the Lord's day, appropriating the same to holy exercises both in publick and private without unnecessary divertise- 30 ments; it being certain and by long experience found, that the observation thereof is a special means of preserving

c This was added because we knew what had been done, and was like to be done again. BAXTER.

d This was added because that the utter neglect of discipline by the over-hot 35 prelates had caused all our perplexities and confusions; and in this point is the chiefest part of our difference with them indeed, and not about ceremonies. BAXTER.

e This was added because abundance of ministers had been cast out in the prelates days, for not reading publickly a book which allowed dancing and such 40 sports on the Lord's day. BAXTER.

and promoting the power of godliness, and obviating prophaneness.

Then for the matters in difference, viz. church-government,
liturgy, and ceremonies, we most humbly represent unto your
majesty :   5

1. First, for church-government; that although upon just
reasons we do dissent from that ecclesiastical hierarchy or
prelacy disclaimed in the covenant, as it was stated and exercised in these kingdoms; yet we do not, nor ever did renounce the true ancient primitive episcopacy or presidency as 10
it was ballanced and managed by a due commixtion of presbyters therewith, as a fit means to avoid corruptions, par-
tiality, tyranny, and other evils which may be incident to the
administration of one single person : which kind of attem-
pered episcopacy or presidency, if it shall by your majesty's 15
grave wisdom and gracious moderation, be in such a manner
constituted, as that the forementioned, and other like evils may
be certainly prevented, we shall humbly submit thereunto.

And in order to an happy accommodation in this weighty
business, we desire humbly to offer unto your majesty some 20
of the particulars which we conceive were amiss in the episcopal government, as it was practised before the year 1640.

1. The great extent of the bishops diocess, which was
much too large for his own personal inspection, wherein he
undertook a pastoral charge over the souls of all those 25
within his bishoprick, which must needs be granted to be
too heavy a burthen for any one man's shoulders : the
pastoral office being a work of personal ministration and
trust, and that of the highest concernment to the souls of
the people, for which they are to give an account to Christ.   30

2. That by reason of this disability to discharge their
duty and trust personally, the bishops did depute the administration of much of their trust, even in matters of spiritual
cognizance, to commissaries, chancellors, and officials, whereof
some were secular persons, and could not administer that 35
power which originally appertaineth to the pastors of the
church.

3. That those bishops who affirm the episcopal office to
be a distinct order by divine right from that of the presbyter,

did assume the sole power of ordination and jurisdiction to themselves.

4. That some of the bishops exercised an arbitrary power, as by sending forth their books of articles in their visitations, 5 and therein unwarrantably enquiring into several things, and swearing the church-wardens to present accordingly. So also by many innovations and ceremonies imposed upon ministers and people not required by law [f]; and by suspending ministers at their pleasure,

10 For reforming of which evils, we humbly crave leave to offer unto your majesty,

1. The late most reverend primate of Ireland his Reduction of episcopacy unto the form of a synodical government, received in the ancient church; as a ground-work towards 15 an accommodation and fraternal agreement in this point of ecclesiastical government: which we the rather do, not only in regard of his eminent piety and singular ability, as in all other parts of learning, so in that especially of the antiquities of the church, but also because therein expedients are offered 20 to the healing of these grievances.

And in order to the same end, we further humbly desire that the suffragans or chorepiscopi, mentioned in the primate's Reduction, may be chosen by the respective synods, and by that election be sufficiently authorized to discharge their trust. 25 That the associations may not be so large as to make the discipline impossible, or to take off the ministers from the rest of their necessary employments.

That no oaths or promises of obedience to the bishops, nor any unnecessary subscriptions or engagements be made neces-30 sary to ordination, institution, induction, ministration, communion or immunities of ministers; they being responsible for any transgression of the law.

And that no bishops nor any ecclesiastical governors, may at any time exercise their government by their own private 35 will or pleasure; but only by such rules, canons, and constitutions, as shall be hereafter by act of parliament ratified and established: and that sufficient provision of law be made to

---

[f] This last clause is wanting in the MS. copy preserved in the Tanner papers.

secure both ministers and people against the evils of arbitrary government in the church.

2. CONCERNING THE LITURGY.

1. We are satisfied in our judgments concerning the law-fulness of a liturgy, or form of publick worship; provided 5 that it be for the matter agreeable unto the word of God, and fitly suited to the nature of the several ordinances, and necessities of the church; neither too tedious in the whole, nor composed of too short prayers, unmeet repetitions or responsals; not to be dissonant from the liturgies of other 10 reformed churches; nor too rigorously imposed; nor the minister so confined thereunto, but that he may also make use of those gifts for prayer and exhortation which Christ hath given him for the service and edification of the church.

2. That inasmuch as the Book of Common Prayer hath in 15 it many things that are justly offensive and need amendment, hath been long discontinued, and very many, both ministers and people, persons of pious, loyal and peaceable minds, are therein greatly dissatisfied; whereupon, if it be again im-posed, will inevitably follow sad divisions, and widening of the 20 breaches which your majesty is now endeavouring to heal; we do most humbly offer to your majesty's wisdom, that for preventing so great evil, and for settling the church in unity and peace, some learned, godly and moderate divines of both perswasions, indifferently chosen, may be imployed to compile 25 such a form as is before described, as much as may be in Scripture words; or at least to revise and effectually reform the old, together with an addition or insertion of some other varying forms in Scripture phrase, to be used at the minis-ter's choice; of which variety and liberty there be instances 30 in the Book of Common Prayer.

3. CONCERNING CEREMONIES.

We humbly represent that we hold our selves obliged, in every part of divine worship, to do all things decently, in order and to edification, and are willing therein to be deter-35 mined by authority in such things as being meerly circum-stantial, are common to humane actions and societies, and are to be ordered by the light of nature and Christian prudence, according to the general rules of the Word, which are always to be observed.

And as to divers ceremonies formerly retained in the Church of England, we do in all humility offer unto your 5 majesty these ensuing considerations:

That the worship of God is in it self perfect, without having such ceremonies affixed thereto ℰ.

That the Lord hath declared himself in the matters that concern his worship to be " a jealous God ;" and this worship 10 of his is certainly then most pure, and most agreeable to the simplicity of the gospel, and to his holy and jealous eyes, when it hath least of humane admixtures in things of themselves confessedly unnecessary adjoyned and appropriated thereunto; upon which account many faithful servants of the Lord, know- 15 ing his word to be the perfect rule of faith and worship, by which they must judge of his acceptance of their services, and must be themselves judged, have been exceeding fearful of varying from his will, and of the danger of displeasing him by additions or detractions in such duties wherein they must 20 daily expect the communications of his grace and comfort, especially seeing that these ceremonies have been imposed and urged upon such considerations as draw too near to the significancy and moral efficacy of sacraments themselves.

That they have, together with popery, been rejected by 25 many of the reformed churches abroad, amongst whom, notwithstanding, we doubt not but the Lord is worshipped decently, orderly, and in the beauty of holiness.

That ever since the reformation they have been matter of contention and endless disputes in this church, and have been 30 a cause of depriving the church of the fruit and benefit which might have been reaped from the labours of many learned and godly ministers, some of whom judging them unlawful, others unexpedient, were in conscience unwilling to be brought under the power of them.

35 That they have occasioned, by the offence taken at them by many of the people, heretofore, great separations from our

---

ℰ To this clause the Tanner MS. adds the following words: " for did they contribute anything to that necessary decency which the apostle requires, we might expect to meet with them in the apostle's time; there being no reason to 40 induce us to the use of them which might not have induced them."

church, and so have rather prejudiced than promoted the
unity thereof; and at this time, by reason of their long
disuse, may be more likely than ever heretofore to produce
the same inconveniencies.

That they are at best but indifferent, and in their nature 5
mutable; and that it is, especially in various exigencies of
the church, very needful and expedient that things in themselves mutable be sometimes actually changed, lest they
should, by perpetual permanency and constant use, be judged
by the people as necessary as the substantials of worship 10
themselves.

And though we do most heartily acknowledge your majesty to be *custos utriusque tabulæ,* and to be supream gover-
nour over all persons, and in all things and causes, as well
ecclesiastical as civil, in these your majesty's dominions, yet 15
we humbly crave leave to beseech your majesty to consider
whether, as a Christian magistrate, you be not as well obliged
by that doctrine of the apostle touching things indifferent, in
not occasioning an offence to weak brethren, as the apostle
himself (then one of the highest officers in the church of Christ) 20
judged himself to be obliged by; and whether the great work
wherewith the Lord hath intrusted your majesty be not rather
to provide by your sacred authority that the things which are
necessary, by virtue of divine command, in his worship should
be duly performed, than that things unnecessary should be 25
made by humane command necessary and penal. And how
greatly pleasing it will be to the Lord that your majesty's
heart is so tenderly and religiously compassionate to such of
his poor servants differing in some small matters, who prefer
the peace of their consciences in God's worship above all their 30
civil concernments whatsoever.

May it therefore please your majesty, out of your princely
care of healing our sad breaches, graciously to grant, that
kneeling at the sacrament of the Lord's supper, and such
holydays as are but of humane institution, may not be im- 35
posed upon such as do conscientiously scruple the observation of them: and that the use of the surplice and cross in
baptism, and bowing at the name of Jesus rather than the
name of Christ or Emanuel, or other names whereby that
divine Person, or either of the other divine Persons, is nomi- 40

nated, may be abolished; these things being, in the judgment of the imposers themselves, but indifferent and mutable, in the judgment of others a rock of offence, and in the judgment of all not to be valued with the peace of the church.

5   We likewise humbly represent unto your most excellent majesty, that divers ceremonies which we conceive have no foundation in the law of the land, as erecting altars, bowing towards them, and such like, have been not only introduced, but in some places imposed; whereby an arbitrary power 10 was usurped, divers ministers of the gospel, though conformable to the established ceremonies, troubled, some reverend and learned bishops offended, the protestants grieved, and the papists pleased, as hoping that those innovations might make way for greater changes.

15   May it therefore please your majesty, by such ways as your royal wisdom shall judge meet, effectually to prevent the imposing and using of such innovations for the future, that so, according to the pious intention of your royal grandfather king James of blessed memory, the publick worship may be 20 free, not only from blame but from suspicion.

In obedience to your majesty's royal pleasure graciously signified to us, we have tendered to your most excellent majesty what we humbly conceive may most conduce to the glory of God, to the peace and reforma-

25   tion of the church, and to the taking away not only of our differences, but the roots and causes of them. We humbly beg your majesty's favourable .acceptance of these our loyal and conscientious endeavours to serve[h] your majesty and the church of Christ, and

30   your gracious pardon if in any thing or expression we answer not your majesty's expectation; professing before your majesty, and before the Lord, the searcher of hearts, that we have done nothing out of strife, vain glory, or emulation, but have sincerely offered what

35   we apprehend most seasonable, as conducing to that happy end of unity and peace which your majesty doth so piously prosecute.

h The words " your majesty and" are wanting in the Tanner MS.

We humbly lay our selves, and these our addresses, at your majesty's feet, professing our unfeigned resolution to live and die your majesty's faithful, loyal and obedient subjects; and humbly implore your gracious majesty, according unto your princely wisdom and 5 fatherly compassion, so to lay your hand upon the bleeding rents and divisions that are amongst us, that there may be an healing of them: so shall your throne be greater than the throne of your fathers; in your days the righteous shall flourish, peace shall run down 10 like a river, and the generations to come shall call you blessed.

III.

His majesty's Declaration to all his loving subjects of his kingdom of England and dominion of Wales concerning ecclesiastical affairs.

CHARLES REX.   15

How much the peace of the state is concerned in the peace of the church, and how difficult a thing it is to preserve order and government in civil, whilst there is no order or government in ecclesiastical affairs, is evident to the world; and this little part of the world, our own dominions, hath had so late 20 experience of it, that we may very well acquiesce in the conclusion, without enlarging ourself in discourse upon it, it being a subject we have had frequent occasion to contemplate upon, and to lament, abroad as well as at home.

In our letter to the speaker of the house of commons from 25 Breda we declared how much we desired the advancement and propagation of the protestant religion; that "neither the unkindness of those of the same faith towards us, nor the civilities and obligations from those of a contrary profession (of both which we have had abundant evidence) could in the 30 least degree startle us, or make us swerve from it, and that nothing can be proposed to manifest our zeal and affection for it, to which we will not readily consent :" and we said then, "that we did hope in due time, ourself to propose somewhat for the propagation of it, that will satisfy the world, 5 that we have always made it both our care and our study, and have enough observed what is most like to bring disadvantage to it." And the truth is, we do think ourself the more competent to propose, and with God's assistance to determine many things now in difference, from the time we 10 have spent, and the experience we have had in most of the reformed churches abroad, in France, in the Low Countries, and in Germany, where we have had frequent conferences with the most learned men, who have unanimously lamented the great reproach the protestant religion undergoes from 15 the distempers and too notorious schisms in matters of religion in England : and as the most learned amongst them have always with great submission and reverence acknowledged and magnified the established government of the Church of England, and the great countenance and shelter 20 the protestant religion received from it, before these unhappy times ; so many of them have with great ingenuity and sorrow confessed, that they were too easily misled by misinformation and prejudice into some disesteem of it, as if it had too much complied with the church of Rome ; whereas they 25 now acknowledge it to be the best fence God hath yet raised against popery in the world ; and we are persuaded they do with great zeal wish it restored to its old dignity and veneration.

When we were in Holland, we were attended by many 30 grave and learned ministers from hence, who were looked upon as the most able and principal assertors of the presbyterian opinions ; with whom we had as much conference, as the multitude of affairs which were then upon us would permit us to have, and to our great satisfaction and comfort 35 found them persons full of affection to us, of zeal for the peace of the church and state, and neither enemies, as they have been given out to be, to episcopacy or liturgy, but modestly to desire such alterations in either, as without shaking foundations, might best allay the present distempers, which the

indisposition of the time and the tenderness of some men's
consciences had contracted. For the better doing whereof,
we did intend, upon our first arrival in this kingdom, to call
a synod of divines, as the most proper expedient to provide a
proper remedy for all those differences and dissatisfactions 5
which had or should arise in matters of religion ; and in the
mean time, we published in our declaration from Breda, "a
liberty to tender consciences, and that no man should be
disquieted or called in question for differences of opinion in
matter of religion, which do not disturb the peace of the 10
kingdom ; and that we shall be ready to consent to such an
act of parliament, as upon mature deliberation shall be
offered to us, for the full granting that indulgence."

Whilst we continued in this temper of mind and resolution,
and have so far complied with the persuasion of particular 15
persons, and the distemper of the time, as to be contented
with the exercise of our religion in our own chapel, according
to the constant practice and laws established, without enjoining that practice, and the observation of those laws in the
churches of the kingdom ; in which we have undergone the 20
censure of many, as if we were without that zeal for the
church which we ought to have, and which by God's grace
we shall always retain ; we have found ourself not so candidly
dealt with as we have deserved, and that there are unquiet
and restless spirits, who without abating any of their own 25
distemper in recompense of the moderation they find in us,
continue their bitterness against the church, and endeavour
to raise jealousies of us, and to lessen our reputation by their
reproaches, as if we were not true to the professions we have
made : and in order thereunto, they have very unseasonably 30
caused to be printed, published, and dispersed throughout the
kingdom a declaration heretofore printed in our name during
the time of our being in Scotland, of which we shall say no
more than that the circumstances, by which we were enforced
to sign that declaration, are enough known to the world ; 35
and that the worthiest and greatest part of that nation did
even then detest and abhor the ill usage of us in that particular, when the same tyranny was exercised there by the
power of a few ill men, which at that time had spread itself

over this kingdom; and therefore we had no reason to expect
that we should at this season, when we are doing all we can
to wipe out the memory of all that hath been done amiss by
other men, and, we thank God, have wiped it out of our own
5 remembrance, have been ourself assaulted with those reproaches, which we will likewise forget.

Since the printing this declaration, several seditious pamphlets and queries have been published and scattered abroad to
infuse dislike and jealousies into the hearts of the people, and
10 of the army; and some who ought rather to have repented
the former mischief they have wrought, than to have endeavoured to improve it, have had the hardiness to publish,
that the doctrine of the church, against which no man, with
whom we have conferred, hath excepted, ought to be re-
15 formed as well as the discipline.

This over passionate and turbulent way of proceeding, and
the impatience we find in many for some speedy determination in these matters, whereby the minds of men may be
composed, and the peace of the church established, hath
20 prevailed with us to invert the method we had proposed to
ourself, and even in order to the better calling and composing
of a synod (which the present jealousies will hardly agree
upon) by the assistance of God's blessed Spirit which we
daily invoke and supplicate, to give some determination our-
25 self to the matters in difference, until such a synod may be
called as may without passion or prejudice give us such
further assistance towards a perfect union of affections, as
well as submission to authority, as is necessary: and we are
the rather induced to take this upon us, by finding upon the
30 full conference we have had, with the learned men of several
persuasions, that the mischiefs, under which both the church
and state do at present suffer, do not result from any formed
doctrine or conclusion which either party maintains or avows,
but from the passion and appetite and interest of particular
35 persons, who contract greater prejudice to each other from
those affections, than would naturally rise from their opinions;
and those distempers must be in some degree allayed, before
the meeting in a synod can be attended with better success
than their meeting in other places, and their discourses in

pulpits have hitherto been; and till all thoughts of victory are laid aside, the humble and necessary thoughts for the vindication of truth cannot be enough entertained.

We must for the honour of all those of either persuasion, with whom we have conferred, declare, that the professions 5 and desires of all for the advancement of piety and true godliness are the same; their professions of zeal for the peace of the church the same; of affection and duty to us the same: they all approve episcopacy; they all approve a set form of liturgy; and they all disprove and dislike the 10 sin of sacrilege, and the alienation of the revenue of the church; and if upon these excellent foundations, in submission to which there is such a harmony of affections, any superstructures should be raised, to the shaking those foundations, and to the contracting and lessening the blessed gift 15 of charity, which is a vital part of Christian religion, we shall think ourself very unfortunate, and even suspect that we are defective in that administration of government with which God hath intrusted us.

We need not profess the high affection and esteem we 20 have for the Church of England as it is established by law, the reverence to which hath supported us with God's blessing against many temptations; nor do we think that reverence in the least degree diminished by our condescensions, not peremptorily to insist on some particulars of ceremony, which 25 however introduced by the piety and devotion and order of former times, may not be so agreeable to the present, but may even lessen that piety and devotion, for the improvement whereof they might happily be first introduced, and consequently may well be dispensed with; and we hope this 30 charitable compliance of ours will dispose the minds of all men to a cheerful submission to that authority, the preservation whereof is so necessary for the unity and peace of the church; and that they will acknowledge the support of the episcopal authority to be the best support of religion, by 35 being the best means to contain the minds of men within the rules of government: and they who would restrain the exercise of that holy function within the rules which were observed in the primitive times, must remember and consider that the ecclesiastical power being in those blessed times always subordinate and subject to the civil, it was likewise proportioned to such an extent of jurisdiction, as was most agreeable to that; and as the sanctity and simplicity and 5 resignation of that age did then refer many things to the bishops, which the policy of succeeding ages would not admit, at least did otherwise provide for, so it can be no reproach to primitive episcopacy, if where there have been great alterations in the civil government, from what was then, there have 10 been likewise some difference and alteration in the ecclesiastical, the essence and foundation being still preserved. And upon this ground, without taking upon us to censure the government of the church in other countries, where the government of the state is different from what it is here, or 15 enlarging ourself upon the reasons why, whilst there was an imagination of erecting a democratical government here in the state, they should be willing to continue an aristocratical government in the church, it shall suffice to say, that since by the wonderful blessing of God the hearts of this whole 20 nation are returned to an obedience to monarchic government in the state, it must be very reasonable to support that government in the church, which is established by law, and with which the monarchy hath flourished through so many ages, and which is in truth as ancient in this island as the 25 Christian monarchy thereof, and which hath always in some respects or degrees been enlarged or restrained, as hath been thought most conducing to the peace and happiness of the kingdom; and therefore we have not the least doubt, but that the present bishops will think the present concessions 30 now made by us to allay the present distempers, very just and reasonable, and will very cheerfully conform themselves thereunto.

I. We do in the first place declare our purpose and resolution is and shall be to promote the power of godliness, to 35 encourage the exercises of religion both public and private, and to take care that the Lord's day be applied to holy exercises, without unnecessary divertisements; and that insufficient, negligent, and scandalous ministers be not permitted in the church; and that as the present bishops are known to be men of great and exemplary piety in their lives, which they have manifested in their notorious and unexampled sufferings during these late distempers, and of great and known sufficiency of learning, so we shall take special care, by the assistance of God, to prefer no men to that office 5 and charge, but men of learning, virtue, and piety, who may be themselves the best examples to those who are to be governed by them; and we shall expect and provide the best we can, that the bishops be frequent preachers, and that they do very often preach themselves in some church of their dio- 10 cese, except they be hindered by sickness, or other bodily infirmities, or some other justifiable occasion, which shall not be thought justifiable if it be frequent.

II. Because the dioceses, especially some of them, are thought to be of too large extent, we will appoint such a 15 number of suffragan bishops in every diocese, as shall be sufficient for the due performance of their work.

III. No bishop shall ordain, or exercise any part of jurisdiction which appertains to the censures of the church, without the advice and assistance of the presbyters; and no 20 chancellors, commissaries, or officials, as such, shall exercise any act of spiritual jurisdiction in these cases, viz. excommunication, absolution, or wherein any of the ministry are concerned, with reference to their pastoral charge. However our intent and meaning is to uphold and maintain the profes- 25 sion of the civil law so far and in such matters, as it hath been of use and practice within our kingdoms and dominions; albeit as to excommunication, our will and pleasure is, that no chancellor, commissary, or official shall decree any sentence of excommunication, or absolution, or be judges in 30 those things wherein any of the ministry are concerned, as is aforesaid. Nor shall the archdeacon exercise any jurisdiction without the advice and assistance of six ministers of his archdeaconry, whereof three to be nominated by the bishop, and three by the election of the major part of the presbyters 35 within the archdeaconry.

IV. To the end that the deans and chapters may be the better fitted to afford counsel and assistance to the bishops, both in ordination and the other offices mentioned before, we

will take care that those preferments be given to the most
learned and pious presbyters of the diocese; and moreover,
that an equal number (to those of the chapter) of the most
learned, pious, and discreet presbyters of the same diocese,
5 annually chosen by the major vote of all the presbyters of
that diocese present at such elections, shall be always advising and assisting, together with those of the chapter, in all
ordinations, and in every part of jurisdiction, which appertains to the censures of the church, and at all other solemn
10 and important actions in the exercise of the ecclesiastical
jurisdiction, wherein any of the ministry are concerned : provided that at all such meetings the number of the ministers
so elected, and those present of the chapter shall be equal,
and not exceed one the other, and that to make the numbers
15 equal, the juniors of the exceeding number be withdrawn,
that the most ancient may take place; nor shall any suffragan
bishop ordain, or exercise the forementioned offices and acts
of spiritual jurisdiction, but with the advice and assistance of
a sufficient number of the most judicious and pious presbyters
20 annually chosen as aforesaid within his precincts : and our
will is that the great work of ordination be constantly and
solemnly performed by the bishop and his aforesaid presbytery, at the four set times and seasons appointed by the
church for that purpose.

25   V. We will take care that confirmation be rightly and
solemnly performed, by the information and with the consent
of the minister of the place; who shall admit none to the
Lord's supper, till they have made a credible profession of
their faith, and promised obedience to the will of God,
30 according as is expressed in the considerations of the rubric
before the Catechism; and that all possible diligence be used
for the instruction and reformation of scandalous offenders,
whom the minister shall not suffer to partake of the Lord's
table, until they have openly declared themselves to have
35 truly repented and amended their former naughty lives, as is
partly expressed in the rubric, and more fully in the canons;
provided there be place for due appeals to superior powers.
But besides the suffragans and their presbytery, every rural
dean (those deans, as heretofore, to be nominated by the

bishop of the diocese) together with three or four ministers
of that deanery, chosen by the major part of all the ministers
within the same, shall meet once in every month, to receive
such complaints as shall be presented to them by the ministers or churchwardens of the respective parishes; and also to 5
compose all such differences betwixt party and party as shall
be referred unto them by way of arbitration, and to convince
offenders, and reform all such things as they find amiss, by
their pastoral reproofs and admonitions, if they may be so
reformed; and such matters as they cannot by this pastoral 10
and persuasive way compose and reform, are by them to be
prepared for, and presented to the bishop; at which meeting
any other ministers of that deanery may, if they please, be
present and assist.   Moreover, the rural dean and his assistants are in their respective divisions to see, that the children 15
and younger sort be carefully instructed by the respective
ministers of every parish, in the grounds of Christian religion,
and be able to give a good account of their faith and knowledge, and also of their Christian conversation conformable
thereunto, before they be confirmed by the bishop, or ad- 20
mitted to the sacrament of the Lord's supper.

VI. No bishop shall exercise any arbitrary power, or do or
impose any thing upon the clergy or the people, but what is
according to the known law of the land.

VII. We are very glad to find, that all with whom we
have conferred, do in their judgments approve a liturgy, or 25
set form of public worship to be lawful; which in our judgment for the preservation of unity and uniformity we conceive
to be very necessary: and though we do esteem the liturgy
of the Church of England, contained in the Book of Common
Prayer, and by law established, to be the best we have seen; 30
and we believe that we have seen all that are extant and used
in this part of the world, and well know what reverence most
of the reformed churches, or at least the most learned men in
those churches have for it; yet since we find some exceptions
made against several things therein, we will appoint an equal 35
number of learned divines of both persuasions, to review the
same, and to make such alterations as shall be thought most
necessary, and some additional forms (in the Scripture phrase

as near as may be) suited unto the nature of the several parts
of worship, and that it be left to the minister's choice to use
one or other at his discretion.   In the mean time, and till
this be done, although we do heartily wish and desire, that
5 the ministers in their several churches, because they dislike
some clauses and expressions, would not totally lay aside the
use of the Book of Common Prayer, but read those parts,
against which there can be no exception ; which would be the
best instance of declining those marks of distinction, which
10 we so much labour and desire to remove ; yet in compassion
to divers of our good subjects, who scruple the use of it as
now it is, our will and pleasure is, that none be punished or
troubled for not using it, until it be reviewed, and effectually
reformed, as aforesaid.

15   VIII. Lastly, concerning ceremonies, which have administered so much matter of difference and contention, and which
have been introduced by the wisdom and authority of the
church, for edification and the improvement of piety, we shall
say no more, but that we have the more esteem of all, and
20 reverence for many of them, by having been present in many
of those churches, where they are most abolished, or discountenanced ; and it cannot be doubted, but that as the universal
church cannot introduce one ceremony in the worship of
God, that is contrary to God's word expressed in the Scrip-
25 ture, so every national church, with the approbation and
consent of the sovereign power, may, and hath always introduced such particular ceremonies, as in that conjuncture of
time are thought most proper for edification and the necessary improvement of piety and devotion in the people, though
30 the necessary practice thereof cannot be deduced from Scripture ; and that which before was, and in itself is indifferent,
ceases to be indifferent, after it is once established by law :
and therefore our present consideration and work is to
gratify the private consciences of those, who are grieved with
35 the use of some ceremonies, by indulging to and dispensing
with their omitting those ceremonies, not utterly to abolish
any which are established by law, (if any are practised contrary to law, the same shall cease,) which would be unjust,
and of ill example ; and to impose upon the conscience of

some, for the satisfaction of the conscience of others, which is otherwise provided for. As it could not be reasonable that men should expect, that we should ourself decline, or enjoin others to do so, to receive the blessed sacrament upon our knees, which in our conscience is the most humble, most devout, and most agreeable posture for that holy duty, because some other men, upon reasons best, if not only, known to themselves, choose rather to do it sitting or standing; we shall leave all decisions and determinations of that kind, if they shall be thought necessary for a perfect and entire unity and uniformity throughout the nation, to the advice of a national synod, which shall be duly called after a little time, and a mutual conversation between persons of different persuasions hath mollified those distempers, abated those sharpnesses, and extinguished those jealousies, which make men unfit for those consultations; and upon such advice, we shall use our best endeavour, that such laws may be established, as may best provide for the peace of the church and state. Provided that none shall be denied the sacrament of the Lord's supper, though they do not use the gesture of kneeling in the act of receiving.

In the mean time, out of compassion and compliance towards those who would forbear the cross in baptism, we are content that no man shall be compelled to use the same, or suffer for not doing it; but if any parent desire to have his child christened according to the form used, and the minister will not use the sign, it shall be lawful for that parent to procure another minister to do it; and if the proper minister shall refuse to omit that ceremony of the cross, it shall be lawful for the parent, who would not have his child so baptized, to procure another minister to do it, who will do it according to his desire.

No man shall be compelled to bow at the name of Jesus, or suffer in any degree for not doing it, without reproaching those who out of their devotion continue that ancient ceremony of the church.

For the use of the surplice, we are contented that all men be left to their liberty to do as they shall think fit, without suffering in the least degree for wearing or not wearing it;

provided that this liberty do not extend to our own chapel,
cathedral or collegiate churches, or to any college in either
of our universities, but that the several statutes and customs
for the use thereof in the said places be there observed as
5 formerly.

And because some men, otherwise pious and learned, say
they cannot conform unto the subscription required by the
canon, nor take the oath of canonical obedience; we are
content, and it is our will and pleasure (so they take the
10 oaths of allegiance and supremacy) that they shall receive
ordination, institution, and induction, and shall be permitted
to exercise their function, and to enjoy the profits of their
livings, without the said subscription or oath of canonical
obedience; and moreover, that no persons in the universities
15 shall for the want of such subscription be hindered in the
taking of their degrees. Lastly, that none be judged to
forfeit his presentation or benefice, or be deprived of it, upon
the statute of the thirteenth of queen Elizabeth, chapter the
twelfth, so he read and declare his assent to all the articles
20 of religion, which only concern the confession of the true
Christian faith, and the doctrine of the sacraments comprised
in the Book of Articles in the said statute mentioned. In a
word, we do again renew what we have formerly said in our
declaration from Breda, for the liberty of tender consciences,
25 that no man shall be disquieted or called in question for differences of opinion in matters of religion, which do not disturb the peace of the kingdom: and if any have been disturbed in that kind since our arrival here, it hath not proceeded from any direction of ours.
30 To conclude, and in this place to explain what we mentioned before, and said in our letter to the house of commons
from Breda, that " we hoped in due time, ourself to propose
somewhat for the propagation of the protestant religion, that
will satisfy the world, that we have always made it both our
35 care and our study, and have enough observed what is most
like to bring disadvantage to it;" we do conjure all our loving
subjects to acquiesce in and submit to this our declaration
concerning those differences, which have so much disquieted
the nation at home, and given such offence to the protestant

churches abroad, and brought such reproach upon the protestant religion in general, from the enemies thereof; as if upon obscure notions of faith and fancy, it did admit the practice of Christian duties and obedience to be discountenanced and suspended, and introduce a license in opinions 5 and manners, to the prejudice of the Christian faith. And let us all endeavour, and emulate each other in those endeavours, to countenance and advance the protestant religion abroad, which will be best done by supporting the dignity and reverence due to the best reformed protestant church at 10 home; and which being once freed from the calumnies and reproaches it hath undergone from these late ill times, will be the best shelter for those abroad, which will by that countenance both be the better protected against their enemies, and be the more easily induced to compose the differences amongst 15 themselves, which give their enemies more advantage against them: and we hope and expect that all men will henceforward forbear to vent any such doctrine in the pulpit, or to endeavour to work in such manner upon the affections of the people, as may dispose them to an ill opinion of us and the 20 government, and to disturb the peace of the kingdom; which if all men will in their several vocations endeavour to preserve with the same affection and zeal we ourself will do, all our good subjects will by God's blessing upon us enjoy as great a measure of felicity as this nation hath ever done, and 25 which we shall constantly labour to procure for them, as the greatest blessing God can bestow upon us in this world. Given at our court at Whitehall this twenty-fifth day of October, MDCLX.

IV.

The king's warrant for the conference at the Savoy. 30

CHARLES the Second, by the grace of God, king of England, Scotland, France and Ireland, defender of the faith, &c. To our trusty and well-beloved the most reverend

father in God accepted archbishop of York, the right reverend
fathers in God Gilbert bishop of London, John bishop of
Durham, John bishop of Rochester, Henry bishop of Chichester, Humphrey bishop of Sarum, George bishop of Wor-
5 cester, Robert bishop of Lincoln, Benjamin bishop of Peterburgh, Bryan bishop of Chester, Richard bishop of Carlisle,
John bishop of Exeter, Edward bishop of Norwich, and to
our trusty and well-beloved the reverend Anthony Tuckney
Dr. in divinity, John Conant Dr. in divinity, William Spur-
10 stow Dr. in divinity, John Wallis Dr. in divinity, Thomas
Manton Dr. in divinity, Edmund Calamy batchelor in divinity, Richard Baxter clerk, Arthur Jackson clerk, Thomas
Case, Samuel Clark, Matthew Newcomen clerks, and to our
trusty and well-beloved Dr. Earles dean of Westminster,
15 Peter Heylin Dr. in divinity, John Hacket Dr. in divinity,
John Barwick Dr. in divinity, Peter Gunning Dr. in divinity,
John Pearson Dr. in divinity, Thomas Pierce Dr. in divinity,
Anthony Sparrow Dr. in divinity, Herbert Thorndike batchelor in divinity, Thomas Horton Dr. in divinity, Thomas
20 Jacomb Dr. in divinity, William Bates, John Rawlinson
clerks, William Cooper clerk, Dr. John Lightfoot, Dr. John
Collins, Dr. Benjamin Woodbridge, and William Drake clerk,
greeting. Whereas by our Declaration of the five and twentieth of October last concerning ecclesiastical affairs, we did
25 amongst other things express an esteem of the liturgy of the
Church of England, contained in the Book of Common Prayer,
and yet since we find some exceptions made against several
things therein, we did by our said Declaration declare we
would appoint an equal number of learned divines of both
30 perswasions, to review the same, and to make such alterations therein as shall be thought most necessary, and some
additional forms in the Scripture phrase, as near as might
be, suited to the nature of the several parts of worship; we
therefore in accomplishment of our said will and intent, and
35 of our continued and constant care and study for the peace
and unity of the churches within our dominions, and for the
removal of all exceptions and differences, and the occasions
of such differences and exceptions from amongst our good
subjects for or concerning the said Book of Common Prayer,

or any thing therein contained, do by these our letters patents require, authorize, constitute and appoint you the said accepted archbishop of York, Gilbert bishop of London, John bishop of Durham, John bishop of Rochester, Henry bishop of Chichester, Humphrey bishop of Sarum, George bishop of 5 Worcester, Robert bishop of Lincoln, Benjamin bishop of Peterburgh, Bryan bishop of Chester, Richard bishop of Carlisle, John bishop of Exeter, Edward bishop of Norwich, Anthony Tuckney, John Conant, William Spurstow, John Wallis, Thomas Manton, Edmund Calamy, Richard Baxter, Ar- 10 thur Jackson, Thomas Case, Samuel Clark and Matthew Newcomen, to advise upon and review the said Book of Common Prayer, comparing the same with the most ancient liturgies which have been used in the church, in the primitive and purest times : and to that end to assemble and meet together, 15 from time to time, and at such times, within the space of four kalender months now next ensuing, in the masters lodgings in the Savoy in the Strand in the county of Middlesex, or in such other place or places as to you shall be thought fit and convenient, to take into your serious and grave considera- 20 tions, the several directions, rules and forms of prayer, and things in the said Book of Common Prayer contained, and to advise and consult upon and about the same, and the several objections and exceptions which shall now be raised against the same. And if occasion be, to make such reasonable and 25 necessary alterations, corrections and amendments therein, as by and between you the said archbishop, bishops, doctors, and persons hereby required and authorized to meet and advise as aforesaid, shall be agreed upon to be needful or expedient for the giving satisfaction unto tender consciences, and 30 the restoring and continuance of peace and unity, in the churches under our protection and government ; but avoiding, as much as may be, all unnecessary ¹ alterations of the forms and liturgy wherewith the people are already acquainted, and have so long received in the Church of England. And 35 our will and pleasure is, that when you the said archbishop,

¹ In some copies (as in Kennet's Register, Wilkins' Conc., &c.) this is "abbreviations." In Baxter's Life, written by himself, it is "alterations." Nicholls notices both readings.

bishops, doctors and persons authorized and appointed by these our letters patents, to meet, advise and consult upon and about the premises, as aforesaid, shall have drawn your consultations to any resolution and determination, which you 5 shall agree upon as needful or expedient to be done for the altering, diminishing or enlarging the said Book of Common Prayer, or any part thereof, that then you forthwith certifie and present unto us in writing, under your several hands, the matters and things whereupon you shall so determine, 10 for our approbation; and to the end the same, or so much thereof as shall be approved by us, may be established. And forasmuch as the said archbishop and bishops, having several great charges to attend, which we would not dispense with, or that the same should be neglected upon any great 15 occasion whatsoever, and some of them being of great age and infirmities, may not be able constantly to attend the execution of the service and authority hereby given and required by us in the meetings and consultations aforesaid, we will therefore, and do hereby require and authorize you the 20 said Dr. Earles, Peter Heylin, John Hacket, John Barwick, Peter Gunning, John Pearson, Thomas Pierce, Anthony Sparrow, and Herbert Thorndike, to supply the place or places of such of the said archbishop and bishops (other than the said Edward bishop of Norwich) as shall by age, sickness, 25 infirmity, or other occasion, be hindred from attending the said meetings or consultations, (that is to say,) that one of you the said Dr. Earles, Peter Heylin, John Hacket, Johr Barwick, Peter Gunning, John Pearson, Thomas Pierce, Anthony Sparrow, and Herbert Thorndike shall from time to 30 time supply the place of each one of them, the said archbishop and bishops, other than the said Edward bishop of Norwich, which shall happen to be hindred, or to be absent from the said meeting or consultations, and shall and may advise, consult, and determine, and also certifie and execute, 35 all and singular the powers and authorities before mentioned, in and about the premises, as fully and absolutely, as such archbishop or bishops, which shall so happen to be absent, should or might do by vertue of these our letters patents, or any thing therein contained, in case he or they were personally present. And whereas in regard of the distance of some, the infirmities of others, the multitude of constant imployments, and other incidental impediments, some of you the said Edward bishop of Norwich, Anthony Tuckney, John Conant, 5 William Spurstow, John Wallis, Thomas Manton, Edmund Calamy, Rich. Baxter, Arthur Jackson, Thomas Case, Samuel Clark, and Matthew Newcomen may be hindred from the constant attendance in the execution of the service aforesaid; we therefore will, and do hereby require and authorize you 10 the said Tho. Horton, Thomas Jacomb, William Bates, John Rawlinson, William Cooper, John Lightfoot, John Collins, Benjamin Woodbridge, and William Drake to supply the place or places of such the commissioners last above mentioned, as shall by the means aforesaid, or any other occa- 15 sion, be hindred from the said meetings and consultations; (that is to say) that one of you the said Thomas Horton, Thomas Jacomb, William Bates, John Rawlinson, William Cooper, Dr. Lightfoot, Dr. Collins, Mr. Woodbridge, and Mr. Drake shall from time to time supply the place of each one of 20 the said commissioners last mentioned, which shall happen to be hindred, or be absent from the meetings and consulta- tions; and shall and may advise, consult and determine, and also certifie and execute all and singular the powers and au- thorities before mentioned, in and about the premises, as fully 25 and absolutely as such of the said last mentioned commission- ers, which shall so happen to be absent, should or might do by vertue of these our letters patents, or any thing therein con- tained, in case he or they were personally present.

In witness whereof we have caused these our letters to be made patents. Witness our self at Westminster, the five and 30 twentieth day of March, in the thirteenth year of our reign.

> Per ipsum Regem
> BARKER.

V.

The exceptions against the Book of Common Prayer.

ACKNOWLEDGING with all humility and thankfulness, his majesty's most princely condescention and indulgence, to very many of his loyal subjects, as well in his majesty's most 5 gracious declaration, as particularly in this present commission, issued forth in pursuance thereof; we doubt not but the right reverend bishops, and all the rest of his majesty's commissioners intrusted in this work, will, in imitation of his majesty's most prudent and Christian moderation and cle-10 mency, judge it their duty (what we find to be the apostles' own practice) in a special manner to be tender of the churches peace, to bear with the infirmities of the weak, and not to please themselves, nor to measure the consciences of other men by the light and latitude of their own, but seriously and 15 readily to consider and advise of such expedients, as may most conduce to the healing of our breaches, and uniting those that differ.

And albeit we have an high and honourable esteem of those godly and learned bishops and others, who were the 20 first compilers of the publick liturgy, and do look upon it as an excellent and worthy work, for that time, when the Church of England made her first step out of such a mist of popish ignorance and superstition wherein it formerly was involved ; yet considering that all human works do gradually arrive at 25 their maturity and perfection, and this in particular being a work of that nature, hath already admitted several emendations since the first compiling thereof :

It cannot be thought any disparagement or derogation either to the work it self, or to the compilers of it, or to those 30 who have hitherto used it, if after more than an hundred years, since its first composure, such further emendations be now made therein, as may be judged necessary for satisfying the scruples of a multitude of sober persons, who cannot at all (or very hardly) comply with the use of it, as now it is, 35 and may best sute with the present times after so long an enjoyment of the glorious light of the gospel, and so happy a reformation. Especially considering that many godly and learned men have from the beginning all along earnestly desired the alteration of many things therein, and very many of his majesty's pious, peaceable, and loyal subjects, after so 5 long a discontinuance of it, are more averse from it than heretofore : the satisfying of whom (as far as may be) will very much conduce to that peace and unity which is so much desired by all good men, and so much endeavoured by his most excellent majesty.   10

And therefore in pursuance of this his majesty's most gracious commission, for the satisfaction of tender consciences, and the procuring of peace and unity amongst our selves, we judge meet to propose,

First, that all the prayers, and other materials of the 15 liturgy may consist of nothing *doubtful* or *questioned* amongst pious, learned, and orthodox persons, inasmuch as the professed end of composing them is for the declaring of the unity and consent of all who join in the publick worship ; it being too evident that the limiting of church-communion to things 20 of *doubtful disputation*, hath been in all ages the ground of schism and separation, according to the saying of a learned person [c].

" To load our publick forms with the private fancies upon which we differ, is the most soveraign way to perpetuate 25 schism to the world's end. Prayer, confession, thanksgiving, reading of the Scriptures, and administration of the sacraments in the plainest and simplest manner, were matter enough to furnish out a sufficient liturgy, though nothing either of private opinion, or of church-pomp, of garments, or 30 prescribed gestures, of imagery, of musick, of matter concerning the dead, of many superfluities which creep into the church under the name of *order* and *decency*, did interpose itself. To charge churches and liturgies with things unnecessary, was the first beginning of all superstition, and 35 when scruple of conscience began to be made or pretended, then schism began to break in. If the special guides and fathers of the church would be a little sparing of incumbering

[c] Mr. Hales.

churches with superfluities, or not over-rigid, either in reviving obsolete customs, or imposing new, there would be far
less cause of schism or superstition ; and all the inconvenience were likely to ensue would be but this, they should in so
5 doing yield a little to the imbecillity of their inferiors ; a thing
which St. Paul would never have refused to do.   Mean while
wheresoever false or suspected opinions are made a piece
of church-liturgy, he that separates is not the schismatick ;
for it is alike unlawful to make profession of known, or sus-
10 pected falshood, as to put in practice unlawful or suspected
action."

   II. Further, we humbly desire that it may be seriously considered, that as our first reformers out of their great wisdom
did at that time so compose the liturgy, as to win upon the
15 papists, and to draw them into their church-communion, by
varying as little as they well could from the Romish forms
before in use ; so whether in the present constitution, and
state of things amongst us, we should not according to the
same rule of prudence and charity, have our liturgy so com-
20 posed, as to gain upon the judgments and affection of all
those who in the substantials of the protestant religion are of
the same persuasions with our selves : inasmuch as a more
firm union and consent of all such, as well in worship as in
doctrine, would greatly strengthen the protestant interest
25 against all those dangers and temptations which our intestine
divisions and animosities do expose us unto, from the common adversary.

   III. That the repetitions, and responsals of the clerk and
people, and the alternate reading of the psalms and hymns
30 which cause a confused murmur in the congregation, whereby
what is read is less intelligible, and therefore unedifying, may
be omitted : the minister being appointed for the people in all
publick services appertaining unto God, and the Holy Scriptures, both of the Old and New Testament, intimating the
35 people's part in publick prayer to be only with silence and
reverence to attend thereunto, and to declare their consent in
the close, by saying *Amen.*

   IV. That in regard the litany (though otherwise containing in it many holy petitions) is so framed, that the petitions

x

for a great part are uttered only by the people, which we
think not to be so consonant to Scripture, which makes the
minister the mouth of the people to God in prayer, the particulars thereof may be composed into one solemn prayer to be
offered by the minister unto God for the people.   5

V. That there be nothing in the liturgy which may seem
to countenance the observation of Lent as a religious fast;
the example of Christ's fasting forty days and nights being
no more imitable, nor intended for the imitation of a Christian,
than any other of his miraculous works were, or than Moses 10
his forty days fast was for the Jews: and the act of parliament, 5 Eliz. forbidding abstinence from flesh to be observed
upon any other than a politick consideration, and punishing
all those who by preaching, teaching, writing, or open speeches,
shall notifie that the forbearing of flesh is of any necessity for 15
the saving of the soul, or that it is the service of God, otherwise than as other politick laws are,

VI. That the religious observation of saints-days appointed
to be kept as holy-days, and the vigils thereof, without any
foundation (as we conceive) in Scripture, may be omitted.
That if any be retained, they may be called festivals, and not 20
holy-days, nor made equal with the Lord's-day, nor have any
peculiar service appointed for them, nor the people be upon
such days forced wholly to abstain from work, and that the
names of all others now inserted in the Calender which are
not in the first and second books of Edward the Sixth, may 25
be left out.

VII. That the gift of prayer, being one special qualification
for the work of the ministry bestowed by Christ in order to
the edification of his church, and to be exercised for the
profit and benefit thereof, according to its various and 30
emergent necessity; it is desired that there may be no such
imposition of the liturgy, as that the exercise of that gift be
thereby totally excluded in any part of publick worship.
And further, considering the great age of some ministers
and infirmities of others, and the variety of several ser- 35
vices oft-times concurring upon the same day, whereby it may
be inexpedient to require every minister at all times to read
the whole; it may be left to the discretion of the minister, to

omit part of it, as occasion shall require : which liberty we find to be allowed even in the first Common Prayer Book of Edward VI.

VIII. That in regard of the many defects which have been observed in that version of the Scriptures, which is used throughout the liturgy (manifold instances whereof may be produced, as in the epistle for the first Sunday after Epiphany, taken out of Romans xii. 1, " Be ye changed in your shape ;" and the epistle for the Sunday next before Easter, taken out of Philippians ii. 5, " Found in his apparel as a man ;" as also the epistle for the fourth Sunday in Lent, taken out of the fourth of the Galatians, " Mount Sinai is Agar in Arabia, and bordereth upon the city which is now called Jerusalem." The epistle for St. Matthew's day taken out of the second epistle of Corinth. and the 4th, " We go not out of kind." The gospel for the second Sunday after Epiphany, taken out of the second of John, " When men be drunk." The gospel for the third Sunday in Lent, taken out of the 11th of Luke, " One house doth fall upon another." The gospel for the Annunciation, taken out of the first of Luke, " This is the sixth month which was called barren," and many other places) ; we therefore desire instead thereof the new translation allowed by authority may alone be used.

IX. That inasmuch as the holy Scriptures are able to make us wise unto salvation, to furnish us throughly unto all good works, and contain in them all things necessary, either in doctrine to be believed, or in duty to be practised ; whereas divers chapters of the apocryphal books appointed to be read, are charged to be in both respects of dubious and uncertain credit : it is therefore desired, that nothing be read in the church for lessons, but the holy Scriptures of the Old and New Testament.

X. That the minister be not required to rehearse any part of the liturgy at the communion-table, save only those parts which properly belong to the Lord's supper ; and that at such times only when the said holy supper is administred.

XI. That as the word " minister," and not priest or curate, is used in the Absolution, and in divers other places ; it may throughout the whole book be so used instead of those two

words; and that instead of the word " Sunday," the word
" Lord's-day" may be every where used.

XII. Because singing of psalms is a considerable part of
publick worship, we desire that the version set forth and
allowed to be sung in churches may be amended; or that we 5
may have leave to make use of a purer version.

XIII. That all obsolete words in the Common Prayer, and
such whose use is changed from their first significancy, as
" aread" used in the gospel for the Monday and Wednesday
before Easter; " Then opened he their wits," used in the 10
gospel for Easter Tuesday, &c. may be altered unto other
words generally received and better understood.

XIV. That no portions of the Old Testament, or of the
Acts of the Apostles, be called " epistles," and read as such.

XV. That whereas throughout the several offices, the 15
phrase is such as presumes all persons (within the communion of the church) to be regenerated, converted, and in an
actual state of grace, (which, had ecclesiastical discipline been
truly and vigorously executed, in the exclusion of scandalous
and obstinate sinners, might be better supposed; but there 20
having been, and still being a confessed want of that, (as in
the liturgy is acknowledged,) it cannot be rationally admitted
in the utmost latitude of charity:) we desire that this may
be reformed.

XVI. That whereas orderly connection of prayers, and of 25
particular petitions and expressions, together with a competent length of the forms used, are tending much to edification, and to gain the reverence of people to them; there
appears to us too great a neglect of both, of this order, and
of other just laws, of method.   30

PARTICULARLY.

1. The collects are generally short, many of them consisting but of one, or at most two sentences of petition; and
these generally ushered in with a repeated mention of the
name and attributes of God, and presently concluding with 35
the name and merits of Christ; whence are caused many
unnecessary intercisions and abruptions, which when many
petitions are to be offered at the same time, are neither

agreeable to scriptural examples, nor suited to the gravity and seriousness of that holy duty.

2. The prefaces of many collects have not any clear and special respect to the following petitions; and particular petitions are put together, which have not any due order, nor evident connection one with another, nor suitableness with the occasions upon which they are used, but seem to have fallen in rather casually, than from an orderly contrivance.

It is desired, that instead of those various collects, there may be one methodical and intire form of prayer composed out of many of them.

XVII. That whereas the publick liturgy of a church should in reason comprehend the sum of all such sins as are ordinarily to be confessed in prayer by the church, and of such petitions and thanksgivings as are ordinarily by the church to be put up to God, and the publick catechisms or systems of doctrine, should summarily comprehend all such doctrines as are necessary to be believed, and these explicitly set down; the present liturgy as to all these seems very defective.

PARTICULARLY.

1. There is no preparatory prayer in our address to God for assistance or acceptance; yet many collects in the midst of the worship have little or nothing else.

2. The Confession is very defective, not clearly expressing original sin, nor sufficiently enumerating actual sins, with their aggravations, but consisting only of generals; whereas confession being the exercise of repentance, ought to be more particular.

3. There is also a great defect as to such forms of publick praise and thanksgiving as are suitable to gospel-worship.

4. The whole body of the common-prayer also consisteth very much of meer generals: as, " to have our prayers heard—to be kept from all evil, and from all enemies, and all adversity, that we might do God's will;" without any mention of the particulars in which these generals exist.

5. The Catechism is defective as to many necessary doctrines of our religion; some even of the essentials of Christianity not mentioned except in the Creed, and there not so explicite as ought to be in a catechism.

XVIII. Because this liturgy containeth the imposition of 5 divers ceremonies which from the first reformation have by sundry learned and pious men been judged unwarrantable, as

1. That publick worship may not be celebrated by any minister that dare not wear a surpless.

2. That none may baptise, nor be baptised, without the 10 transient image of the cross, which hath at least the semblance of a sacrament of human institution, being used as an ingaging sign in our first and solemn covenanting with Christ, and the duties whereunto we are really obliged by baptism, being more expresly fixed to that airy sign than 15 to this holy sacrament.

3. That none may receive the Lord's supper that dare not kneel in the act of receiving; but the minister must exclude all such from the communion: although such kneeling not only differs from the practice of Christ and of his apostles, 20 but (at least on the Lord's day) is contrary to the practice of the catholick church for many hundred years after, and forbidden by the most venerable councils that ever were in the Christian world. All which impositions are made yet more grievous by that subscription to their lawfulness which 25 the canon exacts, and by the heavy punishment upon the nonobservance of them which the act of uniformity inflicts.

And it being doubtful whether God hath given power unto men, to institute in his worship such mystical teaching signs, which not being necessary *in genere,* fall not under the rule of 30 " doing all things decently, orderly, and to edification," and which once granted will, upon the same reason, open a door to the arbitrary imposition of numerous ceremonies of which St. Augustine complained in his days; and the things in controversie being in the judgment of the imposers con- 35 fessedly indifferent, who do not so much as pretend any real goodness in them of themselves, otherwise than what is derived from their being imposed, and consequently the imposition ceasing, that will cease also, and the worship of God not become indecent without them.

Whereas on the other hand, in the judgment of the
5 opposers, they are by some held sinful, and unlawful in themselves; by others very inconvenient and unsuitable to the simplicity of gospel worship, and by all of them very grievous and burthensome, and therefore not at all fit to be put in ballance with the peace of the church, which is more
10 likely to be promoted by their removal than continuance: considering also how tender our Lord and Saviour himself is of weak brethren, declaring it much better for a man to have a "milstone hang'd about his neck, and be cast into the depth of the sea, than to offend one of his little ones:"
15 and how the apostle Paul (who had as great a legislative power in the church as any under Christ) held himself obliged by that common rule of charity, "not to lay a stumbling block, or an occasion of offence before a weak brother, chusing rather not to eat flesh whiles the world stands" (though
20 in itself a thing lawful) "than offend his brother for whom Christ died;" we cannot but desire that these ceremonies may not be imposed on them who judge such impositions a violation of the royalty of Christ, and an impeachment of his laws as insufficient, and are under the holy awe of that which
25 is written, Deut. xii. 32; "What thing soever I command you, observe to do it; thou shalt not add thereto, nor diminish from it;" but that there may be either a total abolition of them, or at least such a liberty, that those who are unsatisfied concerning their lawfulness or expediency, may not be
30 compelled to the practice of them, or subscription to them; but may be permitted to enjoy their ministerial function, and communion with the church without them.

The rather because these ceremonies have for above an hundred years been the fountain of manifold evils in this
35 church and nation, occasioning sad divisions between ministers and ministers, as also between ministers and people, exposing many orthodox, pious, and peaceable ministers to the displeasure of their rulers, casting them on the edge of the penal statutes, to the loss not only of their livings and

liberties, but also of their opportunities for the service of
Christ and his church; and forcing people either to worship
God in such a manner as their own consciences condemn, or
doubt of, or else to forsake our assemblies, as thousands have
done. And no better fruits than these can be looked for 5
from the retaining and imposing of these ceremonies, unless
we could presume, that all his majesty's subjects should have
the same subtilty of judgment to discern even to a ceremony
how far the power of man extends in the things of God,
which is not to be expected; or should yield obedience to all 10
the impositions of men concerning them, without inquiring
into the will of God, which is not to be desired.

We do therefore most earnestly entreat the right reverend
fathers and brethren, to whom these papers are delivered,
as they tender the glory of God, the honour of religion, the 15
peace of the church, the service of his majesty in the accomplishment of that happy union, which his majesty hath so
abundantly testified his desires of, to joyn with us in impor-
tuning his most excellent majesty, that his most gracious
indulgence, as to these ceremonies, granted in his royal 20
Declaration, may be confirmed and continued to us and our
posterities, and extended to such as do not yet enjoy the
benefit thereof.

XIX. As to that passage in his majesty's commission,
where we are authorized, and required to compare the present 25
liturgy with the most ancient liturgies which have been used
in the church in the purest and most primitive times; we
have in obedience to his majesty's commission, made enquiry,
but cannot find any records of known credit, concerning any
entire forms of liturgy, within the first three hundred years, 30
which are confessed to be as the most primitive, so the purest
ages of the church, nor any impositions of liturgies upon
any national church for some hundreds of years after. We
find indeed some liturgical forms fathered upon St. Basil,
St. Chrysostome, and St. Ambrose, but we have not seen 35
any copies of them, but such as give us sufficient evidence to
conclude them either wholly spurious, or so interpolated,
that we cannot make a judgment which in them hath any
primitive authority.

Having thus in general expressed our desires, we come now to particulars, which we find numerous and of a various nature; some, we grant, are of inferior consideration, verbal rather than material, (which, were they not in the publick 5 liturgy of so famous a church, we should not have mentioned,) others dubious and disputable, as not having a clear foundation in Scripture for their warrant: but some there be that seem to be corrupt, and to carry in them a repugnancy to the rule of the Gospel; and therefore have administred 10 just matter of exception and offence to many, truly religious and peaceable; not of a private station only, but learned and judicious divines, as well of other reformed churches as of the church of England, ever since the reformation.

We know much hath been spoken and written by way of 15 apology in answer to many things that have been objected; but yet the doubts and scruples of tender consciences still continue or rather are increased. We do humbly conceive it therefore a work worthy of those wonders of salvation, which God hath wrought for his majesty now on the throne, 20 and for the whole kingdom, and exceedingly becoming the ministers of the gospel of peace, with all holy moderation and tenderness to endeavour the removal of every thing out of the worship of God which may justly offend or grieve the spirits of sober and godly people. The things themselves 25 that are desired to be removed, not being of the foundation of religion, nor the essentials of publick worship, nor the removal of them any way tending to the prejudice of the church or state: therefore their continuance and rigorous imposition can no ways be able to countervail the laying 30 aside of so many pious and able ministers, and the unconceivable grief that will arise to multitudes of his majesty's most loyal and peaceable subjects, who upon all occasions are ready to serve him with their prayers, estates, and lives.

For the preventing of which evils we humbly desire that 35 these particulars following may be taken into serious and tender consideration.

CONCERNING MORNING AND EVENING PRAYER.

Rubrick.

That morning and evening prayer shall be used in the accustomed place of the church, chancel, or chappel, except it be otherwise determined by the ordinary of the place; and the chancel shall remain as in times past.

Exception.

We desire that the words of the first rubrick may be expressed as in the book established by authority of parliament 5 and 6 Edw. VI. thus; " The morning and evening prayer shall be used in such place of the church, chappel, or chancel, and the minister shall so turn him, as the people may best hear,

and if there be any controversie therein, the matter shall be referred to the ordinary."

Rubrick.

And here is to be noted, that the minister, at the time of the communion, and at other times, in his ministration, shall use such ornaments in the church, as were in use by authority of parliament, in the second year of the reign of Edward the Sixth, according to the act of parliament.

Exception.

Forasmuch as this rubrick seemeth to bring back the cope, albe, &c., and other vestments forbidden by the Common Prayer Book, 5 and 6 Edw. VI. and so our reasons alledged against ceremonies under our eighteenth general exception, we desire it may be wholly left out.

Rubrick.

The Lord's Prayer after the Absolution ends thus, " Deliver us from evil."

Exception.

We desire that these words, " For thine is the kingdom, the power and the glory, for ever and ever. Amen," may

be always added unto the Lord's Prayer; and that this prayer may not be enjoyned to be so often used in morning and evening service.

Rubrick.

And at the end of every psalm throughout the year, and likewise in 5 the end of *Benedictus, Benedicite, Magnificat,* and *Nunc Dimittis,* shall be repeated, "Glory be to the Father," &c.

10

Exception.

By this rubrick, and other places in the Common Prayer books, the *Gloria Patri* is appointed to be said six times ordinarily in every morning and evening service, frequently eight times in a morning, sometimes ten, which we think carries with it at least an appearance of that vain repetition which Christ forbids; for the avoiding of which appearance of evil, we desire it may be used but once in the morning, and once in the evening.

Rubrick.

15 In such places where they do sing, there shall the Lessons be sung, in a plain tune, and likewise the Epistle and Gospel.

20

Exception.

The Lessons, and the Epistles, and Gospels, being for the most part neither psalms nor hymns, we know no warrant why they should be sung in any place, and conceive that the distinct reading of them with an audible voice tends more to the edification of the church.

Rubrick.

Or this canticle, *Bene-*
25 *dicite omnia opera.*

Exception.

We desire that some psalm or scripture hymn may be appointed instead of that apocryphal.

IN THE LETANY.

Rubrick.

30 From all fornication, and all other deadly sin.

Exception.

In regard that the wages of sin is death; we desire that this clause may be thus altered; "From fornication, and all other heinous, or grievous sins."

Rubrick.	*Exception.*
From battel, and mur-ther, and sudden death.	Because this expression of "sudden death" hath been so often excepted against, we

desire, if it be thought fit, it may be thus read : " From battel and murther, and from dying suddenly, and unpre-pared."

Rubrick.	*Exception.*
That it may please thee to preserve all that travel by land or by water, all women labouring with child, all sick persons, and young children, and to shew thy pity upon all prisoners and captives.	We desire the term "all" may be advised upon, as seeming liable to just excep-tions ; and that it may be considered, whether it may not better be put indefinitely, "those that travel," &c. ra-ther than universally.

THE COLLECT ON CHRISTMAS DAY.

Rubrick.	*Exception.*
Almighty God, which hast given us thy only be-gotten Son, to take our nature upon him, and this day to be born of a pure virgin, &c.	We desire that in both collects the word " this day" may be left out, it being according to vulgar accepta-tion a contradiction.

Rubrick.

Then shall follow the collect of the Nativity, which shall be said conti-nually unto new-years-day.

THE COLLECT FOR WHITSUNDAY.

Rubrick.

God which upon this day, &c.

Rubrick.

The same collect to be read on Monday and Tuesday in Whitson-week.

5   *Rubrick.*

The two collects for St. John's day, and Innocents, the collects for the first day in Lent, for the fourth
10 Sunday after Easter, for Trinity Sunday, for the sixth and twelfth Sunday after Trinity, for St. Luke's day, and Michaelmas day.

Exception.

We desire that these collects may be further considered and abated, as having in them divers things that we judge fit to be altered.

THE ORDER FOR THE ADMINISTRATION OF THE LORD'S SUPPER.

Rubrick.

15 So many as intend to be partakers of the holy communion shall signifie their names to the curate over-
night, or else in the morning before the beginning
20 of morning prayer, or immediately after.

Exception.

The time here assigned for notice to be given to the minister is not sufficient.

Rubrick.

And if any of these be a notorious evil liver, the curate, having knowledge
25 thereof, shall call him and advertize him in any wise not to presume to the Lord's table.

Exception.

We desire the ministers' power both to admit and keep from the Lord's table, may be according to his majesty's declaration, 25th Oct., 1660, in these words, "The minister shall admit none to the Lord's supper till they have made a credible profession of their faith, and promised obedience to the will of God,
30 according as is expressed in the considerations of the rubrick before the Catechism; and that all possible diligence be used

for the instruction and reformation of scandalous offenders, whom the minister shall not suffer to partake of the Lord's table until they have openly declared themselves to have truly repented and amended their former naughty lives, as is partly expressed in the rubrick, and more fully in the 5 canons."

Rubrick.

Then shall the priest rehearse distinctly all the ten commandments, and the people kneeling, shall after every commandment ask God's mercy for transgressing the same.

Exception.

We desire,

1. That the preface prefixed by God himself to the 10 ten commandments may be restored.

2. That the fourth commandment may be read as in Exod. xx., Deut. v., " He 15 blessed the Sabbath-day."

3. That neither minister nor people may be enjoyned to kneel more at the reading of this than of other parts of Scriptures, the rather because many ignorant persons are thereby induced to use the ten commandments as a prayer. 20

4. That, instead of those short prayers of the people intermixed with the several commandments, the minister, after the reading of all, may conclude with a suitable prayer.

Rubrick.

After the Creed, if there be no sermon, shall follow one of the homilies already set forth, or hereafter to be set forth by common authority.

After such sermon, homily, or exhortation, the curate shall declare, &c.,

Exception.

We desire that the preach- 25 ing of the word may be strictly enjoined, and not left so indifferent, at the administration of the sacraments; as also that ministers may not 30 be bound to those things which are as yet but future and not in being.

Two of the sentences here cited are apocryphal, and four 35 of them more proper to draw

and earnestly exhort them to remember the poor, saying one or more of these sentences following.

out the people's bounty to their ministers, than their charity to the poor.

5 Then shall the churchwardens, or some other by them appointed, gather the devotion of the people.

Collection for the poor may be better made at or a little before the departing of the communicants.

Exhortation.

10 We be come together at this time to feed at the Lord's supper, unto the which in Gods behalf I bid you all that be here 15 present, and beseech you, for the Lord Jesus Christ sake, that ye will not refuse to come, &c.

If it be intended that these exhortations should be read at the communion, they seem to us to be unseasonable.

The way and means thereto is first to examine your lives and conversations; and if ye shall perceive your offences to be such as be not only against God, 20 but also against your neighbours, then ye shall reconcile your selves unto them, and be ready to make restitution and satisfactions.

And because it is requisite that no man should 25 come to the holy communion but with a full trust in God's mercy and with a quiet conscience.

We fear this may discourage many from coming to the sacrament, who lye under a doubting and troubled conscience.

Before the Confession.

30 Then shall this general confession be made in the

We desire it may be made by the minister only.

name of all those that are minded to receive the holy communion either by one of them, or else by one of the ministers, or by the priest himself.

Before the Confession.	*Exception.*
Then shall the priest or the bishop (being present) stand up, and turning himself to the people, say thus.	The minister turning himself to the people is most convenient throughout the whole ministration.

Before the preface on Christmas day, and seven days after.

Because thou didst give Jesus Christ, thine only Son, to be born as this day for us, &c.

Upon Whitsunday, and six days after.

According to whose most true promise, the Holy Ghost came down this day from heaven.

First, we cannot peremptorily fix the nativity of our Saviour to this or that day particularly. Secondly, it seems incongruous to affirm the birth of Christ and the descending of the Holy Ghost to be on this day for seven or eight days together.

Prayer before that which is at the consecration.

Grant us that our sinful bodies may be made clean by his body, and our souls washed through his most precious blood.

We desire, that whereas these words seem to give a greater efficacy to the blood than to the body of Christ, they may be altered thus, "That our sinful souls and bodies may be cleansed through his precious body and blood."

Prayer at the consecration.

Hear us, O merciful Father, &c., who in the same night that he was betrayed 5 took bread, and when he had given thanks, he brake it, and gave to his disciples, saying, Take, eat, &c.

We conceive that the manner of the consecrating of the elements is not here explicite and distinct enough, and the minister's breaking of the bread is not so much as mentioned.

Rubrick.

10 Then shall the minister first receive the communion in both kinds, &c., and after deliver it to the people in their hands, 15 kneeling; and when he delivereth the bread, he shall say, "The body of our Lord Jesus Christ, which was given for thee, preserve 20 thy body and soul unto everlasting life, and take and eat this in remembrance," &c.

We desire, that at the distribution of the bread and wine to the communicants, we may use the words of our Saviour as near as may be, and that the minister be not required to deliver the bread and wine into every particular communicant's hand, and to repeat the words to each one in the singular number, but that it may suffice to speak them to divers jointly, according to our Saviour's example.

We also desire that the kneeling at the sacrament (it being not that gesture which the apostles used, though Christ was personally present 25 amongst them, nor that which was used in the purest and primitive times of the church) may be left free, as it was 1 and 2 Edw., "As touching kneeling, &c., they may be used or left as every man's devotion serveth, without blame."

Rubrick.

30 And note, that every parishioner shall commu-

Exception.

Forasmuch as every parishioner is not duly qualified

Y

nicate at the least three times in the year, of which Easter to be one, and shall also receive the sacraments and other rites, according to the orders in this book appointed.

for the Lord's supper, and those habitually prepared are not at all times actually disposed, but many may be hindered by the providence of 5 God, and some by the distemper of their own spirits, we desire this rubrick may be either wholly omitted, or thus altered:

"Every minister shall be bound to administer the sacrament of the Lord's supper at least thrice a year, provided 10 there be a due number of communicants manifesting their desires to receive.

"And we desire that the following rubrick in the Common Prayer-book, in 5 and 6 Edw., established by law as much as any other part of the Common Prayer-book, may be re-15 stored for the vindicating of our church in the matter of kneeling at the sacrament (although the gesture be left indifferent): "Although no order can be so perfectly devised but it may be of some, either for their ignorance and infirmity, or else of malice and obstinacy, misconstrued, de-20 praved, and interpreted in a wrong part; and yet, because brotherly charity willeth that, so much as conveniently may be, offences should be taken away; therefore are we willing to do the same. Whereas it is ordained in the Book of Common-prayer, in the administration of the Lord's supper, that 25 the communicant kneeling should receive the holy communion, which thing being well meant for a signification of the humble and grateful acknowledging of the benefits of Christ given unto the worthy receivers, and to avoid the prophanation and disorder which about the holy communion might 30 else ensue, lest yet the same kneeling might be thought or taken otherwise, we do declare, that it is not meant thereby that any adoration is done or ought to be done either unto the sacramental bread or wine there bodily received, or unto any real or essential presence there being of Christ's natural 35 flesh and blood: for as concerning the sacramental bread and wine, they remain still in their very natural substances, and

therefore may not be adored, for that were idolatry to be abhorred of all faithful Christians; and as concerning the natural body and blood of our Saviour Christ, they are in heaven, and not here, for it is against the truth of Christ's
5 natural body to be in more places than in one at one time."

OF PUBLIC BAPTISM.

There being divers learned, pious and peaceable ministers who not only judge it unlawful to baptize children whose parents both of them are atheists, infidels, hereticks, or un-
10 baptised, but also such whose parents are excommunicate persons, fornicators, or otherwise notorious and scandalous sinners; we desire they may not be enforced to baptize the children of such, until they have made due profession of their repentance.

15   *Before Baptism.*

Rubrick.	*Exception.*
Parents shall give notice over night, or in the morning.	We desire that more timely notice may be given.
Rubrick.	*Exception.*
And the godfathers, and the godmothers, and the people with the children, &c.	Here is no mention of the parents, in whose right the child is baptised, and who are fittest both to dedicate it unto God, and to covenant for it: we do not know that any

25 persons except the parents, or some others appointed by them, have any power to consent for the children, or to enter them into covenant. We desire it may be left free to parents, whether they will have sureties to undertake for their children in baptism or no.

Rubrick.

Ready at the font.

In the first Prayer.

By the baptism of thy welbeloved Son, &c., didst sanctify the flood Jordan, and all other waters, to the mystical washing away of sin, &c.

The third Exhortation.

Do promise by you that be their sureties.

The Questions.

Doest thou forsake, &c.
Doest thou believe, &c.
Wilt thou be baptized, &c.

Exception.

We desire it may be so placed as all the congregation may best see and hear the whole administration. 5

It being doubtful whether either the flood Jordan or any other waters were sanctified to a sacramental use by Christ's being baptized, and 10 not necessary to be asserted, we desire this may be otherwise expressed.

We know not by what right the sureties do promise and 15 answer in the name of the infant: it seemeth to us also to countenance the anabaptistical opinion of the necessity of an actual profession of 20 faith and repentance in order to baptism. That such a profession may be required of parents in their own name, and now solemnly renewed when they present their children 25 to baptism, we willingly grant: but the asking of one for another is a practice whose warrant we doubt of; and therefore we desire that the two first interrogatories may be put to the parents to be answered in their own names, and the last propounded to the parents or pro-parents thus, " Will 30 you have this child baptized into this faith?"

The second Prayer before Baptism.

May receive remission of sins by spiritual regeneration.

This expression seeming inconvenient, we desire it may be changed into this; " May be regenerated and receive 35 the remission of sins."

In the Prayer after Baptism.

That it hath pleased thee to regenerate this infant by thy Holy Spirit.

We cannot in faith say, that every child that is baptized is "regenerated by God's Holy Spirit;" at least it is a disputable point, and therefore we desire it may be otherwise expressed.

After Baptism.

5 Then shall the priest make a cross, &c.

Concerning the cross in baptism, we refer to our 18th general.

OF PRIVATE BAPTISM.

We desire that baptism may not be administred in a private place at any time, unless by a lawful minister, and in 10 the presence of a competent number : that where it is evident that any child hath been so baptised, no part of the administration may be reiterated in publick, under any limitations : and therefore we see no need of any liturgy in that case.

OF THE CATECHISM.

15   *Catechism.*

1 *Quest.* What is your name, &c.

2 *Quest.* Who gave you that name?

20   *Ans.* My godfathers and my godmothers in my baptism.

3 *Quest.* What did your godfathers and godmothers 25 do for you in baptism?

2 *Ans.* In my baptism, · wherein I was made a

Exception.

We desire these three first questions may be altered ; considering that the far greater number of persons baptized within these twenty years last past, had no godfathers or godmothers at their baptism; the like to be done in the seventh question.

We conceive it might be more safely expressed thus; "Wherein I was visibly admitted into the number of the members of Christ, the

child of God, a member of Christ, and an inheritor of the kingdom of heaven.

children of God, and the heirs (rather than ' inheritors') of the kingdom of heaven."

Of the Rehearsal of the Ten Commandments.

10 *Ans.* My duty towards God is to believe in him, &c.

We desire that the commandments be inserted according to the new translation of the Bible.

In this answer there seems to be particular respect to the several commandments of the first table, as in the following answer to those of the second. And therefore we desire it may be advised upon, whether to the last word of this answer may not be added, " particularly on the Lord's day," otherwise there being nothing in all this answer that refers to the fourth commandment.

14 *Quest.* How many sacraments hath Christ ordained, &c. ?

Ans. Two only as generally necessary to salvation.

That these words may be omitted, and answer thus given; " Two only, baptism and the Lord's supper."

19 *Quest.* What is required of persons to be baptized ?

Ans. Repentance, whereby they forsake sin; and faith, whereby they stedfastly believe the promises of God, &c.

20 *Quest.* Why then are infants baptized when by reason of their tender age they cannot perform them?

We desire that the entring infants into God's covenant may be more warily expressed, and that the words may not seem to found their baptism upon a really actual faith and repentance of their own; and we desire that a promise may not be taken for a performance of such faith and repentance : and especially, that it be not asserted that they perform these by the promise of their sureties, it being to the seed of believers that the cove-

Ans. Yes: they do perform by their sureties, who promise and vow them both in their names.

nant of God is made; and not (that we can find) to all that have such believing sureties, who are neither parents nor pro-parents of the child.

5 In the general we observe, that the doctrine of the sacraments which was added upon the conference at Hampton-Court, is much more fully and particularly delivered than the other parts of the Catechism, in short answers fitted to the memories of children, and thereupon we offer it to be con-
10 sidered :

First, Whether there should not be a more distinct and full explication of the Creed, the Commandments, and the Lord's Prayer.

Secondly, Whether it were not convenient to add (what
15 seems to be wanting) somewhat particularly concerning the nature of faith, of repentance, the two covenants, of justification, sanctification, adoption, and regeneration.

OF CONFIRMATION.

The last Rubrick before the
20   *Catechism.*

And that no man shall think that any detriment shall come to children by deferring of their confirm-
25 ation, he shall know for truth, that it is certain by God's word, that children being baptized, have all things necessary for their
30 salvation, and be undoubtedly saved.

Although we charitably suppose the meaning of these words was only to exclude the necessity of any other sacraments to baptized infants; yet these words are dangerous as to the misleading of the vulgar, and therefore we desire they may be expunged.

Rubrick after the Catechism.

So soon as the children can say in their mother-

We conceive that it is not a sufficient qualification for

tongue the Articles of the
Faith, the Lord's Prayer,
and the Ten Command-
ments, and can answer
such other questions of
this short Catechism, &c.
then shall they be brought
to the bishop, &c. and the
bishop shall confirm them.

confirmation, that children be
able *memoriter* to repeat the
Articles of the Faith, commonly called ˙the Apostles'
Creed, the Lord's Prayer, and 5
the Ten Commandments, and
to answer to some questions
of this short Catechism ; for
it is often found that children
are able to do all this at four 10
or five years old. 2dly, It
crosses what is said in the
third reason of the first rubrick before confirmation, concerning the usage of the church in times past, ordaining that
confirmation should be ministred unto them that were of 15
perfect age, that they being instructed in the Christian religion, should openly profess their own faith, and promise to
be obedient to the will of God.   And therefore (3dly) we
desire that none may be confirmed but according to his
Majesty's Declaration, viz., " That confirmation be rightly 20
and solemnly performed by the information, and with the
consent of the minister of the place."

Rubrick after the Catechism.

Then shall they be
brought to the bishop by
one that shall be his god-
father or godmother.

This seems to bring in another sort of godfathers and
godmothers, besides those 25
made use of in baptism ; and
we see no need either of the
one or the other.

*The Prayer before the Impo-
sition of Hands.*

Who hast vouchsafed to
regenerate these thy ser-
vants by water and the
Holy Ghost, and hast given
unto them the forgiveness
of all their sins.

This supposeth that all the
children who are brought to 30
be confirmed have the Spirit
of Christ, and the forgiveness
of all their sins ; whereas a
great number of children at
that age, having committed 35
many sins since their baptism,

do shew no evidence of serious repentance, or of any special saving grace; and therefore this confirmation (if administred to such) would be a perilous and gross abuse.

Rubrick before the Imposition
5   *of Hands.*

Then the bishop shall lay his hand on every child severally.

This seems to put a higher value upon confirmation than upon baptism or the Lord's supper; for according to the rubrick and order in the Common Prayer Book, every deacon may baptize, and every 10 minister may consecrate and administer the Lord's supper, but the bishop only may confirm.

The Prayer after Imposition
of Hands.

We make our humble 15 supplications unto thee for these children; upon whom, after the example of thy holy apostles, we have laid our hands, to certifie them 20 by this sign of thy favour and gracious goodness towards them.

We desire that the practice of the apostles may not be alledged as a ground of this imposition of hands for the confirmation of children, both because the apostles did never use it in that case, as also because the Articles of the Church of England declare it to be a " corrupt imitation of the apostles' practice," Acts xxv.

We desire that imposition of hands may not be made, as here it is, a sign to certifie children of God's grace and favour 25 towards them; because this seems to speak it a sacrament, and is contrary to that fore-mentioned 25th article, which saith, that " confirmation hath no visible sign appointed by God."

The last Rubrick after Con-
firmation.

30   None shall be admitted to the holy communion,

We desire that confirmation may not be made so ne-

until such time as he can say the Catechism, and be confirmed.

cessary to the holy communion, as that none should be admitted to it unless they be confirmed.

OF THE FORM OF SOLEMNIZATION OF MATRIMONY.   5

The man shall give the woman a ring, &c. ———— shall surely perform and keep the vow and covenant betwixt them made, whereof this ring given and received is a token and pledge, &c.

Seeing this ceremony of the ring in marriage is made necessary to it, and a significant sign of the vow and covenant betwixt the parties; and 10 Romish ritualists give such reasons for the use and institution of the ring, as are either frivolous or superstitious; it is desired that this 15 ceremony of the ring in marriage may be left indifferent, to be used or forborn.

The man shall say, With my body I thee worship.

This word "worship" being much altered in the use of it 20 since this form was first drawn up; we desire some other word may be used instead of it.

In the name of the Father, and of the Son, and of the Holy Ghost.

These words being only used in baptism, and here in 25 the solemnization of matrimony, and in the absolution

of the sick; we desire it may be considered, whether they should not be here omitted, least they should seem to favour those who count matrimony a sacrament.   30

Till death us depart.

This word "depart" is here improperly used.

Rubrick.

Then the minister or clerk going to the Lord's table, shall say or sing this psalm.

Exception.

We conceive this change of place and posture mentioned 35 in these two rubricks is needless, and therefore desire it may be omitted.

Next Rubrick.

The psalm ended, and the man and the woman kneeling before the Lord's table, the priest standing at the table, and turning his face, &c.

5 | *Collect.* | *Exception.*

Consecrated the state of matrimony to such an excellent mystery.

Seeing the institution of marriage was before the fall, and so before the promise of Christ, as also for that the said passage in this collect seems to countenance the opinion 10 of making matrimony a sacrament, we desire that clause may be altered or omitted.

Rubrick.   *Exception.*

Then shall begin the communion, and after the 15 Gospel shall be said a sermon, &c.

This rubrick doth either enforce all such as are unfit for the sacrament to forbear marriage, contrary to Scripture, which approves the marriage of all men; or else compels all that marry to come to the Lord's table, though never so unprepared; and therefore we desire it may be omitted, the rather because that marriage festivals are too often accompanied with such divertisements as are unsuitable to those Christian duties, which ought to be before and follow after the receiving of that holy sacrament.

Last Rubrick.

The new married persons the same day of their 20 marriage must receive the holy communion.

25 | OF THE ORDER FOR THE VISITATION OF THE SICK.

Rubrick before Absolution.   *Exception.*

Here shall the sick person make a special confession, &c., after which con- 30 fession the priest shall absolve him after this sort:

Forasmuch as the conditions of sick persons be very various and different, the minister may not only in the exhortation, but in the prayer also be directed to apply

Our Lord Jesus Christ, &c., and by his authority committed to me, I absolve thee.

himself to the particular condition of the person, as he shall find most suitable to the present occasion, with due regard had both to his spiritu- 5 al condition and bodily weakness ; and that the absolution may only be recommended to the minister to be used or omitted as he shall see occasion.

That the form of absolution be declarative and conditional, as, " I pronounce thee absolved," instead of, " I absolve thee," 10 " if thou doest truly repent and believe."

OF THE COMMUNION OF THE SICK.

Rubrick.

But if the sick person be not able to come to church, yet is desirous to receive the communion in his house, then he must give knowledge over-night, or else early in the morning, to the curate ; and having a convenient place in the sick man's house, he shall there administer the holy communion.

Consider, that many sick persons either by their igno- 15 rance or vicious life, without any evident manifestation of repentance, or by the nature of the disease disturbing their intellectuals, be unfit for re- 20 ceiving the sacrament. It is proposed, that the minister be not enjoyned to administer the sacrament to every sick person that shall desire it, 25 but only as he shall judge expedient.

OF THE ORDER FOR THE BURIAL OF THE DEAD.

We desire it may be expressed in a rubrick, that the prayers and exhortations here used are not for the benefit of 30 the dead, but only for the instruction and comfort of the living.

First Rubrick.

The priest meeting the corpse at the church-stile, shall say, or else the priest and clerk shall sing, &c.

We desire that ministers may be left to use their discretion in these circumstances, 35 and to perform the whole service in the church, if they think fit, for the preventing of these inconveniences which many times both ministers and people are exposed unto by standing in the open air.

The second Rubrick.

5   When they come to the grave the priest shall say, &c.

Forasmuch as it hath pleased Almighty God, of 10 his great mercy to take unto himself the soul of our dear brother here departed; we therefore commit his body to the ground in sure and certain hope of resurrection to eternal life.

These words cannot in truth be said of persons living and dying in open and notorious sins.

15   *The first Prayer.*

We give thee hearty thanks for that it hath pleased thee to deliver this our brother out of 20 the miseries of this sinful world, &c.

These words may harden the wicked, and are inconsistent with the largest rational charity.

That we with this our brother, and all other departed in the true faith of thy holy Name, may have our perfect confirmation and bliss.

25   *The last Prayer.*

That when we depart this life, we may rest in him, as our hope is this our brother doth.

These words cannot be used with respect to those persons who have not by their actual repentance given any ground for the hope of their blessed estate.

OF THE THANKSGIVING OF WOMEN AFTER CHILD-BIRTH, COMMONLY CALLED CHURCHING OF WOMEN.

The woman shall come unto the church, and there shall kneel down in some convenient place nigh unto the place where the table stands, and the priest standing by her shall say, &c.

In regard that the women's kneeling near the table is in many churches inconvenient, 5 we desire that these words may be left out, and that the minister may perform that service either in the desk or pulpit. 10

Rubrick.

Then the priest shall say this psalm, 121.

Exception.

This psalm seems not to be so pertinent as some other, viz. as psalm 113. and psalm 128. 15

O Lord, save this woman thy servant.

Ans. Which putteth her trust in thee.

It may fall out that a woman may come to give thanks for a child born in adultery or fornication, and therefore we desire that something may be 20 required of her by way of profession of her humiliation, as well as of her thanksgiving.

Last Rubrick.

The woman that comes to give thanks, must offer the accustomed offerings.

This may seem too like a Jewish purification, rather 25 than a Christian thanksgiving.

The same Rubrick.

And if there be a communion, it is convenient that she receive the holy communion.

We desire this may be interpreted of the duly qualified; for a scandalous sinner may 30 come to make this thanksgiving.

Thus have we in all humble pursuance of his majesty's most gracious endeavours for the publick weal of this church,

drawn up our thoughts and desires in this weighty affair, which we humbly offer to his majesty's commissioners for their serious and grave consideration; wherein we have not the least thought of depraving or reproaching the Book of
5 Common Prayer, but a sincere desire to contribute our endeavours towards the healing the distempers, and (as soon as may be) reconciling the minds of brethren. And inasmuch as his majesty hath in his gracious declaration and commission mentioned new forms to be made and suted to the several
10 parts of worship; we have made a considerable progress therein, and shall (by God's assistance) offer them to the reverend commissioners with all convenient speed. And if the Lord shall graciously please to give a blessing to these our endeavours, we doubt not but the peace of the church
15 will be thereby setled, the hearts of ministers and people comforted and composed, and the great mercy of unity and stability (to the immortal honour of our most dear soveraign) bestowed upon us and our posterity after us.

VI.

The Answer of the Bishops to the Exceptions of the Ministers.

20   1. BEFORE we come to the proposals it will be perhaps necessary to say a word or two to the preface, wherein they begin with a thankful acknowledgment of his majestie's most princely condescension; to which we shall only say, that we conceive the most real expression of their thankfulness had
25 been a hearty compliance with his maties earnest and passionate request for the use of the present liturgy, at least so much of it as they acknowledge by these papers to be lawful: how far they have in this expressed their thankfulness the world sees, we need not say.

2. It can be no just cause of offence to mind them of their duty, as they do us of ours, telling us it is our duty to imitate the apostles' practice in a special manner, to be tender of the churches peace, and to advise of such expedients, as may conduce to the healing of breaches, and uniting those that 5 differ. For preserving of the churches peace we know no better nor more efficacious way than our set liturgy; there being no such way to keep us from schism, as to speak all the same thing, according to the apostle.

3. This experience of former and latter times hath taught 10 us; when the liturgy was duly observed we lived in peace; since that was laid aside there hath been as many modes and fashions of public worship, as fancies. We have had continual dissentions, which variety of services must needs produce, whilst every one naturally desires, and endeavours 15 not only to maintain, but to prefer his own way before all others; whence we conceive there is no such way to the preservation of peace, as for all to return to the strict use and practice of the form.

4. And the best expedients to unite us to that again, and 20 so to peace, are, besides our prayers to the God of peace, to make us all of one mind in a house, to labour to get true humility, which would make us think our guides wiser and fitter to order us than we ourselves, and Christian charity, which would teach us to think no evil of our superiors, but to 25 judge them rather careful guides and fathers to us; which being obtained, nothing can be imagined justly to hinder us from a ready compliance to this method of service appointed by them, and so live in unity.

5. If it be objected that the liturgy is in any way sinful 30 and unlawful for us to join with, it is but reason that this be first proved evidently before any thing be altered; it is no argument to say that multitudes of sober pious persons scruple the use of it, unless it be made to appear by evident reasons that the liturgy gave the just grounds to make such 35 scruples. For if the bare pretence of scruples be sufficient to exempt us from obedience, all law and order is gone.

6. On the contrary, we judge that if the liturgy should be altered, as is there required, not only a multitude but the

generality of the soberest and most loyal children of the
Church of England would justly be offended, since such an
alteration would be a virtual confession that this liturgy were
an intolerable burthen to tender consciences, a direct cause
5 of schism, a superstitious usage (upon which pretences it
is here desired to be altered) ; which would at once both
justify all those which have so obstinately separated from it,
as the only pious tender-conscienced men, and condemn all
those that have adhered to that, in conscience of their duty
10 and loyalty, with their loss or hazard of estates, lives, and
fortunes, as men superstitious, schismatical, and void of
religion and conscience. For this reason and those that
follow, we cannot consent to such an alteration as is desired,
till these pretences be proved ; which we conceive in no wise
15 to be done in these papers, and shall give reasons for this
our judgment.

Prop. 1. §. 1. To the first general proposal we answer,
That as to that part of it which requires that the matter of
the liturgy may not be private opinion or fancy, that being
20 the way to perpetuate schism ; the church hath been careful
to put nothing into the liturgy, but that which is either
evidently the word of God, or what hath been generally
received in the catholic church ; neither of which can be
called private opinion, and if the contrary can be proved, we
25 wish it out of the liturgy.

§. 2. We heartily desire that, according to this proposal,
great care may be taken to suppress those private conceptions of prayers before and after sermon, lest private
opinions be made the matter of prayer in public, as hath
30 and will be, if private persons take liberty to make public
prayers.

§. 3. To that part of the proposal that the prayers may
consist of nothing doubtful or questioned by pious, learned,
and orthodox persons, they not determining who be those
35 orthodox persons ; we must either take all them for orthodox
persons, who shall confidently affirm themselves to be such,
and then we say first, the demand is unreasonable, for some
such as call themselves orthodox have questioned the prime
article of our Creed, even the Divinity of the Son of God,

z

and yet there is no reason we should part with our Creed for that. Besides, the proposal requires impossibility; for there never was, nor is, nor can be such prayers made, as have not been, nor will be questioned by some who call themselves pious, learned, and orthodox. If by orthodox be meant 5 those who adhere to Scripture and the catholic consent of antiquity, we do not yet know that any part of our liturgy hath been questioned by such.

§. 4. To those generals " loading public form with church pomp, garments, imagery, and many superfluities that creep 10 into the church under the name of order and decency, in-cumbering churches with superfluities, over rigid reviving of obsolete customs, &c." we say that if these generals be intended as applicable to our liturgy in particular, they are gross and foul slanders, contrary to their profession, 15 (page ult.) and so either that or this contrary to their con-science; if not, they signify nothing to the present business, and so might with more prudence and candour have been omitted.

Prop. 2. It was the wisdom of our reformers to draw up 20 such a liturgy as neither Romanist nor protestant could justly except against; and therefore as the first never charged it with any positive errors, but only the want of something they conceived necessary, so it was never found fault with by those to whom the name of protestants most properly 25 belongs, those that profess the Augustan confession: and for those who unlawfully and sinfully brought it into dislike with some people, to urge the present state of affairs as an argument why the book should be altered, to give them satisfaction, and so that they should take advantage by their 30 own unwarrantable acts, is not reasonable.

Prop. 3, 4. The 3d and 4th proposals may go together, the demand in both being against responsals and alternate readings, in hymns and psalms and litany, &c., and that upon such reason as doth in truth enforce the necessity of 35 continuing them as they are, namely for edification. They would take these away, because they do not edify; and upon that very reason they should continue, because they do edify, if not by informing of our reasons and understandings (the prayers and hymns were never made for a catechism), yet by quickening, continuing, and uniting our devotion, which is apt to freeze or sleep, or flat in a long continued prayer or form: it is necessary therefore for the edifying of us therein to be 5 often called upon and awakened by frequent Amens, to be excited and stirred up by mutual exultations, provocations, petitions, holy contentions and strivings, which shall most shew his own, and stir up others' zeal to the glory of God. For this purpose alternate reading repetitions and responsals 10 are far better than a long tedious prayer. Nor is this our opinion only, but the judgment of former ages, as appears by the practice of ancient Christian churches, and of the Jews also: (Socrat. l. vi. c. 8. Theodor. l. ii. c. 24. 2 Chron. vii. 1, 4. Ezra iii. 11.) But it seems, they say, to be against the 15 Scripture, wherein the minister is appointed for the people in public prayers, the people's part being to attend with silence, and to declare their assent in the close by saying Amen: if they mean that the people in public services must only say this word Amen, as they can no where prove it in the 20 Scriptures, so it doth certainly seem to them that it can not be proved; for they directly practise the contrary in one of their principal parts of worship, singing of psalms, where the people bear as great a part as the minister. If this way be done in Hopkins, why not in David's Psalms; if 25 in metre, why not in prose; if in a psalm, why not in a litany?

Prop. 5. §. 1. It is desired that nothing should be in the liturgy which so much as seems to countenance the observation of Lent as a religious fast; and this as an expedient to 30 peace; which is in effect to desire that this our church may be contentious for peace' sake, and to divide from the church catholic, that we may live at unity among ourselves. For St. Paul reckons them amongst the lovers of contention, who shall oppose themselves against the customs of the churches 35 of God. That the religious observation of Lent was a custom of the churches of God, appears by the testimonies following. Chrys. Serm. xi. in Heb. x. Cyrill. Catec. Myst. 5. St. Aug. Ep. 119. "ut 40 dies ante Pascha observentur, ecclesiæ consuetudo roboravit." And St. Hierom ad Marcel. says it was

" secundum traditionem apostolorum :" this demand then tends
not to peace but dissention. The fasting forty days may be
in imitation of our Saviour for all that is here said to the
contrary; for though we cannot arrive to his perfection, ab-
staining wholly from meat so long, yet we may fast 40 days 5
together, either Cornelius' fast, till 3 of the clock afternoon,
or St. Peter's fast till noon, or at least Daniel's fast, abstain-
ing from meats and drinks of delight, and thus far imitate
our Lord.

§. 2. Nor does the act of parliament 5 Eliz. forbid it; we 10
dare not think a parliament did intend to forbid that which
Christ's church hath commanded. Nor does the act determine any thing about Lent fast, but only provide for the
maintenance of the navy, and of fishing in order thereunto,
as is plain by the act. Besides we conceive that we must 15
not so interpret one act as to contradict another, being still
in force and unrepealed. Now the act of 1 Eliz. confirms the
whole liturgy, and in that the religious keeping of Lent,
with a severe penalty upon those who shall by open words
speak any thing in derogation of any part thereof: and 20
therefore that other act of 5 Eliz. must not be interpreted
to forbid the religious keeping of Lent.

Prop. 6. The observation of saints' days is not as of
divine but ecclesiastical institution, and therefore it is not
necessary that they should have any other ground in Scrip- 25
ture than all other institutions of the same nature, so that
they be agreeable to the Scripture in the general end, for the
promoting piety. And the observation of them was ancient, as appears by the rituals and liturgies, and by the joint
consent of antiquity, and by the ancient translation of the 30
Bible, as the Syriac and Ethiopic, where the lessons appointed for holydays are noted and set down; the former of
which was made near the apostles' times. Besides our Saviour
himself kept a feast of the churches institution, viz. the feast
of the dedication (St. John x. 22.). The chief end of these 35
days being not feasting, but the exercise of holy duties,
they are fitter called holydays than festivals: and though
they be all of like nature, it doth not follow that they are
equal. The people may be dispensed with for their work

after the service, as authority pleaseth. The other names are left in the calendar, not that they should be so kept as holydays, but they are useful for the preservation of their memories, and for other reasons, as for leases, law-
5 days, &c.

Prop. 7. §. 1. This makes all the liturgy void, if every minister may put in and leave out at his discretion.

§. 2. The gift or rather spirit of prayer consists in the inward graces of the Spirit, not in extempore expressions,
10 which any man of natural parts, having a voluble tongue and audacity, may attain to without any special gift.

§. 3. But if there be any such gift, as is pretended, it is to be subject to the prophets and to the order of the church.

§. 4. The mischiefs that come by idle, impertinent, ridi-
15 culous, sometimes seditious, impious, and blasphemous expressions, under pretence of the gift, to the dishonor of God and scorn of religion, being far greater than the pretended good of exercising the gift, it is fit that they who desire such liberty in public devotions, should first give the church
20 security, that no private opinions should be put into their prayers, as is desired in the first proposal; and that nothing contrary to the faith should be uttered before God, or offered up to him in the church.

§. 5. To prevent which mischief the former ages knew no
25 better way than to forbid any prayers in public, but such as were prescribed by public authority. Con. Carthag. Can. 106. Milev. Can. 12.

Prop. 9. As they would have no saints' days observed by the church, so no apocryphal chapter read in the church,
30 but upon such a reason as would exclude all sermons as well as apocrypha; viz. because the holy Scriptures contain in them all things necessary, either in doctrine to be believed, or in duty to be practised. If so, why so many unnecessary sermons? why any more but reading of Scriptures? If not-
35 withstanding their sufficiency sermons be necessary, there is no reason why these apocryphal chapters should not be as useful, most of them containing excellent discourses, and rules of morality. It is heartily to be wished that sermons were as good. If their fear be that by this mean, those books may

come to be of equal esteem with the canon, they may be
secured against that by the title which the church hath put
upon them, calling them apocryphal: and it is the churches
testimony which teacheth us this difference, and to leave
them out were to cross the practice of the church in former 5
ages.

Prop. 10. That the minister should not read the communion service at the communion table, is not reasonable
to demand, since all the primitive church used it, and if we
do not observe that golden rule of the venerable council of 10
Nice, "Let ancient customs prevail, till reason plainly
requires the contrary," we shall give offence to sober Christians by a causeless departure from catholic usage, and a
greater advantage to enemies of our church, than our brethren, I hope, would willingly grant. The priest standing at 15
the communion table seemeth to give us an invitation to the
holy sacrament, and minds us of our duty, viz. to receive
the holy communion, some at least every Sunday; and though
we neglect our duty, it is fit the church should keep her
standing.   20

Prop. 11. It is not reasonable that the word minister
should be only used in the liturgy. For since some parts
of the liturgy may be performed by a deacon, others by none
under the order of a priest, viz. absolution, consecration, it
is fit that some such word as priest should be used for those 25
offices, and not minister, which signifies at large every one
that ministers in that holy office, of what order soever he be;
the word curate signifying properly all those who are trusted
by the bishops with cure of souls, as anciently it signified, is
a very fit word to be used, and can offend no sober person. 30
The word Sunday is ancient, (Just. Mart. Ap. 2.) and therefore not to be left off.

Prop. 12. Singing of psalms in metre is no part of the
liturgy, and so no part of our commission.

Prop. 15. "The phrase is such, &c." The church in her 35
prayers useth no more offensive phrase than St. Paul uses,
when he writes to the Corinthians, Galatians, and others,
calling them in general the churches of God, sanctified in
Christ Jesus, by vocation saints, amongst whom notwith-

standing there were many, who by their known sins (which
the apostle endeavoured to amend in them) were not properly
such, yet he gives the denomination to the whole from the
greater part, to whom in charity it was due, and puts the
5 rest in mind what they have by their baptism undertaken
to be, and what they profess themselves to be; and our
prayers and the phrase of them surely supposes no more than
that they are saints by calling, sanctified in Christ Jesus, by
their baptism admitted into Christ's congregation, and so
10 to be reckoned members of that society, till either they shall
separate themselves by wilful schism, or be separated by
legal excommunication; which they seem earnestly to desire,
and so do we.

Prop. 16. §. 1. The connection of the parts of our liturgy
15 is conformable to the example of the churches of God before
us, and have as much dependence as is usually to be seen in
many petitions of the same psalm; and we conceive the
order and method to be excellent, and must do so, till they
tell us what that order is which prayers ought to have, which
20 is not done here.

§. 2. The collects are made short as being best for devotion, as we observed before, and cannot be accounted faulty,
for being like those short but prevalent prayers in Scripture:
" Lord, be merciful to me a sinner:" " Son of David, have
25 mercy on us:" " Lord, encrease our faith."

§. 3. Why the repeated mention of the name and attributes
of God should not be most pleasing to any godly person, we
cannot imagine; or what burden it should seem, when David
magnified one attribute of God's mercy 26 times together,
30 (psalm xxxvi.) Nor can we conceive why the name and
merits of Jesus with which all our prayers should end, should
not be as sweet to us as to former saints and martyrs, with
which here they complain our prayers do so frequently end.
Since the attributes of God are the ground of our hope of
35 obtaining all our petitions, such prefaces of prayers as are
taken from them, though they have no special respect to the
petitions following, are not to be termed unsuitable, or said
to have fallen rather casually than orderly.

Prop. 17. §. 1. Exc. 1. There are besides a preparative

exhortation several preparatory prayers: "Despise not, O Lord, humble and contrite hearts;" which is one of the sentences in the preface: and this; "That those things may please him, which we do at this present;" at the end of the Absolution. And again immediately after the Lord's Prayer before the psalmody: "O Lord, open thou our lips, &c."

§. 2. Exc. 2. This which they call a defect, others think they have reason to account the perfection of the liturgy, the offices of which being intended for common and general services, would cease to be such by descending to particulars, as in confession of sin; while it is general, all persons may and must join in it, since in many things we offend all. But if there be a particular enumeration of sins, it cannot be so general a confession, because it may happen that some or other may by God's grace have been preserved from some of those sins enumerated, and therefore should by confessing themselves guilty, tell God a lie; which needs a new confession.

§. 3. As for original sin, though we think it an evil custom springing from false doctrine, to use any such expressions as may lead people to think that to the persons baptized (in whose persons only our prayers are offered up) original sin is not forgiven in their holy baptism; yet for that there remains in the regenerate some relics of that which are to be bewailed, the church in her confession acknowledgeth such desires of our own hearts as render us miserable by following them: That there is no health in us: that without God's help our frailty can not but fall: that our mortal nature can do no good thing without him: which is a clear acknowledgment of original sin.

§. 4. Exc. 3. We know not what public prayers are wanting, nor do they tell us; the usual complaint hath been, that there were too many. Neither do we conceive any want of public thanksgivings; there being in the liturgy Te Deum, Benedictus, Magnificat, Benedicite, Glory be to God on high, Therefore with Angels and Archangels, The doxology, Glory be to the Father, &c. all peculiar, as they require, to Gospel worship, and fit to express our thanks and honour to God upon every particular occasion; and occasional thanksgivings after the litany, of the frequency whereof themselves elsewhere complain, who here complain of defect. If there be any forms wanting, the church will provide.

§. 5. Exc. 4. They complain that the liturgy contains too many generals, without mention of the particulars; and the instances are such petitions as these: That we may do God's will: to be kept from all evil: almost the very terms of the petitions of the Lord's Prayer: so that they must reform that, before they can pretend to mend our liturgy in these petitions.

§. 6. Exc. 5. We have deferred this to the proper place, as you might have done.

Prop. 18. §. 1. We are now come to the main and principal demand as is pretended, viz. the abolishing the laws which impose any ceremonies, especially three, the surplice, the sign of the cross, and kneeling. These are the yoke which, if removed, there might be peace. It is to be suspected, and there is reason for it from their own words, that somewhat else pinches, and that if these ceremonies were laid aside, and these or any other prayers strictly enjoined without them, it would be deemed a burden intolerable: it seems so by No. 7, where they desire that when the liturgy is altered, according to the rest of their proposals, the minister may have liberty to add and leave out what he pleases. Yet because the imposition of these ceremonies is pretended to be the insupportable grievance, we must of necessity either yield that demand, or shew reason why we do not; and that we may proceed the better in this undertaking, we shall reduce the sum of their complaint to these several heads, as we find them in their papers: the law for imposing these ceremonies they would have abrogated for these reasons:

1. §. 2. It is doubtful whether God hath given power to men to impose such signified signs, which though they call them significant, yet have in them no real goodness in the judgment of the imposers themselves, being called by them things indifferent; and therefore fall not under St. Paul's rule of "omnia decenter," nor are suitable to the simplicity of the Gospel worship.

2. §. 2. Because it is a violation of the royalty of Christ, and an impeachment of his laws as insufficient, and so those that are under the law of Deut. xii. " Whatsoever I command you, observe to do ; you shall take nothing from it, nor add any thing to it ;" you do not observe these.

3. §. 3. Because sundry learned, pious, and orthodox men have ever since the reformation judged them unwarrantable ; and we ought to be, as our Lord was, tender of weak brethren, not to offend his little ones, nor to lay a stumblingblock before a weak brother.

4. §. 4. Because these ceremonies have been the fountain of many evils in this church and nation, occasioning sad divisions betwixt minister and minister, betwixt minister and people, exposing many orthodox preachers to the displeasure of rulers. And no other fruits than these can be looked for from the retaining these ceremonies.

§. 3. rule 1. Before we give particular answer to these several reasons, it will be not unnecessary to lay down some certain general premises or rules, which will be useful in our whole discourse. 1. That God hath not given a power only, but a command also, of imposing whatsoever should be truly decent and becoming his public service, (1 Cor. xiv.) After St. Paul had ordered some particular rules for praying, praising, prophesying, &c., he concludes with this general canon, Let all things be done εὐσχημόνως, in a fit scheme, habit, or fashion, decently ; and that there may be uniformity in those decent performances, let there be a τάξις, rule or canon for that purpose.

§. 4. rule 2. Not inferiors but superiors must judge what is convenient and decent. They who must order that all be done decently, must of necessity first judge what is convenient and decent to be ordered.

§. 5. rule 3. These rules and canons for decency made and urged by superiors are to be obeyed by inferiors, till it be made as clear that now they are not bound to obey, as it is evident in general, that they ought to obey superiors. For if the exemption from obedience be not as evident as the command to obey, it must needs be sin not to obey.

§. 6. rule 4. Pretence of conscience is no exemption from

obedience; for the law, as long as it is a law, certainly binds to obedience, (Rom. xiii.) " Ye must needs be subject." And this pretence of a tender gainsaying conscience cannot abrogate the law, since it can neither take away the authority 5 of the law-maker, nor make the matter of the law in itself unlawful. Besides, if pretence of conscience did exempt from obedience, laws were useless; whosoever had not list to obey, might pretend tenderness of conscience, and be thereby set at liberty; which if once granted, anarchy and confusion must 10 needs follow.

§. 7. rule 5. Though charity will move to pity, and relieve those that are truly perplexed or scrupulous, yet we must not break God's command, in charity to them; and therefore we must not perform public services undecently or disorderly 15 for the ease of tender consciences.

§. 8. ans. 1. These premised, we answer to your first reason that those things which we call indifferent, because neither expressly commanded nor forbidden by God, have in them a real goodness, a fitness and decency, and for that cause are 20 imposed, and may be so by the rule of St. Paul, (1 Cor. xiv.) by which rule, and many others in Scripture, a power is given to men to impose signs, which are never the worse surely, because they signify something that is decent and comely: and so it is not doubtful whether such power be given. 25 It would rather be doubtful whether the church could impose such idle signs, if any such there be, as signify nothing.

§. 9. ans. 2. To the second, that it is not a violation of Christ's royalty to make such laws for decency, but an exercise of his power and authority, which he hath given to the 30 church: and the disobedience to such commands of superiors is plainly a violation of his royalty. As it is no violation of the king's authority, when his magistrates command things according to his laws; but disobedience to the command of those injunctions of his deputies is violation of his authority. 35 Again, it can be no impeachment of Christ's laws as insufficient, to make such laws for decency, since our Saviour, as is evident from the precepts themselves, did not intend by them to determine every minute and circumstance of time, place, manner of performance, and the like, but only to command

in general the substance of those duties, and the right ends
that should be aimed at in the performance, and then left
every man in particular (whom for that purpose he made
reasonable) to guide himself by rules of reason, for private
services : and appointed governors of the church to determine 5
such particularities for the public. Thus our Lord commanded prayers, fasting, &c. : for the times and places of
performance he did not determine every of them, but left
them to be guided as we have said. So that it is no impeachment of his laws as insufficient, to make laws for determining 10
those particulars of decency, which himself did not, as is
plain by his precepts, intend to determine, but left us
governors for that purpose ; to whom he said, "As my Father
sent me, even so send I you ;" and "Let all things be done
decently and in order :" of whom he hath said to us, "Obey 15
those that have the oversight over you :" and told us that
if we will not hear his church, we must not be accounted as
Christians, but heathens and publicans. And yet nevertheless
they will not hear it and obey it in so small a matter as a
circumstance of time, place, habit, or the like, which she 20
thinks decent and fit, and yet will be accounted for the best
Christians, and tell us that it is the very awe of God's law
(Deut. xii. 32.) that keeps them from obedience to the
church in these commands ; not well considering that it
cannot be any adding to the word of God, to command things 25
for order and decency which the word of God commands to
be done, so as they be not commanded as God's immediate
word, but as the laws of men ; but that it is undeniably
adding to the word of God to say that superiors may not
command such things, which God hath no where forbidden, 30
and taking from the word of God to deny that power to men,
which God's word hath given them.

§. 10. ans. 3. The command for decent ceremonies may
still continue in the church notwithstanding the xii. of Deut.
and so it may too for all the exceptions taken against them 35
by sundry learned, pious, and orthodox persons, who have
judged them, they say, unwarrantable. And if laws may be
abrogated as soon as those that list not to obey will except
against them, the world must run into confusion. But those

that except are weak brethren, whom by Christ's precept and
example we must not offend. If by weak we understand
ignorant, they would take it ill to be so accounted; and it is
their own fault if they be, there having been much written as
5 may satisfy any that have a mind to be satisfied. And as
king James of blessed memory said at Hampton Court,
" If after so many years preaching of the Gospel, there be any
yet unsatisfied, I doubt it proceeds rather out of stubbornness of opinion than out of tenderness of conscience." If by
10 tenderness of conscience they mean a fearfulness to sin, this
would make them most easy to be satisfied, because most
fearful to disobey superiors. But suppose there be any so
scrupulous, as not satisfied with what hath been written, the
church may still without sin urge her command for these
15 decent ceremonies, and not be guilty of offending her weak
brother; for since the scandal is taken by him, not given by
her, it is he that by vain scrupulocity offends himself, and
lays the stumblingblock in his own way.

§. 11. The case of St. Paul, not eating of flesh, if it
20 offended his brother, is nothing to the purpose; who there
speaks of things not commanded either by God or by his
church, neither having in them any thing of decency, or
significancy to serve in the church. St. Paul would deny
himself his own liberty, rather than offend his brother; but
25 if any man breaks a just law or custom of the church, he
brands him for a lover of schism and sedition. 1 Cor. xi. 16.

§. 12. ans. 4. That these ceremonies have occasioned many
divisions is no more fault of theirs, than it was of the Gospel
that the preaching of it occasioned strife betwixt father and
30 son, &c. The true cause of those divisions is the cause of
ours, which St. James tells us is lust, and inordinate desires
of honours or wealth, or licentiousness, or the like. Were
these ceremonies laid aside, there would be the same divisions,
if some who think Moses and Aaron took too much upon
35 them, may be suffered to deceive the people, and to raise in
them vain fears and jealousies of their governors; but if all
men would, as they ought, study peace and quietness, they
would find other and better fruits of these laws of rites and

ceremonies, as edification, decency, order, and beauty, in the service and worship of God.

§. 13. There hath been so much said not only of the lawfulness, but also of the conveniency of those ceremonies mentioned, that nothing can be added. This in brief may here suffice for the surplice; that reason and experience teaches that decent ornaments and habits preserve reverence, and are held therefore necessary to the solemnity of royal acts, and acts of justice, and why not as well to the solemnity of religious worship. And in particular no habit more suitable than white linen, which resembles purity and beauty, wherein angels have appeared, (Rev. xv.) fit for those, whom the Scripture calls angels: and this habit was ancient. Chrys. Ho. 60 ad po. Antioch.

§. 14. The cross was always used in the church "in immortali lavacro," (Tertull.) and therefore to testify our communion with them, as we are taught to do in our Creed, as also in token that we shall not be ashamed of the cross of Christ, it is fit to be used still, and we conceive cannot trouble the conscience of any that have a mind to be satisfied.

§. 15. The posture of kneeling best suits at the communion as the most convenient, and so most decent for us, when we are to receive as it were from God's hand the greatest of seals of the kingdom of heaven. He that thinks he may do this sitting, let him remember the prophet Mal. Offer this to the prince, to receive his seal from his own hand sitting, see if he will accept of it. When the church did stand at her prayers, the manner of receiving was "more adorantium," (S. Aug. ps. xcviii. Cyril. Catech. Mystag. 5.) rather more than at prayers, since standing at prayer hath been generally left, and kneeling used instead of that (as the church may vary in such indifferent things). Now to stand at communion, when we kneel at prayers, were not decent, much less to sit, which was never the use of the best times.

§. 16. That there were ancient liturgies in the church is evident: S. Chrysostom, S. Basil and others; and the Greeks tell us of St. James, much elder than they. And though we find not in all ages whole liturgies, yet it is certain that there

were such in the oldest times, by those parts which are
extant ; as " Sursum corda" &c., " Gloria Patri" &c., " Benedicite," " Hymnus Cherubinus" &c., " Vere dignum et jus-
tum" &c., " Dominus vobiscum. Et cum spiritu tuo," with
5 divers others. Though those that are extant may be interpolated, yet such things as are found in them all consistent
to catholic and primitive doctrine, may well be presumed to
have been from the first, especially since we find no original
of these liturgies from general councils.

10   CONCERNING MORNING AND EVENING PRAYER.

§. 1. rub. 1. We think it fit that the rubric stand as it is,
and all to be left to the discretion of the ordinary.

§. 2. rub. 2. For the reasons given in our answer to the
18th general, whither you refer us, we think it fit that the
15 rubric continue as it is.

§. 3. Lord's Pr. " Deliver us from evil." These words,
" for thine is the kingdom," &c., are not in St. Luke, nor in
the ancient copies of St. Matt., never mentioned in the ancient
comments, nor used in the Latin church, and therefore ques-
20 tioned whether they be part of the gospel ; there is no reason
that they should be always used.

§. 4. Lord's Pr. often used. It is used but twice in the
morning and twice in the evening service ; and twice cannot
be called often, much less so often. For the litany, communion, baptism, &c., they are offices distinct from morning
25 and evening prayer, and it is not fit that any of them should
want the Lord's Prayer.

§. 5. Glor. Patri. This doxology being a solemn confession
of the blessed Trinity, should not be thought a burden to any
Christian liturgy, especially being so short as it is ; neither is
30 the repetition of it to be thought a vain repetition, more than
" his mercy endureth for ever," so often repeated, psal. cxxxvi.
We cannot give God too much glory, that being the end of
our creation, and should be the end of all our services.

§. 6. p. 15. rub. 2. " In such places where they do sing"
35 &c. The rubric directs only such singing as is after the manner of distinct reading, and we never heard of any incon-

venience thereby, and therefore conceive this demand to be needless.

§. 7. Benedicite. This hymn was used all the church over, (Conc. Tolet. can. 13.) and therefore should be continued still as well as Te Deum (Ruffin. Apol. cont. Hieron.) or Veni 5 Creator, which they do not object against as apocryphal.

IN THE LITANY.

§. 1. The alterations here desired are so nice, as if they that made them were given to change.

§. 2. "From all other deadly sin," is better than "from 10 all other heinous sin" upon the reason here given, because the wages of sin is death.

§. 3. "From sudden death" as good as "from dying suddenly;" which therefore we pray against, that we may not be unprepared. 15

§. 4. "All that travel" as little liable to exceptions as "those that travel," and more agreeable to the phrase of Scripture, (1 Tim. i. 2,) "I will that prayers be made for all men."

§. 5. p. 16. The 2nd Collect, &c. We do not find, nor do 20 they say, what is to be amended in these collects; therefore to say any thing particularly were to answer to we know not what.

THE COMMUNION SERVICE.

§. 1. p. 17. Kyries. To say, "Lord, have mercy upon us," after every commandment is more quick and active than to 25 say it once at the close; and why Christian people should not upon their knees ask their pardon for their life forfeited for the breach of every commandment, and pray for grace to keep them for the time to come, they must be more than ignorant that can scruple. 30

§. 2. p. 18. Homilies. Some livings are so small that they are not able to maintain a licensed preacher; and in such and the like cases this provision is necessary. Nor can any reason be given, why the minister's reading a homily, set forth by common authority, should not be accounted preaching of the word, as well as his reading (or pronouncing by heart) a homily or sermon of his own or any other man's.

§. 3. Sentences. The sentences tend all to exhort the people to pious liberality, whether the object be the minister or the poor; and though some of the sentences be apocryphal, they may be useful for that purpose. Why collection for the poor should be made at another time, there is no reason given, only change desired.

§. 4. p. 19. 3 Exhort. The first and third exhortations are very seasonable before the communion, to put men in mind how they ought to be prepared, and in what danger they are to come unprepared, that if they be not duly qualified, they may depart and be better prepared at another time.

§. 5. Exc. 1. " We fear this may discourage many." Certainly themselves cannot desire that men should come to the holy communion with a troubled conscience, and therefore have no reason to blame the church for saying, " it is requisite that men come with a quiet conscience," and prescribing means for quieting thereof. If this be to discourage men, it is fit they should be discouraged and deterred and kept from the communion, till they have done all that is here directed by the church, which they may well do, considering that this exhortation shall be read in the church the Sunday or holyday before.

§. 6. Minister's turning. The minister's turning to the people is not most convenient throughout the whole ministration. When he speaks to them, as in Lessons, Absolution, and Benedictions, it is convenient that he turn to them. When he speaks for them to God, it is fit that they should all turn another way, as the ancient church ever did; the reasons of which you may see Aug. lib. 2. de Ser. Dom. in monte.

§. 7. Exc. 3. It appears by the greatest evidences of antiquity, that it was upon the 25th day of December. S. Aug. in Psal. 132.

§. 8. " That our sinful bodies" &c. It can no more be said those words do give greater efficacy to the blood than to the body of Christ, than when our Lord saith, " This is my blood which is shed for you and for many for the remission of sins," &c. and saith not so explicitly of the body.

A a

§. 9. Com. Kneel. It is most requisite that the minister deliver the bread and wine into every particular communicant's hand, and repeat the words in the singular number; for so much as it is the propriety of sacraments to make particular obsignation to each believer, and it is our visible pro- 5 fession, that, by the grace of God, Christ tasted death for every man.

§. 10. Kneel at Sacr. Concerning kneeling at the sacrament we have given account already; only thus much we add, that we conceive it an error to say that the Scripture 10 affirms the apostles to have received not kneeling. The posture of the paschal supper we know; but the institution of the holy sacrament was after supper; and what posture was then used, the Scripture is silent. The rub. at the end of the 1 Ed. C. that leaves kneeling, crossing, &c. indifferent, 15 is meant only at such times as they are not prescribed and required. But at the eucharist kneeling is expressly required in the rub. following.

§. 11. Com. three times a year. This desire to have the parishioners at liberty, whether they will ever receive the 20 communion or not, savours of too much neglect and coldness of affection towards the holy sacrament. It is more fitting that order should be taken to bring it into more frequent use, as it was in the first and best times. Our rub. is directly according to the ancient Council of Eliberis, C. 81. 25 (Gratian de Consecrat.) No man is to be accounted a good catholic Christian that does not receive three times in the year. The distempers which indispose men to it must be corrected, not the receiving of the sacrament therefore omitted. It is a pitiful pretence to say they are not fit, and 30 make their sin their excuse. Formerly our church was quarreled at for not compelling men to the communion; now for urging men. How should she please!

§. 12. This rub. is not in the liturgy of queen Elizabeth, nor confirmed by law; nor is there any great need of re- 35 storing it, the world being now in more danger of profanation than of idolatry. Besides the sense of it is declared sufficiently in the 28th article of the Church of England. The time appointed we conceive sufficient.

PUBLIC BAPTISM.

§. 1. " Until they have made due profession of repentance"
&c.   We think this desire to be very hard and uncharitable,
punishing the poor infants for the parents' sakes, and giving
5 also too great and arbitrary a power to the minister to judge
which of his parishioners he pleaseth atheists, infidels, heretics, &c., and then in that name to reject their children from
being baptised.   Our church concludes more charitably, that
Christ will favorably accept every infant to baptism, that is
10 presented by the church according to our present order.   And
this she concludes out of holy Scriptures (as you may see in
the office of baptism) according to the practice and doctrine
of the catholic church.   (Cypr. Ep. 59. August. Ep. 28. et de
verb. Apost. Serm. 14.)

15 §. 2. The time appointed we conceive sufficient.

§. 3. p. 23. " And then the godfathers" &c.   It is an erroneous doctrine, and the ground of many others, and of many
of your exceptions, that children have no other right to baptism than in their parents' right.   The churches primitive
20 practice (S. Aug. Ep. 23.) forbids it to be left to the pleasure
of parents, whether there shall be other sureties or no.   It is
fit we should observe carefully the practice of venerable antiquity, as they desire, Prop. 18.

§. 4. The font usually stands, as it did in primitive times,
25 at or near the church door, to signify that baptism was the
entrance into the church mystical; " we are all baptised into
one body" (1 Cor. xii. 13); and the people may hear well
enough.   If Jordan and all other waters be not so far sanctified by Christ, as to be the matter of baptism, what authority
30 have we to baptise?   And sure his baptism was " dedicatio
baptismi."

§. 5. It hath been accounted reasonable, and allowed by
the best laws, that guardians should covenant and contract
for their minors to their benefit.   By the same right the
35 church hath appointed sureties to undertake for children,
when they enter into covenant with God by baptism.   And
this general practice of the church is enough to satisfy those
that doubt.

§. 6. p. 24. " Receive remission of sins by spiritual regeneration." Most proper, for baptism is our spiritual regeneration, (St. John iii.) "Unless a man be born again of water and the Spirit" &c. And by this is received remission of sins, (Acts ii. 3,) " Repent and be baptised every one of you, for 5 the remission of sins." So the Creed : " One baptism for the remission of sins."

§. 7. p. 24. " We cannot in faith say that every child that is baptised is regenerate" &c. Seeing that God's sacraments have their effects, where the receiver doth not " ponere 10 obicem," put any bar against them (which children cannot do) ; we may say in faith of every child that is baptised, that it is regenerated by God's Holy Spirit; and the denial of it tends to anabaptism, and the contempt of this holy sacrament, as nothing worthy, nor material whether it be 15 administered to children or no. Concerning the cross we refer to our answer to the same in general.

PRIVATE BAPTISM.

§. 8. " We desire that baptism may not be administered in a private place;" and so do we, where it may be brought 20 into the public congregation. But since our Lord hath said, (St. John iii.) " Unless one be born of water and the Holy Ghost, he cannot enter into the kingdom of heaven," we think it fit that they should be baptised in private, rather than not at all. It is appointed now to be done by the lawful 25 minister.

Nor is any thing, done in private, reiterated in public, but the solemn reception into the congregation, with the prayers for him, and the public declaration before the congregation, of the infant, now made by the godfathers, that the whole 30 congregation may testify against him, if he does not perform it ; which the ancients made great use of.

OF THE CATECHISM.

§. 1. p. 26. ans. 3. Though divers have been of late baptised without godfathers, yet many have been baptised with 35

them; and those may answer the questions as they are; the
rest must answer according to truth. But there's no reason
to alter the rule of the Catechism for some men's irregula-
rities.

5	§. 2. ans. 2. We conceive this expression as safe as that
which they desire, and more fully expressing the efficacy of
the sacrament, according to St. Paul, the 26 and 27 Gal. iii.,
where St. Paul proves them all to be children of God, because
they were baptised, and in their baptism had put on Christ:
10 "if children, then heirs," or, which is all one, "inheritors,"
Rom. viii. 17.

§. 3. p. 26. 10. com. We conceive the present translation to
be agreeable to many ancient copies: therefore the change to
be needless.

15	§. 4. p. 27. "My duty towards God," &c. It is not true
that there is nothing in that answer which refers to the fourth
commandment: for the last words of the answer do orderly
relate to the last commandment of the first table, which is
the fourth.

20	§. 5. "Two only as generally necessary to salvation," &c.
These words are a reason of the answer, that there are two
only, and therefore not to be left out.

§. 6. "We desire that the entering of infants," &c. The
effect of children's baptism depends neither upon their own
25 present actual faith and repentance (which the Catechism
says expressly they cannot perform,) nor upon the faith and
repentance of their natural parents or pro-parents, or of their
godfathers or godmothers; but upon the ordinance and institution of Christ. But it is requisite that when they come
30 to age they should perform these conditions of faith and repentance, for which also their godfathers and godmothers
charitably undertook on their behalf. And what they do for
the infant in this case, the infant himself is truly said to do,
as in the courts of this kingdom daily the infant does answer
35 by his guardian; and it is usual for to do homage by proxy, and
for princes to marry by proxy. For the further justification
of this answer, see St. Aug. Ep. 23. ad Bonifac. " Nihil
aliud credere, quam fidem habere: ac per hoc cum responde-
tur parvulum credere, qui fidei nondum habet effectum, re-

spondetur fidem habere propter fidei sacramentum, et con-
vertere se ad Deum propter conversionis sacramentum. Quia
et ipsa responsio ad celebrationem pertinet sacramenti. Itaque parvulum, etsi nondum fides illa, quæ in credentium
voluntate consistit, tamen ipsius fidei sacramentum, fidelem 5
facit."

§. 7. p. 28. The Catechism is not intended as a whole body
of divinity, but as a comprehension of the articles of faith,
and other doctrines most necessary to salvation; and being
short, is fittest for children and common people, and as it was 10
thought sufficient upon mature deliberation, and so is by us.

CONFIRMATION.

§. 1. rub. 1. It is evident that the meaning of these words
is, that children baptised, and dying before they commit
actual sin, are undoubtedly saved, though they be not con- 15
firmed: wherein we see not what danger there can be of
misleading the vulgar by teaching them truth. But there
may be danger in this desire of having these words expunged,
as if they were false; for St. Austin says he is an infidel that
denies them to be true. Ep. 23. ad Bonifac.　　　　　　　20

§. 2. rub. "After the Catechism we conceive that it is not
a sufficient qualification," &c. We conceive that this qualification is required rather as necessary than as sufficient; and
therefore it is the duty of the minister of the place (can. 61)
to prepare children in the best manner to be presented to the 25
bishop for confirmation, and to inform the bishop of their
fitness, but submitting the judgment to the bishop, both of
this and other qualifications; and not that the bishop should
be tied to the minister's consent. Comp. this rub. to the
second rub. before the Catechism, and there is required what 30
is further necessary and sufficient.

§. 3. ex. 1. "They see no need of godf." Here the compilers of the liturgy did, and so doth the church, that there
may be a witness of the confirmation.

§. 4. ex. 2. "This supposeth that all children," &c. It 35
supposeth, and that truly, that all children were at their baptism regenerate by water and the Holy Ghost, and had given
unto them the forgiveness of all their sins; and it is chari-

tably presumed that notwithstanding the frailties and slips of their childhood they have not totally lost what was in baptism conferred upon them ; and therefore adds, " Strengthen them, we beseech thee, O Lord, with the Holy Ghost the 5 Comforter, and daily encrease in them their manifold gifts of grace," &c. None that lives in open sin ought to be confirmed.

§.5. p.30. rub. "Before the imposition of hands," &c. Confirmation is reserved to the bishop " in honorem ordinis," to 10 bless being an act of authority. So it was of old : St. Hierom, Dial. adv. Lucifer. says it was "totius orbis consensio in hanc partem :" and St. Cyprian to the same purpose, Ep. 73 ; and our church doth every where profess, as she ought, to conform to the catholic usages of the primitive times, from which 15 causelessly to depart argues rather love of contention than of peace. The reserving of confirmation to the bishop doth argue the dignity of the bishop above presbyters, who are not allowed to confirm, but does not argue any excellency in confirmation above the sacraments. St. Hierom argues the 20 quite contrary (ad. Lucif. c. 4) : That because baptism was allowed to be performed by a deacon, but confirmation only by a bishop, therefore baptism was most necessary, and of the greatest value : the mercy of God allowing the most necessary means of salvation to be administered by inferior orders, and 25 restraining the less necessary to the higher, for the honour of their order.

§. 6. ex. 1. Prayer after the imposition of hands is grounded upon the practice of the apostles (Heb. vi. 2, and Acts viii. 17) ; nor doth 25 article say that confirmation is a corrupt 30 imitation of the apostles' practice, but that the five commonly called sacraments have ground partly of the corrupt following the apostles, &c., which may be applied to some other of these 5, but cannot be applied to confirmation, unless we make the church speak contradictions.

35 §. 7. ex. 2. We know no harm in speaking the language of holy Scripture (Acts viii. 15), "they laid their hands upon them, and they received the Holy Ghost." And though imposition of hands be not a sacrament, yet it is a very fit sign, to

certify the persons what is then done for them, as the prayer speaks.

AFTER CONFIRMATION.

There is no inconvenience that confirmation should be required before the communion, when it may be ordinarily obtained. That which you here fault, you elsewhere desire. 5

§. 1. p. 31. The ring is a significant sign, only of human institution, and was always given as a pledge of fidelity and constant love : and here is no reason given why it should be taken away ; nor are the reasons mentioned in the Roman 10 ritualists given in our Common Prayer Book.

§. 2. p. 32. ex. 1. These words, "in the name of the Father, Son, and Holy Ghost," if they seem to make matrimony a sacrament, may as well make all sacred, yea civil, actions of weight to be sacraments, they being usual at the 15 beginning and ending of all such. It was never heard before now that those words make a sacrament.

§. 3. They go to the Lord's table because the communion is to follow.

§. 4. col. "Consecrated the estate of matrimony to such an 20 excellent mystery," &c. Though the institution of marriage was before the fall, yet it may be now, and is, consecrated by God to such an excellent mystery as the representation of the spiritual marriage between Christ and his church (Ep. v. 23). We are sorry that the words of Scripture will not please. 25 The church, in the 25 article, hath taken away the fear of making it a sacrament.

§. 5. p. 33. rub. "The new married persons the same day of their marriage must receive the holy communion." This inforces none to forbear marriage, but presumes (as well it 30 may) that all persons marriageable ought to be also fit to receive the holy sacrament ; and marriage being so solemn a covenant of God, they that undertake it in the fear of God will not stick to seal it by receiving the holy communion, and accordingly prepare themselves for it. It were more Christian 35 to desire that those licentious festivities might be suppressed, and the communion more generally used by those that marry:

the happiness would be greater than can easily be expressed. " Unde sufficiunt ad enarrandum felicitatem ejus matrimonii, quod ecclesia conciliat, et confirmat oblatio." Tertull. l. 2. ad uxorem.

VISITATION OF THE SICK.

§. 1. "For as much as the condition," &c. All which is here desired is already presumed, namely, that the minister shall apply himself to the particular condition of the person; but this must be done according to the rule of prudence and
10 justice, and not according to his pleasure. Therefore, if the sick person shew himself truly penitent, it ought not to be left to the minister's pleasure to deny him absolution, if he desire it. Our church's direction is according to the 13 canon of the venerable council of Nice, both here and in the
15 next that follows.

§. 2. The form of absolution in the liturgy is more agreeable to the Scriptures than that which they desire, it being said in St. John xx., " Whose sins you remit, they are remitted," not, Whose sins you pronounce remitted; and the
20 condition needs not to be expressed, being always necessarily understood.

§. 3, p. 34. ex. 1. It is not fit the minister should have power to deny this viation, or holy communion, to any that humbly desire it according to the rubric; which no man dis-
25 turbed in his wits can do, and whosoever does must in charity be presumed to be penitent, and fit to receive.

THE BURIAL OF THE DEAD.

§. 1. rub. 1. It is not fit so much should be left to the discretion of every minister; and the desire that all may be
30 said in the church, being not pretended to be for the ease of tender consciences, but of tender heads, may be helped by a cap better than a rubric.

§. 2. p. 35. We see not why these words may not be said of any person whom we dare not say is damned, and it were
35 a breach of charity to say so even of those whose repentance we do not see: for whether they do not inwardly and heartily repent, even at the last act, who knows? and that God will

not even then pardon them upon such repentance, who dares
say? It is better to be charitable, and hope the best, than
rashly to condemn.

CHURCHING WOMEN.

§. 1. p. 36. ex. 1. It is fit that the woman performing espe- 5
cial service of thanksgiving should have a special place for
it, where she may be perspicuous to the whole congregation,
and near the holy table, in regard of the offering she is there
to make. They need not fear popery in this, since in the
church of Rome she is to kneel at the church door.　　10

§. 2. ex. 2. The psalm 121 is more fit and pertinent than
those others named, as 113, 128, and therefore not to be
changed.

§. 3. ex. 3. If the woman be such as is here mentioned, she
is to do her penance before she is churched.　　15

§. 4. ex. 4. Offerings are required as well under the gospel
as the law; and amongst other times most fit it is, that oblations should be when we come to give thanks for some special
blessing. Psal. lxxvi. 10, 11. Such is the deliverance in
childbearing.　　20

§. 4. ex. 5. This is needless, since the rub. and common
sense require that no notorious person be admitted.

THE CONCESSIONS.

§. 1. We are willing that all the epistles and gospels be
used according to the last translation.　　25

§. 2. That when any thing is read for an epistle which is
not in the epistles, the superscription shall be, " For the
epistle."

§. 3. That the Psalms be collated with the former translation, mentioned in rubr., and printed according to it.　　30

§. 4. That the words "this day," both in the collects and
prefaces, be used only upon the day itself; and for the following days it be said, " as about this time."

§. 5. That a longer time be required for signification of the
names of the communicants: and the words of the rubric be 35
changed into these, " at least some time the day before."

§. 6. That the power of keeping scandalous sinners from

the communion may be expressed in the rubr. according to the 26 and 27 canons; so the minister be obliged to give an account of the same immediately after to the ordinary.

§. 7. That the whole preface be prefixed to the command-5 ments.

§. 8. That the second exhortation be read some Sunday or holyday before the celebration of the communion, at the discretion of the minister.

§. 9. That the general confession at the communion be pro-10 nounced by one of the ministers, the people saying after him, all kneeling humbly upon their knees.

§. 10. That the manner of consecrating the elements be made more explicit and express, and to that purpose those words be put into the rubr., "Then shall he put his hand 15 upon the bread and break it," "then shall he put his hand unto the cup."

§. 11. That if the font be so placed as the congregation can not hear, it may be referred to the ordinary to place it more conveniently.

20 §. 12. That those words, "Yes, they do perform those," &c., may be altered thus, "Because they promise them both by their sureties," &c.

§. 13. That the words of the last rubr. before the Catechism may be thus altered, "that children being baptised have all 25 things necessary for their salvation, and dying before they commit any actual sins, be undoubtedly saved, though they be not confirmed."

§. 14. That to the rubr. after confirmation these words may be added, "or be ready and desirous to be confirmed."

30 §. 15. That those words, "with my body I thee worship," may be altered thus, "with my body I thee honour."

§. 16. That those words, "till death us depart," be thus altered, "till death us do part."

§. 17. That the words "sure and certain" may be left out.

VII.

*The disputation in which the episcopal divines were opponents
and the ministers respondents.*

A true and perfect copy of the whole disputation at the
Savoy, that was managed by the episcopal divines as
opponents, to prove that there is nothing sinful in the 5
liturgy.   Published to make intelligible the fragment
already published by the lord bishop of Worcester, under
the hands of Dr. Pierson and Dr. Gunning; and so much
of his lordship's book against Mr. Baxter as concerneth
that disputation.   Printed in the year 1662.   10

Oppon. My assertion is, Nothing contained in the liturgy
is sinful.

This general assertion I am ready to make good in all
particulars, in which our brethren shall think fit to charge
the liturgy with sinfulness.   15

And because our brethren have as yet by way of disputation charged no other part of it with the imputation of sinfulness, but that which concerneth kneeling at the communion,
therefore my first assertion as to that particular is this; The
command contained in the liturgy concerning kneeling at the 20
communion is not sinful.

This truth I am ready to prove by several arguments.
First, This only command [The minister shall deliver the
communion to the people in their hands kneeling] is not
sinful: The command contained in the liturgy concerning 25
kneeling at the communion is this only command [The
minister &c.]   Ergo, The command contained in the liturgy
concerning kneeling at the communion is not sinful.

Resp. Neg. major.

Oppon. Prob. major.   30

That command which commandeth only an act in itself
lawful, is not sinful: This only command [The minister shall

deliver &c.] commandeth only an act in itself lawful: Ergo, This only command [The minister shall deliver &c.] is not sinful.

Resp. Neg. major and minor.

5 Oppon. Prob. major.

That command which commands an act in itself lawful and no other act or circumstance unlawful, is not sinful: That command which commands only an act in itself lawful, commands an act in itself lawful, and no other act or circumstance

10 unlawful: Ergo, That command which commandeth only an act in itself lawful, is not sinful.

Resp. 1. We deny the major; and for brevity give a double reason of our denial: one is, because that may be a sin " per accidens" which is not so in itself, and may be unlawfully commanded, though that accident be not in the command.

15 Another is, that it may be commanded under an unjust penalty.

2. We deny the minor for both the same reasons.

Oppon. Prob. minor.

The delivery of the communion to persons kneeling is an

20 act in itself lawful: This only command [The minister shall deliver &c.] commandeth only the delivery of the communion to persons kneeling: Ergo, This only command [The minister shall deliver &c.] commandeth only an act in itself lawful.

Resp. We distinguish of delivering to persons kneeling: it

25 signifieth either exclusively (to those and no other), or not exclusively, (to other). In the first sense we deny the major; in the second sense we deny the minor.

Oppon. You deny both our propositions for two reasons, both the same: we make good both our propositions, not-

30 withstanding both your reasons.

The major first. That command which commandeth an act in itself lawful, and no other act, whereby any unjust penalty is enjoined, nor any circumstance, whence, directly or "per accidens," any sin is consequent, which the commander ought

35 to provide against, is not sinful: That command which commandeth an act in itself lawful, and no other act or circumstance unlawful, commandeth an act in itself lawful, and no other act, whereby any unjust penalty is enjoined, nor

any circumstance whence, directly or " per accidens," any sin
is consequent, which the commander ought to provide against :
Ergo, That command which commands an act in itself lawful,
and no other act or circumstance unlawful, is not sinful.

Resp. 1. The proposition denied is not in the conclusion. 5

The major is denied, because the first act commanded
may be " per accidens" unlawful, and be commanded by an
unjust penalty, though no other act or circumstance commanded be such.

Oppon. The minor next.   That command which com- 10
mandeth an act in itself lawful, and no other act whereby
any unjust penalty is enjoined, nor any circumstance whence,
directly or " per accidens," any sin is consequent, which the
commander ought to provide against, commands an act in
itself lawful, and no other act or circumstance unlawful : 15
That command which commands only an act in itself lawful,
commandeth an act in itself lawful, and no other act whereby
any unjust penalty is enjoined, nor any circumstance whence,
directly or " per accidens," any sin is consequent, which the
commander ought to provide against : Ergo, That command 20
which commands only an act in itself lawful, commands an act
in itself lawful, and no other act or circumstance unlawful.

Oppon. We prove our major, notwithstanding your reason
alleged.

That command which hath in it all things requisite to the 25
lawfulness of a command, and particularly cannot be guilty
of commanding an act " per accidens" unlawful, nor of commanding an act under any unjust penalty, is not sinful,
notwithstanding your reason alleged : That command which
commandeth an act in itself lawful, and no other act, whereby 30
any unjust penalty is enjoined, nor any circumstance whence,
directly or " per accidens," any sin is consequent which the
commander ought to provide against, hath in it all things
requisite to the lawfulness of a command, and particularly
cannot be guilty of commanding an act "per accidens" unlawful, 35
nor of commanding an act under any unjust penalty : Ergo,
That command which commandeth an act in itself lawful, and
no other act whereby any unjust penalty is enjoined, nor any
circumstance whence, directly or "per accidens," any sin is

consequent, which the commander ought to provide against, is not sinful, notwithstanding your reason alleged.

Resp. The minor is .denied upon the same reasons, which you do nothing to remove. Such a command hath not in it 5 all things requisite to the lawfulness of a command, because though no other act be commanded, whereby an unjust penalty is enjoined, yet still the first act may be commanded " sub pœna injusta:" and though no other act or circumstance be commanded that is a sin "per accidens," yet the first act 10 itself commanded may be a sin " per accidens."

Oppon. Either our minor is true, notwithstanding your reason, or else the first act may be a command commanding an unjust punishment, and be an act lawful : or the first act itself being lawful in itself and all circumstances, may yet 15 be a sin "per accidens," against which the commander ought to provide : " Posterius utrumque falsum," both the latter members are false : " Ergo, prius verum," therefore the first is true.

Resp. 1. Neg. major. Because 1. The subject is changed : 20 you were to have spoken of the first act commanded, and you speak of the first act commanding, in the first member ; you should have said [else the first act may be commanded " sub pœna injusta," and yet be in itself lawful] ; which is true.

2. Because in the second member, where you should have 25 spoken only of the commanded circumstances of the act, you now speak of all its circumstances, whether commanded or not.

*3. We undertook not to give you all our reasons ; the minor may be false upon many other reasons. And were your major 30 reduced in the points excepted against, we should deny the minor as to both members.

And we should add to our reasons. 1. That command which commandeth an act in itself lawful and only such, may yet be sinful privatively, by omission of some necessary part, 35 some mode or circumstance.

2. It may sinfully restrain, though it sinfully command not.

3. It may be sinful "in modis," commanding that universally, or indefinitely, or particularly, or singularly, that should be

otherwise; though in the circumstances, properly so called, of the act, nothing were commanded that is sinful.

4. It may through culpable ignorance be applied to undue subjects, who are not circumstances: as if a people that have the plague be commanded to keep assemblies for worship, the 5 lawgiver being culpably ignorant that they had the plague. Many more reasons may be given.

Oppon. We make good our major by shewing that the subject is not changed; thus: If whensoever the first act is commanded "sub pœna injusta," and no other act is com- 10 manded, whereby any unjust penalty is enjoined, (which were your words,) the first act commanding must command an unjust punishment (which were ours), then we have not changed the subject: But the antecedent is true, therefore the consequent.   15

CHAPTER VIII.

The revision of the liturgy in the reign of Charles II.

THE conference held at the Savoy terminated on
the 24th day of July, 1661, by the expiration of
5 the four months, to which the commission had been
limited. But a convocation had begun to sit in the
mean time, and the bishops had already made preparations for such changes as they deemed expedient, in
the Book of Common Prayer, and the general govern-
10 ment of the church.

It appears from the king's Declaration of October,
1660, that his first intention was to summon a synod
immediately on his return to England; and that he
abandoned that intention, when he became better
15 acquainted with the state of religious parties, resolving
to conduct the proper inquiries himself, and to come
to a decision on his own authority. This resolution
was probably taken for the purpose of gratifying the
dissenters, as they could not expect any favour in a
20 convocation from which they would in great measure
be excluded. But it was supported by many other
considerations. All parties acknowledged, at least in
principle, that the clergy, who had been ejected from
their livings, must be restored; and it was a conse-
25 quence almost inevitable, that a convocation, appointed after such changes, and under the operation of
kindred influences, would represent extreme opinions,

B b

and be little qualified either to make permanent arrangements for the church, or to act in harmony with the convention-parliament. The same impression seems to have continued at a later period; and it was not until a strong memorial had been addressed to the 5 chief minister of state, shewing the necessity for convening the clergy of the two provinces on the meeting of the new parliament, that archbishop Juxon was empowered to issue his mandate for the assembling of a convocation at St. Paul's, on the 8th of May, 1661. 10

The first business undertaken in this convocation was to draw up a form of prayer for the 29th of May, the anniversary at once of the king's birth and of the restoration of the monarchy. In the third session the bishops of Salisbury (Henchman), Peterborough (Laney), 15 and St. Asaph (Griffith), were directed, in conjunction with six members of the lower house, to prepare an office for the baptism of adults, such an office having become necessary from the increase of anabaptism, and the great neglect of religious ordinances, which 20 had recently prevailed. It was completed before the 31st of May, and on that day received its approbation from the house of bishops. In the eighth, and some following sessions, the bishops, having obtained two royal licenses for that and other purposes, made some 25 progress in examining portions of a code of canons. In the session of the 21st of November, the first session that took place after the close of the Savoy conference, they entered upon the consideration of the Book of Common Prayer, and directed the bishops of 30 Durham (Cosin), Ely (Wren), Oxford (Skinner), Rochester (Warner), Salisbury (Henchman), Worcester (Morley), Lincoln (Sanderson), and Gloucester (Nicholson), to proceed without loss of time in preparing it for

their revision.   So earnest, however, were they in this
matter, and· so clearly directed in their judgment, as
well by the recent discussions, as by the strong expression of public opinion, that by means which will be
5 explained hereafter they were able at once to super-
sede their newly-appointed committee, and to make
considerable progress in the revision of the liturgy at
the same meeting.   On the day following they held
two sessions for the same purpose, and on Saturday,
10 the 23rd of November, a portion of the Book of
Common Prayer, containing the corrections of the
bishops, was delivered to the prolocutor of the lower
house, with an injunction that they should proceed to
examine it with all possible expedition.   The lower
15 clergy were not surpassed in zeal and promptitude by
their superiors.   Three days afterwards, when the bishops had finished their labours, and placed the second
moiety in the hands of the prolocutor, the clergy of the
lower house delivered back the first. portion, together
20 with their schedule of amendments.   With labourers
so earnest and so friendly the whole work was speedily
completed, though not before great impatience had
been shewn by the king and the two houses of parliament[a].   A new preface was adopted, the calendar
25 was reconstructed, a form of prayer provided for use at
sea, and on the 13th of December a committee, consisting of members of both houses, was instructed to
make a diligent examination and last revision of the

[a] In one of the same sessions (the 40th) the bishops came unani-
30 mously to a vote in favour of some constant forms of prayer to be
used before and after sermons.   By so doing they were extinguishing the last, and perhaps the most earnest, hope of the nonconformists for an opportunity of exercising, what they styled, the gift
of prayer.   For prudential reasons, however, the bishops did not
35 carry their resolution into effect.   See Kennet, Register, p. 576.

whole book, incorporating some new collects which
had been read and approved in the same session.
Little now remained to be done. A form[b] of thanksgiving for God's general mercies, composed and presented by bishop Reynolds, was read and discussed, a 5
form of words for subscribing the Book was drawn
up in committee and approved by the house, and
finally on the 20th of December, 1661, the Book of
Common Prayer was adopted and subscribed by the
clergy of both houses of convocation and of both pro- 10
vinces[c].

Our attention would now be directed, according to
the order of time, to the proceedings of the newly-
elected parliament; but there are still some acts of the
convocation connected with our subject, which it will 15
be most convenient to notice in this place. It appears
that on the 29th of January, 1662, a copy of the bill
now pending in parliament for the observance of the
liturgy was read and examined in the bishops' house;
on the 5th of March they deputed the bishops of St. 20
Asaph (Griffith), Carlisle (Sterne), and Chester (Walton), with the concurrence of the lower house, to revise

b The general thanksgiving is commonly ascribed to bishop Sanderson; but there is no direct authority for doing so. The account 25
given by Isaac Walton, which after all is not sufficiently precise to
be used in evidence, is clearly the statement of a partial and credu-
lous friend. If a general thanksgiving had already been approved
by the bishops, it is scarcely probable that any form of the same
kind would have been introduced by bishop Reynolds; and as there 30
is no notice that his form was rejected, or that any other was supplied afterwards, it seems not improbable that the general thanksgiving, which we now use, was the composition of bishop Reynolds.

c For this occasion the two houses of convocation at York had
been united (the bishops in person, and the lower clergy by means 35
of a deputation) with the two houses of the province of Canterbury.

certain alterations[d] which had been made in the Book
of Common Prayer during its progress through parliament; on the 8th of March, Mr. Sancroft (afterwards
archbishop of Canterbury) was directed to superintend
5 the printing of the book, and Mr. Scattergood and
Mr. Dillingham to correct the press; and on the 18th
of the same month the president of the upper house
reported to the assembled clergy that the lord chancellor, in his own name and on behalf of the lords in
10 general, presented their thanks to both houses of con-

d " Emendationes sive alterationes alias in libro Publicarum Precum per domum parliamenti factas." Such is the account of the
matter given in the records of the upper house. (Synodus Angli-
cana, App. p. 103.) But it is probable that this resolution of the
15 bishops was prospective; with reference to alterations, which might
possibly be made afterwards, and not to any which had then been
actually made. For on the 5th of March it was much too early for
any alterations to have been agreed upon; as the Prayer Book had
then been only eight days in the possession of the house of lords,
20 and the bill of uniformity, of which it was a part, was not passed in
that house till the 9th of April. There is no notice of such alterations at any time in the lords' journals, and the only vote there recorded respecting the liturgy is of the date of March 17, and is on
the question simply, whether the book transmitted from the king
25 should be annexed to the act. Upon the whole it may fairly be inferred that no alterations were made by the lords, and it is known
that none were made by the house of commons.

It appears, also, that on the 21st of April, when the house of commons was still engaged with the act of uniformity, the bishops were
30 desirous of substituting the word "children" for the word "persons
[not baptized]" and consulted the lord chancellor as to the best
method of doing it. (Syn. Angl. App. p. 109.) It is not known
whether any further steps were taken in the matter: but the application would seem to imply that no precedent had then been given
35 them of changes made by either house of parliament; and if the desire of the bishops had reference, as is probable, to the last rubric
of "public baptism for such as be of riper years," it is evident that
that alteration was not made.

vocation for the great care and industry they had shewn in revising the Book of Common Prayer[e].

It was not possible that a house of commons, actuated by the powerful motives that prevailed at the time of the restoration, and consisting in a great 5 degree of persons who were embittered against the

[e] " The following is an extract from one of the MSS. in the Lambeth library (vol. 577) written with abp. Sancroft's hand, giving an account of the individuals employed in the alterations now made in the liturgy, taken from the journals of the lower house of convo- 10 cation. As those journals no longer exist, perhaps this is the only record remaining of the persons who were employed in the work.

" ' Out of the Journal of the Lower House of Convocation.

" Fr. Mundie, Actuary.

" 1661, May 16. Chosen to attend the bishops at Elie House 15 the next morning at 8 o'clock, concerning a form of prayer for May 29th, the prolocutor and eight more, scilicet, the deans of Sarum (Dr. Baily), Chichester (Dr. Henshaw), Peterborough (Dr. Rainbow), and Norwich (Dr. Crofts) ; the archdeacon of Surry (Dr. Pearson), of Canterbury (Dr. George Hall), Dr. Creed, and Dr. 20 Martin.

" May 18. Chosen to attend the bishops for the review of the book for the 30th of January, the dean of Gloucester (Dr. Brough), of Lichfield (Dr. Paul), the archdeacon of St. Albans (Dr. Frank), Dr. Crowther, the dean of Christ Church, Oxford (Dr. Fell), Dr. 25 Fleetwood, Dr. Pory, archdeacon of Middlesex, Dr. Gunning.

" To attend the bishops at the Savoy on Monday next at 3 o'clock afternoon, to consult about the form of baptizing the adults, the dean of Westminster (Dr. Earl), of Worcester (Dr. Oliver), archdeacon of Sudbury (Dr. Sparrow), archdeacon of Wilts (Dr. Creed), 30 Dr. Heywood, Dr. Gunning.

" May 22. Precibus peractis, ordered that each keep his place, that but one speak at once, and that without interruption ; none to use long speeches ; to have a constant verger.

" May 24. A prayer or collect to be made for the parliament 35 sitting, and one for the synod ; referred to Dr. Pory and the archbishop's other chaplains to draw up and present the same to this house the next session.

recent course of government, should be calm spectators of the proceedings at the Savoy conference.   In
those proceedings were renewed many questions, some
directly and others by implication, which had furnished
5 materials for the debates of the long parliament, and
had led by an easy descent to their most fatal measures.   There was no case, in short, whether they

" May 31. Dr. Pory introduxit formam precationum pro parlia-
mento et synodo. The approbation of them referred to the dean
10 of Wells (Dr. Creighton), Dr. Creed, Dr. Pearson, Dr. Crowther,
and the archbishop's two chaplains.

" June 7. A form of prayer (juxta edictum regium), with humiliation for the immoderate rain, and thanksgiving for the change
thereof by fair weather, referred to eight of this house (who are to
15 attend four bishops at Elie House this afternoon), scilicet, the dean
of Winton (Dr. Alexander Hyde), the dean of Sarum (Dr. Bailie),
the dean of Wells (Dr. Creighton), Dr. Priaulx, Dr. Gulston, Dr.
Preston, Dr. Rawley.'

" Doubts have been entertained respecting the persons who framed
20 the prayer for the parliament, as it now stands in our liturgy ; but
these doubts are cleared up by the above cited extracts from the
convocation books, which shew that the prayer was prepared and
introduced for the approbation of the convocation by ' Dr. Pory (then
archdeacon of Middlesex) and the archbishop's other chaplains.'
25 The fact, however, is that the prayer, though now for the first time
introduced into the liturgy, was not entirely new. A prayer for
the parliament, with the same beginning and ending, and particularly
containing the expression, ' our religious and gracious king,' was
inserted in a form of prayers put forth in the time and under the
30 authority of Charles I. on the first breaking out of the troubles in
1628 [but see above, p. 233.] and from this the prayer, which now
forms part of the liturgy, was partly formed." Dr. D'Oyly's note
on the Life of abp. Sancroft, vol. i. p. 113.

The prayer for the parliament appeared for the first time in its
35 present shape in a form of prayer appointed for a general fast on the
12th of June, 1661, special mention of it being made in the title-
page. It was thence transferred by the convocation to the Book of
Common Prayer.

regarded the recent history of disorder, or the theory
of a settled government, that would, in the convictions
of the royalists, combine a greater number of hazards,
and rekindle more certainly the flames of discord, than
the remodeling of the church and the public ritual.[5]
So strongly did these sentiments prevail in the house
of commons, that on the 25th of June, when the long
list of exceptions and the new liturgy, presented at
the conference, had already created a strong impression against the nonconformists, a committee was[10]
appointed to make search for the original of king
Edward's second Service-book, and "to provide for an
effectual conformity to the liturgy of the church for
the time to come." This was followed up by resolute
measures, when it was found that there was now no[15]
prospect of any reasonable compliance on the part of
the nonconformists. On the 9th of July, a "bill for
the uniformity of public prayer and administration of
the sacraments" was read for the third time, and together with a copy of the Prayer Book, printed in[20]
1604, was passed and sent to the upper house. It is
not known what was the issue of their inquiries respecting the second Service-book of king Edward. It
is probable as the book is not uncommon now, that a
copy of it was produced, and was not found to be suffi-[25]
ciently in accordance with the higher tone of ordinances, which since the days of Elizabeth had more
generally prevailed. However this may be, it may
certainly be presumed that the edition of 1604 was
selected in preference to any recent edition, for the[30]
purpose of avoiding the alleged alterations of archbishop Laud, alterations, of which the commons would
form their opinion from general report, and the evil
reputation he had contracted of popish tendencies.

This, at least, is evident, that they had no intention of gratifying the nonconformists in any of their wishes.

But the lords were contented to wait till the conference should have closed, and some measure should 5 be proposed to them, recommended by the votes of the clergy and the confirmation of the crown.   It appears that of the bill sent up to them on the 9th of July no notice was taken for some time, except that its reading was appointed for a day on which they did not 10 assemble.   But on the 14th day of February, 1662, the same bill, after a copy⁵ had already been submitted to the bishops, was read for the first time by the lords, and three days afterwards it passed through the second reading, and was placed in the hands of a 15 select committee.   The Book of Common Prayer, however, was not yet delivered to them; and the committee having inquired on the 13th of February, with strong symptoms of impatience, whether they should still wait for it, or should " proceed upon the book 20 brought from the commons," they received a royal message on the 25th of the same month, together with an authentic copy of the corrected Prayer Book confirmed under the great seal.   After much subsequent discussion respecting some provisos transmitted by his 25 majesty, and other clauses introduced in behalf of ejected ministers and for other purposes, the bill, with its many amendments, was passed by the lords on the

---

⁵ It appears that the bishops deliberated upon this bill in their house of convocation on the 29th of January, (Syn. Angl. App. p. 98); 30 but, as they had been restored to their places in the house of lords on the 20th of November, 1661, the question was probably introduced by one or more of their own body, with a view to their entering into some common understanding respecting it, and so acting in concert in the house of lords.

9th day of April, 1662, and returned to the house of commons[h].

It appears that the commons were jealous of the preference given to the corrected[i] Book of Common Prayer over the edition of 1604, and suspecting that some differences might have been introduced between the two periods when the books were respectively printed, directed a close comparison to be made between them. On the 16th of April they proceeded so far in their fear of change, as to make it a question whether they should not reconsider the corrections made in convocation; and though they decided to adopt them without further examination, the division was only of 96 to 90 in their favour. In order to save the dignity of the house, they afterwards divided on the question whether they had the power of reconsidering such corrections, and then obtained a vote in the affirmative.

It is not necessary to enumerate the many and important clauses of the act itself, which have no direct bearing on the state of the liturgy. Lord Clarendon says that the provision requiring re-ordination from all ministers who had not been episcopally ordained, and which, though enjoined by the governors of the church, had not hitherto been made imperative by the legislature, was introduced by the lords and adopted after much earnest debate. The practical result was, that

h Lord Clarendon says, (Life, vol. ii. p. 130,) that the " act began first in the house of peers." But it is clear from the journals that the peers proceeded on the bill which had been sent up to them from the commons before their adjournment.

i The corrected book was probably a copy of the printed edition of 1634 (at which time Laud was archbishop of Canterbury) with the corrections inserted.

"very many of those who had received presbyterian orders" submitted : but the clause was doubtless very offensive to the more rigid nonconformists, as it not only involved an acknowledgment of many errors, but 5 also compelled them to forego the feeling they entertained against episcopacy, a feeling the more difficult to surrender, as it was a combination of argument and of hatred. Equally offensive was the clause that required "assent and consent to be declared to all and 10 every thing contained in the Book of Common Prayer;" and more certain was it to occasion separation from the church, as the minds of men had long been employed on the question, and the strong currents of the times had compelled them to make direct and public 15 avowal of their opinions. But the greatest embarrassment arose from the royalist convictions of the commons. They required from all persons in holy orders, and every schoolmaster on receiving his appointment, a declaration[k] that it was not lawful, on any pretence 20 whatever, to take arms against the king; that they

k Respecting this declaration lord Clarendon speaks as follows (Life, vol. ii. p. 135.) : "The framing and forming this clause had taken up very much time, and raised no less passion in the house of commons; and now it came among the lords it was not less trouble- 25 some. It added to the displeasure and jealousy against the bishops, by whom it was thought to be prepared and commended to their party in the lower house." It appears that there was much reason for this suspicion : for in their session of the 12th of April, three days after the bill was sent to the commons, the bishops debated 30 " de subscriptionibus clericorum instituendorum et ludimagistrorum licentiandorum et tribus articulis 36 canone, &c. Dominus Episcopus London Præsidens, &c. de et cum consensu, &c., curam commisit reverendis Patribus Dominis Episcopis Sarum et Coven' et Lichen' ad consulend' Jurisperitos de concipiend' forma in scriptis 35 in et circa subscriptionem prædict'." Syn. Angl. App. p. 108.

would conform to the liturgy as by law established, and that the oath called the solemn league and covenant was of no obligation, and had been unlawfully imposed. There were few members of either house, who were not devoted, by personal feeling as well as [5] sincere conviction, to the support or rejection of this clause. It brought before them not only the question of their present interests, and the stern sense of what was due to their own consistency, but also the whole history of the past rebellion, and the many scenes of [10] danger in which they had fought and suffered. But the supposed necessity for strong and despotic powers, combined with the general hatred of both houses against the presbyterians, prevailed. The lords endeavoured to mitigate the severity of the clause by [15] some amendments, in which the commons acquiesced; and so, says lord Clarendon, the bill "was presented to the king; who could not well refuse his royal assent, nor did in his own judgment or inclination dislike what was offered to him." [20]

Of the alterations made at this time in the Prayer-book the following are the most important. The Sentences, the Epistles and Gospels, and other extracts from the Bible (except the Psalter, the Ten Commandments, and other portions of the Communion Service) [25] were taken generally from the version of 1611. The Absolution was ordered to be pronounced by the "priest" alone, instead of the "minister." The Book of Bel and the Dragon was re-inserted in the Calendar of Lessons. The prayers for the king, the royal family, [30] the clergy and people, together with the prayers of St. Chrysostom and the Benediction, were printed in the Order both of Morning and Evening Service, instead of being left, as formerly, at the end of the litany.

The Evening Service, which previously began with the Lord's Prayer, was now opened with the Sentences, the Exhortation, the Confession, and Absolution, printed as in the Morning Service.   In the litany
5 the words "rebellion" and "schism" were added to the petition respecting "sedition, privy conspiracy," &c. In a subsequent petition the words " bishops, priests, and deacons" were employed instead of " bishops, pastours, and ministers of the church."   Among the
10 occasional prayers and thanksgivings were now introduced a second prayer for fair weather, the two prayers for the ember weeks, the prayers for the parliament and for all conditions of men, a thanksgiving for restoring public peace at home, and the general thanks-
15 giving.   New collects were appointed for the third Sunday in Advent, and for St. Stephen's day.   The Genealogy, which previously made part of the Gospel for the Sunday after Christmas, was now omitted. A distinct collect, epistle, and gospel, were provided for
20 a sixth Sunday after the Epiphany.   The gospels for the Sunday next before Easter and for Good Friday were shortened, having formerly contained within them respectively the second lesson for the day. In several places, as in one of the collects for Good
25 Friday, in those for the fifth and sixteenth Sundays after Trinity, for St. Simon and St. Jude, and in other places, the word " church¹" was used for " congregation."

¹ The change of the word " congregation" was thought so important with reference to the presbyterians, that in several passages
30 where it was used in its popular sense and " church" was inappropriate, the word " people" was inserted instead of it, to prevent the possibility of mistake.   Even in the ancient preface it was thought necessary that the words " ministers of the congregation" should be altered to " ministers in the congregation," to remove any the

A distinct collect was supplied for Easter-even. The first of the anthems used on Easter-day was added. A distinct epistle was provided for the day of the Purification. The last clause respecting saints departed was added to the prayer [m] for the church 5

remotest presumption, that the expression might appear to give, in favour of the presbyterian form of church-government.

The same principle which had occasioned the use of the word "congregation" in the liturgies of king Edward, led to the use of the same word, rather than the word "church," as a translation of 10 ἐκκλησία, in the earliest English Bibles, viz. Tyndale's and Cranmer's. The Genevan version, which came afterwards, introduced the word "church" in several instances, and the Bishops' Bible in a greater number. It is used generally for the word ἐκκλησία in the version of 1611. See Fulke's Defence &c. p. 225. Parker ed., and Field on 15 the Church, b. i. c. 5. ad fin.

[m] The words "alms and oblations," as contained in the same prayer and in its marginal rubric, require some explanation. It will appear that they both refer to the offerings made in money. In the Book of 1549 no mention is made of either alms or 20 oblations. In 1552 alms only are mentioned; and the prayer is preceded by the following rubric : " Then shall the churchwardens ......gather the devotion of the people, and put the same into the poor man's box; and upon the offering days appointed, every man and woman shall pay to the curate the due and accustomed offerings." 25

The same was continued exactly in the books of 1559, 1607, and 1634. In 1662 the words " and oblations" were added; the preceding rubric was changed thus......" shall receive the alms for the poor and other devotions of the people in a decent basin......and reverently bring it to the priest, who shall humbly present and 30 place it upon the holy table;" and as an explanation of the distinct purposes denoted by the two words "alms and oblations" the following rubric was added at the end of the whole service : " After the divine service ended, the money given at the offertory shall be disposed of to such pious and charitable uses as the minister and 35 churchwardens shall think fit. Wherein if they disagree, it shall be disposed of as the ordinary shall appoint."

At the same revision, and immediately before the prayer for the church militant, was also added this rubric : " And when there is a

militant. The rubric was added as to "covering what
remaineth of the elements with a fair linen cloth."
The order in council respecting kneeling at the Lord's
supper, which had been introduced in 1552 and re-
5 moved by queen Elizabeth, was restored, with this
alteration; instead of "any real and essential presence
there being of Christ's natural flesh and blood," it is
now read, "any corporal presence of Christ's natural
flesh and blood." A new office was appointed for the
10 "baptism of such as are of riper years;" and some
alterations made in the other offices of baptism. The
preface to Confirmation was curtailed, and the clause
respecting the undoubted salvation[n] of baptized infants
dying before the commission of actual sin, was placed
15 after the office for Infant Baptism. Some changes were
made in the offices for Confirmation and Matrimony;
and in the rubric at the end of the latter, the receiving
the communion on the day of the marriage was no longer
made imperative. In the Visitation of the Sick the
20 words "if he humbly and heartily desire it" were

communion, the priest shall then place upon the table so much
bread and wine as he shall think sufficient." It was proposed in
Mr. Sancroft's book (see infra) that the rubric should run thus:
" the priest shall then offer up and place upon the table;" but the
25 words "offer up" were not adopted. Had it been otherwise, a
different interpretation might have been suggested for the word
" oblations."

[n] This was one of the greatest grievances complained of by the
dissenters, being, as they said, a declaration that that is certain
30 by God's word, which at best can only be proved as a probable
deduction from it. Baxter was so inexorable on this point, as to
maintain, "That of the forty sinful terms for a communion with
the church party, if thirty-nine were taken away, and only that
rubric, concerning the salvation of infants dying shortly after their
35 baptism, were continued, yet they could not conform." Long's
Vox Cleri, an. 1690. p. 18.

added to the rubric respecting absolution: the Benediction also and the prayers that follow, appear now
for the first time.   In the Order for Burial the first
rubric respecting persons unbaptized or excommunicate
was added.   Forms of prayer were supplied to be used 5
at sea: and, lastly, offices° were provided for the 30th

° The statute 3 James I. c. 1. provided for the religious observance of the 5th of November; the stat. 12 Charles II. c. 30. (confirmed by 13 Charles II. stat. 1. c. 7.) for the religious observance
of the 30th of January; the stat. 12 Charles II. c. 14. (confirmed 10
by 13 Charles II. stat. 1. c. 11.) for the religious observance of the
29th of May; but in no one of these statutes was any direction
given as to a service to be appointed for the day, that appointment
being left in each case to the king in council under his royal supremacy and the powers declared in the statute 1 Eliz. c. 2.   These 15
several services were accordingly considered and arranged, under the
king's license for that purpose, in the convocation of 1662, and when
the Book of Common Prayer was published according to the act of
uniformity, they were annexed to it in obedience to the following
order: "Charles R. Our will and pleasure is that these three forms 20
of prayer and service made for the 5th of November, the 30th of
January, and the 29th of May, be forthwith printed and published,
and for the future annexed to the Book of Common Prayer and
Liturgy of the Church of England, to be used yearly on the said
days in all cathedral and collegiate churches and chapels, in all 25
chapels of colleges and halls within both our universities, and of our
colleges of Eton and Winchester, and in all parish churches and
chapels within our kingdom of England, dominion of Wales and
town of Berwick upon Tweed. Given at our court at Whitehall the
2nd day of May in the 14th year of our reign. By his majesty's 30
command, Edward Nicholas." A similar order has been issued at
the beginning of each successive reign. Alterations have been made
in these services at different times by royal authority: as for instance
in the reign of James II. when the form provided for the 29th of
May underwent many alterations besides those which were rendered 35
necessary by the death of Charles II; and in the reign of William
and Mary, when prayers composed by bishops Patrick and Sprat
were added to the service of the 5th of November, to commemorate

of January and 29th of May, and the old service for
the 5th of November was corrected. These and many

the landing of king William. In neither of these two cases does the
convocation appear to have been consulted. In the first of them,
5 the new form was issued with the following notice : "James R. The
form of prayer with thanksgiving heretofore appointed for the 29th of
May, relating in several passages of it to the birth and person of our
most dearly beloved brother king Charles II. and so upon occasion
of his death being necessarily to be altered, and it being now by our
10 special command to the bishops so altered and settled to our satisfaction as a perpetual office of thanksgiving for the standing mercies of
that day ; our express will and pleasure is" &c. &c. In the second
case the alterations made in the service for the 5th of November
were approved by the royal commission of the year 1689, but were
15 not submitted to the convocation of that period, on account of the
strong opposition that the court had experienced from the clergy of
the lower house.

Prayers and thanksgivings for the anniversary of the sovereign's
accession have been added to the usual service of the day in every
20 reign since the time of the Reformation. The form provided in the
time of queen Elizabeth may be seen in Strype's Ann. vol. ii. p. 2.
p. 65. But after the interruption occasioned by the great rebellion
a new form was compiled by command of king James II. and was
put forth with the following notice : " James R. Whereas not only
25 the pious Christian emperors in ancient times, but also of late our
own most religious predecessors, kings of this realm, did cause the
days on which they began their several reigns to be publicly celebrated every year (so long as they reigned) by all their subjects with
solemn prayers and thanksgiving to Almighty God : this pious
30 custom received lately a long and doleful interruption upon occasion
of the barbarous murder of our most dear father of blessed memory,
which changed the day, on which our late most dear brother succeeded to the crown, into a day of sorrow and fasting : but now we
thinking fit to revive the former laudable and religious practice, and
35 having caused a form of prayer and thanksgiving to be composed
by our bishops for that purpose ; our will and pleasure is" &c. &c.
This form with some considerable alterations made in the time of
queen Anne, has been issued at the beginning of each succeeding
reign, and depends altogether upon the royal authority.

C C

other minor alterations[P], amounting as Dr. Tenison computed to about 600 in number, were made in the Book of Common Prayer by the convocation of 1662, and were finally ratified by the act of uniformity[q].

[P] It is commonly stated (see Burnet, Own Times, vol. i. p. 333.5 Neal's Purit. vol. iii. p. 97.) that the festivals of St. Barnabas and the Conversion of St. Paul were now added for the first time to the Calendar. But this is not the case. The collects, &c. for both days are to be found in the editions of 1549, 1552, and so downwards, although in some cases, as in Grafton's edition of 1552, the name of 10 Barnabas has been omitted by mistake in the Calendar. It appears however that in the Romish church these two apostles were not placed in the same order with the rest; and even in our own church we find bishop Wren in the year 1636 giving directions that "ministers forget not to read the collects, epistles, and gospels 15 appointed for the Conversion of St. Paul and for St. Barnaby's day." Docum. Ann. No. cxliii.

[q] One alteration made at this time is reserved for a note, as requiring some explanation. In the consecration of a bishop the form of words addressed to him on the imposition of hands had 20 previously been, "Take the Holy Ghost, and remember that thou stirre up the grace of God which is in thee by imposition of hands; for God hath not given us the spirit of feare, but of power, and love, and sobernesse." It was altered to the present form, which begins thus: "Receive the Holy Ghost, for the office and work of 25 a bishop in the church of God," &c. A corresponding addition was also made to the words employed in the ordering of priests. It will readily be conjectured that the change was made for the purpose of marking more strongly the commission given to a bishop as distinct from that of a priest; a question on which it will have been observed 30 that after various success in other contests, the church-party never suffered themselves to be vanquished. But the matter will be better understood from the following letter of Dr. Humfrey Prideaux (afterwards dean of Norwich) written to one of archbishop Sancroft's chaplains, and bearing date Nov. 25, 1687. (Tanner, MSS. 35 vol. xxix. No. 73.)

"I being of late much assaulted here with papers from the papists, have thought it my duty to leave none of them unanswered; and in one concerning the validity of our orders, having many cavils

It will be observed that in this long enumeration
there is no mention of any of those characteristic
points which had been the subjects of strife and
division in the church from the earliest days of puri-
5 tanism : that the use of the Apocrypha, the expressions
complained of in the litany, and in the services for
baptism, marriage, and burial, the rubric with regard
to vestments, the kneeling at the communion, the cross
in baptism, the ring in marriage, the declaration as to
10 infants dying immediately after baptism, the absolution
for the sick, though some of them slightly modified,
continued in principle the same. All these and several
others had been conceded by the committee of 1641 ;
they had also been virtually withdrawn by the royal
15 declaration of October 1660 ; and some of them had
been abandoned by the bishops in the Savoy conference. But they were all of them retained and confirmed by the act of uniformity, on the plea that the
nonconformists had lost whatever claim they might

20 objected against them on the account of the alteration in the words
of ordination made in the review of our liturgy anno 1662, among
other things in my answer I told them that this alteration was not
made with any respect to our controversy with them, but to silence
a cavil of the presbyterians, who from our ordinal pretended to
25 prove against us that there was no difference between the two
functions, because the words of ordination said nothing to him [as
a bishop] in the old ordinal which he had not afore as a priest.
And this I well remember to have read somewhere to have been the
sole occasion of adding those further explanatory words now in our
30 ordinal. But in answer to this they tell me that it was not occasioned by the presbyterians, but by two books then wrote called
Erastus Senr. and Erastus Junr.; which having arguments unanswerable against the validity of our orders from the defect of the
forms by which they were administered, we had no other way to
35 solve the difficulty but by mending the fault they took notice of.   •
The favour that I now beg of you is, that you would be pleased to

once have had for consideration and forbearance, and
that the other party, consisting at once of the orthodox
and the royalists, saw nothing in such alterations but
inconvenience and error. And this feeling was so
strong both in convocation and in parliament, that 5
several changes of an opposite character were approved,
which could not fail to be galling to the presbyterians.
The substitution of " church" for " congregation," the
specific mention of " bishops, priests, and deacons,"
instead of a more general designation, the re-intro- 10
duction of Bell and the Dragon into the Calendar, and

inform yourself from my ld. archbp. (who was I understand much
concerned in all that was then done) how this affair went, and on
what motives that explanatory addition was made, and also, if you
can, whether these two books were published before or after the 15
conclusion of that affair, and if you will be pleased to communicate
to me what information you can get herein, you will very much
oblige," &c. &c.

It is not known what answer was given to this letter : but the
change had been recommended among the MSS. corrections of Mr. 20
Sancroft's book (see infra p. 390. l. 7.), where it was proposed that
after the word " Holy Ghost" should be inserted " by whom the
office and authority of a bishop is now committed unto thee." It is
clear also that it was for the purpose of meeting the objections of the
presbyterians rather than the Romanists, not only from the general 25
state of controversy at the time, but from this consideration also,
that it is strictly to the point in the former case, and irrelevant in
the other. The objection of the presbyterians was, " We do not find
in Scripture any ordination to the office of a bishop differing from
the ordination of an elder" (Smectymnuus, an. 1641) ; whereas the 30
objection of the Romanists was, " the protestants have no true
priests, because they have not the form of ordaining priests which
was and is in the catholic church," (see abp. Bramhall on Protestant
Ordination, an. 1657.) The book entitled Erastus Senior was published in the year 1662, and was therefore subsequent to the time 35
when the corrections of the Prayer-book were finally approved and
adopted in the convocation.

other similar alterations, though none of them new in
principle, seemed designed to convince the nonconformists that instead of any wish to admit them to
further power or privilege within the church, there
5 was a distinct and settled desire to restrain or exclude
them. So strongly did they themselves feel this conviction, that it was proposed[r] on their behalf in the
house of lords, that the existing liturgy should be
continued, and all the corrections made in convocation
10 should be abandoned.

The fear, which the commons seem to have contracted, that occasion would be taken for introducing
into the liturgy the religious sentiments of archbishop
Laud and his school of theologians, was not altogether
15 without foundation. It might in the first instance
have been suggested by the remembrance of what was
done in the reign of king Charles I. when, under the
directions of the archbishop and bishop Wren, the
liturgy was revised for the use of the episcopal church
20 of Scotland. But it had stronger grounds[s] to support
it. There is still in existence a copy of the edition of
1634 with a great number of corrections in manuscript

[r] Lord Clarendon's Life, vol. ii. p. 128.
[s] It is worthy of notice that in the form of prayer for the 30th of
25 January, which was put forth in the preceding year (1661) by royal
authority, these words appeared in one of the collects, but were
erased by the convocation, when the service was afterwards revised
and annexed to the liturgy : " We beseech thee to give us all grace
to remember and provide for our latter end, by a careful studious
30 imitation of this thy blessed saint and martyr, and all other thy
saints and martyrs that have gone before us, that we may be made
worthy to receive benefit by their prayers, which they in communion
with thy church catholic offer up unto thee for that part of it here
militant and yet in fight with and danger from the flesh." (See
35 Bodl. A. 2. 8. Linc.)

prepared for this convocation, and carrying so much the appearance of completeness and authority, as to contain minute instructions for the printer. The corrections are all of them in the handwriting of Mr. Sancroft, who was at that time chaplain to the bishop[5] of Durham (Cosin), and was soon afterwards appointed by the convocation to superintend the Prayer-book in its progress through the press. The copy itself, it may fairly be presumed, was drawn up by Mr. Sancroft[t]

[t] By the kind assistance of professor Jenkyns, a diligent search[10] has been made among the letters and papers of bp. Cosin, now preserved at Durham, for any light they might enable us to throw upon this transaction. But nothing has been found in connexion either with the conference or the convocation. "The letters relate principally, indeed almost entirely, to the bishop's own private mat-[15] ters and the affairs of the sea. There are none either to or from Mr. Sancroft. He is incidentally mentioned in one or two, where it is said, ' Mr. Sandcroft is gone to Cambridge.' Letter dated Apr. 10, 1661. ' On Sunday Mr. Sandcroft preached at Whitehall afore his majestie, and was much applauded.' Letter dated Jun. 28,[20] 1661. There are comparatively few letters in bp. Cosin's own handwriting." But among the letters preserved by archbishop Sancroft and now in the Tanner Collection in the Bodleian, is one written to him from Auckland by one of bp. Cosin's chaplains, and dated June 16, 1662, shewing the great interest the bishop felt in[25] the progress of the Prayer-book under Mr. Sancroft's superintendance. "My lord desires at all times to know particularly what progress you make in the Common Prayer."

In the same collection (Tanner, MSS. vol. xlix. No. 181) is a letter from Mr. Sancroft to his brother, written March 10, 1662,[30] immediately after he was appointed by the convocation to superintend the printing of the Prayer-book, and shewing that it was not the first employment in which he had been engaged in their service. "On Saturday I sent to take a passage in the Cambridge coach. . . . but before I slept, I found myself stopt by those who have a right[35] to command me. I know not well when this new business will be at an end ; nor can foresee, whether I shall be licensed to attend my lord into the north when he goes, which will be presently after Easter."

under the direction of bishops Cosin[u] and Wren, and was produced in the convocation of the 21st of November, when the committee, of which these bishops were the leading members, seem to have reported that
5 the preparations were already made, and that the whole house might proceed immediately to the work of revision.   However this may be, the corrections contain, together with many important improvements, strong indications of such sentiments respecting the
10 real presence in the eucharist, and prayers for the dead, as were entertained by the bishops above mentioned, and became afterwards the distinguishing creed of the non-juring clergy.   Doubtless the liturgy provided for Scotland was before them when they made
15 their corrections in the English Service.   It is clear that they were indebted to it in several of their alterations; although they have constantly improved

[u] There is in bp. Cosin's library at Durham a copy of the Prayer-book printed in 1619 by Barker and Bill, containing great numbers
20 of corrections in MS., which are commonly said to have been written by bp. Cosin himself.   Archdeacon Sharp (Disc. on the Rubric, p. 28.) speaks of it as follows: " A large prayer book with marginal annotations and alterations in his own [bp. Cosin's] handwriting. By the several directions given therein to the printer it seems to
25 have been designed as a corrected copy for the printer to follow." From the same friend who has been mentioned in the preceding note, I learn that the book " though prepared for the printer, as appears from the directions on a blank leaf at the beginning, is any thing but a fair copy, being full of erasures and corrections not always easy to
30 make out." This however is certain, that the corrections in Sancroft's book correspond exactly in fourteen of their most remarkable passages, in which they have been collated, with the book at Durham; and we may fairly assume that Sancroft's book was the fair copy taken from the other, with corrections and additions, as in the case
35 of the Ordination Services, which are contained and altered in Sancroft's book, but are altogether wanting in the Durham volume.

upon it, in some instances taking a higher, in others
a more subdued tone of doctrine and expression.   But
the presence of these manuscript corrections will easily
account for the speed with which the task of revision
was completed.   The book indeed does not contain the 5
prayers for the parliament and for all conditions of
men, the general thanksgiving, the prayers added to
the visitation of the sick, and some others; for they
came from other sources, and had not yet been submitted to the convocation.   But it appears to have 10
supplied the greatest portion of the other new matter
that was finally adopted. ᵛ With the exception of such
cases as would have brought in new grounds of controversy, the corrections suggested in Mr. Sancroft's
book, though frequently modified or reconstructed in 15
their progress, were for the most part approved by the
convocation, and incorporated in the future liturgy.

ᵛ Of the corrections in Mr. Sancroft's book, which would seem to
belong to the Laudian school of theology, the following are speci-
mens: the rubric respecting the consecrated elements which remain 20
after distribution; the alteration made in the admonition respecting
kneeling at the communion; the following rubric at the beginning
of the communion service: "The table always standing in the
midst at the upper end of the chancel (or of the church, where a
chancel is wanting) and being at all times covered with a carpet of 25
silk, shall also have at the communion time a fair white linen cloth
upon it with paten, chalice, and other decent furniture, meet for the
high mysteries there to be celebrated." Rubric after the sentences;
"The priest shall then offer up and place upon the table," &c.
Prefix to the prayer for the church militant; "Let us offer up our 30
prayers and praises for the good estate of Christ's catholic church."
Proposal to restore the prayer of oblation from king Edward's first
Service-book. Rubric at the end of the communion service; "though
wafer bread, pure and without any figure upon it, shall not be forbidden," &c.   All these, with the exception of the two first, were 35
rejected.

CHAPTER IX.

The attempt made to revise the liturgy in the reign of
William and Mary.

THE result of the Savoy conference, although it
depressed the condition of the nonconformists and
delayed indefinitely the accomplishment of their wishes,
did not put an end either to their hopes or their exertions.　They lost indeed at that period many of their
more temperate and more valuable supporters, who
were induced, partly by a feeling of despair, but still
more by a sense of duty, to join the ranks of the conformists.　Such persons, however, had always pitched
their tone of theology so low, that they could continue
to act in some degree with their former friends, even
after they had declared themselves in favour of the
establishment.　Of these Dr. Tillotson was the most
remarkable, as well on account of his own personal
character, as for the high station that he soon acquired;
and it will readily be conceived that his services were
more effective in favour of the nonconformists, when
they could no longer claim him as a member of their
body.　True to his original persuasion, and anxious to
enlarge the boundaries of the church, not so much
perhaps from any clear views of ultimate advantage, as
from the generalizing temper and spirit of his mind, he
lost no opportunity, during the two reigns that placed

the greatest impediments in his way, for advocating
and promoting the comprehension of dissenters. The
most memorable occasion occurred early in the year
1668, when he and Dr. Stillingfleet united with Bates,
Manton, and Baxter, in preparing terms of accommo- 5
dation to be brought forward in parliament under the
auspices of lord keeper Bridgman and chief baron
Hale. These terms were constructed after the model
of the king's declaration from Breda in the year
1660, with an especial provision for the case of presby- 10
terian orders; and the subject was introduced to the
parliament on the 10th of February, 1668, by the following admonition from the throne: "One thing more
I hold myself obliged to recommend to you at this present; which is, that you would seriously think of some 15
course to beget a better union and composure in the
minds of my protestant subjects in matters of religion."
But the recent confusions and the proceedings of the
Savoy conference were so fresh in the memory of the
nation, and the project was so unacceptable to the 20
great body of its representatives, that the first *resolution adopted by the commons was an address to his
majesty in favour of the existing act of uniformity;
and this was soon followed by another address from
the whole house against papists and nonconformists, 25
with an intimation that they could not enter upon the
subject of his majesty's admonition, until he had issued
a proclamation in accordance with their wishes.

Decided as was the hostility of the house of commons on this occasion, the cause of the nonconformists 30
gained an important advantage in the banishment of
lord Clarendon, and the forming of the administration
commonly known by the name of the Cabal. In the

* Commons' Journals, Feb. 10. and March 4, 1664.

year 1673 a bill for the relief of the dissenters passed
through the house of commons, and was read a third
time with amendments in the upper house, but was not
finally adopted before the parliament was prorogued.
5 They had lost the assistance of an able and resolute
prelate on the death of bishop Wilkins in 1672, and
had not yet received the open and unreserved support
[b] of bishop Croft, whose treatise entitled "The naked
Truth," itself anonymous, but soon ascribed to its real
10 author, was not published before the year 1675; but
bishops [c] Pearson, Morley, and Ward were alleged to

[b] Bishop Morley in a private letter to archbishop Sheldon writes
thus of bishops Wilkins and Croft: "I discoursed at large with
him of Chester whom I never knew so well before as I do now; for
15 I thought him to be much more learned and rational than I find he
is and much less peevish and perverse in point of opinion than I
find he is also, so that I have no hope he will ever do any good at
all in the church.—As for the bishop of Hereford I think his affections to be better than his understanding, and therefore having heard
20 what he said of oaths in the parliament house I do not wonder that
he maintained in the pulpit the souls being ex traduce (as one that
heard him told me he did on Ashwednesday) which philosophy I
take to be of very dangerous consequence in divinity." Sheldon
papers. Letters. March 1. 166¾.

25 [c] This is the statement of Baxter, who insinuates at the same
time of the two latter that they were insincere and dishonest, (Life
by Sylv. b. i. p. 3. p. 84.) But bishop Ward appears to have been
constantly unfavourable to the dissenters. In the year 1662, immediately after his appointment to the see of Exeter, he expressed him-
30 self as both surprised and gratified at their "spirit of giddiness" in
withdrawing themselves from the church. (Tanner MSS. vol. xlviii.
No. 43.) In 1671 he is noticed by Baxter himself as requiring
exact conformity throughout his diocese of Salisbury; and in 1683
he compelled Dr. Whitby, who was at that time his chaplain, to
35 make a public retractation of some sentiments that he had published
in favour of dissenters. It would be unreasonable to suppose that
any bishop, after all that had passed, would be desirous of taking
part in a negotiation of which Baxter was to be a principal
conductor.

be favourably inclined to them, many peers, especially
the earls of Carlisle, Halifax, and Orrery, were known
to be friendly to them, and the duke of Buckingham,
the most powerful patron of the times, not only wrote
pamphlets in their behalf, but also brought forward, in 5
the year 1675, a specific motion for their relief. Nevertheless whenever they appeared to be making progress,
there always arose some new and countervailing ob-
struction. It was early in this year that Dr. Tillotson,
finding his efforts unsuccessful, and fearing that any 10
further perseverance would do injury both to himself
and to the cause in which he had engaged, wrote the
following[d] letter to Baxter (April 11, 1675.)

"I took the first opportunity after you were with us
to speak to the bishop of Sal—— who promised to 15
keep the matter private, and only to acquaint the bishop
of Ch—— with it, in order to a meeting. But upon

---

[d] Baxter's Life by Sylv. p. 3. p. 157. Life by Calamy, p. 343.
Dr. Stillingfleet still continued to negotiate in favour of the dissenters, as we learn from the following statement in Long's Vox 20
Cleri, p. 3. "In the year 1681, when Dr. Stillingfleet, now bishop
of Worcester, made large overtures to gratify the dissenters, viz.
that the cross in baptism might be either taken off, or confined to
public baptism, and left to the choice of the parents; that such as
could not kneel might be permitted to stand at the reception of the 25
sacrament of the Lord's supper; that the surplice should be taken
away; that at baptism the fathers should be permitted to join with
the sponsors in offering the child to baptism, or desire them publicly
to present their child, and the charge be given to them both; that
they should be required to subscribe only to thirty-six of the Arti- 30
cles; that there should be a new translation of the Psalms for parish
churches; that the apocryphal lessons should be exchanged for
scriptural; that the rubric should be corrected; with many other
condescensions; they were all thrown, as it were, with spite in his
teeth, by those that answered his sermon and proposals, with an 35
'Habeat sibi et suis.'"

some general discourse, I plainly perceived several
things could not be obtained. However he promised
to appoint a time of meeting; but I have not heard
from him since. I am unwilling my name should be
5 used in this matter; not but that I do most heartily
desire an accommodation, and shall always endeavour
it. But I am sure it will be a prejudice to me, and
signify nothing to the effecting of the thing; which, as
circumstances are, cannot pass in either house, without
10 the concurrence of a considerable part of the bishops
and the countenance of his majesty: which at present
I see little reason to expect."

And this leads to the consideration of another agent
in the intricacies of this period, which may account for
15 much of the embarrassment we meet with, and is the
more necessary to be noticed, because, though really
powerful in itself, it assumed a mysterious or exagge-
rated shape from the obscurity that surrounded it.
The king had always been disposed in favour of the
20 Romish communion, and having become uneasy under
the constraint that was imposed upon him, resolved, in
the beginning of the year 1669, to enter into engagements in favour of that church, and to bind himself
down in such a manner, that he could not afterwards
25 escape from them. In this resolution he may have had
something of that forlorn reliance on the infallibility of
Rome, which has frequently acted as a spell on men of
feeble understanding or debased habits; but he was
also attracted by the opportunity it would afford for
30 the exercise of adroitness and dissimulation, and the
complete occupation he would obtain for the cravings
of a jaded and insatiable mind. He declared accordingly to his brother the duke of York, to lord Arundel,
lord Arlington, and sir T. Clifford, all of them willing

instruments in such an enterprise, that he wished to have their "advice[d] about the ways and methods fitted to be taken for the settling the catholic religion in his kingdoms; telling them withal that he was to expect to meet with many and great difficulties in bringing it 5 about, and that he chose rather to undertake it now, when he and his brother were in their full strength, and able to undergo any fatigue. This he spake with great earnestness and even with tears in his eyes; and added, that they were to go about it as wise men and 10 good catholics ought to do."

Now a motive of this kind, acting with a powerful and constant force upon the measures of the court, could not fail to affect the projects of the nonconformists, frequently crossing their path, and interrupting 15 their progress, but more frequently directing them towards the accomplishment of their wishes, and only abandoning them when they were beginning to be confident of success. In this game of artifice and delusion the court had a manifest advantage over their strange 20 confederates. Both parties were clear and precise in their plans, but the one had no reservations, and could not even disguise their weaknesses, while the other maintained the appearance of sincerity, and yet concealed the very object for which they entered into the 25 alliance. The court therefore, shrouded in its own secresy, and practised in the arts of dissimulation, was able to advance or retard the cause of the nonconformists, to dazzle them with transient gleams of success, or distract them with a variety of discordant purposes, with- 30 out forfeiting the advantage, whenever it was wanted, of their cooperation. But the disappointments, which the court was constantly inflicting, it was doomed in

[d] Clarke's Life of James II. vol. i. p. 442.

its turn to sustain. From the commencement of the reign of Charles, the dissenters had strong suspicions of his Romish tendencies. As early as the year 1660, when the king had granted an audience to divines of 5 both parties for the purpose of considering the declaration he was preparing to issue, and lord Clarendon was instructed to add a further clause, which in its effects would have extended to the Romanists the right of meeting for religious worship, Baxter, with an honesty 10 of purpose that sometimes made amends for his obstinacy, informed his majesty, that he and his friends did not seek to include either papists or Socinians within the conditions of toleration. Such continued to be the flux and reflux of these important transactions during 15 the whole of the reign of Charles II., the court and the dissenters continually expressing their reliance upon each other, and as continually defeating their respective projects; and this state of things may furnish an additional excuse for the friends of the church, 20 who appeared to look with unconcern upon so formidable a combination, but knew in reality that at such a period it would only issue in disappointment to their opponents, and an increase of strength to themselves.

With the life of Charles terminated the reign of 25 darkness and dissimulation. James II. was so open in his acknowledgment of popery, and so indefatigable in his endeavours to promote it, that both churchmen and dissenters, being compelled to take measures for their own security, contracted, though not without 30 much reluctance, affinities for each other. But in the alliance that followed, the two parties were not equally conspicuous in the services they rendered, or the advantage they derived from it. The open war of reason and argument, that was proclaimed immediately against

popery, was conducted exclusively by churchmen, and
redounded the more to their credit from the contrast
afforded by the silence of their auxiliaries. And yet
the dissenters were wanting neither in earnestness nor
in talent; but seeing plainly that their weapons were 5
already wielded by the hands of the strong, they were
contented to remain inactive, although their interests
as a party would suffer. This was one great article in
their claims for consideration; and it was supported
by the growing respect they manifested for the national 10
church, as the great pillar of the protestant faith, and
by their steadiness in resisting the bribes and blandish-
ments of the court. And certainly in the same proportion in which exertions had been made to seduce
them, they drew upon themselves by their uniform 15
resistance the heavy indignation of their sovereign.
" The kingdom and the court," say the Stuart MSS.,
" were filled with incendiaries, whose constant endeavours were to scatter fears and jealousies, and draw
suspicions from every step his majesty made, and above 20
all to pervert that royal and Christian one of granting
liberty of conscience, and to insinuate a belief that it
was only in order to supplant religion and then destroy
it. And now the dissenters too did not only concur
in this, but valued themselves upon the strength and 25
penetration of their judgments, that they could foresee
and discover that to have been the original motive and
end of it; and that all the mitigations to them was
only for the sake of the papists; by that means making
the throne dreadful even when it was the seat of mercy. 30
They soon therefore joined hands and voices with the
church of England party, so far at least as to rail
against the church of Rome, and talk of nothing but

c Clarke's Life of James II. vol. ii. p. 169.

fire and faggot, as if Smithfield had been all in a blaze, when the king's tenderness made it his principal care, that there should not be the least fine inflicted for religion's sake : but this (they were told) might be 5 catalogued amongst their other thankful returns, for the king's snatching them out of the fire, and losing his credit with the church party for having gathered those vipers from the dunghill, where the laws had laid them, and cherishing them in his bosom till they 10 stung him with reproaches, as false as they were villainous and ungrateful."

It might naturally be conceived that a change had been gradually coming over the spirit of the times in favour of the nonconformists. The dread of a republic 15 had subsided, the arrogance of the dissenters had quailed, the recollection of the protectorate had vanished, and instead of them had risen up from the increasing power of the papacy a spectre, as hideous as if it had been the creation of extreme terror, and 20 yet as formidable as substance and reality could make it. It is evident that their common and imminent danger had inspired a general feeling in favour of a more complete combination between churchmen and nonconformists, a combination which might not only 25 qualify them for their approaching conflict, but might convert their mutual confidence as comrades into the basis of a lasting and cordial friendship. The memorable petition presented by the seven bishops to king James II. in the year 1688 made open declaration, 30 that there was no want of " due tenderness to dissenters, in relation to whom they were willing to come to such a temper, as should be thought fit, when that matter should be considered and settled in parliament and convocation." Archbishop Sancroft, in the articles[f]

f Docum. Annals, vol. ii. p. 325.

that he issued to the bishops of his province immediately after his trial, enjoined the clergy to have a "very tender regard to our brethren the protestant dissenters," and to manifest it by habits of friendly intercourse; concluding his articles with this most comprehensive[g] injunction, "that they warmly and most affectionately exhort them to join with us in daily fervent prayer to the God of peace for an universal blessed union of all reformed churches both at home and abroad against our common enemies; that all they, who do confess the [10] holy name of our dear Lord, and do agree in the truth of his holy word, may also meet in one holy communion, and live in perfect unity and godly love." He also joined in the Declaration issued from Guildhall on the 11th of December 1688, when an engagement [15] was made to assist the prince of Orange, and one of the great objects specified was, "a due liberty to protestant dissenters." But the strongest token of his concurrence is given on the authority of his intimate friend the bishop of St. Asaph (Lloyd); as will appear [20] from the following statement of bishop Patrick in the history of his own life. "On the 14th of January I went in the afternoon to the dean of St. Paul's house (Dr. Tillotson), where I met the bishop of St. Asaph, the dean of Canterbury (Dr. Sharp), the dean of Nor- [25] wich (Dr. Fairfax), and Dr. Tenison, to consult about such concessions as might bring in dissenters to our communion. For which the bishop of St. Asaph[g]

g This is one of the many instances in which it is impossible to ascertain, amidst the secresy and mystery of his proceedings, what [30] were the real designs of archbishop Sancroft. His position was certainly one of the greatest hazard and perplexity; but as it appears from a review of his conduct that it was consistent throughout, it is the more surprising that if he had a definite plan from the first, as we might reasonably suppose that he had, he should not only have [35]

told us he had the archbishop of Canterbury's leave.
We agreed that a bill should be prepared to be offered
by the bishops, and we drew up the matter of it in ten
or eleven heads."

5   And yet it is not probable that the archbishop approved of concessions for admitting dissenters within
the church, although he appears in the present instance
to have aided the prevailing sentiment in their favour.
In his own principles he was adverse to a creed, which,
10 as he would probably have described it, was ambiguous
in meaning, and destructive of authority: from his
habits of business and his close observation of man-

concealed it from his friends, but have knowingly left them to draw
inferences respecting it, which it was far from his intentions to realize.
15 The only favourable interpretation is that he had no fixed determination at the first, and that his plans growing upon him as events
proceeded, and always contracting a bias from the tendency of his
own character, were after all only a combination of circumstances,
however carefully and prudently adjusted.
20   Other accounts of the part which the archbishop took in favour
of dissenters may be seen in the visitation charge of bp. Burnet, published in 1704; in the speech delivered by Dr. Wake, then bishop
of Lincoln, at the trial of Dr. Sacheverel, in the year 1710 (Docum.
Ann. vol. ii. p. 320); in Baxter's Life, by Calamy, p. 426, and in
25 the following extract from the diary of Mr. Wharton, one of his
grace's chaplains (D'Oyly's Sancroft, vol. ii. p. 134), who states that
the communication was made to him by the bishop of St. Asaph, on
the 25th of June, 1688, as they were going to Lambeth: " Miram
rerum catastrophen adesse, cui, si ipse sociique episcopi, præsenti
30 pontificiorum rabie erepti, superfuerint, omni modo curaturos, ut
ecclesia sordibus et corruptelis penitus exueretur, ut sectariis refor-
matis reditus in ecclesiæ sinum exoptati occasio ac ratio concede-
retur, si qui sobrii et pii essent; ut pertinacibus interim jugum
levaretur, extinctis penitus legibus mulctatoriis; utque cancellari-
35 orum officialium et curiarum ecclesiasticarum abusus funditus tolle-
rentur. Fuse isthæc declaravit episcopus, dum ab hospitio ejus ad
Thamesis ripam in vehiculo uno deveheremur; ille enim Lametham
pergebat."

kind, he had persuaded himself that concessions, if
they conciliated a few opponents, would alienate as
many friends, and leave a result of additional inse-
curity. But his extreme caution,· and the retirement
into which he was driven, partly by his infirmities, but 5
more by his critical position in the politics of the
times, deprive us of any direct materials for judging
of his views on the subject of a comprehension. The
following letter, however, addressed to him on the 3rd
of September, 1688, by bishop Turner (of Ely), a pre- 10
late who had always enjoyed his confidence and friendship, who had shared with him in his recent persecution, and was destined to be a partner in his future
deprivation, may fairly be employed as a clue to his
private sentiments. It will be observed that the letter 15
was written about a month after the archbishop had
addressed his articles of conciliation to the bishop[h]
of Ely as well as to his other suffragans.

"One reason of my labouring so much in this point to
introduce frequent communions and make them numerous is 20
really this : it grows every day plainer to me that many of
our divines, men of name and note (I pray God there be not
some[i] bishops with them in the design) intend upon any
overture for comprehension (when time shall serve) to offer
all our ceremonies in sacrifice to the dissenters, kneeling at 25
the sacrament and all. This makes it necessary for us to
increase as much as possible the number of those who, as

h Tanner MSS. vol. xxviii. No. 121. Of the influence which this
prelate, together with the bishops of Norwich and Chichester, had
with the primate, a remarkable instance is given by Wharton in his 30
diary, D'Oyly's Sancroft, vol. ii. p. 137. Birch's Tillotson, p. 156.
i This probably refers to the bishop of St. Asaph (Lloyd), whom
we find a few months afterwards engaged with Tillotson, Patrick,
and others, in preparing concessions for a bill of comprehension.
Patrick's Life, p. 141.   35

true lovers of devotion and decency in it, may contend even for multitude and interest in the nation with those that would strip this poor church of all her ornaments. It is point of offence taken at them that will be most insisted upon one day.
5 Let it appear, then, that it will give offence to innumerable better Christians, if we part with them. Upon the whole matter this is our harvest time, and our time of laying up for another evil day (besides this which is upon us); and the best provision against it would be this, to gather, and, as it
10 were, incorporate the very very many that sit loose but not averse from us, by putting them into this way of regular devotion."

The rights of an hereditary throne, and the oath already taken for its support, considerations that
15 pressed heavily and painfully on the minds of great numbers of churchmen, and prevented them from acknowledging the authority of king William, were of little weight in the estimation of dissenters, whose notions of government, whether in church or in state,
20 were laid on a different foundation. It was natural, therefore, that the new sovereign, however necessary it was to secure the good-will of the establishment, should endeavour to retain the services and to strengthen the attachment of the nonconformists. In the declaration
25 that he issued as prince of Orange, he promised to "endeavour a good agreement between the church of England and all protestant dissenters, and to cover and secure all those who would live peaceably under the government, from all persecution upon the account
30 of their religion." We may infer from these words that he looked forward with more confidence to a toleration of dissent, than to any removal of it by means of a coalition. His tone became still more moderate as he proceeded. To the dissenting ministers
35 of London, who presented earnest and ostentatious

addresses to the king and his consort, every personal
attention was shewn; but they received no greater assurance of support than a promise "to use all endeavours for the obtaining of an union that was necessary
for the edifying of the church." The first step taken [5]
in their favour was recommended, not so much on the
plea of religious unity, as on the value of their future
services in support of the newly-established government. In a speech to the two houses of parliament on
the 16th of March, 1689, the king said, "as I doubt [10]
not but you will sufficiently provide against papists, so
I hope you will leave room for the admission of all
protestants that are willing and able to serve." But
this appeal in favour of toleration, though designed to
follow in the train of the other measures adopted by [15]
the parliament, was unavailing for the removal of the
sacramental test; which, though originally levelled
against papists, had excluded many classes of dissenters
from places and offices of trust. The clause containing
this important proposal was rejected in the upper [20]
house by a large majority, and when brought forward
in another and less objectionable shape, still passed in
the negative. However cautiously these matters were
conducted on the part of the crown, it is evident that
there was already germinating such an element of [25]
discord, as would occasion a separation between the
two rival parties, whose temporary alliance had been
owing to the unnatural character of the last reign, and
could not be dissevered without extreme danger to
any plans of comprehension.   [30]

In the mean time, and without any further observations from the throne for the purpose of introducing
them, two other bills were laid before the lords, the
one "for uniting their majesties' protestant subjects,"

the other "for exempting their majesties' protestant subjects, dissenting from the church of England, from the penalties of certain laws." Bishop Compton (of London) gave notice of them to the archbishop in the
5 following words: "We[k] are now entering upon the

[k] Tanner MSS. vol. xxvii. No. 41. The following letter, addressed March 16, 1690, to the bishop of London, was preserved by archbishop Sancroft among his papers, and headed by this notice in his handwriting: "Dr. T. S. to the B. of L." It ex-
10 presses in strong language the opinion which the primate appears to have had of bishop Compton.

(Tanner MSS. vol. xxvii. No. 105.)

" I write this to your lordship out of a principle of true Christian charity. There is a report which runs from one end of the town to
15 the other, and your unworthy compliances under all sorts of government for these forty years make it easily credible, that not contenting yourself to have renounced your faith and allegiance, and the personal homage done to the king at his coronation, you are writing a book to justify the taking the new oaths, and thereby endeavour-
20 ing, as much as in you lies, to involve the whole nation in the guilt of perjury. Your enemies cannot wish you a greater mischief, nor desire a better advantage against you. Now, though there be no great fear that your arguments will have any evil influence upon the sober and understanding and judicious members of our holy mother,
25 the church of England, which I doubt not, God, who has wonderfully preserved her from the fury and violence of papists, will as wonderfully preserve, maugre the defection of some of her bishops, from the malice and rage of presbyterians and anabaptists, and other wild sectaries, who with united force are now labouring hard
30 to ruin her, under the spurious and popular, but most scandalous and unjustifiable pretensions of comprehension and toleration : yet, as a friend, I advise you to forbear, if not for the peace of this poor afflicted church and the honour of the episcopal order, at least for your own ease and reputation. For assure yourself the weakness,
35 the fallaciousness, the impiety of your design shall be fully exposed and laid open to the view of the whole world. But if, notwithstanding this friendly and faithful advice, to gratify your new friends the earl of Macclesfield, and the party lately come out of Holland,

bill of comprehension, which will be followed by the
bill of toleration. These are two great works in
which the being of our church is concerned; and I
hope you will send to the house for copies. For
though we are under a conquest[1], God has given us 5
favour in the eyes of our rulers, and we may keep up
the church if we will." The first of these bills, having
been for some time in the hands of a committee, was
debated before the house on the 4th of April, 1689;
and the question being put, "whether to agree with 10
the committee in leaving out the clause about the
indifferency of the posture at the receiving the sacrament," the votes were equal, and according to usage

you shall still persist in the resolution which you have taken up, you
would do well, for fear somebody else should do it for you, to print 15
at the same time your discourse in defence and justification of the
ecclesiastical commission, together with your reasons, such as they
are, for reading the king's declaration for liberty of conscience: to
which your letters to the bishop of Chester will serve as a very fit
and proper appendix.   20

"I pray God make you throughly and truly sensible of your
horrid prevarications, and of the many and great mischiefs which
you have done the Church of England, and give you grace to make
some satisfaction to her for them before you die; which is the hearty
prayer of your lordship's unfeigned friend and monitor, B. C."   25

1 This notion of a conquest, though supported by some of the
court party, became soon afterwards very odious, and met with the
condemnation of the two houses of parliament. Bishop Burnet's
Pastoral Letter to his clergy having indirectly supported it, was
censured by the house of commons in January 1692, and ordered to 30
be burnt by the common executioner. On the 24th of that month
the lords came to this resolution (see Kennet's Hist. vol. iii. p. 650,
col. 2.), "That the assertion of king William and queen Mary's
being king and queen by conquest was highly injurious to their
majesties, and inconsistent with the principles on which this govern- 35
ment is founded, and tending to the subversion of the rights of the
people."

the clause passed in the negative. As there were present on that occasion sixty-four lay peers and only seven bishops, this vote, in opposition to the strongest political motives, and the direct influence of the court, may be taken as decisive of the opinions entertained by the higher classes of society on the important question of church-government. The conscience of the dissenters was placed in the balance against the authority of the church, and was not of sufficient weight and substance to preponderate. And this estimate did not arise from any extreme tenderness for the church in its spiritual character; for on the following day, when the debate was respecting a royal commission of bishops, and others of the clergy, it was proposed that the words " and laity" should be added, and the proposal was only rejected[m], in conformity with the same principle, on an equality of votes. The bill, however, was ultimately passed by the lords on the 8th of April. On the 18th of the same month they also passed the bill for the toleration of dissenters, and sent it to the house of commons.

The latter of these two bills, after undergoing several amendments, was passed by the commons on the 17th of May, and finally received the royal assent on the 24th of the same month. They had signified their readiness to proceed in the consideration of this measure at the same time that they virtually rejected the

---

[m] It appears that the same bill was again submitted to parliament a few years afterwards, and a copy of it, as drawn up at that time, which has been found among the Burnet papers now preserved in the Bodleian, is printed at length in the next chapter. It probably was the same bill, in respect to religious matters, which had been drawn up in 1668 under the auspices of lord keeper Bridgman and chief baron Hale, and in accordance with the declaration issued by king Charles II. for liberty of conscience.

bill of comprehension, by petitioning the king to
summon a convocation, as the more proper assembly
for discussing ecclesiastical questions. The use of the
surplice, the right posture at the eucharist, and other
regulations adopted by the church, could not, in their 5
judgment, be submitted to the will of parliament,
although they had obtained their force from the act of
the legislature, until they had been considered by the
clergy in their convocation. In this sentiment the
lords afterwards concurred; and a joint address was 10
presented to the throne, praying that " according to
the ancient practice and usage of this kingdom in time
of parliament, his majesty would be graciously pleased
to issue forth his writs, as soon as conveniently might
be, for calling a convocation of the clergy of this 15
kingdom, to be advised with in ecclesiastical matters."
This address was adopted on the 16th of April.

A sentiment of this nature, entertained so cordially
by the house of commons, could not be matter of
indifference to the great body of the clergy. It was 20
opposed, indeed, by the nonconformists, under the persuasion that their demands would not meet with so
favourable a hearing in a convocation, where they
would be discussed on ecclesiastical grounds, as in a
parliament, which would conduct its debates on prin- 25
ciples of civil policy. But an opposition from that
quarter would only make the clergy the more resolute
in requiring that matters, strictly ecclesiastical, should
be discussed in the first instance by an assembly of
their own order; and this feeling was so strong, and 30
the sense of its justice was so general, that Dr. Tillotson[n], though anxious to promote the cause of the

---

[n] It is plain that with the objects he had in view, a person even
of his sanguine temper must have despaired of their success when

nonconformists, yielded to the necessity of the case, and urged his royal master, whose confidence he now enjoyed, to issue his writs for the meeting of a convocation.

5 To make, however, all arrangements requisite for such an assembly, and to give the projected measures some degree of prepossession in their favour, a commission was issued on the 13th of September to ten

he urged the summoning of a convocation. Such, at least, was the
10 strong opinion of Dr. Calamy and bishop Burnet, the latter of whom entered into all the designs of Tillotson, but with a much smaller mixture of reserve or caution. The opinion of the former is stated at length in his Life of Baxter (p. 446); and the following conversation, reported by sir John Reresby in his Memoirs (p. 343, edit.
15 1734), is decisive as to the opinion of bishop Burnet : " A few days afterwards being with lord privy seal (marquis of Halifax), the bishop of Salisbury came in and complained heavily of the slow proceedings of the house of commons, saying the Dutch would clap up a peace with France, if they did not mend their pace ; observed that
20 the Church of England was in the fault ; and expressed himself as if he thought they meant a kindness to king James by their method of procedure. Lord privy seal agreed with him in his sentiments, and added that the church people hated the Dutch, and had rather turn papists than receive the presbyterians among them ; but that, on
25 the other hand, these were to the full as rank and inveterate against those, and would mar all their business by their inadvertence with regard to their bill of comprehension and their ill-timing of other bills : in short, that they would disgust those from whom they looked for indulgence. They were both angry with the commons' address
30 to the king the day before, desiring him to support and defend the Church of England according to his former declaration, and to call a convocation of the clergy, which the bishop said would be the utter ruin of the comprehension scheme."

This view, however, of Dr. Tillotson's opinion respecting a convo-
35 cation is opposed to the statement of Dr. Nicholls (Appar. ad defens. p. 93) ; who represents him as anxious that a convocation should be employed, and unconscious that it would throw any difficulty in the way, beyond the natural slowness of its proceedings.

bishops, and twenty other divines, requiring them to
"prepare such alterations of the liturgy and canons,
and such proposals for the reformation of ecclesiastical
courts, and to consider such other matters as might
most conduce to the good order, and edification, and 5
unity of the Church of England, and to the reconciling
as much as possible of all differences." The members
of this commission were Dr. Lamplugh, archbishop of
York, Drs. Compton, Mew, Lloyd, Sprat, Smith, sir
Jonathan Trelawny, Burnet, Humfreys, and Stratford, 10
bishops of London, Winchester, St. Asaph, Rochester,
Carlisle, Exeter, Salisbury, Bangor, and Chester; Drs.
Stillingfleet, Patrick, Tillotson, Meggot, Sharp, Kidder,
Aldrich, Jane, Hall, Beaumont, Montague, Goodman,
Beveridge, Batteley, Alston, Tenison, Scott, Fowler, 15
Grove, and Williams. Among these divines, the most
eminent of the period, are included many persons who
could not be supposed to be favourable to the wishes
and designs of the government; but they were doubtless selected in most instances with an especial refer- 20
ence to their declared principles of moderation, and
the measures they might be thought likely to support.
That Dr. Tillotson had no fears as to their general
sentiments may be inferred from the following paper,
that he drew up on the same day when the commission 25
was issued:

"*Concessions*° *which will probably be made by the Church of
England for the union of protestants; which I sent to the
earl of Portland by Dr. Stillingfleet, Sept. 13th,* 1689.

"1. That the ceremonies enjoined or recommended in the 30
liturgy or canons be left indifferent.

° Birch's Life of Tillotson, p. 182.

"2. That the liturgy be carefully reviewed, and such alterations and changes be therein made, as may supply the defects, and remove, as much as is possible, all ground of exception to any part of it, by leaving out the apocryphal lessons, and correcting the translation of the Psalms used in the public service, where there is need of it; and in many other particulars.

"3. That instead of all former declarations and subscriptions to be made by ministers, it shall be sufficient for them, that are admitted to the exercise of their ministry in the Church of England, to subscribe one general declaration and promise to this purpose, viz. that we do submit to the doctrine, discipline, and worship of the Church of England, as it shall be established by law, and promise to teach and practise accordingly.

"4. That a new body of ecclesiastical canons be made, particularly with a regard to a more effectual provision for the reformation of manners both in ministers and people.

"5. That there be an effectual regulation of ecclesiastical courts to remedy the great abuses and inconveniences which by degrees and length of time have crept into them; and particularly that the power of excommunication be taken out of the hands of lay officers and placed in the bishop, and not to be exercised for trivial matters, but upon great and weighty occasions.

"6. That for the future those who have been ordained in any of the foreign reformed churches, be not required to be re-ordained here, to render them capable of preferment in this church.

"7. That for the future none be capable of any ecclesiastical benefice or preferment in the Church of England that shall be ordained in England otherwise than by bishops; and that those who have been ordained only by presbyters shall not be compelled to renounce their former ordination. But because many have and do still doubt of the validity of such ordination, where episcopal ordination may be had, and is by law required, it shall be sufficient for such persons to receive ordination from a bishop in this or the like form: ' If thou art not already ordained, I ordain thee,' &c.; as in case a doubt be made of any one's baptism, it is appointed by the liturgy that he be baptised in this form, ' If thou art not baptised, I baptise thee,'" &c.

It would be unreasonable to suppose that the general sentiments of the nation were in favour of so great an 5 amount of change.   The English character was too deeply impregnated with a love of facts and details, to approve of the comprehensive views and sanguine expectations of Dr. Tillotson, and too proud of its own nationality to acquiesce in the wishes of a sovereign, 10 whose great services had been almost forgotten in the dread of his foreign predilections.   The wishes of sober and considerate men may be read in the following letter[p] addressed at that time by Dr. Comber, precentor of York, and afterwards dean of Durham, to 15 bishop Patrick (then of Chichester) who was one of the most distinguished members of the commission (dated York, Oct. 19, 1689):

" I heartily rejoice that you are in this new commission, wherein I hope both your true affection to the church and 20 charity to dissenters who are capable of being obliged will appear.   But unless they are wiser and better tempered above than many are in these parts, our condescensions will only help them with arguments to upbraid us, not incline them to part with one opinion in order to a coalition.   'Tis 25 true there are some few moderate presbyterians, who always communicated with us on occasion, and the alterations they desire are not many nor dangerous to our constitution. They will submit to a conditional re-ordination, to this very liturgy with some slight amendments, and some of them to surplice 30 and cross : yea they approve and practise kneeling at the sacrament.   But the greater part of dissenters here are Independents, who seem incapable of any thing but toleration, and cannot be taken in but by such concessions as will shake

[p] Tanner MSS. vol. xxvii. No. 76.   35

the foundations of our church: and possibly by attempting to gain such as after all will be false friends, we may drive out many true ones both of the considerable clergy and laity also. I perceive the late success of that party in Scotland 5 against episcopacy, and the opinion of their numbers and interest here hath lately advanced their pretences to liberty of conscience into hopes of legal establishment and dominion over all others; to which I know the great pillars of our church will be cautious how they contribute. And till they 10 be well assured what these gentlemen would have, and also fully satisfied that their desires are consistent with our establishment and safety, I hope they will give them no encouragement. I know very little in our liturgy against which they could ever make one wise objection, and nothing 15 but what hath been and may be justified. Yet to gain friends or comply with consciences really tender something may be abated. But alas! what content will that give to them, when Clarkson (whose book I am now answering) writes against all set forms, as having their original in ignorant and 20 superstitious ages, and as things unknown in the primitive times. These things at this time of day, together with their giving presbyterian orders openly to many with design to perpetuate the schism, may justly make us stand our ground till they who have neither gospel nor antiquity, neither law 25 nor reason of their side, come some more paces toward us. My lord, I should not presume to write this if it were only my own sense; but it is the agreeing sentiment of all the members of this our northern convocation which I have met with; and that I hope will excuse this freedom, because it is 30 convenient your lordship should know how affairs go here."

Great reliance was doubtless placed on the firmness of bishop Patrick, because in his theological writings he had always manifested a leaning towards the strongest views of doctrine and discipline, and in 35 "A friendly Debate between a Conformist and a Non-conformist," published originally in 1668 and republished in 1683, with a reply to some censures of sir

M. Hale, he had openly declared that he was adverse
to the scheme of comprehension. This reliance was
not without reason: for independently of the temptations offered by high preferment, the critical state of
the church in the latter years of James II., the repul- 5
sion insensibly created by the active warfare in which
the clergy were engaged with the Romanists, and the
earnest wish to promote as high a tone of theology as
possible in the measures of the new reign, may fairly
be allowed to have brought Dr. Patrick within the influ- 10
ence of the prevailing current, without any impeachment
of his integrity or religious principles. He may be taken
as representing that class of divines, now numerous
and deserving of the greatest respect, who had originally been opposed to any important concessions, from the 15
belief that they would not tend to edification, but had
gradually been induced by an approximation on their
own part, and still more by a greater spirit of deference
on the part of dissenters, to concur in promoting the
projected union.   20

The proceedings of this commission may be stated
in the brief report of it contained in bishop Patrick's
narrative⁹ of his own life.

"On the 3d of October the commission about ecclesiastical
affairs was to be opened in Jerusalem Chamber. I came 25
about 10 o'clock, and there were near twenty of the thirty
commissioners present. It gave them power to consider what
alterations were fit to be made in the liturgy and canons;
and what regulations in the ecclesiastical courts; and how to
reform the manners of the clergy; to be offered to the con- 30
vocation, and to the parliament, and to the king. We sat
till about one o'clock, and debated several things about the
mending of the old translation of the reading Psalms and
Apocrypha; and ordered another meeting next Wednesday.

<hr/>

⁹ P. 149. ed. Oxf. 1839.

" On the 16th of October the commissioners sat again, and had a long dispute with the bishop of Rochester; who argued both against the commission itself, and against our preparing any thing before the convocation met. We stayed there till
5 one; and the bishop of London, of Worcester, and several others, came to my house and dined with me, and we went over a good part of the amendments we proposed to make in the liturgy, till it was night. And the next morning they came hither again, to consider the rest of the liturgy at my
10 house, and stayed till almost twelve.

" The next day we met in the Jerusalem Chamber, where we had appointed a general meeting of the commissioners. The bishop of Rochester absented himself. When we had read over all that we had to offer about the several offices, we
15 proceeded to consider of the three ceremonies, and came to a conclusion that the sign of the cross in baptism should be left indifferent, which was expressed in such words as we hoped would satisfy our own people. None dissented; but the bishop of Winchester (Mew), and the dean of Christ
20 Church (Aldrich), and the dean of Gloucester (Jane), went out as soon as we began that debate.

" On the 21st we met again in the Jerusalem Chamber, and though several absented themselves, we proceeded, and sat there till past six o'clock. The next day we met again at
25 ten o'clock, and sat till between four and five. And so they did several days after. I was desired in the end of the month to join with the bishops of London and Rochester in making some new prayers for the 5th of November, when together with the gunpowder-treason, we commemorate the king's
30 landing to give us a new deliverance.

" On the 26th the bishop of Rochester came to me, and told me he could not be at leisure to make the prayer which the bishop of London had committed to his care, but desired me to do it; which I did the next day. On the 27th the com-
35 missioners sat from three till between six and seven. On the 30th I revised all the service for the 5th of November, and we sat again as long as before, in the Jerusalem Chamber: and so we did the next day, when we considered the offices of Visitation of the Sick and Commination.

"The bishops went to wait on the king on the 4th of November, to wish him many happy years. The bishop of London spake in the name of the rest; and the king's answer was, ' I desire to live for no other end, but to serve this nation and this church.' In the afternoon we met again to consider the business of re-ordination; which held us a long time; and then we went over some of the collects, till almost seven o'clock. Many more meetings we had, which I shall not mention."

It may be inferred from this statement, and the inference is confirmed by other evidence, that the alterations recommended by this commission were numerous and important. Their report however was not offered to the convocation; and the document itself, being left in the custody of Dr. Tenison, was never allowed to be made public. For the secresy that he observed he urged as his excuse that the "proposals" would give no satisfaction on either side, but be rather a handle for mutual reproaches; one side upbraiding their brethren for having given up so much; and the other justifying their nonconformity, because those concessions were too little, or however, were not passed into law." Doubtless he remembered in what manner the dissenters had employed for their own purposes the resolutions[s] adopted by the committee of divines in the year 1641, and the bitter and resentful feeling created in the minds of the conformists by the publication of them.

---

[r] Kennet, Comp. Hist. vol. iii. p. 591, note. It might reasonably be supposed that this document would be placed by archbishop Tenison in the library at Lambeth. In the year 1727 it was in the hands of the bishop of London (Gibson), and an extract was obtained from it at that time by Dr. Waterland, (see Waterland's Works, vol. iv. p. 305, note.) A search has been made for this document, but without success.

[s] See p. 241.

A cause so zealously and ably supported, recommended by the influence of the court, and urged forward by all persons belonging to the two large descriptions of the sanguine and the turbulent, was yet des-
5 tined to meet with fatal obstructions, some transmitted from former times, and others of recent origin. It will have been observed that the question of reordination had occupied much of the time and attention of the king's commissioners. It had long been considered,
10 and was now agreed upon, as the ground on which the battle between the two parties was to be fought, containing within it space and provocation enough for all the ecclesiastical differences, and adding the further recommendation that many vital questions of state
15 policy would be flung into the contest. Till the passing of the act of uniformity in the reign of Charles II, the ordination conveyed by presbyters, though resisted by the governors of the church, had never been disowned by the legislature; and of all the provisions of
20 that act the clause that required episcopal ordination was the most embarrassing to the nonconformists. It was with the greatest difficulty that they could be induced to forego their demand for the complete reversal of it, and allow of some conditional measure, such as a
25 fresh dedication in addition to their own orders, corresponding with the practice adopted in the case of a doubtful baptism. This latter kind of measure had been introduced into all the bills of comprehension, and was sought to be recommended[t] on the authori-
30 ty of such names as bishop Overall and archbishop Bramhall, names that might be expected to meet with

[t] Birch's Life of Tillotson, p. 184. Nicholls' Appar. ad Def. Eccl. Angl. p. 97.

respect and deference from all classes of theologians. But the question was of too vital a nature to be decided on mere authority, some of the strongest advocates for comprehension being the most resolute in behalf of ordination from the hands of bishops. In an able pamphlet, now usually ascribed to dean Prideaux[u], but generally given at the time to Dr. (afterwards bishop) Kidder, is the following passage, manifestly shewing that although a decided advocate for the nonconformists, he looked upon episcopal ordination as among the essentials of the church of Christ. "We, as divines, are best able to do it, as it ought, without prejudice to the church; whereas if we cast it into the hands of laymen, they may, instead of altering circumstantials, strike at essentials, and so make a breach upon the religion itself to the undoing of all. And although this should be avoided, as I fear it will not in some particulars I could instance, as particularly in that of our orders, yet the least mischief we can expect will be totally to extinguish all convocations for the future, and resolve the whole power of the church into the two houses of parliament."

But beyond all these considerations, however important in themselves, collateral circumstances added greatly to the dread that was felt of the presbyterian

---

[u] It is ascribed to dean Prideaux on the authority of his son (Univ. Dict. art. H. Prideaux); but in the copy left by bishop Barlow to the Bodleian is the following notice in the handwriting of the bishop, "Writt by Dr. Kidder, dean of Peterburgh, who had beene a dissenter."   Bishop Kennet, at a different period, supposed it to have been written by Dr. Tillotson, (Complete History, vol. iii. p. 591.) It appears, however, from the proceedings of the lower house of convocation, that there were two pamphlets with the same title of "Letter relating to the Convocation."

leaven. The violences already committed in Scotland, threatening in their consequences to spread the flames of a religious war throughout the whole of the empire, made men connect the wild and ferocious 5 spirit of the northern insurgents with the question of church-government. The episcopal party in Scotland had certainly been treated with great severity. They had no stated liturgy in general use among them, and they allowed the validity of presbyterian orders; qua- 10 lities these, which might fairly have been expected to give them some favour in the eyes of their adversaries. But being directly dependent upon the crown, and addicted, however temperately, to the use of forms and ceremonies, they were branded as a political party, 15 and held in the same abomination with papists. The treatment they met with was as cruel as if it had proceeded from a spirit of revenge, and became accordingly a solemn warning to all their brethren whose warfare, like theirs, was against the presbytery. We 20 may safely affirm that the downfall of episcopacy in the north was one of the principal causes that preserved to the Church of England at this period its ancient integrity in doctrine and discipline.

Another important event in connection with the de- 25 mands of the dissenters was the toleration they had recently obtained from parliament. As long as they could allege in their behalf that they were deprived of their rights, although they were peaceable and loyal citizens, and driven from their native country, although they 30 were among the most affectionate of its children, they created a presentiment in their favour which nothing short of either political hatred or religious enthusiasm could withstand. Among men in general, accordingly, their case was irresistible and was constantly making converts. But when they were allowed to conduct their worship according to their own discretion, their claims appeared to have been satisfied, and the question was not only at an end, but had also been adjudged according to their own principles. To demand, 5 then, that they should still be admitted within the pale of the church was at once to require the greater body to submit to the wishes of the smaller, and to force the consciences of their opponents under the pressure of external authority; and these were concessions 10 which no reasonable men would grant them, and they themselves were debarred by their own past conduct from asking. The whole case had lapsed from themselves and vested in the adverse party: so that the conformists were left to determine it as a simple ques-15 tion of prudence, whether it was better to diminish the number of their adversaries, or to preserve agreement among their own members.

But the most important difficulty in the way of a comprehension arose from the schism that was now 20 taking place in the church itself. Driven from their preferments on account of the greater degree of sanctity they attached to the nature of an oath, and carrying with them the reputation of devotedness to their spiritual duties and indifference about their secular 25 interests, the non-jurors were objects of universal respect and concern. To the claims they possessed upon all classes they added the more distinct recommendations of a precise and dogmatic adherence to the established faith, and a jealousy of all foreign innovations. 30 They formed accordingly a centre round which were assembled, together with a large body of most respectable churchmen, all those who were attached to the ancient dynasty, and many others whose moving principle was hatred to the existing government. It would have been dangerous to the safety of the church, and fatal to the cause of the revolution, to have supplied so powerful a party with the further plea that the 5 national religion had been adulterated.   So strong and so general was this feeling among the friends of the nonconformists, that bishop Burnet expresses himself on the subject in the following manner[x]: " If we had made alterations in the rubric and other parts of the 10 Common Prayer, they [the Jacobite clergy] would have pretended that they still stuck to the ancient church of England, in opposition to those who were altering it, and setting up new models: and as I do firmly believe that there is a wise Providence that watches 15 upon human affairs, and directs them, chiefly those that relate to religion ; so I have with great pleasure observed this in many instances relating to the revolution.   And upon this occasion I could not but see that the Jacobites among us, who wished and hoped that 20 we should have made those alterations, which they reckoned would have been of great advantage for serving their ends, were the instruments of raising such a clamour against them, as prevented their being made. For by all the judgments we could afterwards make, 25 if we had carried a majority in the convocation for alterations, they would have done us more hurt than good."

These considerations, added to the conscientious objections that were felt in many quarters against any 30 kind of change, produced their natural effect upon the members of the convocation.   That assembly met in the month of December, and the business that first engaged their attention, the appointment of a prolo-

---

[x] Own Times, vol. iv. p. 59.

cutor in the lower house, furnished a favourable opportunity for trying the strength of the two contending
parties, and bringing all their differences, whether
ecclesiastical or civil, to an issue. The court party
proposed Dr. Tillotson as their candidate, and certainly 5
could not have found among their ranks a person
better qualified to represent their principles, or to recommend them by the lustre of his talents and virtues.
The candidate of the opposite party was Dr. Jane, dean
of Gloucester, and regius professor of divinity at Ox- 10
ford, who was known to be a divine of great reading
and resolution, and supposed[y] to be fitted for the work
of a fierce opposition by personal feelings of resentment. He was elected by a large majority; and his
election, coupled with the strong political influence 15
that was employed in promoting it, gave sufficient intimation that no measures proposed by the court would
be likely to meet with acceptance from the great body
of the clergy. This intimation was soon followed by
an act, not only forcible in itself, but pregnant with 20
much latent hostility. When the bishops sent down
an address acknowledging the protection his majesty
had afforded to religion in general, and especially to
their own established form of it, but so expressed as to
include the church of England under the general title 25
of protestant churches, the lower house required the ·
expression to be altered, on the avowed principle that
they disowned all communion with foreign churches.
The case was too manifest to be misunderstood. The
upper house, lacking its full proportion of bishops, and 30
deprived of its metropolitan, could not exercise its
usual influence over the clergy in general; and the
king readily adopted the only alternative remaining

[y] See Life of Dr. H. Prideaux, p. 55.

to him, of discontinuing[z] the session, and preventing any future renewal of the strife by successive prorogations.

[z] Among the losses sustained by the church on the breaking up of this convocation was the following : " There was provided a family book to be authorized by this convocation. It contained directions for family devotions, with several forms of prayer for worship every morning and evening, suited to the different circumstances of the families in which they were to be used..... Some years afterwards Dr. Prideaux pressed archbishop Tenison to publish this book, telling him that he thought it would not want its effect, if it was published by his authority only ; though he was of opinion with his grace, that it would be best done with the concurrence of the convocation, could that be safely obtained ; which he thought it could not, on account of the great divisions among the clergy and the spirit of opposition, which then appeared in too many of them against their superiors. This book hath since had the misfortune to be lost ; for being put into the hands of Dr. Williams, bishop of Chichester, it was some how mislaid, and after his death could never be retrieved." Life of Dr. H. Prideaux, p. 61, &c.

CHAPTER X.

*Documents connected with the attempted revision of
William and Mary.*

I. Commission of William and Mary for the review of the liturgy,
1689. From Kennet's Complete History, vol. iii. p. 590.

II. Letter from lord Nottingham to bishop Burnet, requiring him
to attend as one of the king's commissioners. From the original
among the Burnet papers in the Bodleian.

III. Proceedings of the commission of 1689. From Dr. Calamy's
Life of Baxter, p. 452.

IV. Proceedings of the commission of 1689. From Dr. Nicholls'
Apparatus ad Defens. Eccles. Angl. p. 95.

V. The particular acts and adjournments of the convocation of
1689. From Mr. Long's Vox Cleri, printed anno 1690, p. 59.
(Comp. Wilk. Conc. vol. iv. p. 619.)

VI. Letter to Dr. Tillotson, bearing date Oct. 5, 1689. From
the MS. library at Lambeth. Gibs. 930, No. 183.

VII. An act for uniting his majesty's protestant subjects. From
a MS. among the Burnet papers in the Bodleian.

I.

Commission of William and Mary for the review of the liturgy,
1689.

WHEREAS the particular forms of divine worship, and
5   the rites and ceremonies appointed to be used therein,
are things in their own nature indifferent and alterable, and
so acknowledged ; it is but reasonable that upon weighty
and important considerations, according to the various exigencies of times and occasions, such changes and alterations
10 should be made therein, as to those that are in place and
authority should from time to time seem either necessary or
expedient :

And whereas the Book of Canons is fit to be reviewed, and
made more suitable to the state of the church : and whereas
15 there are defects and abuses in the ecclesiastical courts and
jurisdictions; and particularly there is not sufficient provision made for the removing of scandalous ministers, and for
the reforming of manners either in ministers or people : and
whereas it is most fit that there should be a strict method
20 prescribed for the examination of such persons as desire to
be admitted into holy orders, both as to their learning and
. manners :

We therefore out of our pious and princely care for the
good order and edification and unity of the Church of Eng-
25 land, committed to our charge and care ; and for the reconciling as much as is possible, of all differences among our
good subjects ; and to take away all occasions of the like for
the future, have thought fit to authorize and empower you,
&c. &c., and any nine of you, whereof three to be bishops, to
30 meet from time to time, as often as shall be needful, and to
prepare such alterations of the liturgy and canons, and such
proposals for the reformation of ecclesiastical courts, and to
consider of such other matters, as in your judgments may
most conduce to the ends abovementioned.

II.

*Letter from lord Nottingham to bishop Burnet, requiring him to
attend as one of the king's commissioners. (From the original
among the Burnet papers in the Bodleian.)*

Whitehall, Sep. 19, 1689.   5

My Lord,

The king commands me to acquaint your lop. that he has
thought fitt to issue a commission under the great seal of
England to certaine bishops, deans, and others of the clergy,
to prepare such alterations and amendments of the liturgy 10
and canons, and such proposalls for the reformation of ecclesiasticall courts, and to consider such other matters as may
most conduce to the good order, edification, and unity of the
Church of England, soe that their resolutions may be in a
readiness to be offered to the convocation at their next meet- 15
ing, and when approved by them may be presented to his
majesty and the two houses of parliament, that if it shall be
judged fitt, they may be establisht in due form of law.

I am further commanded to acquaint your lop. that you
are appointed one of the commissioners, and that the bishops 20
and clergy in and about the citty doe think Thursday the
third of October next will be the most convenient day for the
first meeting in or near London; at which you are desired to
be present.

I am, my lord,   25
Your lops. most humble servant,
NOTTINGHAM.

Lord bishop of Salisbury.

III.

[a] *An account of the proceedings of the commissioners to prepare matters for the approaching convocation in* 1689. *Communicated to Dr. Calamy by a friend.* (*Calamy's Life of Baxter,*
5   p. 452.)

THE committee being met in the Jerusalem Chamber, a dispute arose about the authority and legality of the court. (The bishop of Rochester, though he had so lately acted in an illegal one, being one of those that questioned it.)   The
10 grounds of this scruple were the obligations the clergy lay under by act of parliament of king Henry VIII. not to enter into any debates, about making any alterations in church affairs without the king's special and immediate privacy, and direction first given concerning such alterations.   It was
15 answered that that must be done either by an act of the king's own judgment, or by a private cabal, (both which ways would be very exceptionable,) or else by his majesty's commission to a certain number of ecclesiastics, to consult about and prepare what was necessary to be altered, as it was in
20 the present case.   For moreover, the commissioners pretended not to make these alterations obligatory by virtue of a law, but only to get them ready to lay before the convocation : the very reports being not so much as to be referred to the privy council, lest they might be subject to be canvassed and
25 cooked by lay hands.   However, the bishops of Winchester and Rochester, Dr. Jane and Dr. Aldrich, withdrew dissatisfied ; and the rest, after a list of all that seemed fit to be changed was read over, proceeded very unanimously and with-

---

[a] A MS. copy of this account is in the Tanner Collection, (vol. cclxxxii. No.
30 222.) in a volume containing many papers in the handwriting of abp. Sancroft. Whether this MS. were preserved by the archbishop, or only by bishop Tanner, it clearly may be considered as of high authority, in the absence of the original document confided to Dr. Tenison.   It is remarkable that no notice is taken in it of the important point of reordination, which the commissioners certainly debated,
35 and according to the statement of Dr. Nicholls, were willing to concede.

out any heats in determining as follows, (each article as soon as agreed upon being signed by the bishop of London,) viz.

That the chanting of divine service in cathedral churches shall be laid aside, that the whole may be rendered intelligible to the common people.   5

That besides the Psalms, being read in their course as before, some proper and devout ones be selected for Sundays.

That the apocryphal lessons and those of the Old Testament, which are too natural, be thrown out, and others appointed in their stead by a new calendar, which is already 10 fully settled, and out of which are omitted all the legendary saints' days, and others not directly referred to in the service book.

That not to send the vulgar to search the canons, which few of them ever saw, a rubric be made, setting forth the use- 15 fulness of the cross in baptism, not as an essential part of that sacrament, but only a fit and decent ceremony. However, if any do, after all, in conscience scruple it, it shall be omitted by the priest.

That likewise if any refuse to receive the sacrament of the 20 Lord's supper kneeling, it may be administered to them in their pews.

That a rubric be made declaring the intention of the Lent fasts to consist only in extraordinary acts of devotion, not in distinction of meats. And another to state the meaning of 25 Rogation Sundays and Ember weeks; and appoint that those ordained within the " quatuor tempora" do exercise strict devotion.

That the rubric which obliges ministers to read or hear common prayer publicly or privately every day, be changed to 30 an exhortation to the people to frequent those prayers.

That the Absolution in morning and evening prayer may be read by a deacon, the word " priest" in the rubric being changed into " minister ;" and those words " and remission" be put out as not very intelligible.   35

That the Gloria Patri shall not be repeated at the end of every Psalm, but of all, appointed for morning and evening prayer.

That those words in the Te Deum, " thine honourable,

true and only Son," be thus turned, " thine only begotten Son," honourable being only a civil term, and no where used " in sacris."

The Benedicite shall be changed into the [a] 128th Psalm, and
5 other Psalms likewise appointed for the Benedictus and Nunc dimittis.

The Versicles after the Lord's Prayer, &c. shall be read kneeling, to avoid the trouble and inconveniences of so often varying postures in the worship.   And after these words,
10 " Give peace in our time, O Lord," shall follow an answer, promissory of somewhat on the people's part, of keeping God's laws, or the like ; the old response being grounded on the predestinating doctrine taken in too strict an acceptation.

15   All high titles or appellations of the king, queen, &c. shall be left out of the prayers, such as " most illustrious, religious, mighty," &c. and only the word " sovereign" retained for the king and queen.

Those words in the prayer for the king, " Grant that he
20 may vanquish and overcome all his enemies," as of too large an extent, if the king engage in an unjust war, shall be turned thus ; " Prosper all his righteous undertakings against thy enemies," or after some such manner.

Those words in the prayer for the clergy, " who alone
25 workest great marvels," as subject to be ill-interpreted by persons vainly disposed, shall be thus, " who art the author of all good gifts."   And those words, " the healthful spirit of thy grace," shall be, " the holy spirit of thy grace," healthful being an obsolete word.

30   The prayer which begins, " O God, whose nature and property," shall be thrown out, as full of strange and impertinent expressions, and besides not in the original, but foisted in since by another hand.

The collects for the most part are to be changed for those
35 the bishop of Chichester has prepared ; being a review of the old ones with enlargements, to render them more sensible and affecting ; and what expressions are needful, so to be retrenched.

---

[a] The Psalm intended was probably the 148th.

If any minister refuse the surplice, the bishop, if the people desire it, and the living will bear it, may substitute one in his place that will officiate in it: but the whole thing is left to the discretion of the bishops.

If any be desirous to have godfathers and godmothers 5 omitted, and their children presented in their own names to baptism, it may be granted.

About the Athanasian Creed they came at last to this conclusion: that lest the wholly rejecting it should by unreasonable persons be imputed to them as Socinianism, a rubric 10 shall be made, declaring the curses denounced therein not to be restrained to every particular article, but intended against those that deny the substance of the Christian religion in general.

Whether the amendment of the translation of the reading 15 Psalms, (as they are called,) made by the bishop of St. Asaph and Dr. Kidder, or that in the Bible shall be inserted in the Prayer Book, is wholly left to the convocation to consider of and determine.

In the litany, communion service, &c. are some alterations 20 made, as also in the canons, which I cannot yet learn so particular account of, as to give them you with the rest; as perhaps I may hereafter be able to do.

IV.

[b]*An account of the proceedings of the commissioners of* 1689, *by* 25 *Dr. Nicholls.* (*Apparatus ad Defens. Eccles. Angl. p.* 95.)

Imperato operi viri reverendi se protinus accingunt, et in Liturgia denuò limanda labores auspicantur. Primùm in examen vocatur Calendarium, ex quo lectionibus Apocryphis exturbatis, Canonicæ Scripturæ capita suffecta sunt, cum majore 30

---

[b] This account is understood to have been obtained by Dr. Nicholls from the papers of bishop Williams (of Chichester) who was one of the commissioners. Kennet, Comp. Hist. vol. iii. p. 591.

populi fructu perlegenda. Symbolum quod vulgo Sancti
Athanasii dicitur, quia a multis improbatur propter atrocem
de singulis, secus quam hic docetur credentibus, sententiam
ministri arbitrio permittitur, ut pro apostolico mutetur. Col-
5 lectæ in totum anni cyclum de novo elaborantur, ad epistolæ et
evangelii doctrinam congruentius factæ ; et cum tanta verborum elegantia atque splendore, tantaque Christianæ mentis vi
atque ardore compositæ sunt, ut nihil possit animos audientium magis afficere et accendere, et eorum mentes ad Deum
10 evehere. Eas primum contexuit, summus hujus rei artifex,
Simon Patricius ; ulteriorem vim sanguinem spiritumque ad-
hibebat Gilbertus Burnetius ; eas denique cum magno judicio,
singulis verbis diligenter expensis, examinante Edvardo Stil-
linfleto ; ultimam limam addente ac verbis enodibus et dulcis
15 facilisque eloquentiæ fluentis iterum perpoliente Joanne Til-
lotsonio. Novam Psalmorum versionem ornabant originibus
congruentiorem ; eam curam sibi plerumque vindicante
Richardo Ciddero, viro in linguis orientalibus versatissimo.
Singulas dictiones et vocabula, quæ sparsim per Liturgiam
20 improbarant illius hostes, exquisita indagine collegit Thomas
Tenisonius ; in eorum loca suffectis verbis perspicuis et dis-
tinctis, nec a morosiori aliquo cavillandis. Alia quædam pro-
posita sunt, sed quæ integre ad synodum referenda judica-
bantur. Primùm ut crux baptismalis seu infantium frontibus
25 signetur, seu prorsus omittatur, penes parentes sit eligere.
Deinde si non-conformista minister ad Ecclesiam revertatur,
novis mysteriis vulgari ritu non iterum initiandus, sed ordina-
tione quadam conditionali potius insigniendus, uti nobis in
usu est baptismum infantibus, de quorum baptizatione non
30 admodum compertum est, inferre ; benedictione episcopi ad-
dita, ut mos erat apud antiquos, clericos ab hæreticis ordi-
natos recipiendi (Dionys. Alex. ap. Euseb. Hist. Eccl. l. 7.
c. 2. Concil. Nic. 1. Can. 8. Just. sive Author Resp. ad orthodox. resp. 18. Theod. Hist. Eccl. l. 1. c. 8.) In sacris ordinibus
35 tali modo conferendis exemplo præiverat vir de ecclesia optime
meritus Dominus Bramallus, Hiberniæ Primas, cum Scotos
Presbyteros in Ecclesiam reciperet.

Hæc eorum summa erat quæ in hoc congressu viri doctis-
simi moliebantur.

.V.

The particular acts and adjournments of the convocation from Dec. 4th, 1689.

THE litany was read by a bishop for some days in Latin, there being only this supplication added after the prayers for 5 the bishops:

"That it may please thee to inspire with thy Holy Spirit this convocation, and to preside over it, to lead us into all truth, which is according to godliness.

At other times, when there was no sermon, this prayer for 10 the parliament was constantly used:

"Most gracious God, who dost rule all men, and govern all things, be graciously present, we beseech thee, with the three estates of the kingdom in parliament assembled, under the government of our most gracious princes William and Mary; 15 assist them with the spirit of counsel and peace, whereby they may be preserved in one mind and accord, and also may be inspired with the love of thee, and study the publick welfare: that whatsoever laws, by their joint suffrages shall be obtained, being established by our lord and lady the king and 20 queen, may establish righteousness and peace to us, and confirm them to our posterities for ever, to the encrease of all virtue, and the eternal glory of thy name, by and for Jesus Christ our Lord and Saviour."

Then follow'd these five collects; I. The collect on St. 25 Simon and St. Jude's day: "O Almighty God, who hast built thy church upon the foundation of the apostles and prophets," &c.

II. The collect for Good Friday: "Almighty and everlasting God, by whose Spirit," &c. 30

III. Collect: "Almighty God, who by thy Son Jesus Christ didst give to the holy apostles many excellent gifts, and commandedst them earnestly to feed thy flock, make, we beseech thee, all bishops and pastors diligently to preach thy holy word, and the people obediently to follow the same, that they 35 may receive the crown of everlasting glory, through Jesus Christ our Lord. *Amen.*"

IV. The collect on the fifth Sunday after Trinity: "Grant, we beseech thee," &c.

5 V. Collect: "O Lord God, the Father of lights, and Fountain of all wisdom, we thy humble and unworthy servants, prostrating ourselves at thy footstool, beseech thee, that we who are here met together in thy name, under the government of our most gracious king William and queen Mary,

10 being assisted by thy heavenly grace, may so search out, meditate, handle and discern all things which may promote thy honour and glory, and the good of thy church, that thy Spirit, which heretofore did preside over the counsil of the apostles, may also preside over this our counsil, and lead us

15 into all that truth which is according to godliness; that we who have worthily and seriously, utterly renounced the errours of our holy reformation, the corruptions and superstitions, together with the papal tyranny which heretofore did here abound, may all of us firmly and constantly hold the apostolic

20 and truly catholick faith, and without fear, may duly serve thee with a pure worship, through Jesus Christ our Lord. *Amen.*"

Then follows the prayer of St. Chrysostome: "Almighty God, who hast given us grace at this time," &c.

25 Then the members of the convocation were called over: An alphabetical catalogue of all the names of the members of the upper and lower house of this present convocation.

William lord bishop of St. Asaph.
Geor. Bright, D.D. dean of St. Asaph.
30 Samuel Davies, L.D. proctor for the chapter.
William lord bishop of St. Asaph, archdeacon of St. Asaph.
Griffin Lloyd, B.D. John Edwards, M.A. proctors for the clergy.

Bath and Wells.

35 Ralph Bathurst, D.D. dean of Bath and Wells.
Rich. Busby, D.D. proctor for the chapter.
Edwin Sandys, A.M. Edw. Waple, B.D. archdeacon of Wells [Bath], Taunton.

William Clement, A.M. Giles Pooley, A.M. proctors for the clergy.

Humphrey lord bishop of Bangor.
John Jones, D.D. dean of Bangor.
Rol. Foulks, A.M. proctor for the chapter. 5
Humphrey lord bishop of Bangor, archdeacon of Bangor and Anglesey.
Fran. Lloyd, A.M. archdeacon of Merioneth.
Robert Wynne, A.M. John Williams, A.M. proctors for the clergy. 10

Gilbert lord bishop of Bristol.
William Levett, D.D. dean of Bristol.
Steph. Crespion, A.M. proctor for the chapter.
John Feilding, D.D. archdeacon of Dorset.
Roger Mander, D.D. Rich. Roderick, B.D. proctors for 15 the clergy.

Canterbury.

John Tillotson, D.D. then dean of Canterbury, now dean of St. Paul's, London.
——————— proctor for the chapter. 20
John Batteley, archdeacon of Canterbury.
Geo. Thorpe, D.D. John Cooke, A.M. proctors for the clergy.

Simon lord bishop of Chichester.
Francis Hawkins, D.D. dean of Chichester. 25
Zach. Cradock, D.D. proctor for the chapter.
Josias Pleydell, A.M. archdeacon of Chichester.
Joseph Sayer, B.D. archdeacon of Lewes.
Conyers Richardson, A.M. David Morton, D.D. proctors for the clergy. 30

Thomas lord bishop of St. David's.
John Ellis, D.D. præcentor.
Spencer Lucy, A.M. proctor for the chapter.
Tim. Halton   archdeacon of St. David's.
Geo. Owen,   deacon   marthen. 35

Tho. Stainoe, B. D. archdeacon of Brecknock.

Joh. Williams, A. M. archdeacon of Cardigan.

Tho. Sandys, A. M. Will. Powell, A. M. proctors for the Clergy.

5　　　　　　　　　　*Ely.*

John Spencer, D. D. dean of Ely.

John Moore, D. D. proctor for the chapter.

Will. Saywell, D. D. archdeacon of Ely.

Sam. Blith, D. D. Nicholas Gouge, A. M. proctors for the
10 clergy.

———

Jonathan lord bishop of Exeter.

Rich. Annesley, D. D. dean of Exon.

Geo. Hooper, D. D. proctor for the chapter.

Edw. Lake, D. D. archdeacon of Exeter.

15　Edw. Drew, A. M. archdeacon of Cornwall.

Fra. Fulwood, D. D. archdeacon of Totnes.

Will. Read, A. M. archdeacon of Sarum.

John James, D. D. Tho. Long, senior, B. D. proctors for
the clergy.

20　　　　　　　　　*Glocester.*

Will. Jane, D. D. dean of Gloucester, prolocutor.

Rich. Duke, A. M. proctor for the chapter.

Tho. Hide, D. D. archdeacon of Glocester.

Abraham Gregory, D. D. Rich. Parsons, L. D. proctors for
25 the clergy.

———

Herbert lord bishop of Hereford.

Geo. Benson, D. D. dean of Hereford.

Tho. Rogers, D. D. proctor for the chapter.

Sam. Benson, A. M. archdeacon of Hereford.

30　Adam Ottley, A. M. archdeacon of Salop.

Will. Johnson, D. D. Rich. Bulkley, A. M. proctors for the
clergy.

———

William lord bishop of Landaffe.

Henry Bull, D. D. archdeacon of Landaffe.

35　Jonathan Edwards, proctor for the chapter.

William Frampton, A. M. —— Jenkins, A. M. proctors for the clergy.

———

Thomas lord bishop of Lichfield and Coventry.
Lancelot Addison, D. D. dean of Lichfield.
John Willes, D. D. proctor for the chapter.   5
Lancelot Addison, D. D. archdeacon of Coventry.
Fran. Ashenhurst, A. M. archdeacon of Darby [Stafford, Salop].
Barnabas Poole, A. M. Jo. Kimberly, A. M. proctors for the clergy.   10

———

Thomas lord bishop of Lincoln.
Daniel Brevint, D. D. dean of Lincoln.
John Inet, A. M. Samuel Fuller, D. D. proctors for the chapter.
Tho. Oldys, L. B. archdeacon of Lincoln.   15
John Hutton, A. M. archdeacon of Stow.
Byrom Eaton, D. D. archdeacon of Leicester.
John Hammond, D. D. archdeacon of Bucks.
John Gery, L. D. archdeacon of Huntington.
John Skelton, A. M. archdeacon of Bedford.   20
James Gardiner, D. D. Rob. Edwards, B. D. proctors for the clergy.

———

Henry lord bishop of London, president.
J. Tillotson, D. D. now dean of St. Paul's.
Will. Stanley, D. D. proctor for the chapter.   25
Thomas Tenison, D. D. archdeacon of London.
John Goodman, D. D. archdeacon of Essex.
Charles Alston, D. D. archdeacon of Middlesex.
Will. Beveridge, D. D. archdeacon of Colchester.
John Cole, A. M. archdeacon of St. Albans.   30
Gregory Hascard, D. D. Rob. Grove, D. D. proctors for the clergy.

Norwich.

John Sharpe, D. D. then dean of Norwich, now dean of Canterbury.   35

Nath. Hodges, A. M. proctor for the chapter.
John Conant, D. D. archdeacon of Norwich.
Edw. Reynolds, D. D. archdeacon of Norfolk.
John Spencer, D. D. archdeacon of Sudbury.
5   Humph. Prideaux, D. D. archdeacon of Suffolk.
John Connald, A. M. John Eachard, D. D. proctors for
the clergy.

Oxford.

Hen. Aldrich, D. D. dean of Christ Church.
10   Hen. Smith, D. D. proctor for the chapter.
Timothy Halton, D. D. archdeacon of Oxon.
John Mill, D. D. Henry Maurice, D. D. proctors for the
clergy.

Peterborough.

15   Rich. Kidder, D. D. dean of Peterbour.
John Patrick, A. M. proctor for the chapter.
Tho. Woolsey, D. D. archdeacon of Northampt.
Matthew Hutton, B. D. Nath. Whalley, A. M. proctors for
the clergy.

----

20   Thomas lord bishop of Rochester.
Hen. Ullock, D. D. dean of Rochester.
Fran. Brevall, D. D. proctor for the chapter.
Tho. Plume, D. D. archdeacon of Rochester.
Rich. Holden, A. M. Joseph Yates, A. M. proctors for the
25 clergy.

Gilbert lord bishop of Salisbury.
Tho. Price, D. D. dean of Sarum.
Rob. Woodward, L. D. proctor for the chapter.
Will. Richards, B. D. archdeacon of Sarum.
30   Tho. Lambert, D. D. archdeacon of Berks.
Tho. Ward, L. D. archdeacon of Wilts.
John Younger, D. D. Thomas Wyat, D. D. proctors for
the Clergy.

Westminster.

35   Thomas lord bishop of Rochester, dean of Westminster.

Edw. Pelling, D. D. proctor for the chapter.
Rich. Busby, D. D. archdeacon of Westminster.

Peter lord bishop of Winchester.
Rich. Meggott, D. D. dean of Winton.
Will. Hawkins, D. D. proctor for the chapter.   5
Tho. Clutterbuck, D. D. archdeacon of Winchester.
Tho. Sayer, D. D. archdeacon of Surrey.
Will. Harrison, D. D. Geo. Hooper, D. D. proctors for the
clergy.

> Windsor.   No return.   10
> Wolverhampton.   No return.

Edward lord bishop of Worcester.
Geo. Hicks, D. D. dean of Worcester.
R. Battle, A. M. proctor for the chapter.
John Fleetwood, A. M. archdeacon of Worcester.   15
John Jephcott, D. D. Tho. Hodge, A. M. proctors for the
clergy.

And after this the prolocutor was chosen: the persons
named were Dr. Tillotson, dean of St. Paul's, and Dr. Jane,
the king's professor in Oxford: Dr. Jane had the majority 20
of voices; yet great endeavours were used to prefer the dean,
whose party having argued much for it, but saw themselves
overcome, did at last yield to the election of Dr. Jane, the
votes for him being double to the others. The first thing
that was done in the convocation, after the chusing the pro- 25
locutor, was Dec. 4th, when the commission from the king
was read, there being present twelve bishops; the commission
was as follows:

" William and Mary, by the grace of God, king and queen
of England, Scotland, France, and Ireland, defenders of the 30
faith, &c. to all to whom these presents shall come, greeting;
whereas, in and by one act of parliament made at Westminster, in the 25th year of the reign of king Henry the VIIIth,
reciting, That whereas the king's humble and obedient subjects the clergy of this realm of England, had not only ac- 35
knowledged according to the truth that the convocations
of the same clergy were always, had been, and ought to be

assembled only by the king's writ, but also submitting themselves to the king's majesty, had promised in *verbo sacerdotis,*
that they would never from thenceforth presume to attempt,
alledge, claim, or put in ure, or enact, promulge, or execute
5 any new canons, constitutions, ordinances provincial or others,
or by whatsoever other name they should be called, in the convocation, unless the said king's most royal assent and license
might to them be had, to make, promulge, and execute the
same; and that the said king did give his royal assent and
10 authority in that behalf. It was therefore enacted by the
authority of the said parliament, according to the said submission and petition of the said clergy, among other things,
that they, nor any of them, from thenceforth should enact,
promulge, or execute any such canons, constitutions, or ordi-
15 nances provincial, by whatsoever name they might be called,
in their convocations in time coming, which always should be
assembled by authority of the king's writ, unless the same
clergy might have the king's most royal assent and license,
to make, promulge, and execute such canons, constitutions,
20 and ordinances, provincial or synodal, upon pain of every one
of the said clergy doing contrary to the said act, and being
thereof convict, to suffer imprisonment, and make fines at the
king's will.

"And further, by the said act it is provided, that no canons,
25 constitutions, or ordinances should be made or put in execution within this realm, by authority of the convocations of
the clergy, which should be contrariant or repugnant to the
king's prerogative royal, or the customs, laws, or statutes of
this realm, any thing contained in the said act to the contrary
30 thereof notwithstanding.

"And lastly, it is also provided by the said act, That such
canons, constitutions, ordinances and synodals, provincial,
which then were already made, and which then were not contrariant or repugnant to the laws, statutes and customs of
35 this realm, nor to the damage or hurt of the king's prerogative royal, should then still be used and executed as they
were before the making of the said act, until such time as
they should be viewed, searched, or otherwise ordered and
determined by the persons mentioned in the said act, or the

most part of them, according to the tenor, form, and effect of the said act, as by the said act, among divers other things more fully and at large, it doth and may appear.

" And whereas the particular forms of divine worship, and rites and ceremonies appointed to be used therein, being 5 things of their own nature indifferent and alterable, and so acknowledged, it is but reasonable that upon weighty and important considerations, according to the various exigency of times and occasions, such changes and alterations should be made therein, as to those that are in place and authority 10 should, from time to time, seem either necessary or expedient.

" And whereas the Book of Canons is fit to be reviewed, and made more suitable to the state of the church: and whereas there are divers defects and abuses in the ecclesiastical courts and jurisdictions; and particularly there is not sufficient pro- 15 vision made for the removing of scandalous ministers, and for the reformation of manners either in ministers or people; and whereas it is most fit that there should be a strict method prescribed for the examination of such persons as desire to be admitted into holy orders, both as to their learning and 20 manners: know ye, that we, for divers urgent and weighty causes and considerations us thereunto moving, of our especial grace, certain knowledge, and meer motion, have by virtue of our prerogative royal, and supreme authority in causes ecclesiastical, given and granted, and by these presents do give and 25 grant, full, free, and lawful liberty, license, power, and authority unto the right rev. Father in God Henry lord bishop of London, president of this present convocation for the province of Canterbury, (upon the suspension of the lord archbishop of Canterbury,) during this present parliament now assembled; 30 and in his absence to such other bishops as shall be appointed president thereof, and to the rest of the bishops of the same province, and to all deans of cathedral churches, archdeacons, chapters, and colleges, and the whole clergy of every several diocese within the said province: that they the said lord 35 bishop of London, or other president of the said convocation, and the rest of the bishops, and other the said clergy of this present convocation within the said province of Canterbury, or the greatest number of them, whereof the president of the

said convocation to be always one, shall and may from time
to time during this present parliament, confer, treat, debate,
consider, consult, and agree of and upon such points, matters,
causes and things as we, from time to time, shall propose, or
5 cause to be proposed, by the said lord bishop of London, or
other president of the said convocation, concerning alterations
and amendments of the liturgy and canons, and orders, ordinances and constitutions for the reformation of ecclesiastical
courts; for the removing of scandalous ministers; for the
10 reformation of manners either in ministers or people; and for
the examination of such persons as desire to be admitted into
holy orders, and all such other points, causes and matters as
we shall think necessary and expedient, for advancing the
honour and service of Almighty God, the good and quiet of
15 the church, and the better government thereof. And we do
also by these presents, give and grant unto the said lord
bishop of London, or other president of the said convocation,
and to the rest of the bishops of the said province of Canterbury, and unto all deans of cathedral churches, archdeacons,
20 chapters, and colleges, and the whole clergy of every several
diocese within the said province, full, free, and lawful liberty,
license, power and authority, that they the said lord bishop
of London, or other president of the said convocation, and
the rest of the said bishops and other the clergy of the same
25 province, or the greatest number of them that shall be present
in person, or by their proxies, shall and may, from time to
time, draw into forms, rules, orders, ordinances, constitutions
and canons, such matters as to them shall seem necessary and
expedient for purposes abovementioned; and the same set
30 down in writing, from time to time, to exhibit and deliver, or
cause to be exhibited and delivered unto us, to the end that
we, as occasion shall require, may thereupon have the advice
of our parliament; and that such, and so many of the said
canons, orders, ordinances, constitutions, matters, causes, and
35 things as shall be thought requisite and convenient by our
said parliament, may be presented to us in due form for our
royal assent, if upon mature consideration thereof we shall
think fit to enact the same. In witness whereof we have
caused these our letters to be made patent: witness ourselves

at Westminster the 30th day of November, in the fifth year
of our reign.

"Per Breve de privato Sigello,   BURKER.
"Vera Copia, J. C."
"N. P."   5

His majesty's gracious message to the convocation, sent
by the earl of Nottingham, as followeth:

"WILLIAM R.

"His majesty has summon'd this convocation, not only
because 'tis usual upon holding of a parliament, but out of a 10
pious zeal to do every thing that may tend to the best
establishment of the Church of England, which is so eminent
a part of the reformation, and is certainly the best suited to
the constitution of this government; and therefore does most
signally deserve, and shall always have both his favour and 15
protection; and he doubts not, but that you will assist him
in promoting the welfare of it, so that no prejudices, with
which some men may have laboured to possess you, shall
disappoint his good intentions, or deprive the church of
any benefit from your consultations. His majesty therefore 20
expects, that the things that shall be proposed, shall be
calmly and impartially considered by you, and assures you,
that he will offer nothing to you but what shall be for the
honour, peace, and advantage both of the protestant religion
in general, and particularly of the Church of England."   25

The Bishops' address.

"We your majesty's most dutiful subjects, the bishops and
clergy of the province of Canterbury, in convocation assembled, having received your majesty's gracious message, together with a commission from your majesty by the earl of 30
Nottingham, hold ourselves bound in gratitude and duty,
to return our most humble thanks and acknowledgments of
the grace and goodness expressed in your majesty's message,
and the zeal you shew in it for the protestant religion in
general, and the Church of England in particular, and of the 35
trust and confidence reposed in us by this commission: we

look on these marks of your majesty's care and favour as the
continuance of the great deliverance Almighty God wrought
for us by your means, in making you the blessed instrument
of preserving us from falling under the cruelty of popish
5 tyranny ; for which as we have often thanked Almighty God,
so we cannot forget that high obligation and duty which we
owe to your majesty ; and on these new assurances of your
protection and favour in our church, we beg leave to renew
the assurance of our constant fidelity and obedience to your
10 majesty, whom we pray God to continue long and happily to
reign over us."

This address was not approved of by the lower house, who
thought they had the priviledge (wanting the books of presidents) to present one of their own drawing ; but that not
15 being admitted, it was voted by the lower house to make
some amendments ; which were not agreed on till after a
conference with the bishops, the lower house insisting that
they would confine themselves to the king's declaration, and
to what concerned especially the Church of England ; where-
20 upon a conference was desired, and a committee appointed to
attend the lords : the conference was managed chiefly between
the bishop of Salisbury and the prolocutor ; the bishop urged
that the Church of England was not distinguished from other
protestant churches but by its hierarchy and revenues, and
25 that it was an equivocal expression ; for if popery should
prevail it would be called the Church of England still. To
which the prolocutor answered, that the Church of England
was distinguished by its doctrine as it stands in the articles,
liturgy, and homilies, as well as by its hierarchy, and that
30 the term of protestant churches was much more equivocal,
because Socinians, anabaptists, and quakers assumed that title.
After this we heard no more reply, but a committee of convocation in the lower house having drawn up another form, it
was consented to. And thanks were given to the prolocutor
35 for managing the conference.

And the address, as agreed on to be presented, was as
followeth :

· " We your majesty's most loyall and most dutiful subjects
the bishops and clergy of the province of Canterbury, in con-

vocation assembled, having received a most gracious message from your majesty by the earl of Nottingham, hold ourselves bound in duty and gratitude, to return our most humble acknowledgments for the same; and for the pious zeal and care your majesty is pleased to express therein for the 5 honour, peace, advantage, and establishment of the Church of England: whereby we doubt not, the interest of the protestant religion in all other protestant churches, which is dear to us, will be the better secured under the influence of your majesty's government and protection. And we crave 10 leave to assure your majesty that in pursuance of that trust and confidence you repose in us, we will consider whatsoever shall be offered to us from your majesty, without prejudice, and with all calmness and impartiality; and that we will constantly pay the fidelity and allegiance which we have all 15 sworn to your majesty and the queen; whom we pray God to continue long and happily to reign over us."

This address was presented on Thursday the 12th of Dec. in the Banquetting-chamber.

His majesty's most gracious answer to the bishops' 20 address, &c.

"My lords,

"I take the address very kindly from your convocation: you may depend upon it, that all I have promised, and all that I can do for the service of the Church of England, I will do: 25 and I give you this new assurance, that I will improve all occasions and opportunities for its service."

I. In the adjournments it was first debated, what proxies each man might have from those that were absent: and it was agreed, that one man might have four. 30

II. Whether those bishops that had arch-deaconries annexed to their bishopricks might grant proxies to any member of the lower house of convocation to vote for them.

III. Whether such proctors for the clergy, as had not appeared, might grant their proxies; which was resolved in 35 the affirmative, presidents being found for the same.

Then it was complained, that the convocation wanted the

books of presidents belonging to the convocation; and it
being said, that the bishop of Asaph and dean Tillotson had
such books, they were desired to bring them in; which was
done, and a committee appointed to inspect them, and report
5 what presidents could be found that might concern the convocation, which is yet under examination. It was proposed,
that a committee might be continued during the adjournment, to prepare things against their meeting; but this was
denied. Complaint was made of some dangerous books
10 printed contrary to the canons, as that against the Creed of
Athanasius; which was sent to the bishops to be censured
by them. A reverend person made a speech on the behalf of
the bishops under suspension, that something might be done
to qualify them to sit in convocation, but so as the convoca-
15 tion might not incur any danger; which being not in their
cognizance it was waved, and left to farther consideration.

THE MINUTE PARTICULARS OBSERVED IN THE PROCEEDINGS
OF THE CONVOCATION, 4th DECEMBER, 1689.

Prayers being ended, the king's commission brought in with
20 a message by the earl of Nottingham, both which being read,
the bishops went to Jerusalem-chamber, from whence they
sent a copy of the king's message, with the form of an address,
to which they desired the concurrence of this house.

Dean of Windsor, St. Paul's, Exon, desired by this house
25 to attend the lords, to know whether they were all consenting
to the said address, and likewise to pray a copy of the said
commission. They reported from the lords, that they were
consenting to the said address, and order'd to be sent down
to this house, and desir'd their concurrence; and that they
30 would order a copy of the commission. Then a question
arose, whether this house should concur with the form recommended by the bishops, or address the king in their own
form.

Resolv'd by this house, To return thanks to the king in a
35 form of their own.

Dean of Peterborough, dean of Christ Church, desir'd to
attend the lords with this resolution.

Order'd, That nothing of any moment be agreed upon, or

pass into an act, till the old books of former convocations be brought in.

Order'd, That Mr. Pleydell's proxy be withdrawn.

The bishops desiring a conference,

Order'd, That the dean of Christ Church, Chichester, Lich- 5 field, Bristol, St. Paul's, Peterborough, Drs. Hooper, Maurice, Willis, be desir'd to attend the lords, to acquaint them, that the house consents to a conference, and have appointed managers, but desire a longer time to prepare instructions for them.   10

The lords appointed Friday morning, nine of the clock, to be attended about the conference.

Order'd, That the same persons, together with the prolocutor, deans of Windsor, Exon, Dr. Battely, and archdeacon Fielding be appointed a committee to draw up instructions 15 to-morrow at 9 o'clock.

Adjourned to the 6th.

6 December. Prayers ended, the old books, and the copy of the commission brought in. The committee brought in an address, with alterations, with the reasons why they cannot 20 concur with the bishops in their form, in these words, " We are desirous to confine our address to his majesty's most gracious message, and to those things only therein which concern the Church of England;" which reasons being approved of and agreed to by this house, it was carried up to the lords 25 by the said committee, who reported from their lordships, That what alterations this house makes in their lordships' address ought to be specified in the respective lines thereof in particular exceptions.

Order'd, That the form of amendments sent down by the 30 lords be referred to the same committee, to meet to-morrow at eight of the clock at Dr. Busby's chamber, saving this house's right of proceedings, in their own way, in this and the like cases, where there is no precedent to the contrary.

Order'd, That the house adhere to the reason of their 35 amendments, which was offered to the lords.

Order'd, That Drs. Tenison, Fuller, Beveredge, Hamond, Halton, Thorpe, Parsons, Gregory, Grove, Saywell, Alston, Mander, Woodward, Goodman, Busby, Younger, Moore,

Stanley, Mr. Kimberly, Richardson, Ottley, Buckley, and
Skelton, be appointed a committee to inspect the old books
belonging to the convocation, and where they find them defective to offer new orders for the approbation of this house,
5 eleven whereof to be a quorum, and to meet at three this
afternoon at Dr. Tenison's library.

Adjourned till to-morrow.

7 December. Prayers ended, the committee return'd the
bishops' form of address alter'd according to the order of the
10 house yesterday, which being approv'd of by this house, they
were desir'd to carry it up to the lords.

Adjourned till 9.

9 Decemb. Prayers ended, the committee return'd the
bishops' form of address, alter'd according to the order of the
15 house on Friday, which being approved of, they were again
to carry it up to the lords (being prevented by the adjournment on Wednesday from attending their lordships with it):
who brought down three reasons from their lordships why
the express mention of the Protestant religion should be in-
20 serted in the address, which are as follows : " 1. Because it
is the known denomination of the common doctrine of the
western part of Christendom, in opposition to the errors and
corruptions of the church of Rome. 2. Because the leaving
out this may have ill consequences, and be liable to strange
25 constructions both at home and abroad, among protestants
as well as papists.   3. Because it agrees with the general
reason offer'd by the clergy for their amendments, since this
is expressly mentioned in the king's message, and in this the
church of England being so much concerned, the bishops
30 think it ought still to stand in the address." Then a question arose, whether the consideration of these reasons should
be refer'd to a committee, or debated in a full house.

Resolv'd, That it be debated.

After the debate the house agreed that after these words
35 in the address, (viz.) " the establishment of the church of
England," it be immediately added, " whereby we doubt not
the interest of all the protestant churches, which is dear to
us, will, under the influence of your majesty's government, be
the better secured."

Order'd, The lords desiring a committee from this house
to inspect the old books, that Drs. Tenison, Maunder, Woodward, Halton, Moore, Gregory, Mr. Skelton, and Ottley, be
appointed a committee to attend the lords this afternoon at
five o'clock, to inspect the old books.   5

Adjourn'd till to-morrow.

10 Decemb. Prayers ended, a message came down from
the lords for the managers to attend their lordships; who
reported from their lordships, that they desire the reason of
this house, why instead of the "protestant religion" they in- 10
sert "protestant churches."

Order'd, That the same managers be appointed to draw up
their reasons immediately; who return'd their reason in these
words: "We being the representatives of a form'd established church, do not think fit to mention the word religion 15
any further than it is the religion of some form'd established
church," which reason being approved, it was carried up to
the lords.

The lords returned the amendments with some alterations,
in these words: "After the words 'establishment of the 20
church of England,' add 'whereby we doubt not the interest
of the protestant religion in this and all other protestant
churches, which is dear to us, will be the better secured
under your majesty's government and protection.'"

Order'd by the house, That the words "this and" be 25
omitted. The prolocutor, at the request of the house, gave
an account of the conference with the lords.

Order'd, That the thanks of the house be given to the prolocutor for managing the conference with the lords.

Adjourn'd till to-morrow.   30

11 Decemb. Prayers ended, the prolocutor reported from
the lords, that they had agreed to all the amendments with
this house, and that they would give this house an account
this morning when it would be a fit time to wait upon his
majesty with the said address. Then the house desir'd the 35
prolocutor to attend the lords and humbly to represent to
their lordships, that there are severall books of very dangerous consequence to the Christian religion, and the church of
England particularly; notes upon Athanasius Creed, and two

letters relating to the present convocation, newly come abroad; and to desire their lordships' advice, in what way, and how far, safely, without incurring the penalty of the statute 25 H. VIII., the convocation may proceed in the
5 preventing the publishing the like scandalous books for the future, and inflicting the censure of the church, according to the canons provided in that behalf, upon the authors of them. Then the prolocutor acquainted the house that their lordships received the message very kindly and promised to take it into
10 consideration; and also that this house is desired to attend their lordships at the banquetting house to-morrow, at three of the clock to present the said address to his majesty.

Adjourn'd to Friday.

13 Decemb. Prayer ended.

15 Adjourn'd till to-morrow.

Prayers ended, a copy of the king's answer to the address sent down from the lords.

The prolocutor acquainted the house that the president had declared his sence of the ill consequence of those books
20 that were sent up from this house to their lordships: and that upon enquiry, he could not receive any satisfaction how far the convocation might proceed in that affair, but he would, as far as lay in him, take further order about it.

Agreed by this house, That the prolocutor return thanks
25 to the president for the care he hath taken about our proposal concerning the books, and to desire his lordship to proceed further in it.

Then it was proposed by the lords to appoint a committee of both houses to sit during the recess.
30 After some debate,

Resolved, That this house does not consent to appoint any committee during the said recess.

Adjourn'd to the 24th of Jany.

VI.

Letter to Dr. Tillotson, bearing date Oct. 5, 1689. (From the MS. Library at Lambeth. Gibs. 930. No. 183.)

Reverend Sir,

THOUGH I am a stranger to your person, yet I am none to [5] your character, and so cannot but hope you'll pardon the confidence of this address. The great design now on foot of making alterations in the liturgy, &c. in which you are reported to have a share, is what occasions the talk and raises the expectation of the whole nation. May the great God of [10] heaven and earth bless the endeavours of all who are or shall be concerned in it, that they may indeed issue in the encrease of true piety, order, and peace. As such attempts are not certainly over hastily to be made, so, when they are made, they ought not, in my opinion, to be with a too niggardly [15] hand. Every thing at such a season should be enquired into and throughly considered which may at all be thought necessary to promote the good ends proposed. On account of this conceit of mine (for that perhaps is the name it deserves), I now put the following questions into your hands, which I must [20] beg you, sir, favourably to receive; since I design'd to offer, and I hope have offered, them with that humility and submission which become one of the meanest among the sons of the established church of England.

I. Since the age seems so averse to frequent repetitions in [25] divine worship, whether the Lord's Prayer, Gloria Patri, &c. may not be more seldom used? whether, too, a greater variety of prayers may not be allowed, two or three different forms being set down upon every occasion, that he who officiates may sometimes take one and sometimes another? and whether [30] even the whole evening service may not be made to differ from that of the morning?

II. Since short collects do not very well suit the humour of the people, whether several of those in our liturgy may not be contrived into one? as, for instance, those of petition [35] together, intercession together, &c.

III. Whether a prayer for preservation be not wanting in our Common Prayer Book, as it now is, wherein particular

persons (on their giving notice) may be commended to the divine protection, a thing frequently desired in some places, especially port-towns? also another for the sick or afflicted, to be used when the litany is read; there being none ap-
5 pointed at those times?

IV. Whether some psalms, proper to express our ordinary wants, and to be thankful in for general blessings, or else anthems to the same effect, made up of select expressions of Scripture, would not do well in the room of the Magnificat,
10 Nunc dimittis, and even the Benedictus?

V. Whether the prayers for the king and queen may not be put in such general words as will be applicable to all circumstances? we being, as it is well known, not long since crampt by a form, not without some seeming advantage to
15 our enemies, and scandal to some of our friends?

VI. Whether the lessons out of the Apocrypha may not be omitted? the version of the Psalms in the C. P. B. exchanged for that of the Bible? the present singing psalms laid by, and new ones made and allow'd? Doubtless there
20 are men in this age who are able to put the Psalms into numbers fit to be ordinarily sung; with all the advantages of wit and exactness, as well as a natural easiness and plainness. Though some have already done well, there is nothing yet extant, methinks, which is complete of that kind. A good
25 translation in metre would remove one of the justest exceptions against our worship, contribute much to devotion, and in all likelihood be received at this juncture with little or no jealousy or outcry of the people.

VII. Whether the whole office of Visiting the Sick, also
30 the use of Common Prayer by the minister in his own family, may not be left indifferent? the office of Burial (till discipline be duly exercised) made more applicable to some loose Christians who die in our communion? the Athanasian Creed left out, some of the expressions of it being harsh to vulgar
35 ears, and being hardly of the antiquity pretended to?

VIII. As for the surplice, sign of the cross, bowing at the name of Jesus, kneeling at the sacrament, reading the second service at the communion table, the rubric about the salvation of infants at the end of the office of baptism, it need not,

I think, be made a question whether something is not to be allowed to the weakness of some of our brethren. But then, that a change in these (and indeed several other) things may not seem to reflect on our former practice, as well as that of the ancient church, whether some preface or declaration may 5 not be proper more fully to shew the true reasons on which the church first retained and now makes alterations about them!

IX. Whether some express allowance be not convenient of several things which now in many places are grown customary without one! Such are, Sermons in the afternoon, The 10 liberty which is taken in the prayer before sermons, A short prayer of the minister's own composing after sermons, The neglect of wearing square caps, hoods, &c.

X. Whether the promises of the sureties in the office of Baptism might not be made a little more intelligible to ordi- 15 nary people! Whether, too, the Church Catechism might not be as useful if some controverted things in the beginning, and some school definitions toward the end of it, were left out! And whether a larger catechism may not be fitly appointed to be learned after the former ?   20

XI. Whether a person's declaring his resolution to submit to the use of the liturgy may not serve as well as the assent and consent which have been so much cavill'd at ?

XII. Whether some expedients are not to be found out further to restore the credit of episcopacy among the vulgar, 25 and redeem the reverence due to that (as I am persuaded) divine institution? such may be, The primitive way of election restored ; Some effectual restriction of (if not the power, at least) the scandalous oppressions and sometimes debaucheries of their lay officers ; All imaginable caution in pronounc- 30 ing church censures ; More frequent visitations of the bishop himself, but without charge to the inferior clergy or churchwardens ; Confirmations, Cognizance of presentments, &c. in less haste than what is too customary, and with greater solemnity ; The punishment of offenders in such a way, that 35 the honour of religion may manifestly appear the end of the prosecution, and not the profit of the officers ; perhaps, too, a little more regard to the judgment of the Πρεσβυτέριον, which anciently was of council to the bishop.

L

XIII. Whether some more effectual provisions ought not to be made to prevent the being, if it be possible, of so much as one scandalous minister, provisions which may influence the universities, patrons, givers of testimonials and titles, 5 examiners, and the bishop himself; also after admission to cures, the churchwardens, deans rural, neighbouring ministers, archdeacons? Could we hope, too, for some way to advance poor vicarages, a law for the better recovery of dues, and a settled maintenance in corporations; doubtless they would be 10 found serviceable to this as well as other good purposes.

XIV. Whether after the occasions of offence are removed, and the church doors set as open as any reasonable dissenters can desire, the making of some gentle law may not be proposed as necessary to discourage the growth of atheism and 15 heresy?

XV. Whether it would not be an act of charity in those reverend persons who meet by virtue of the present commission, to make the distressed condition of a neighbour church matter of their humble petition to those who are able to 20 relieve her? Though some particular men have been guilty of imprudence and errors, that therefore a sacred order and a national church should be offered up as a sacrifice, seems not very reasonable.

I have thus ventured to give you the trouble of the fore- 25 going queries, and I leave it to you, sir, to make what use of them you think fit. Perhaps some of them are utterly to be rejected, and others may lead to things impracticable any where but in a new Atlantis. However, if I have hinted but so much as one single thing, which shall be thought service- 30 able towards the honour of religion and the long desired tranquillity, I shall think my labour very well rewarded. I am, with all that respect is due to your great merit,

Reverend Sir,
Your very humble servant,

35   Oct. 5, 1689.   U. M.

For the reverend Dr. Tillotson, dean of St. Paul's,
   London.

VII.

An act for uniting his majesty's protestant subjects. (*From a MS. among the Burnet papers in the Bodleian.*)

WHEREAS the peace of the state is highly concerned in the peace of the church, which therefore at all times, but espe- 5 cially in this conjuncture, is most necessary to be preserved : in order, therefore, to remove occasion of differences and dissatisfactions which may arise from protestants, Be it enacted by the king's most excellent majesty, by and with the advice and consent of the lords spiritual and temporal, and of the 10 commons in this present parliament assembled, and by the authority of the same, that in order to the being a minister of this church, or the taking, holding, or enjoying any ecclesiastical benefice or promotion in the same, no other subscriptions or declarations shall, from henceforward, be required of 15 any person, but only the declaration mentioned in a statute made in the 30th year of the late king Charles the Second, entituled "An act for the more effectual preserving the king's person and government, by disabling papists from sitting in either houses of parliament," and also this declaration follow- 20 ing : "I, A. B. d oapprove of the doctrine and worship of the Church of England as containing all things necessary to salvation, and I submit to the government thereof by law established." And be it further enacted by the authority aforesaid, that in order to the being collated or instituted into 25 any benefice or promotion, no more nor other oaths shall be required to be taken by any person than only the oaths of fidelity mentioned in the late statute made in the first year of the reign of king William and queen Mary, entituled "An act for removing or preventing all questions or disputes con- 30 cerning the assembling or sitting of this present parliament," and also the oath of simony, any statute or canon to the contrary notwithstanding.

And be it further enacted by the authority aforesaid, that the two declarations aforesaid shall be made and subscribed, 35

and the said oaths of fidelity taken in the presence of the
bishop or his chancellor, or the guardian of the spiritualities,
by every person who is to receive any holy orders, or that is
to have a license to preach any lecture, or that is to be col-
5 lated or instituted into any benefice, or that is to be admitted
into any ecclesiastical dignity or promotion, before such his
ordination, licensing, collation, institution, or admission.

And be it further enacted, that every person that shall
have from henceforward, or take any degree in either of the
10 universities, or any fellowship, headship, or professor's place
in the same, shall before his admission to that degree or fellowship, or headship, or professor's place, subscribe the aforesaid declarations, and take the said oaths of fidelity in the
presence of the vice-chancellor or his deputy: and every per-
15 son, likewise, that shall be admitted master of any free-school
shall make the said declaration and take the said oaths in
the presence of the bishop or chancellor of the diocese.

And be it further enacted, that the making and subscribing the said declarations, and taking the said oaths as afore-
20 said, shall be as sufficient to all intents and purposes aforesaid,
as if the parties had made all other declarations and subscriptions, and taken all other oaths which they should have taken
by virtue of any law, statute, or canon whatsoever.

And be it further enacted by the authority aforesaid, that
25 from henceforth no minister shall be obliged to wear a surplice in the time of reading prayers, or performing any other
religious office, except only in the king's chapels, and in all
cathedral and collegiate churches and chapels in this realm of
England and dominion of Wales.

30 And be it further enacted by the authority aforesaid, that
no minister shall henceforward be obliged to use the sign of
the cross in baptism, nor any parent obliged to have his child
christened by the minister of the parish, if the said minister
will not use or omit the sign of the cross according to the de-
35 sire of the parent, who in that case may procure some other
minister to do it.

And be it further enacted by the authority aforesaid, that
no minister or ecclesiastical person shall oblige any body to

find godfathers for any child to be baptised so long as the
parent or parents be there to fill their place.

And be it further enacted by the authority aforesaid, that
no minister who shall officiate in the administration of the
sacrament of the Lord's supper, shall deny or refuse it to 5
any person that desires to be admitted to the same, although
such person shall not receive it kneeling.

And be it further enacted by the authority aforesaid, that
no minister ordained only by presbyters since the year of our
Lord 1660, shall be admitted to any benefice or promotion 10
unless he receive a second imposition of hands from some
bishop, to recommend him to the grace of God for the work
or exercise of his office, in the place or charge unto which he
is called ; and the bishop shall frame his words and testimo-
nial accordingly, to the mutual satisfaction of himself and the 15
ordained, till a form on purpose be by a convocation and a
law established.

And forasmuch as the excellent government of the church
by bishops, as it was reformed and established in Edward the
Sixth and queen Elizabeth's days, is to be still upheld, and
several things in regard to the books of the liturgy, and of 20
ordering priests and deacons, and consecrating bishops, and
of the ecclesiastical constitutions or canons, and in regard to
the exercise of discipline and otherwise, do require redress,
reduction, or improvement, in order whereunto it pleased
king William and queen Mary to grant a commission to 25
thirty persons, bishops, deans, and doctors of the church, who
made some good progress therein : Be it further enacted by
the authority aforesaid, that those commissioners shall be
filled up, and hereby further authorized and required to proceed to the perfecting that work, and to add what they think 30
else needful, to the end that whatsoever is wanting in this
act for the further satisfaction of the dissenter may be supplied by them, and then present what is done to his majesty
to be communicated to a convocation and a parliament, when
and how he shall think meet, according to his most excellent 35
wisdom.

CONCLUSION.

THE commission issued by king William is the last attempt made by authority for the revision of the liturgy. But though so completely frustrated in that memorable case, the project has at all subsequent periods met with supporters among the sanguine, the anxious, and the intemperate; and in one instance, if not in others, has been brought distinctly before the governors of the church for their consideration. Archbishop Cornwallis was petitioned in the year 1772 by several clergymen[a], some of whom afterwards obtained high stations in the church, to sanction a review of the liturgy and articles, with a request " that their wishes might be signified to the rest of the bishops that every thing might be done, which could be prudently and safely done, to promote those important and salutary purposes." The archbishop's answer given on the 11th of February, 1773, was in the following words: " I

[a] Among the petitioners were Drs. Porteus, Yorke, and Percy, afterwards bishops of London, Ely, and Dromore. See Hodgson's Life of Bishop Porteus, p. 38. In the British Museum is a Collection of volumes, 39 in number, bequeathed to it in the year 1766 by a Bedfordshire clergyman of the name of Jones, which contain the most copious materials for a revision of the liturgy, and illustrate at the same time the boundless extravagance to which a love of alterations is sometimes carried. (Addit. MSS. 5368—5407.)

have consulted severally my brethren the bishops; and it is the opinion of the bench in general, that nothing can in prudence be done in the matter that has been submitted to their consideration."

To obtain then from this history of conferences such practical instruction as may direct us in our proceedings for the future, it may be well to consider, as the conclusion of the whole subject, whether it is necessary or desirable to make any further attempt at revising the Book of Common Prayer. It may readily be granted that there are regulations, as to the conducting of the services, which might be improved, and words and phrases in the services themselves, which when addressed to modern ears, require to be explained. To use the language of a living prelate, whose authority rests upon his personal qualifications, no less than upon his exalted station; "lapse of time has rendered some phrases obsolete, or strange, or improper: condemnation of heretical opinions may have been expressed in stronger terms than is necessary or convenient: the selection of lessons might certainly be improved, and better adapted to the customary times of attendance on public worship. Above all it would seem productive of many advantages if the limits of that discretion, already given to the officiating minister in certain parts of the service, were extended, subject only to the interference of canonical advice and authority, whenever it might be thought expedient to check too great a latitude[b]."

Now in a liturgy, the component parts of which may be considered as coeval with the first ages of Christianity, and as having met with general acceptance

[b] Charge delivered in the diocese of Llandaff in the year 1833. p. 27.

and veneration at all subsequent periods, the necessity
for a revision cannot seriously be entertained, except
on one extreme and extravagant supposition. It cannot
be entertained on any consideration of the liturgy in
5 itself, but solely on the supposition, that the people,
for whose use it is designed, and on whose judgment,
humanly speaking, its fate is to depend, have so far
receded from its confession of faith, or tone of devotion,
as to find it discordant and irreconcilable with their
10 sentiments. But such a supposition it would be irrelevant and unprofitable to discuss.

To the further question whether a revision is desirable, an answer must be sought not so much from the
general principles of a ritual, or the wants of a mixed
15 congregation, as from the practical difficulties inseparable from such an undertaking. The change must
be made, if at all, by means of three distinct assemblies, a commission, a convocation, and a parliament,
their united concurrence being indispensable, although
20 the approbation of any one of them would seem to be
almost unattainable. Suppose a commission to have
met, and to consist of divines selected partly from the
stations they occupied, and partly from their known
approval, in general terms, of the projected measure.
25 It is highly improbable that they would adopt any
given amount of alterations, without a conviction on
the part of some, that more concessions were required,
and of others, that too many had been granted already:
it is certain that before they had reached that point in
30 their progress, they would have met with questions
involving cases of conscience, and articles of faith,
and would not have been able to solve them without
differences of opinion on matters essential. But suppose
that by the careful selection of the commissioners, or

by their extraordinary forbearance, these first difficulties are surmounted, and the proposition, drawn out
and matured, is ready to be laid before the two houses
of convocation. That body is not merely in the probable
character of its individual members, but still more in 5
its corporate nature and constitution, opposed to such
a change, and morally incapable of consenting to it.
But suppose again by some remarkable coincidence,
these further obstacles are overcome, and a schedule
of alterations has been adopted by the representatives 10
of the clergy. Then succeeds a parliament, not following the precedent of former times, and giving their
sanction to the projected changes without examination,
but submitting probably every point to discussion, and
deciding on principles entirely different from those of 15
the two assemblies that had preceded them. Forthwith
arise inquiries as to the nature and extent of the
powers of convocations; dissertations on the alliance
between the church and the state; assertions of sove-
reignty on the one side, and of divine authority on 20
the other; inquiries running back into the remotest
periods of constitutional history, and losing themselves
in the wide ocean of absolute rights. And if the
foresight of all, or any, of these confusions were not
sufficient to deter reasonable men from calling them 25
out of chaos, there must still be obtained a combination
of external circumstances, such as it would be matter
for surprise to find singly even in tranquil times, but
to find them all concurring at one period, and that too
a period of great excitement, would surpass the boldest 30
flights of rational speculation. There must still be
a combination of such circumstances, as a church
possessed of power but willing to relinquish it, an ag-
gregation of dissenters harmonious among themselves,

and with feelings of respect and deference towards
churchmen, a large mass of spectators looking calmly
on the progress of change, without accelerating or disturbing it, and lastly a paternal government seeking
5 only the moral welfare of the people, and laying aside
all views of party or personal aggrandisement.

It would scarcely be possible to imagine occasions
more favourable for such an undertaking than the
times of the restoration and the revolution, when the
10 church, the dissenters, and the government might be
expected to concur in promoting some scheme of comprehension. And yet, in both those instances, there
were many essential differences never fully developed,
that would, by their emergence, have prevented a coa-
15 lition, even had not the plan suffered shipwreck in the
outset, on such unforeseen and incidental dangers as
the predominance of a few impracticable dissenters in
the one instance, and the intervention of the non-jurors
in the other.

20 Let it be remembered, also, on the part of nonconformists, that whenever objection is made against any
expressions as ambiguous or indefinite, other parties, of
different and even opposite opinions, will be as ready
as they themselves are, to offer amendments. In such
25 a case, the result will probably be that phrases, which
had previously afforded a common shelter to both, will
be made precise and contracted in accordance with the
wishes of the more rigid interpreters. Let it be remembered that if one party complain of a strict ad-
30 herence to forms and a tendency towards superstition,
another party, more compact, more learned and more
resolute, may call for the restoration[c] of prayers and

---

[c] See the two Liturgies of King Edward VI. compared. Pref.
p. xxxv.

usages, which once found a place in the liturgy, and were removed by the fathers of the reformation as too nearly allied to Romanism. It is the natural progress of controversy, the numbers of a party going on inversely with the refinement of opinion, that discussion begets 5 distinction, and distinction is followed by exclusion.

The revision of king Charles II, memorable as a passage of history, is no less instructive as an example. Beginning in a sense of thankfulness that the times of trouble were at an end, in a generous spirit of forgive- 10 ness for past sufferings, and in a prevailing disposition to renounce private interests and to include all reasonable worshippers within one common ritual, it terminated in a stricter interpretation of religious faith, in more rigorous requirements of ecclesiastical discipline, 15 and in an increased amount of civil disabilities. And this result was probably warranted, and certainly excusable, under the peculiar aspect of the times; but it was owing in a great degree to the rash and intemperate proceedings of the nonconformists, who had caused the 20 floodgates of inquiry to be thrown open, and were the first to be carried away by the torrent,

THE END.

CPSIA information can be obtained at www.ICGtesting.com
Printed in the USA
241328LV00005B/5/P